新SAT
速战速决

（美）Chunan Chen ◎ 主编

5 套完整新SAT试题 **+** 详细解析 直接获得第一手体验

6 位美国 一线教育专家 合力打造

全景式解读 *2016 SAT* 新变革，新SAT备考首选

中国出版集团
中译出版社

图书在版编目（CIP）数据

新 SAT 速战速决 /（美） 陈春安主编；（美） 陈春安等编 .
—北京 ：中译出版社， 2015.7
ISBN 978-7-5001-4193-8

Ⅰ .①新… Ⅱ .①陈… Ⅲ .①英语－高等学校－入学考试
－美国－自学参考资料 Ⅳ .① H310.41

中国版本图书馆 CIP 数据核字 （2015） 第 163698 号

出版发行／中译出版社
地　　　址／北京市西城区车公庄大街甲 4 号物华大厦六层
电　　　话／（010） 68002527　68359813
邮　　　编／100044
传　　　真／（010） 68357870
电子邮箱／ book@ctph.com.cn
网　　　址／ http://www.ctph.com.cn

策划编辑／吴良柱　吴 蓉
责任编辑／姜 军　刘黎黎　郭 欢
封面设计／靳 婧

印　　刷／北京合众伟业印刷有限公司
经　　销／新华书店

规　　格／ 889×1194 毫米　1/16
印　　张／ 30
字　　数／ 480 千字
版　　次／ 2016 年 8 月第 2 版
印　　次／ 2016 年 8 月第 2 次

ISBN 978-7-5001-4193-8　　定价：98.00 元

前言

作为世界各国高中生申请美国名校学习及奖学金的重要参考，SAT考试的每次变革都牵动人心。2016年SAT改革的号角已经吹响。此次改革是SAT考试自2005年起的首次重大变化，将对传统的考试形式进行颠覆性的改革和洗牌。

关于改革后的SAT考试，College Board（美国大学理事会）总裁David Coleman指出，新SAT更接近美国的高中和大学课程（the future SAT would be more closely tied to high school and college curriculums.）。也就是说新SAT考试侧重考查学生是否具备学科阅读、篇章分析、论证分析等大学学术生活与未来工作所要求的较强能力，并希望借此帮助学生尽快地适应大学生活和职业发展。而对中国学生而言，应该有意识地训练自己的逻辑思维能力和分析问题、解决问题的能力，因为新SAT非常重视考生能否在现实情境中解决问题。另外，培养扎实的语言能力并通过阅读积累加深对美国社会和文化的理解也非常有必要。

具体来说，涉及到SAT考试内容的8大变革措施包括：在上下文中考词汇、生僻单词的考查大幅减少；掌握证据，在某些题目中找出答案所对应的原文证据；essay部分改为选考，要求学生分析一篇文章，解释作者所运用的论证策略；数学部分将会集中于三个方面：代数的核心知识、解决问题和分析数据的能力以及高等数学的入门准备知识；阅读与语法考查基于现实情境；加大历史、社会研究与科学等方面的分析能力的考查；阅读选文中加入美国建国文献或者由其引发的重大全球对话；错误答案不再扣分。

SAT考试变革在即，市面上针对改革后的新SAT备考资料却极其匮乏，最为考生熟悉的也就是由College Board官方发布的 *The Official SAT Study Guide*，即《SAT官方指南》这本厚如典籍的"大部头"。考生需要对新SAT考试有个简洁直观的了解，并通过试题感受变革后的区别。考虑到这一点，我和我的美国同仁们决定带国内的考生踏上试水之旅，抢先获得第一手体验。为此，新航道特意在美国专门组建了强大的研发团队。整个团队根植于美国本土，由具有多年教学经验的教育专家领衔编写，更汇集了多位一线教师，确保了该书与高中课程的有效接轨。团队自主研发、自主命题、精心选材，精巧设题，打造出了《新SAT速战速决》这本新SAT模拟试题集。

具体来说，本书的优势在于：

1. 美籍名师编写，品质保证。 众所周知，SAT被称为"美国高考"，从文章选材到题目设置无一不印刻着深深的美国烙印。只有亲临一线的教育专家、浸淫美国文化多年的教育者才能深刻把握 SAT 考试的精髓。所以本土化创作团队的重要性不言而喻。该书的创作团队来自于美国本土，由知名美籍教育专家领衔编写，保证了 SAT 的纯正和地道，品质值得信赖。

2. 模拟试题仿真度极高，融合 8 大改革。该书全面面向 2016 年新 SAT 考试，书中更是重磅推出了 5 套高仿真模拟试题。依据 8 大变革，这 5 套题在阅读文章选材方面增加了社会研究、历史文献相关题材的比重，并特别增加了对于图表、数据的分析，从而贴近高中生课内所学知识内容，也更加贴近学生在未来实际的大学学习中遇到的学习情景；数学方面加大了应用题的比重，聚焦于实际应用，意在提高学生解决真实生活中问题的能力；5 篇 Essay 的阅读文章涵盖了美国施政纲领、经典人权演讲以及其他引起全球大讨论的热点问题。所选文章都是经典的立论文段，宜读宜论，更能考查学生分析例证方法、论点展开、修辞方法的能力。

3. 精炼解析＋高分范文，自学好帮手。"题目＋解析"是一本试题集的标配。对于那些靠自学备考的考生来说，精准、到位的解析更是解疑答惑的必备之选。本书中的 5 套题，每一道题都配有解析，essay 部分也提供了高分范文。解析精炼、精准，绝非冗长赘言。范文论证得当，遣词地道，对初次面对新 SAT 作文形式的考生来说具有极大的参考价值。

4. 版式精巧，完美实战体验。题目采用双栏设计，每个 section 独立起页，配有 College Board 官方提供的答题卡。总之，这 5 套题的每一个细节无一不向实战看齐，确保你在练习过程中的体验完全匹敌真实考试。"于细微处见真章"，品质体现在每一个细节之中，希望能通过这些设计，给考生一个绝佳的实战体验。

《新 SAT 速战速决》誓打造仿真度极高的模拟试题，成为《SAT 官方指南》之外最具含金量的新 SAT 试题集。希望通过这 5 套题的实战演练，可以帮助大家建立对新 SAT 直接的观感，从而更好地迎接 2016 的新变革。

自古以来，改革代表了未知与挑战，只有最勇敢的人才会迎难而上，并享受最大的成果。新的 SAT 时代即将来临，作为第一批试水者，我为你们感到骄傲，愿这本书能够在你们追寻梦想的途中助你们一臂之力。早日实现留学美国的梦想！

新航道国际教育集团总裁兼校长

2015 年 7 月 16 日

CONTENTS
目 录

新 SAT 简介

New SAT Practice Tests

Answer Explanations

新SAT简介

重新设计的 SAT 新在何处

很早以前，美国各大学录取新生时都很头疼：由于全国所有高中开设的课程不一，即使课程相同内容也各异，再加上评分标准不同，招来的新生往往悬殊太大。从高中甲招来的 4.5GPA 学生比从高中乙招来的 3.5GPA 学生水平差一大截的现象司空见惯。于是 College Board 从 1927 年开始推行 SAT，使高校招生有一个统一的标准。虽然美国的 SAT 不是"一考定终生，"但它确实成为了各高等学校录取新生的主要依据之一。八十八年来，为了与时俱进，SAT 经历了无数变革，比较大的有三十多次。近年来，SAT 依然受到来自各方面的批评不断，许多人认为它与美国的高中教学脱节，与高等教育脱节，与美国社会脱节。一些 SAT"状元"来到大学后并不能很快适应大学的学习。特别是从国外招来的一些 SAT 高分学生对美国的历史、地理、文化和社会知之甚少，常常需要恶补。这些现象说明现在的 SAT 未能准确检测高中毕业生对大学学习或职业训练的准备情况。2014 年，College Board 终于决定对 SAT 进行一次伤筋动骨的改造。经过近两年的准备，重新设计的 SAT 将于 2016 年 3 月开始全面铺开。

新的 SAT 新在何处呢？与现在的 SAT 比较，它从形式到内容都有很大的变化。

首先，SAT 被重新设计为三个部分：以证据为基础的阅读与写作（Evidence-based Reading and Writing）、数学 (Math) 和短文写作（Essay Writing）。第一部分包括阅读考试（Reading Test）及写作和语言考试（Writing and Language Test）。数学也分为两个部分，一部分不可使用计算器，另一部分可使用计算器。以证据为基础的阅读与写作和数学共 153 题，总分为 400 – 1600。短文写作为选考，分数另计。计分为三个部分：阅读、分析和写作，各为 1 – 4 分。每篇短文由两人阅卷，所以总分为 2 – 8 分。为鼓励考生尽可能回答所有问题，计分时只计正确答案，答错不再扣分。

在内容上，考题将聚焦于对大学的学习和未来的成功至关重要的东西。归纳起来，有以下几个新的特点：

新 SAT 将十分重视许多不同学科的文本中重要的、广泛使用的词汇和短语（relevant words）。考生要依据上下文确定这些词语的词义或喻义。虽然这对一些考生来说有一定的难度，但他们在中小学阶段的学习以及 SAT 备考过程中学会的这种技能将使他们获益终生。因此，考生再也不必拿着卡片死记硬背那些考过即忘的冷僻词汇。他们只需做好每天的功课，养成认真阅读的好习惯，多多练习，做到熟能生巧。

既然读和写的部分被称为 Evidence-based Reading and Writing，当然就要重证据。考生不可凭自己的经验或主观看法选择答案。往往一道题要你选择作者的观点或目的，紧接着一道题要你指出文章中什么证据支持你的选择。如果你认真阅读，一对皆对；如果是自己想当然，一错皆错。写的部分主要考句子结构和用词，有时错在原文，有时错在选择答案。

短文写作虽是选考，但这正好是许多考生一显身手的地方。而且，许多大学一定会希望看到考生的短文写作评分。考生必须先阅读一篇文章，然后要分析作者是如何立论并说服读者或听众的。考生必须指出作者是如何使用证据、推理、修辞手段等等来支持其论点的。这样的短文写作，不仅对中小学英语教学中的广泛阅读、细致分析、清晰写作给予了强力支持，而且又很接近于学生在大学阶段无论文科或理工科都经常要做的作业。

数学考试将不再追求广度，转而注重深度，集中于解答应用题、进行数据分析、核心代数和被称为"高等数学通行证"的那些方面，包括几何与三角函数。College Board 认为掌握这些方面的知识是进入大学学习和职业训练之前的必要准备。

在新 SAT 考试中，考生将要面对的是基于真实世界的问题，即与他们将来在大学的学习和未来的工作直接相关的问题。在读写部分，考生必须认真阅读各种文本，包括小说与非小说，图表与数据，以及在自然科学、社会科学及其他领域常见的那些文章。考生不仅被要求改错，还要能编辑改进属于人文、历史、社会科学和职业等各领域的文章。数学部分则要求考生能应用多个步骤解答一些自然科学、社会科学和职业领域真实生活中的问题。比如给你一个真实的情景，然后提出几个问题，要求你深入分析，认真思考，然后用数学方法进行解答。

重新设计的 SAT 要求考生运用阅读、写作、语言和数学的技能对科学和历史 / 社会研究各学科的问题作答。这将有助于他们今后在大学里和工作中运用这些技能去理解科学发现、政治发展、全球事件以及卫生环保等领域的问题。在新 SAT 的各个部分，考生将遇到这些领域的比较有难度的文章和图表数据。他们必须读懂这些文章，修改某些部分，使其与图表显示的数据相一致，或者综合文本和图表所提供的信息，解答自然科学与社会科学方面的问题。

重新设计的 SAT 将特别注重美国的建国文献，包括独立宣言，人权法案和联邦文献。College Board 认为，建国文献开启了一场一直延续至今的关于人类文明生活性质的大讨论。建国文献的精神，被后来一些作家、演说家和思想家如 Edmund Burke, Mary Wollstonecraft 和 Mohandas Gandhi 等人不断发扬光大，使这场围绕自由、正义与人的尊严等重要问题的大讨论得以更广泛、更深入地进行。每次考生参加新 SAT 考试，都会遇到美国建国文献或全球大讨论中的重要文件。College Board 希望引导学生认真阅读这些内容丰富、意义深远的精彩文章，让他们不仅能掌握大学学习和未来就业所必需的技能，而且也获得一个机会，直接回应与深入探讨知情公民特别关注的那些问题。

总的来看，重新设计的 SAT 反映了 College Board 的良苦用心。当然它也不会是十全十美的。例如，新 SAT 命题的依据是"共同核心标准"（Common Core Standards），可是全美绝大多数州对它都还不熟悉。有人认为，与其说新 SAT "反映"了学生学什么，不如说它"要求"学生学什么，是典型的"尾巴摇动狗"（the tail wagging the dog）；因而对于绝大多数无缘接受专业的 SAT 训练的考生来说是不公平的。

以证据为基础的阅读
EVIDENCE-BASED READING

这个部分要求考生在 65 分钟内阅读 4 篇独立的短文和两篇相关联的短文并回答 52 个问题。短文的篇幅均为 500 至 750 个词，偶尔会附有图表。

从内容来分：文学 1 篇，选自经典或当代美国文学和世界文学；历史与社会研究 1 篇，选自人类学、经济学、教育学、语言学、政治科学和社会学；美国建国文献和全球文明探讨 1 篇，选自美国独立宣言、人权法案、联邦文献或其他国家有关文明与人权探讨的重要著述；自然科学 2 篇，选自地球科学、生物学、化学和物理学等方面的基本概念和最新发展的论文。

每篇短文后有 11 或 12 道题，不仅测试考生是否能快速掌握和理解短文中的信息与大意，更着重的是测试考生是否能分析作者如何立论、如何论证并说服读者听众。另外，两篇相关的短文排在一起则是为了测试考生综合与比较分析的能力。

这 11 或 12 道题并非按难度排列，而是从整体到局部。第 1 道题往往是关于中心思想、主要论点或全篇结构，然后才是有关论据、细节和词义等方面的问题。许多问题都会提示与短文的哪段、哪句或哪行有关。

每篇短文后的问题虽不完全一样，但问题的形式却大致相同。除了问及作者的论点和论文结构之外，每篇都有两个"行文中的词语"(Words in the Context) 问题和两个"论据"（Evidence）问题。

以下三个方面的技巧可帮你在阅读考试中取得更好的成绩。

一、集中精力

许多考生在阅读考试中最大的问题是难于集中精力。即使平时喜爱阅读的人在面对新 SAT 的那些短文时也难免犯困走神。

首先，你必须明白：考 SAT 的阅读同平时在学校里的阅读有着根本不同的目的。在学校里的阅读为的是学习新的知识，记住所读的东西，以便将来考试或工作时用得上。考 SAT 时，你并不需要发现并且记住什么新的知识，你只需在那些短文中寻找问题的答案。由于在规定的时间内可以多次阅读，即使开始漏了什么，以后还可补回来。所以，你大可不必从头到尾去读文章。从问题入手，直奔答案，不仅能防止疲劳，还能收到事半功倍的效果。

二、熟悉结构

如果你能掌握 SAT 阅读考试的短文与考题之间的结构特点，考起来就会轻松得多。以下三个特点特别值得留意：

● 行数提示：百分之八十的考题都会有行数提示，但是你最好不要只看那一行就匆忙答题。为了充分理解上下文，最好阅读上下五行的窗口。

● 先后顺序：除个别问题针对全文外，其他问题基本上是按先后顺序的。例如，如果第 6 题的答案在 20 - 25 行，第 8 题的答案在 35 - 40 行，那么第 7 题的答案应该在 25 – 35 行之间去找。遇到没有行数提示的问题尤其应该这样做。

● 特别词语：问题和短文中有时会出现一些特别词语，或斜体，或大写，或带引号。没有行数提示时这些特别词语可帮你快速判定在哪里去找答案。

三、基本策略

有些考生把考题一翻开，茫茫然不知如何动手。在备考训练中，不妨试试如下几招。

1. 先易后难。

所有短文并非难度相同。例如，一篇侦探小说节选肯定比一篇研究科罗拉多河流域旱灾成因的科学论文容易读得多。另外，有些短文后带行数提示的问题多，当然也就相对容易些。因为有时间限制，先集中精力做容易的，能够提高答题的准确率。将所有短文由易到难排队，然后按此顺序答题。

2. 先读引言。

有的短文配有斜体引言，或介绍背景，或点明主旨。先读这段引言，对全文的理解会大有帮助。

3. 问题入手。

如前所述，SAT 阅读的目的是答题。先读问题，不仅能帮你预测短文大意，还可确定答题顺序。遇到有行数提示的问题，马上将题号标在短文中有关的地方。见到特别词语，可用笔圈起来。

4. 读懂问题。

新 SAT 阅读部分每篇短文开始的一两个考题，总是与全文的中心思想或结构有关。然后所有的问题都与具体的细节相关。不妨先答后面的问题，把全局性的问题留待最后作答。另外，新 SAT 阅读部分的考题通常不是以问题的形式出现。例如：The author's primary reason for mentioning the gadfly is to, 然后给你四个选择。实际上你应该问自己：What is the author's primary reason for mentioning the gadfly?

5. 问什么读什么。

对那些有行数提示的问题，不妨多读前后几行，但应尽快铆定答案。如果你是把全局性的问题留待最后作答，也许你已经基本上读完了全文，而不需要再从头到尾读一遍。

6. 预测答案。

编考题的人总是把正确答案混在三个似是而非的选择中。为了不受干挠，不妨先预测一下答案，然后再看那四个选择。

7. 逆向选择。

有些问题，一眼就能找出正确答案。但很多问题却不会那么简单。因此逆向选择常常能帮你解决问题。原因很简单：选正确答案，是四里挑一；选错误答案，是四里挑三。排除两个，答对的可能性就增加到百分之五十。

练习

DIRECTIONS

For these questions, determine the solution to each question presented and choose the best choice provided. Be sure to fill in the respective circle on your answer sheet.

Questions 1-11 are based on the following passage.

Read the passage from a speech delivered by Patrick Henry on March 23, 1776, to the Second Virginia Convention in Richmond, Virginia, as quoted in William Wirt's Sketches of the Life and Character of Patrick Henry (1817). Then answer questions 1 through 11.

Adapted from "Speech to the Second Virginia Convention" by Patrick Henry

"Ask yourselves how this gracious reception of our petition comports with those warlike preparations which cover our waters and darken
Line our land? Are fleets and armies necessary to a
5 work of love and reconciliation? Have we shown ourselves so unwilling to be reconciled, that force must be called in to win back our love? Let us not deceive ourselves, sir. These are the implements of war and subjugation—the last arguments to
10 which kings resort. I ask gentlemen, sir, what means this martial array, if its purpose be not to force us to submission? Can gentlemen assign any other possible motive for it? Has Great Britain any enemy in this quarter of the world,
15 to call for all this accumulation of navies and armies? No, sir: she has none. They are meant for us: they can be meant for no other. They are sent over to bind and rivet upon us those chains, which the British ministry have been so long
20 forging. And what have we to oppose to them? Shall we try argument? Sir, we have been trying that for the last ten years. Have we any thing

new to offer upon the subject? Nothing. We have held the subject up in every light of which
25 it is capable; but it has been all in vain. Shall we resort to entreaty and humble supplication? What terms shall we find, which have not been already exhausted? Let us not, I beseech you, sir, deceive ourselves longer. Sir, we have done every thing
30 that could be done, to avert the storm which is now coming on. We have petitioned—we have remonstrated—we have supplicated—we have prostrated ourselves before the throne, and have implored its interposition to arrest the tyrannical
35 hands of the ministry and parliament. Our petitions have been slighted; our remonstrances have produced additional violence and insult; our supplications have been disregarded; and we have been spurned, with contempt, from the foot
40 of the throne. In vain, after these things, may we indulge the fond hope of peace and reconcili- ation. There is no longer any room for hope. If we wish to be free—if we mean to preserve inviolate those inestimable privileges for which we have
45 been so long contending—if we mean not basely to abandon the noble struggle in which we have been so long engaged, and which we have pledged ourselves never to abandon, until the glorious object of our contest shall be obtained—
50 we must fight!—I repeat it, sir, we must fight!! An appeal to arms and to the God of Hosts, is all that is left us!"

"They tell us, sir," continued Mr. Henry, "that

7

we are weak—unable to cope with so formidable
55 an adversary. But when shall we be stronger?
Will it be the next week, or the next year? Will
it be when we are totally disarmed; and when a
British guard shall be stationed in every house?
Shall we gather strength by irresolution and
60 inaction? Shall we acquire the means of effectual
resistance, by lying supinely on our backs, and
hugging the delusive phantom of hope, until our
enemies shall have bound us, hand and foot?
Sir, we are not weak, if we make a proper use
65 of those means which the God of nature hath
placed in our power. Three millions of people,
armed in the holy cause of liberty, and in such a
country as that which we possess, are invincible
by any force which our enemy can send against
70 us. Besides, sir, we shall not fight our battles
alone. There is a just God who presides over the
destinies of nations; and who will raise up friends
to fight our battles for us. The battle, sir, is not to
the strong alone; it is to the vigilant, the active,
75 the brave. Besides, sir, we have no election. If we
were base enough to desire it, it is now too late to
retire from the contest. There is no retreat, but in
submission and slavery! Our chains are forged.
Their clanking may be heard on the plains of
80 Boston! The war is inevitable—and let it come!!
I repeat it, sir, let it come!!!" "It is in vain, sir, to
extenuate the matter. Gentlemen may cry, Peace,
Peace— but there is no peace. The war is actually
begun! The next gale that sweeps from the north,
85 will bring to our ears the clash of resounding
arms! Our brethren are already in the field! Why
stand we here idle? What is it that gentlemen
wish? What would they have? Is life so dear, or
peace so sweet, as to be purchased at the price of
90 chains, and slavery? Forbid it, Almighty God!—I
know not what course others may take; but as for
me," cried he, with both his arms extended aloft,
his brows knit, every feature marked with the
resolute purpose of his soul, and his voice swelled
95 to its boldest note of exclamation— "give me
liberty, or give me death!"
　　Speech to the Second Virginia Convention by
Patrick Henry, 1817. Public Domain.

1

The main purpose of Patrick Henry's speech can
be described as
A. explaining why the British king sent his navies
    and armies to the colonies.
B. persuading colonists to fight for freedom and
    independence.
C. asking the British king to withdraw his armed
    forces from the colonies.
D. warning the colonists that a war is coming.

2

Which quotation provides the best support for the
answer to the previous question?
A. "what means this martial array, if its purpose
    be not to force us to submission?"
B. "we are weak—unable to cope with so
    formidable an adversary."
C. "Gentlemen may cry, Peace, Peace— but there
    is no peace."
D. "If we wish to be free, … we must fight - I
    repeat it, sir, we must fight!"

3

According to Patrick Henry's speech, which of
the following is not likely among his opponents'
opinions?
A. We are too weak to fight against a mighty
    British force.
B. Peace is of the top interest of the colonists.
C. The colonies belong to England. Therefore, we
    must obey the king's orders.
D. The British armed forces may not be coming
    to fight against us.

4

According to Patrick Henry, which of the following claims is not true about the situation before the War of Independence?

A. The British forces were much stronger than the colonists.

B. The colonists didn't want a peaceful solution.

C. Some colonists thought that the colonies were not ready for the war yet.

D. The British ministry and parliament had turned down the colonists' request for freedom.

5

Which choice provides the best evidence for the answer to the previous question?

A. Lines 29 – 35 ("We have done … ministry and parliament.")

B. Lines 73 – 75 ("The battle is not … no election."

C. Lines 1 – 7 ("Ask ourselves … win back our love?")

D. Lines 83 – 86 ("The war is … in the field.")

6

In Lines 32 - 33, Henry says of the colonists, ".... we have prostrated ourselves before the throne...." In this context, what does it mean *to prostrate oneself*?

A. to show humbleness and submission

B. to lie down on the ground

C. to use up one's physical and mental resources

D. to put oneself in an advantageous situation

7

What point does Henry seek to make in saying that the colonists have prostrated themselves before the throne?

A. They continue to behave as if they are subjects of the king.

B. They are unknowingly imitating the king's behavior.

C. Their efforts have attracted the sympathy of the king.

D. They would be better advised to stand up to the king.

8

Which statement best describes Henry's views about those who continue to strive for reconciliation with the British?

A. They make the colonists more vulnerable to British tyranny.

B. They are pursuing an alternative course toward the same goal.

C. They have ignored the truth about the British's intentions toward the colonists.

D. They demonstrate admirable loyalty toward the king.

9

As it is used in Line 39 ("We have been spurned"), "spurned" most nearly means

A. disapproved

B. refused rudely

C. ignored

D. disagreed

10

According to his speech, Patrick Henry thought that the colonists had no other choice but to fight because

A. the British king wanted to enslave the colonists.
B. the colonists had tried every other means to avoid a war with the British but did so in vain.
C. the war had already begun and there was no retreat now.
D. all of the above.

11

By saying, "Give me liberty, or give me death!" Patrick Henry means that

A. his fate is in the king's hands.
B. he is not sure whether they will win the war.
C. he wants to fight for freedom and he is not afraid of death.
D. life is more important than liberty.

写作和语言
WRITING AND LANGUAGE

写作和语言部分要求考生像作家那样仔细阅读，发现问题，并遵循英语语法修改文章。考生必须决定是否可以通过改变某些词语、标点或句子顺序而使文章更好。这个部分有 4 篇短文，共 44 道选择题，考试时间为 35 分钟。也就是说，考生要在 9 分钟内读完一篇短文并回答 11 或 12 道题。听起来有点吓人吧？不过每篇短文都在 500 个词左右，难度也不是很大。

短文分属 4 类：

1）职业：如医疗卫生、科技、商业等领域的文章

2）社会研究：包括历史、地理、政治、经济、人类学、社会学、语言学和心理学等领域的文章

3）人文科学：包括文学、艺术、音乐、舞蹈等方面的报导或论文

4）自然科学：包括地球科学、生物学、化学和物理等学科的文章

这 44 道题可分为两类：一类是改错，包括用词、语法和标点；另一类是编辑，主要是修改原文使其更好地表达作者的意思。有些题只针对一个词，另一些题则会针对几个词甚至几个句子，答题时要留意划线部分有多长。注意许多题的 4 个选择答案中 A 总是 No Change "不须改变，"如果你认为原文无错误，就应选 A。

这个全新的写作和语言部分，就是中国学生所熟悉的语法部分，究竟是个什么样子呢？先让我们来看一段样题：

[1] Studying grammar rules **1** <u>seem</u> to be a thing of the past. [2] Instead, most English classes are **2** <u>focus</u> on reading and writing today, with the implicit claim that one learns to write by writing. [3] Also implicit in this claim is the idea that grammar no

1

(A) NO CHANGE
(B) seems
(C) will seem
(D) seemed

2

(A) NO CHANGE
(B) being focused
(C) focused
(D) having focus

11

longer has the practical, **3** objective or, egalitarian cachet that is once did. [4] "Proper speech" does not exist in and of **4** itself; proper speech, instead, is the province of those who consider themselves proper. [5] The age of diagramming sentences and laboring over difference between direct and indirect objects is gone. **5** **6** [6] For all that people complain about it, what is the difference between "who" and "whom" anyway?

3

(A) NO CHANGE
(B) objective or egalitarian,
(C) objective, or egalitarian,
(D) objective, or egalitarian

4

(A) NO CHANGE
(B) itself proper
(C) itself, proper
(D) itself proper,

5

The best placement for sentence 5 would be
(A) where it is now.
(B) after sentence 1.
(C) after sentence 2.
(D) after sentence 3.

6

Which of the following questions would best conclude the paragraph by summarizing one of its main points?
(A) NO CHANGE
(B) Who is to say, after all, that the speech of a particular race, class, or region is any "better" than any other?
(C) Kids hate learning grammar, and teachers hate teaching it, so why bother?
(D) Why is grammar so difficult for native speakers?

基本策略

设想你在与同学互相修改作文，你在修改你同桌的文章。记住两点：

对于没有提示的问题，如以上的 1, 2, 3, 4 题，比较四个选择的不同之处，你就会发现该题是考什么。

对于有提示的问题，一定要仔细看清提示。这部分并不考阅读理解，所以找到提示正确答案的词语或标点符号就行了。

一、比较选择

新 **SAT** 可以考大约 40 个语法概念，但不会提示各题考的是什么。不会问你这里该用逗号吗，或者这里应该用什么时态之类的问题。不过，透过四个选择，出题的人还是为你提供了一些暗示。让我们来看一看第一题的四个选择：

1. (A) NO CHANGE
   (B) seems
   (C) will seem
   (D) seemed

这四个选择都是动词 seem 的不同时态，所以我们只需考虑时态，而不用去想什么标点啊，词序啊之类的事情。

再看第三题：

3. (A) NO CHANGE
   (B) objective or egalitarian,
   (C) objective, or egalitarian,
   (D) objective, or egalitarian

这一次，四个选择都是同样的三个词，不同的是逗号。所以我们知道这个问题是考如何正确地使用逗号，不用考虑这个词是什么意思。

二、寻找暗示

有时候有的考题真会以问句的形式出现。这时候，暗示可能就在问题本身。例如：

15.Which of the following provides the most specific information regarding the range of Montaigne's subjects?
   (A) some of the best-loved essays in the history of French literature
   (B) topics that are still of interest to twenty-first century readers
   (C) a variety of subjects relevant to a sixteenth-century gentleman
   (D) everything from gallstones to great historical events

因为问的是 Which provides the most specific information regarding the range of Montaigne's subjects, 正确答案一定是（D）. Montaigne 是法国历史上最有名的政论家，他的作品浩若繁星。问题中的 "range" 和答案中的 "everything" 就是给我们的暗示。其他选择虽然都有关，但总是有 some, still of interest, 或 relevant to 这些词语来限定范围，因此不能成为正确答案。有时候暗示就在选择中。例如：

22.Which of the following alternatives to the underlined portion would be LEAST acceptable?
   (A) However,
   (B) Nevertheless,
   (C) Therefore，
   (D) Even so,

13

这四个选择都是属于 transition 的词语。其中 (A), (B), (D) 三个属于转折，只有 (C) 是顺接。因为正确答案只有一个，所以只能是 (C).

三、分清类别

一类是词语。记住先看选择再开始。上述样题的第 1、2 两题就是属于这一类：

1. (A) NO CHANGE
   (B) seems
   (C) will seem
   (D) seemed

2. (A) NO CHANGE
   (B) being focused
   (C) focused
   (D) having focus

如前所述，第 1 题的四个选择都是 seem 的不同形式，因此我们必须从行文中看哪个是正确的形式。首先，环顾周围发现其他动词都是现在时，(C) 和（D）就可淘汰。然后找到主语是 studying (不是 rules!)，单数，所以确定 (B) 是正确答案。

第 2 题的四个选择都是动词 focus 的不同形式。因为与 are 连在一起，(A) 和（D）都是语法错误。（B）和（C）在语法上都没错，但（C）更简洁，因此要选（C）。

二类是标点。不少问题与标点符号有关。这类问题主要是看，而不是读，因为标点无声。样题中第 3、4 两题就是属于这类。

3. (A) NO CHANGE
   (B) objective or egalitarian,
   (C) objective, or egalitarian,
   (D) objective, or egalitarian

4. (A) NO CHANGE
   (B) itself proper
   (C) itself, proper
   (D) itself proper,

第 3 题中，除了逗号外，四个选择一字不差。其实你懂不懂这些词都没关系，只须牢记在表列三个以上同类词语时，要用 A, B, and C 或者 A, B, or C 的模式。所以（D）是正确答案。

第 4 题中，也是四个选择一字不差，只是要选择逗号还是分号。我们发现，"Proper speech" does not exist in and of itself 和 proper speech, instead, in the province of those who consider themselves proper 两个部分都有完整的句子结构。因此不能选择逗号，因为逗号不可用来连接句子。也许你觉得应该用句号或者用 and 来连接，你没错。这就说明了为什么要从分析四个选择入手。

14

三类是提问。在写作和语言部分，约有半数的考题带有提示或提问。首先一定要搞清问的是什么。

5. The best placement for sentence 5 would be

   (A) where it is now.

   (B) after sentence 1.

   (C) after sentence 2.

   (D) after sentence 3.

6. Which of the following questions would best conclude the paragraph by summarizing one of its main points?

   (A) NO CHANGE

   (B) Who is to say, after all, that the speech of a particular race, class, or region is any "better" than any other?

   (C) Kids hate learning grammar, and teachers hate teaching it, so why bother?

   (D) Why is grammar so difficult for native speakers?

第 5 题问的是短文中第 5 句应放在哪里合适。该句的大意是 the age of learning grammar has passed. 看看短文中还有没有别的句子表示相同的意思？第 1 句就是。第 2 句表示情况是怎么变化的。所以第 5 句应放在两者之间。顺序是非常清楚的：[1] a thing of the past, [2] the age … is gone, [3] instead… today. 这里根本不需要阅读理解或深入分析，只需理清顺序而已。

第 6 题，选择一个问句来总结这段短文。这段文章首先谈到因为英语教学已将重点放在其他方面，语法教学早已过时；然后又谈到"规范"的问题。理想的结尾应该包含这两个方面。（A）只限于语法一方面，当然不合适。（C）和（D）涉及的问题不在此段文章中，因此也应被排除。只剩下了（B）当然就是正确答案了。注意到"better"了吗？它与 proper 可是遥相呼应啊。

练习

DIRECTIONS

For these questions, determine the solution to each question presented and choose the best answer choices of those provided. Be sure to fill in the respective circle on your answer sheet.

Questions 1 – 10 are based on the following passage.

Adapted from Ana Swanson, "How China used more cement in 3 years than the U.S. did in the entire 20th Century," The Washington Post, Wonkblog, March 24, 2015

China used more cement between 2011 and 2013 than the U.S. used in the entire 20th Century. **1** It's a statistic so mind-blowing that it stunned Bill Gates and inspired heiku. But can it be true, and, if so, how? Yes, China's economy has grown at an extraordinary rate, and it has more than four times as many people as the United States. But the 1900s were America's great period of expansion, the century in which the U.S. built almost **2** all of it's roads and bridges, the Interstate system, the Hoover Dam, and many of the world's tallest skyscrapers. And China and the U.S. are roughly the same size in terms of geographic area, ranking third and fourth in the world, respectively.

3

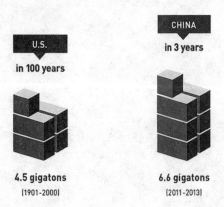

U.S.
in 100 years

CHINA
in 3 years

4.5 gigatons
(1901-2000)

6.6 gigatons
(2011-2013)

Bill Gates GatesBlog

1

(A) NO CHANGE
(B) It is a statistic so mind-blowing that stunned Bill Gates
(C) It is a statistic so mind-blowing it stunned Bill Gates
(D) It is a so mind-blowing statistic that stunned Bill Gates

2

(A) NO CHANGE
(B) all its
(C) all it's
(D) all of its

3

The author uses this graph
(A) to illustrate the whole article.
(B) to illustrate the first paragraph.
(C) to illustrate the second paragraph.
(D) as an independent part.

The statistic seems incredible, but according to government and industry sources, it appears accurate. What's more, once you dive into the figures, they have a surprisingly logical explanation that reveals some fascinating differences between the two countries, and some ominous realities about China.

So how did China use so much cement? First, the country is urbanizing **4** with historic rate, much faster than the U.S. did in the 20th Century. More than 20 million Chinese relocate to cities each year, which is more people than live in downtown New York City, Los Angeles and Chicago combined. This massive change has taken place in less than 50 years. In 1978, less than a fifth of China's population lived in cities. By 2020, that proportion will be 60 percent.

5 Secondly there are a few more facts that make the cement stat even more believable. As Goldman Sachs pointed out in a note, China's population today is only about four times as large as the U.S., but it is 15 times as large as the U.S. was in the early 20th Century, and nine times the size of the U.S. in 1950.

1) In 1950, the world manufactured roughly as much steel as cement; by 2010, steel production had grown by a factor of eight, but cement had gone up by a factor of 25. *2)*And where many houses in the U.S. are made of wood, China suffers from a relative lack of lumber. *3)*Unlike in the U.S., many people in China live in high- or low-rise buildings made out of cement. *4)*The world also experienced a shift in building materials over the 20th Century. **6**

Finally, China's cement industry is much larger than it should be. Many of China's cement manufacturers are state-owned, and they benefit from government support and access to cheap capital. As in other overcapacity state-owned industries — aluminum, steel, and shipbuilding — China's cement sector has undergone a period of explosive growth without much regard for product quality or profit.

This massive cement industry also takes a heavy toll on the environment. **7** Scientists estimate that, the global cement industry, accounts for around 5 percent of the world's carbon emissions, and more than half of the world's cement production capacity is based in China.

When Bill Gates wrote in his blog about China's

4

(A) NO CHANGE
(B) with a historical rate
(C) at a historical rate
(D) at historical rate

5

Which option provides the best transition between paragraphs?
(A) NO CHANGE
(B) On the other hand,
(C) Another reason is,
(D) Beyond China's incredible urbanization,

6

For the sake of cohesion, Sentence 4 should be placed
(A) where it is now.
(B) before sentence 1.
(C) before sentence 2.
(D) before sentence 3.

7

(A) NO CHANGE
(B) Scientists estimate that, the global cement industry accounts
(C) Scientists estimate that the global cement industry accounts
(D) Scientists estimate, that the global cement industry accounts

stunning cement consumption, he pointed out that the issue of materials is **8** key to helping the world's poorest people improve their lives. Replacing mud floors with concrete improves sanitation; paving roads with concrete allows vegetables to get to market, kids to get to school, and the economy to flourish. In China, the building boom **9** has spurred economic growth that has lifted hundreds of millions of people out of poverty.

10 China's massive cement use also points to a darker side of the economy: the waste that occurs with too much top-down economic planning, and the environmental toll of growth at all costs. China's cement splurge is impressive, yes, but it may hold the seeds of a more ominous story.

8

(A) NO CHANGE
(B) key to help the world's poorest people improve
(C) key to help the world's poorest people to improve
(D) key to help the world's poorest people improving

9

(A) NO CHANGE
(B) has spurred economic growth, and that has lifted
(C) has spurred economic growth and that has lifted
(D) has spurred economic growth and has lifted

10

(A) NO CHANGE
(B) Then, China's …
(C) But China's …
(D) And yet, China's …

数学
MATH

数学考试分为两个部分：一部分不准使用计算器，考生必须在 25 分钟之 做完 20 道题。另一部分可以使用计算器，要求考生在 55 分钟之 做完 37 道题。看起来时间有点儿紧，但只要概念清晰、技能熟练，绝大多数考生都不会觉得太难。不过在备考练习时最好留意培养自己的解题速度。

数学考试包括 4 个领域，分别测试如下项目：

领域	测试项目	使用计算器	不使用计算器
核心代数	基本概念，含线型等式与不等式	11 题	8 题
应用题与数据分析	解读数据（性质与数量），分析关系	17 题	0 题
高等数学通行证	高层概念，含二次和高次方程	7 题	9 题
其他	几何、三角、复数	3 题	3 题
合计		38 题	20 题

在这 57 道题中，45 道为选择答案题，其余 12 道为学生自答题。两部分的考题都是选择题在先，自答题在后。所有考题均按由易到难的顺序排列。另外，在可使用计算器的部分还有一道难度较大的应用题，称为 Extended-thinking Question（伸展思考题）。该题要求考生运用所学的数学知识分两步或三步解答现实生活中的一个问题。各类考题计分如下表：

考题分类	计分	%	
使用计算器	选择答案题（30 题）	40%	78%
	学生自答题（8 题）	10%	
不使用计算器	选择答案题（15 题）	38%	22%
	学生自答题（5 题）	12%	
总计		100%	100%

对付这种选择题的数学考试，可用的方法很多，这里仅介绍美国学生中最流行的一种。

代入法

在解答选择题时，许多美国考生会用 **Plug In** 的方法，即代入法。通常分两步走：首先用一个数置换问题中的未知数（不要用 0，1，或者问题中已出现过的数），得到一个答案；然后用这个答案去检查四个选择，淘汰不合者。例如：

6. Xerxes is *x* years old and 4 years older than Zara. How old was Zara 7 years ago?

    (A) *x* – 3

    (B) *x* – 4

    (C) *x* – 7

    (D) *x* – 11

根据题意，设想一个大于 11 的数，比方说 12 吧。划掉题中的 x，改为 12，原题即可变成一道简单的算术题：

Xerxes is 12 years old and 4 years older than Zara. How old was Zara 7 years ago? 12 – 4 – 7 = 1

再检查四个选择：(A) 12 – 3 = 9 (B) 12 – 4 = 8 (C) 12 – 7 = 5 (D) 12 -11 = 1

于是确定（D）是正确答案。无论用什么数代入，20 或者 30，结果都一样。

使用代入法时，一定要搞清已知与未知的关系。例如：

10.Three times x is 2 more than half of y. What is the value of y?

    (A) $6x + 4$

    (B) $\dfrac{3x - 2}{4}$

    (C) $6x - 2$

    (D) $6x - 4$

首先假定 $x = 4$（因为 2 和 3 都已出现在问题中），three times x 就是 12. 因为 12 是 two more than half of y, 那么 half of y 就是 10. 因此 $y = 20$. 然后以此来检验四个选择：

    (A) 6 (4) + 4 = 28 淘汰

    (B) $\dfrac{3(4) - 2}{4}$ = 2.5 淘汰

    (C) 6(4) – 2 = 22 淘汰

    (D) 6(4) – 4 = 20 正确！

所以 (D) 是正确答案。

隐形代入

有时候问题中并未出现一个未知数，但只要能找到相对应的关系，仍可置换。例如：

33. The number of bacteria in petri dish A doubles every 10 minutes. The number of bacteria in petri dish B doubles every 6 minutes. If both petri dishes begin with the same number of bacteria, how many times greater will the number of bacteria in petri dish B be than the number of bacteria in petri dish A after one hour?

如果知道两个试验盘中的细菌数，问题就迎刃而解了。我们可以假定两盘开始时都是 4 个。A 盘 10 分钟后就是 8 个。20 分钟后 16 个。30 分钟后 32 个。40 分钟后 64 个。用同样的方法算出 B 盘中 6、12、18 分钟后 的细菌数……直至 60 分钟后 4,096 个。两下相除，得出答案 16 倍。

对于有关系无数字的问题，代入法可以将无形变有形因而简化问题。对于解答含百分比、比例和几何学的问题，代入法往往都很有效。

答案代入

如果选择答案是数值而不是未知数，而且问题是 How many, How much, 或者 What is the value of 之类，可以用答案直接代入。因为正确答案必定是四中之一，有时候答案代入会比正常计算更容易。来看这个例子：

28.If $\dfrac{(x+6)^2}{x+5} = \dfrac{1}{x+5}$, What is the value of x?

(A) -7

(B) -5

(C) 0

(D) 7

在某些情况下用答案代入时先试中间数，即使不成，也可知道下一步该试大一点的还是小一点的。这里先试（B）-5，结果分子部分没问题，分母部分却不行：$x+5=0$。再试 (C) 0，结果等式不成立，左边大于右边，该试一个使得 $x+6$ 更小的。于是再试 (A) -7，结果成功，确定 (A) 为正确答案。

练习

NO CALCULATOR SECTION

1

In the following equation, what is the value of n?

$$\frac{2(n-4)+2}{3} = \frac{12-(6-n)}{2}$$

A. 50
B. 15
C. 6
D. 30

2

$$2x \geq y - 1$$

Which of the following ordered pairs is NOT a solution to the inequality above?

A. $(1, 2)$
B. $(-1, -3)$
C. $(0, 0)$
D. $(-4, -5)$

3

Which of the following equations has exactly one real solution?

A. $x^2 - 5x + 6 = 0$
B. $x^2 + x - 6 = 0$
C. $x^2 - 4x + 4 = 0$
D. $x^2 + 3x + 2 = 0$

4

The graph below represents the function $y = 2x + b$. Which of the following is a possible equation for x as a function of y?

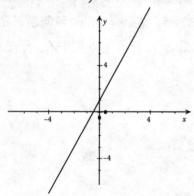

A. $x = \dfrac{y - b}{2}$

B. $x = \dfrac{-y - b}{2}$

C. $x = 2y + b$

D. $x = -2y - b$

CALCULATOR SECTION

5

If $\frac{3}{4}x + 4 = \frac{1}{8}x - 1$, what is the value of x ?

A. 2
B. −8
C. −2
D. $\frac{8}{3}$

6

If $5a = 45$, and $ab = 1$, what is the value of b?

A. $\frac{1}{9}$
B. 9
C. 44
D. 46

7

A Florida gift shop's net profit, in dollars, from the sale of mugs is given by $P(m) = 2.5(m - 50)$, where m is the number of mugs sold. How many mugs must they sell in order to earn a net profit of $650?

A. 150
B. 200
C. 250
D. 310

8

If $x = 3^{2n-1} + 3$ and $y = n + 1$, what is the value of $x - y$ when $n = 1.5$?

9

The table below shows values of the function $f(x) = 2x + b$. If $g(x) = 5x - 9$, what is the value of $g(f(7))$?

x	$f(x)$
−1	6
0	8
1	10
2	12

A. 101
B. 110
C. 22
D. 26

Problems 10 and 11 refer to the following information.

Alison likes to go shopping in the mall in New Jersey because there is no sales tax on clothing there. She bought some shirts, pants and an evening dress with a coupon for a 15% discount of the original price. On her receipt are these words: The More You Buy, The More You Save. Total: $229.50

10

If she buys the same clothes at the same price in her own city, with no discount but a tax of 8% instead, how much more would she have to spend in dollars?

11

Alison's brother Raymond is a computer game lover. Alison decides to buy some games for his birthday. The game store is running a big sale. Final Fantasy is "Buy 2 Get 3rd at Half Price," and the Sims 4 is "Buy 2 Get $20 Off." The tag price for the Sims 4 is 1.5 times of that for Final Fantasy. After calculation, Alison realizes that with the same amount of money, she can get either 3 of the Final Fantasy or 2 of the Sims 4. What is the tag price for the Sims 4?

短文写作
ESSAY

重新设计的 SAT 将短文写作列为选考。如果你申请的大学不要求短文写作考分，那么你可以自行决定是否参加短文写作考试。短文写作考试的分数单列，为 1 – 4 分，不计入 SAT 总分。如果你选择参加短文写作考试，那么你就有一个机会来展示自己理解阅读材料、分析论点论据、有效组织写作的能力。

如前所述，新 SAT 的短文写作考试与以前的 SAT 大不相同。首先，时间由原来的 25 分钟增加到 50 分钟，篇幅也由 2 页增加到 4 页。这样考生可以写得更多，也有更多时间修改自己的作文。其次，命题方式完全变了。以前的短文写作考试要求考生提出自己的论点并有效论证。新的短文写作考试却让考生先认真阅读一篇文章，然后分析文章的作者如何提出论点、如何组织论证、使用什么技巧说服读者听众。要牢记你的任务是评判作者是否对其论点作出了有效论证，而不是表明你是否同意作者的观点。

按照 College Board 的要求，短文写作计分主要考虑三个方面：第一，阅读理解。要想显示你读懂了原文，最好的方法是在你的论文里适当地、有效地引用原文。第二，深入分析。记住，你不能像照相机一样只看外表，要像 X 光机一样透视骨架。只有掌握了文章的结构，才有可能分析作者的论点、论据和论证方法。第三，写作能力。评卷老师主要是看结构，看句法，看用词。结构宜用 5-5- 式，即所谓 Golden Five；全文 5 段（开头 + 主体 3 段 + 结尾），主体每段不少于 5 句。当然，Golden Five 并非金科玉律，考生可以根据时间的限制和内容的需求适当调整主体段数与各段长短。句子要长短搭配，句型宜单句为主、偶有复句。用词要多采用那些有色彩的词，例如：the author *claims*，或者 he *argues*，比 the author *says* 要好得多。

练习

As you read the passage below, consider how Walter E. Williams uses:

- evidence, such as facts or examples, to support claims.

- reasoning to develop ideas and to connect claims and evidence.

- stylistic or persuasive elements, such as word choice or appeals to emotion, to add power to the ideas expressed.

Adapted from Walter E. Williams: Global Warming. Townhall.com March 11, 2015

1   "But the debate is settled. Climate change is a fact," said President Barack Obama in his 2014 State of the Union address. Saying the debate is settled is nonsense, but the president is right about climate change.

2   *GlobalChange.gov* gives the definition of climate change: "Changes in average weather conditions that persist over multiple decades or longer. Climate change encompasses both increases and decreases in temperature, as well as shifts in precipitation, changing risk of certain types of severe weather events, and changes to other features of the climate system." That definition covers all weather phenomena throughout all 4.54 billion years of Earth's existence.

3   You say, "Williams, that's not what the warmers are talking about. It's the high CO_2 levels caused by mankind's industrial activities that are causing the climate change!" There's a problem with that reasoning. Today CO_2 concentrations worldwide average about 380 parts per million. This level of CO_2 concentration is trivial compared with the concentrations during earlier geologic periods. For example, 460 million years ago, during the Ordovician Period, CO_2 concentrations were 4,400 ppm, and temperatures then were about the same as they are today. With such high levels of CO_2, at least according to the warmers, the Earth should have been boiling.

4   Then there are warmer predictions. In the wake of Hurricane Katrina, warmers, such as the Union of Concerned Scientists, made all manner of doomsday predictions about global warming and the increased frequency of hurricanes. According to the Committee for a Constructive Tomorrow, "no Category 3-5 hurricane has struck the United States for a record nine years, and Earth's temperature has not budged for 18 years."

5   Climate change predictions have been wrong for decades. Let's look at some. At the first Earth Day celebration, in 1969, environmentalist Nigel Calder

25

warned, "The threat of a new ice age must now stand alongside nuclear war as a likely source of wholesale death and misery for mankind." C.C. Wallen of the World Meteorological Organization said, "The cooling since 1940 has been large enough and consistent enough that it will not soon be reversed." In 1970, Harvard University biologist George Wald predicted, "Civilization will end within 15 or 30 years unless immediate action is taken against problems facing mankind." Sen. Gaylord Nelson, in Look magazine in April 1970, said that by 1995, "somewhere between 75 and 85 percent of all the species of living animals (would) be extinct."

6   The most disgusting aspect of the climate change debate is the statements by many that it's settled science. There is nothing more anti-scientific than the idea that any science is settled. Very often we find that the half-life of many scientific ideas is about 50 years. For academics to not criticize their colleagues and politicians for suggesting that scientific ideas are not subject to challenge is the height of academic dishonesty.

Write an essay in which you explain how Walter E. Williams builds an argument to persuade his audience that global warming is a false alarm. In your essay, analyze how Williams uses one or more of the features listed in the box above (or features of your own choice) to strengthen the logic and persuasiveness of his argument. Be sure that your analysis focuses on the most relevant features of the passage.

Your essay should not explain whether you agree with Williams's claims, but rather explain how Williams builds an argument to persuade his audience.

ACKNOWLEDGEMENTS FOR THIS SECTION

The passages in this section were adapted from the following sources:

William Wirt, "Sketches of the Life and Character of Patrick Henry," Electronic edition, pp121-123. Originally published by James Webster, Philadelphia, 1817

Ana Swanson, "How China used more cement in 3 years than the U.S. did in the entire 20th century," The Washington Post, Wonkblog, March 24, 2015

Walter E. Williams, "Global Warming," Townhall.com March 11, 2015

Answer Explanations
Exercise

EVIDENCE-BASED READING

1. B

Choice B is the best answer because it reflects the most important idea presented by Patrick Henry over the course of his speech.

2. D

Choice D is the best answer. Patrick Henry points out that their noble goal is freedom, and freedom cannot be obtained by asking for the king's mercy as their experience had already proved.

3. C

Choice C is the best answer because it is not mentioned in Henry's speech, although some colonists did think so.

4. B

Choice B is the best answer because Henry said that they had tried that for the last ten years.

5. A

Choice A is the best answer because this quotation shows what the colonists had already done in the past — nonviolent reconciliation.

6. A

Choice A is the best answer because literally it means to lie with face downward like worshippers do before an idol.

7. D

Choice D is the best answer because, as Henry points out, they had done that for the last ten years but only brought more violence and insult to the colonists.

8. C

Choice C is the best answer because they based their hope on a delusive phantom — that the king is fair — when the British navies and armies were coming.

9. B

Choice B is the best answer as suggested by the words of "with contempt, from the foot of the throne."

10. D

Choice D is the best answer because all of these can be found in Henry's speech.

11. C

Choice C is the best answer because Henry says that we have no choice but to fight if we don't want to be enslaved by the British.

WRITING AND LANGUAGE

1. A

"…so … that " introduces a clause to modify an adj.

2. D

It means "all of the country's …"

3. B

It shows what the first paragraph talks about: How much cement China used in 3 years vs how much the US did in the 20th century.

4. C

"Rate" is a countable noun.

5. D

The previous paragraph talks about China's incredible urbanization as a major fact.

6. B

This is the topic sentence. All other sentences are supporting details.

7. C

The *that* - clause is what the scientists estimate.

8. A

The word "*to*" is a preposition which should be followed by a noun, like *a key to the door*.

9. A

The *that* – clause modifies the noun "economic growth."

10. D

It needs a transition to mark a turning point here, and "*but*" is only a sentence connector.

MATH

1. D

Plug in the answers. Make $n=50$, the left hand side is $\frac{94}{3}$, the right hand side is 28. Make $n=15$, the left hand side is 8, the right hand side is $\frac{21}{2}$. Make $n=6$, the left hand side is 2, the right hand side is 6. Make $n=30$, both sides are 18. Only (D) makes both sides equal.

Algebraically, first simplify the equation to $\frac{2n-6}{3}=\frac{6+n}{2}$. Then multiply both sides by 6, we get $4n-12=18+3n$, move the terms and simplify, we get $n=30$, which is (D).

2. D

Plug in the answers. Only $(-4, -5)$ will violate the inequality: it makes the left hand side -8 and the right hand side -6.

3. C

A quadratic equation $ax^2+bx+c=0$ has exactly one real solution if $\Delta=b^2-4ac=0$. We check the answers. In (A) $\Delta=1$; in (B) $\Delta=25$; in (C) $\Delta=0$; in (D) $\Delta=1$. (C) is the correct answer.

4. A

It is better to solve this directly instead of figuring out the actual value of b. From $y = 2x + b$, subtract b from both sides and exchange the side, we get $2x=y - b$; divide both sides by 2, $x=\frac{y-b}{2}$, which is (A).

5. B

Plug in the answers. Make $x = 2$, the left hand side evaluates to $\frac{11}{2}$, the right hand side evaluates to $-\frac{4}{3}$. Make $x = -8$, both sides evaluate to -2. (B) is the correct answer.

Algebraically, multiply both sides by 8 we get $6x+32=x-8$. Subtract x and then 32 from both sides, we get $5x=-40$. So $x = -8$, which is (B).

6. A

Because $5a = 45$, $a = 9$. Now $ab=9b=1$, so $b=\frac{1}{9}$, which is (A).

7. D

We have $650 = 2.5(m - 50)$. Multiply both side by 4 then divide by 10, $260=m-50$. So $m = 310$.

8. 9.5

$x-y = (3^{2n-1} +3) - (n+1)$

$x-y = (3^{3-1} +3) - (1.5 + 1)$

x-$y = 12 - 2.5 = 9.5$

9. A

First solve for b in the equation $f(x)$. The easiest way is to look at the table and use the second row, where $x = 0$. We find that $b = 8$. So $f(7)=2\times7+8=22$; and $g(f(7))=g(22) = 5 \times 22 - 9=101$, which is (A).

10. 62.1

Find the original price:

$$(1 - 15\%)x = 229.5$$

$$x = 229.5/ 85\% = 270$$

The original price plus 8% tax:

$$270 (1+8\%) = 291.6$$

She actually saved:

$$291.6 - 229.5 = 62.1$$

11. 60

Suppose the tag price for Final Fantasy is x dollars, and that of the Sims 4 is $1.5x$ dollars. The problem states that

$$2.5x=2(1.5x)-20.$$

Solve this we get $x=40$. So the tag price for the Sims 4 is 60 dollars. Note that the above equation holds, no matter that is the tax rate for the computer games.

ESSAY

In the essay "Global Warming," writer Walter E. Williams tackles the conventional wisdom about climate change. Williams urges his audience to reconsider the widely held belief that science has proven the existence of global warming beyond a doubt. In order to demonstrate that apocalyptic predictions about climate change are unfounded, he reframes the definition of climate change, refutes evidence put forth by his opponents, and relies on "us" versus "them" rhetoric.

Williams opens with a reexamination of the term "climate change," which is often used as a synonym for global warming. The very first line of the essay is a quote from President Obama's 2014 State of the Union address stating that "But the debate is settled. Climate change is a fact." By including the word "but" at the beginning of the quotation, the author hints that he is soon to disagree. In the very next sentence, he lays out the stakes of the debate, arguing that it is "nonsense" to claim that the debate over global warming is finished, but conceding that Obama is correct on climate change. This intriguing contrast urges the reader to ponder what is and is not true about climate change. In the following paragraph, Williams elaborates by supplying the globalchange.gov definition of climate change. Instead of specifically referring to global warming, the term climate change encompasses all of the constantly changing weather patterns over Earth's 4.54 billion year history. By showing that climate change has a much broader meaning than the way that it is typically used, Williams sets the stage for his next attack on global warming.

The credibility of global warming advocates is further weakened by a list of several unfulfilled climate change predictions. Williams explains that following Hurricane Katrina, global warming scientists feared that many similarly catastrophic events would soon follow. He counters powerfully by explaining that according to the Committee for a Constructive Tomorrow, no hurricane of similar magnitude has occurred in the nine years following Hurricane Katrina nor has the Earth's temperature changed over the past eighteen years. In the next paragraph, he shows that doomsday climate predictions are not unique to the present day. As recently as 1969, scientists were concerned not with global warming, but with the threat of a new ice age. By citing a string of contradictory, unrealized predictions of climate change calamities, Williams shows how uncertain the science of climate change really is.

The final way that Williams builds his argument is by deriding his opponents with blunt language. In the first paragraph, he rebuffs the idea that the scientific debate over climate change is over by calling it "nonsense" and shortly thereafter he refers to global warming advocates as "warmers." These phrases cast his opponents as illogical. In the final paragraph, he delivers his knockout blow when he declares that claims that global warming is "settled science" are "disgusting." Here he leads the reader to conclude that global warming proponents are not only misinformed, but anti-science. In contrast, he welcomes the reader as a potential ally against unquestioning belief in global warming. In paragraph two, he begins his response to the reader's hypothetical objections with "you say" and in paragraph five, he includes the reader in his analysis with the line "Let's look at some." Williams's word choice portrays his opponents as foolish while simultaneously inviting his readers to join the elite ranks of those who know better.

Walter E. Williams adamantly rejects the notion that science has reached consensus about global warming. For him, the evidence is wildly inconsistent and unpersuasive. By reexamining the definition of climate change, detailing contradictory predictions, and utilizing aggressive language, he makes his case for reopening the debate about global warming.

New SAT
Practice Tests

New SAT Practice Test 1

Reading Test

65 MINUTES, 52 QUESTIONS

Turn to Section 1 of your answer sheet to answer the questions in this section.

DIRECTIONS

Each passage or pair of passages below is followed by a number of questions. After reading each passage or pair, choose the best answer to each question based on what is stated or implied in the passage or passages and in any accompanying graphics (such as a table or graph).

Questions 1-10 are based on the following passage.

This passage is an excerpt from Ray Bradbury's Fahrenheit 451.

IT WAS A PLEASURE TO BURN

IT was a special pleasure to see things eaten, to see things blackened and changed. With the brass nozzle in his fists, with this great python
Line spitting its venomous kerosene upon the world,
5 the blood pounded in his head, and his hands were the hands of some amazing conductor playing all the symphonies of blazing and burning to bring down the tatters and charcoal ruins of history. With his symbolic helmet
10 numbered 451 on his stolid head, and his eyes all orange flame with the thought of what came next, he flicked the igniter and the house jumped up in a gorging fire that burned the evening sky red and yellow and black. He strode in a swarm
15 of fireflies. He wanted above all, like the old joke, to shove a marshmallow on a stick in the furnace, while the flapping pigeon-winged books died on the porch and lawn of the house. While the books went up in sparkling whirls and blew away on a
20 wind turned dark with burning.

Montag's hand closed like a mouth, crushed the book with wild devotion, with an insanity of mindlessness to his chest. The men above were hurling shovelfuls of magazines into the dusty air.

25 They fell like slaughtered birds and the woman stood below, like a small girl, among the bodies.

Montag had done nothing. His hand had done it all, his hand, with a brain of its own, with a conscience and a curiosity in each trembling
30 finger, had turned thief. Now, it plunged the book back under his arm, pressed it tight to sweating armpit, rushed out empty, with a magician's flourish! Look here! Innocent! Look!

He gazed, shaken, at that white hand. He held
35 it way out, as if he were far-sighted. He held it close, as if he were blind.

"Montag! "

He jerked about.

"Don't stand there, idiot!"

40 The books lay like great mounds of fishes left to dry. The men danced and slipped and fell over them. Titles glittered their golden eyes, falling, gone.

"Kerosene! They pumped the cold fluid
45 from the numbered 451 tanks strapped to their shoulders. They coated each book, they pumped rooms full of it.

They hurried downstairs, Montag staggered after them in the kerosene fumes.

50 "Come on, woman!"

The woman knelt among the books, touching the drenched leather and cardboard, reading the gilt titles with her fingers while her eyes accused Montag.

CONTINUE ➡

55 "You can't ever have my books," she said.
"You know the law," said Beatty. "Where's your
common sense? None of those books agree with
each other. You've been locked up here for years
with a regular damned Tower of Babel. Snap
60 out of it! The people in those books never lived.
Come on now! "
She shook her head.
"The whole house is going up;" said Beatty,
The men walked clumsily to the door. They
65 glanced back at Montag, who stood near the
woman.
"You're not leaving her here?" he protested.
"She won't come."
"Force her, then!"
70 Beatty raised his hand in which was concealed
the igniter. "We're due back at the house. Besides,
these fanatics always try suicide; the pattern's
familiar."
Montag placed his hand on the woman's
75 elbow. "You can come with me."
"No," she said. "Thank you, anyway."
"I'm counting to ten," said Beatty. "One. Two."
"Please," said Montag.
"Go on," said the woman.
80 "Three. Four."
"Here." Montag pulled at the woman.
The woman replied quietly, "I want to stay
here"
"Five. Six."
85 "You can stop counting," she said. She opened
the fingers of one hand slightly and in the palm
of the hand was a single slender object.
An ordinary kitchen match.
The sight of it rushed the men out and down
90 away from the house. Captain Beatty, keeping his
dignity, backed slowly through the front door, his
pink face burnt and shiny from a thousand fires
and night excitements. God, thought Montag,
how true! Always at night the alarm comes.
95 Never by day! Is it because the fire is prettier by
night?

The main purpose of the introduction is to
A. persuade the reader to sympathize with
censorship.
B. familiarize the reader with the ideas of the
protagonist.
C. introduce the idea of censorship through
governmental means.
D. discuss the requirements of firefighting in the
future.

The best evidence for the answer to the previous
question occurs
A. in lines 5 to 9, "his hands were the hands of
some amazing conductor…"
B. in lines 3 to 4, "with this great python…"
C. in lines 1 to 2, "it was a special pleasure to see
things eaten…"
D. in lines 18 to 20, "while the books went up…"

3

As used in line 10, "*stolid*" most nearly means:
A. calm, showing little emotion
B. excited, exuberant
C. charred, burned
D. impulsive

The passage most strongly supports the idea that
A. the woman has been under suspicion for
years.
B. the firefighters routinely demean their victims.
C. Montag has a capacity for empathy.
D. books are symbolic of freedom.

CONTINUE

5

The answer to the previous question is best evidenced by
A. lines 56 through 61 "You know the law…"
B. lines 55 and 88 "you can't ever have my books…"
C. line 75 "you can come with me…"
D. lines 90 and 93 "Captain Beatty, keeping his dignity…"

6

It can be best inferred from the passage that Captain Beatty
A. has developed an impersonal approach to his profession.
B. is impetuous and irrational.
C. has an inner source of empathy and compassion.
D. depends on indifference to provide comfort to his profession.

7

As used in Line 53, "*gilt*" most closely means:
A. gold-leafed
B. a sense of onus
C. charred
D. verbose

8

The best evidence for the previous answer occurs in
A. lines 23 and 24 "the men above…"
B. lines 56-57 "where's your common sense…"
C. lines 82-83 "I want to stay here…"
D. line 42 "Titles glittered their golden eyes…"

9

The author uses the simile in line 40, "the books lay like great mounds of fishes left to dry," to exemplify
A. that the firefighters will have second thoughts about burning the books.
B. that the woman will produce a kitchen match to assume control.
C. that the firefighters need to add kerosene to destroy the books.
D. that the books will cease to have life, like fishes out of water.

10

Montag's theft of the book shows his
A. proclivity towards rule breaking.
B. desire to find solace and meaning in the chaos of his job.
C. ability to feel compassionate towards the woman.
D. desire to be caught.

CONTINUE

Questions 11-21 are based on the passage and graph below

-Adapted from The Rwandan Genocide; Modern History Project 2012 https://modernhistoryproject2012. wordpress.com/history-of-hutu-tutsi-relations/

The 19th century brought with it two separate factors that increased racial tensions between the Hutus and Tutsis. These factors were colonisation
Line coupled with land redistribution problems. The
5 land problems created a system of patronage known as Uburetwa or Ubuhake. These words mean "to work for access to land", and conse- quently, implementation of this system made the Hutus who were not part of the nobility serfs that
10 worked on the land. The relationship between the Tutsi and the Hutu started to descend to crude lord-vassal interactions at this point in history, and the arrival of the German colonists in the late 1800's served to add to the problem, as they
15 endorsed the Tutsis' power over the Hutus'. The colonists did a lot to engender the future tensions between the two races. Their worst contribution was racial science.

After World War I, Belgium was given control
20 over Rwanda. The Belgians increased the divide between the Hutus and Tutsis through the use of the eugenics, which was rather popular at the time (i.e. Nazi Germany). Skull measurements showing larger brain size, greater height, and
25 lighter skin tones all reaffirmed the Tutsis' superiority over the Hutus, by providing proof of their apparent greater purity and closer ancestry to Europeans.

The final step that Belgium took was imple-
30 menting coffee production in Rwanda. Peasant farmers, for the large part Hutus, were obligated to grow coffee beans on their land on punishment of death from Tutsi officials in a system of corvée rule. Corvée is a semantic that is one step
35 higher than slavery. The only difference is that in corvée rule, the ruler does not own the servant outright. For example, many Hutu farmers were subjected to a standard 10 lashes daily, before work, so as to remind them to maintain a solid
40 work ethic. Essentially, by the time of Rwandan

independence in 1962, the Hutu were an oppressed race, facing cruelty from a Tutsi elite, who were manipulated by the colonists.

After World War II, Belgium took a different
45 approach to Rwanda. In 1946, Rwanda, then known as Rwanda-Urundi, became a UN trust territory, with Belgium as the administrative authority. In the interest of increased democracy, and under the auspices of the UN, Belgian elite
50 and King Mutara Rudahigwa, the Mwami at the time, started to integrate more Hutus into the administration. King Rudahigwa also abolished the system of Ubuhake. Some Tutsi elite were angered by this, because they assessed the
55 situation as a threat to Tutsi rule (arguably an astute observation).

By 1954, King Rudahigwa insisted total independence for Rwanda and the end of the Belgian occupation. During the independence
60 movement, under the influence of the Roman Catholic Church, a Hutu catechist name Gregoire Kayibanda published the Hutu Manifesto, a document that demanded that political authority be granted to the Hutu majority (when the
65 Belgians leave). This was the basis for the ideology of Hutu Power during the genocide. The Church further encouraged Kayibanda and his associates to form political parties.

While the politics of Rwanda was undergoing
70 radical change, Belgian Commando Colonel, G. Logiest, organized a large group Hutus and killed thousands of Tutsis and forced the exile of hundreds of thousands others. Soon, King Kigeli was also forced into exile, having reigned
75 for only a few months. The newly 'democratized' Rwanda held an election in 1960. Many believed that the Belgians tampered in the results, but ultimately Parmehetu won, and their leader, the aforementioned Gregoire Kayibanda became
80 Prime Minister of the provisional government. On September 25th of the same year, the UN held a referendum in Rwanda in order to determine whether the monarchy should be abolished. Through the referendum process, the abolition
85 of the monarchy won the popular vote, and thus

CONTINUE ➤

ended the reign of the Tutsi Mwami in Rwanda. This gave the Hutus the position of power through Gregoire Kayibanda, the new President and Prime Minister. In 1962, the Belgians

90　left Rwanda and it was officially declared an independent state.

Table 1.Semi- Rigorous Estimates of Rwandan Casualties, Type 1

Source	Total	Tutsis	Hutus
UN-Cmte of Experts 1994	500,000 to I million	NA	NA
Human Rights Watch 1995/99	800,000	500,000	300,000
Africa Rights 1994/95	NA	438,000	NA
Gerard Prunier 1996	850,000	800,000	50,000
Filip Reyntjens 1997	1,050,000-1,150,000	600,000~	40,000~
Rwandan Government 2002 (Census)	1,074,017	998,835	75,182
Rwandan Student Survivors 2004	NA	1,952,078	NA
Rwandan Government 2008 (Survey)	1 million +	700,000	300,000~

-graph copied from www.politicalviolenceataglance.org

11

The primary purpose of the article is to
A. discuss the vassal-serf relationship that existed between the Hutus and Tsutsis.
B. detail the factors contributing to the Rwandan genocide.
C. show how European influence helped the Tsutsis.
D. evaluate UN influence on democratic advances in Rwanda.

12

The term *engender* in line 16 can best be defined as:
A. cause
B. align
C. dispel
D. coerce

13

It can be best inferred from the selection that
A. The United Nations has a long history of involvement in Rwanda.
B. Belgian influence can best be described as neutral.
C. prior to 1946, the United Nations took little interest or action in Rwanda.
D. Mwami rule was popular with the people of Rwanda.

14

The establishment of *corvee* rule best served to
A. change Belgian approaches to the Rwandan system of government.
B. create a more equal distribution of power among Hutus and Tsutsis.
C. force the United Nations into intervening in Rwanda.
D. establish a long-term system of government for future generations.

15

Evidence for question 14 is best provided by which of the following:
A. lines 57-65, "By 1954, King Rudahigwa…."
B. lines 40-43, "Essentially, by the time of Rwandan independence…"
C. lines 48-52, "In the interest of democracy…"
D. lines 69-73, "While the politics of Rwanda was undergoing radical change"

CONTINUE ▶

16

From the graph provided, which of the following is most likely true?

A. Tsutsi influence in government caused over-inflated statistics.

B. There is widespread agreement on the number and demographics of casualties.

C. The United Nations provided accurate accounts of casualties.

D. The statistics in 2002 were most likely inaccurate based upon the other evidence provided.

17

It can be inferred from the passage that the author most likely agrees with which of the following?

A. The influence of European colonists, in effect, caused the Rwandan genocide.

B. European systems of government provided the framework for what would become the Rwandan government.

C. The implementation of coffee production served to foster understanding between land owners and farmers.

D. The system of Ubuhake offered an opportunity for farmers to become land owners.

18

The term *eugenics* in line 22 most closely means:

A. the study of human physiology

B. a lord-vassal system of government

C. racial segregation

D. the belief in racial superiority based upon physical characteristics

19

From the last paragraph, which of the following is most likely true?

A. Col. G. Logiest broke from prior Belgian stances in Rwanda.

B. The Belgian government continued their stance of neutrality.

C. There was an increased level of understanding between Hutu and Tsutsi factions of government.

D. The United Nations' influence in Rwanda was best described as laissez-faire.

20

Evidence for question 19 is best found in:

A. lines 76-80, "Many believed that the Beligians tampered…"

B. lines 73-76, "Soon, King Kigeli was forced into exile…"

C. lines 71-73, "organized a large group of Hutus…"

D. lines 84-86, "Through the referendum process…"

21

The author's tone regarding European influence prior to World War II can best be described as:

A. conciliatory

B. accusatory and angry

C. understanding and grateful

D. grudgingly acceptant

CONTINUE

Questions 22-32 are based on the following passage

-adapted from Dr. Martin Luther King Jr.'s "I Have a Dream" speech, 8/28/1963

There are those who are asking the devotees of civil rights, "When will you be satisfied?" We can never be satisfied as long as the Negro is
Line the victim of the unspeakable horrors of police
5 brutality. We can never be satisfied as long as our bodies, heavy with the fatigue of travel, cannot gain lodging in the motels of the highways and the hotels of the cities. We cannot be satisfied as long as the negro's basic mobility is from a
10 smaller ghetto to a larger one. We can never be satisfied as long as our children are stripped of their self-hood and robbed of their dignity by signs stating: "For Whites Only." We cannot be satisfied as long as a Negro in Mississippi cannot
15 vote and a Negro in New York believes he has nothing for which to vote. No, no, we are not satisfied, and we will not be satisfied until "justice rolls down like waters, and righteousness like a mighty stream."
20 I am not unmindful that some of you have come here out of great trials and tribulations. Some of you have come fresh from narrow jail cells. And some of you have come from areas where your quest – a quest for freedom left
25 you battered by the storms of persecution and staggered by the winds of police brutality. You have been the veterans of creative suffering. Continue to work with the faith that unearned suffering is redemptive. Go back to Mississippi,
30 go back to Alabama, go back to South Carolina, go back to Georgia, go back to Louisiana, go back to the slums and ghettos of our northern cities, knowing that somehow this situation can and will be changed.
35 Let us not wallow in the valley of despair, I say to you today, my friends.

And so even though we face the difficulties of today and tomorrow, I still have a dream. It is a dream deeply rooted in the American dream.
40 I have a dream that one day this nation will rise up and live out the true meaning of its creed:

"We hold these truths to be self-evident, that all men are created equal."

I have a dream that one day on the red hills of
45 Georgia, the sons of former slaves and the sons of former slave owners will be able to sit down together at the table of brotherhood.

I have a dream that one day even the state of Mississippi, a state sweltering with the heat of
50 injustice, sweltering with the heat of oppression, will be transformed into an oasis of freedom and justice.

I have a dream that my four little children will one day live in a nation where they will not
55 be judged by the color of their skin but by the content of their character.

I have a *dream* today!

I have a dream that one day, *down* in Alabama, with its vicious racists, with its
60 governor having his lips dripping with the words of "interposition" and "nullification" — one day right there in Alabama little black boys and black girls will be able to join hands with little white boys and white girls as sisters and brothers.
65 I have a *dream* today!

I have a dream that one day every valley shall be exalted, and every hill and mountain shall be made low, the rough places will be made plain, and the crooked places will be made straight; "and
70 the glory of the Lord shall be revealed and all flesh shall see it together."

This is our hope, and this is the faith that I go back to the South with.

With this faith, we will be able to hew out
75 of the mountain of despair a stone of hope. With this faith, we will be able to transform the jangling discords of our nation into a beautiful symphony of brotherhood. With this faith, we will be able to work together, to pray together, to
80 struggle together, to go to jail together, to stand up for freedom together, knowing that we will be free one day.

22

Which of the following most closely describes the author's perspective on the civil rights movement?

A. passive complacency
B. vehement opposition
C. steadfast resolve
D. silent understanding

23

Evidence for question 22 can best be found

A. in lines 20-21, "I am not unmindful...."
B. in lines 74-75, "With this faith, we will be able to..."
C. in lines 37-39, "And so even though we face..."
D. in lines 1-5, "There are those who are asking..."

24

The term *sweltering* in line 49 most closely means:

A. stifling
B. humid
C. melting
D. coolness

25

The main purpose of the speech being delivered is to

A. discuss the causes of racial divide in the South.
B. assign blame to the current state of racial affairs.
C. offer alternatives to current racial segregation practices.
D. persuade the listener of the virtues of desegregation.

26

The author's view of the future can best be characterized as:

A. anxiously skeptical
B. passionately optimistic
C. cynical
D. angrily accusatory

27

The lines 74-78, "With this faith, we will be able to transform the jangling discords of our nation into a beautiful symphony of brotherhood," best expresses the opinion that

A. societal change comes with considerable risk.
B. current conditions warrant an impartial third party to establish racial change.
C. utilizing current society in a cohesive manner can bring together productive results.
D. the amount of current discord makes change impossible.

28

Support for question 27 can best be found

A. in lines 58-64, "I have a dream that one day, down in Alabama..."
B. in lines 29-34, "Go back to Mississippi..."
C. in lines 68-71, "rough places will be made plain..."
D. in line 74, "With this faith, we will be able to..."

45

CONTINUE ▶

29

The term *exalted* in line 67 best means:

A. raised
B. praised
C. exonerated
D. worshipped

30

The author's feelings towards other activists in the civil rights movement can best be characterized as:

A. judgmental
B. unappreciative and demanding
C. respectful
D. compassionate gratitude

31

This is best exemplified by the statement in

A. lines 20-21, "I am not unmindful…"
B. lines 28-29, "Continue to work with the faith that…"
C. line 35, "Let us not wallow in the valley of despair…"
D. lines 40-41, "I have a dream that one day, this nation…"

32

The author's statement that "a Negro in Mississippi cannot vote and a Negro in New York believes he has nothing for which to vote," most likely means most Negroes believe

A. suffrage is of paramount importance.
B. their actions need to convey the points of the Negro more clearly.
C. few politicians have the ideals of Negroes in mind.
D. universal voting rights are unrealistic.

CONTINUE ➡

Questions 33-42 deal with the paragraph that follows

-adapted from "25 Years of Hubble Space Telescope: A Story of Redemption" by Calla Cofield for space.com, 25 April 2015

NASA unveiled its official anniversary image for the Hubble 25-year celebration. It's a cosmic landscape featuring multicolored gas clouds and
Line dazzling, jewel-like stars — a breathtaking image
5 of a region in space that can teach astronomers about how star clusters form in the universe. When it comes to this equation of beauty plus science, there really isn't another scientific instrument on Earth, or in orbit, that can
10 compete with the Hubble telescope.

"Even the most optimistic person to whom you could have spoken back in 1990 couldn't have predicted the degree to which Hubble would rewrite our astrophysics and planetary science
15 textbooks," NASA Administrator Charles Bolden said at the image-unveiling event. "A quarter-century later, Hubble has fundamentally changed our understanding of our universe, and our place in it."
20 At its current pace, the Hubble telescope produces 10TB of new data per year — enough to fill the entire collection of the Library of Congress, Bolden said. At that same event, Kathy Flanagan, interim director of the Space Telescope
25 Science Institute in Baltimore, which operates Hubble's science program, said scientists using data from the telescope have produced "nearly 13,000" science papers.

This week, NASA hosted a Hubble
30 symposium to discuss major science results from the telescope. The space agency also has hosted Hubble-themed events for the press and the general public, as well as a Friday night (April 24) gala to honor many of the people who made
35 Hubble what it is today. Few, if any other, NASA projects have garnered such an ovation.

The Hubble telescope climbed to its current position at the peak of accomplishment from some deep valleys of near failure.
40 In his book, "The Universe a Mirror: The

Saga of the Hubble Space Telescope and the Visionaries Who Built it," (Princeton University Press, 2008), science writer Robert Zimmerman chronicled the decades-long slog to get the
45 Hubble telescope to where it is today. First, there was the chore of convincing the astronomy community to agree to invest in such a costly project, and then to get Congress to fund it, and to keep funding it during construction. It wasn't
50 just the telescope that suffered during those years; Zimmerman also wrote about people who dedicated themselves to Hubble at the expense of their careers or even their personal lives.

The Hubble Space Telescope was originally
55 scheduled to blast off in 1983 but didn't get off the ground until 1990. Shortly after the telescope's launch, the scientific team realized the images they were receiving were blurry. It turned out that the telescope's mirror was ground ever so
60 slightly to the wrong thickness. (The flaw arose because of a mistake with the testing equipment used during the mirror's construction.)

In 1993, the first Hubble servicing mission installed hardware that could adjust for the
65 flaw in the mirror, and the telescope quickly blossomed to its full potential. It revealed new information at every size scale, from the solar system to the entire observable universe. Hubble has found four new moons around Pluto, demon-
70 strated that galaxies frequently collide and merge together, drastically improved measurements of the age of the universe, and showed that space is not only expanding but spreading out faster and faster.
75 By 2003, Hubble had provided more than a decade of valuable science and beautiful images. At that point, it could have retired and still been labeled a success. But plans were in the works to add two new instruments to Hubble and repair
80 two instruments that had stopped working.

The fifth and thus-far final crewed repair mission to Hubble took place in 2009. That mission is a microcosm of Hubble's life story: full of close calls that nearly spelled disaster for
85 the telescope, like when a bolt holding down

CONTINUE

a handrail wouldn't come loose and nearly prevented the astronauts from getting to one of the instruments that needed fixing.

In the end, the mission was a complete
90 success. The astronauts installed two new instruments, fixed two broken instruments, and installed new batteries, new gyroscopes and a new scientific computer, to prolong Hubble's life. Today, it continues to be one of the most
95 powerful, most in-demand telescopes in the world.

33

It can be assumed that, following the various delays and initial blurry images, the scientific community
A. began contemplating alternative methods of exploring the outer reaches of the solar system.
B. most likely considered Hubble a failure.
C. began scrapping the project in favor of another cutting edge telescope.
D. the problem would go away over a period of time.

34

The term "microcosm" in line 83 is best defined as:
A. particle
B. portion of the universe
C. small example
D. evidence

35

The authors of the article would most likely agree with the statement:
A. Despite the many setbacks and costs, Hubble has exceeded expectations.
B. Though great scientific discoveries have been gained, Hubble is only a modest success.
C. Hubble is nearing the end of its usefulness.
D. Recent advances in scientific exploration have rendered Hubble obsolete.

36

The best evidence for the previous question lies in the statement in
A. lines 54-56, "The Hubble Space Telescope…"
B. lines 37-39, "The Hubble telescope climbed to its current position…"
C. lines 77-78, "At that point, it could have retired…"
D. lines 7-10, "When it comes to this equation…"

37

It can be reasonably inferred from the passage that
A. advances in astrophysics are critical to Hubble's continued success.
B. the extent to which we now understand the universe is primarily due to Hubble.
C. though its contributions are numerable, the conclusions drawn from evidence obtained from Hubble has been inconsistent and marginally reliable.
D. future funding for Hubble is in dire jeopardy.

38

The author describes the 2009 repair mission as, "the fifth and thus-far final" one mainly to illustrate

A. the belief that Hubble will continue to be utilized and, likewise, maintained for many years.

B. the assertion that no further repair missions will be made for this aging and increasingly obsolete piece of scientific equipment.

C. the belief that no further repair missions will be necessary for the expected remaining years of Hubble usefulness.

D. budgetary restrictions will not provide for any further missions to repair Hubble.

39

The term "slog" in line 44 most likely means:

A. arduous task

B. aloofness of spirit

C. haphazard

D. slow, deliberate process

40

The gala celebration of Hubble served, in effect, to recognize

A. the authors of the scholarly articles published with Hubble data.

B. the exploits and accomplishments of the various repair missions.

C. the innovators and initial supporters of Hubble as veritable scientific heroes.

D. the DeIver Looking Glass, which helped correct the initial blurry images.

41

From the passage, which statement is most likely true?

A. Expectations of the scientific community generally engendered a feeling of understanding through Hubble's early setbacks.

B. Researchers who supported Hubble faced considerable odds, both personally and professionally, in even undertaking such a project.

C. Evidence obtained from Hubble has been marginally useful as a means of scientific inquiry and advancement.

D. The delay in Hubble's launch was causative of the various mechanical problems experienced by Hubble.

42

Evidence for question 41 is best found in

A. lines 51-53, "Zimmerman also wrote about…"

B. lines 54-56, "The Hubble Space Telescope was originally…"

C. lines 31-35, "The space agency has also hosted…"

D. lines 58-61, "It turned out…"

CONTINUE ➤

Questions 43-52 deal with the paragraphs below

-adapted from "Great Barrier Reef on brink of devastation in relentless quest for coal", by Dr. Helen Caldicott for The Sydney Morning Herald, 4 February 2014

The rampant destruction of the Great Barrier Reef, given the green light last Friday by the federal government, epitomises the values of our
Line modern world. "Economic development" and
5 "jobs" reign supreme while our reef, one of the seven wonders of the world, a UNESCO World Heritage site, is in great jeopardy.

Home to endangered dugongs, glorious endangered sea turtles and corals, it is seething
10 with life rich in biodiversity containing many potential medications to treat cancer and other diseases. The preservation of this unique treasure is now secondary to the voracious greed on the part of Queensland and federal governments and
15 some individuals to export coal.

By 2030 Australia is predicted to increase its export of coal from 240 million tonnes this year to 787 million tonnes in 2030. Queensland's liquefied natural gas and coal exports are soaring
20 in order to deliver atmospheric-warming carbon fuels to satisfy Chinese and Indian markets.

This fecund zone is of cardinal importance for not only cycling nutrients that sustain all coastal sea-life, but it protects the reef from land-based
25 toxicity that enters the sea. The reef's magnificent natural shield has been impregnated. The acidification of the ocean as a result of global warming further compromises the structure of the corals.

Then there is the problem of noise. The
30 Queensland and federal governments are aware that noise pollution can have a detrimental effect on oceanic wildlife including all the biological processes that take place within the reef itself. Whales, dolphins, sea turtles and dugongs are at
35 risk from noise pollution as they incur cardiovascular and autoimmune stresses. Animals ranging from blue whales to the coral clown fish cease feeding and noise pollution prevents mating.

Yet no government noise regulation has been
40 imposed on industry to curtail the final death

knell for Earth's greatest reef, although the UN convention on Law Of The Sea states that all countries are to lessen under-sea noise pollution, including vessel noise and sub-sea construction
45 equipment.

But as well as noise pollution, the ongoing damage is extraordinary. To create three liquefied natural gas terminals on Curtis Island near Gladstone, 21 million tonnes of material were
50 dredged. This irreparably destroyed the seabed, enormous plumes of sediment were released, fish were killed en masse and the bund wall containing land-dumped dredging was breached, causing a vast toxic algal bloom. Meanwhile,
55 Environment Minister Greg Hunt has authorised the Abbot Point port to dredge 3 million tonnes from the seabed to create six new coal ship berths.

-adapted from "Australia to dump dredged sand in Great Barrier Reef Park", by Euan McKirdy for cnn.com, 31 January 2014

The Australian federal government has
60 approved a plan to dump 3 million cubic meters of dredge spoil in the Great Barrier Reef Park. The dredged material will come from the proposed expansion of the coal port at Abbot Point, south of Townsville on the Queensland
65 coast.

Final approval came from the Great Barrier Reef Marine Park Authority, and is subject to "strict conditions." The proposal, while controversial and opposed by environmental
70 groups including Greenpeace, had already been approved by Federal Environment Minister Greg Hunt last month.

The reef is the largest living structure on the planet, and is a hugely diverse ecosystem
75 stretching 2,300 kilometers along the Queensland coast. The Great Barrier Reef Marine Park is 345,000 square kilometers in size and home to thousands of species of coral, fish, mollusks, jellyfish, sharks and whales.
80 The Authority's General Manager for Biodiversity, Conservation and Sustainable

CONTINUE ➤

Use, Bruce Elliot states that the environmental safeguards — 47 in total — insisted upon by the Authority would protect the reef and seagrasses,
85 along with the social and heritage uses of the marine park.

"By granting this permit application with rigorous safeguards, we believe we are able to provide certainty to both the community and the
90 proponent while seeking to ensure transparent and best practice environmental management of the project," he said.

The Great Barrier Reef was designated a World Heritage Site by UNESCO in 1981 and
95 environmental group Greenpeace warned that the move to allow dumping in the park may lead to that organization listing the site as "in danger" this year.

"This go-ahead for dumping is one more body
100 blow for the Reef which further threatens marine life, its World Heritage status and Australia's tourism and fishing industries," Greenpeace Reef Campaigner Louise Matthiesson said on the group's website.
105 "Green lighting the reef's destruction makes a mockery of the Authority's charter which obliges it to protect the Great Barrier Reef Marine Park and the World Heritage Area."

43

The writing style of passage 1, as it compares to passage 2, can best be described as

A. based largely on information gathered from interview while passage 2 relies heavily on scientific fact.
B. reflecting a more editorial perspective while passage 2 is generally neutral and informative.
C. relying strictly on fact over opinion.
D. presumptuous rather than opinionated.

44

The term "mockery" in line 106 most closely means:

A. example
B. detailed illustration
C. supportive argument
D. sarcastic joke

45

The author of passage 1's assertion that the Great Barrier Reef has been given the "green light for destruction" and is in dire jeopardy is primarily aimed at

A. alerting the public to eventual dangers inherent in the dredging and shipping operations approved by the federal government.
B. detailing ineffective governmental regulation and the country's failure to implement United Nations stipulations.
C. sparking discussion regarding the potential dangers of vast toxic algal bloom and methods to combat such an event.
D. discussing the biodiversity and ecological systems inhabiting the Great Barrier Reef.

CONTINUE ➡

46

The best evidence for the answer to the previous question is found in:
A. lines 12-15, "The preservation of this unique treasure…"
B. lines 22-25, "This fecund zone is of cardinal importance…"
C. lines 46-50, "But as well as noise pollution…"
D. lines 25-28, "The reef's magnificent natural shield…"

47

Passage 2 accurately predicts which of the potential ecological dangers detailed in Passage 1:
A. a sharp decrease in profits for the fishing industry
B. departure of various forms of sea life, including whales, dugongs, and sea turtles from the reef due to noise pollution
C. dredge spoils affecting aspects of marine life and the tourism/fishing industries
D. increases in vast, toxic algal blooms

48

The term "fecund" in line 22 most likely means:
A. increasingly polluted
B. shrinking
C. diverse
D. productive and fertile

49

From information obtained in Passage 2, governmental regulators most likely feel
A. satisfied and optimistic regarding avoiding potential environmental dangers.
B. cautious and wary of future environmental encroachment by industry in the Great Barrier Reef.
C. encouraged by the return of diverse species to the reef due to government enforced environmental regulations.
D. guarded from pro-environmental agencies opposed to dredging and coal shipping in Australia.

50

Evidence for the previous question is best found in
A. lines 99-102, "The go-ahead for dumping…"
B. lines 80-86, "The Authority's General Manager…"
C. lines 73-76, "The reef is the largest living structure…"
D. lines 105-108, "Green lighting the reef's destruction…"

CONTINUE ▶

51

The authors of Passages 1 and 2 most likely share which potential negative outcome?

A. the effects of overfishing on the biodiversity of the Great Barrier Reef and other critical structures
B. oil spills resulting from increasing shipping procedures in the open market
C. increasing greenhouse gases and western demand for oil and coal will further affect the intricate ecosystems of their country
D. higher demand for consumable products will deplete our natural resources

52

Which of the following situations is most analogous to lines 22-28, "This fecund zone is of cardinal importance...":

A. the concerns over the effects of deforestation of the Amazon Rain Forest and the related effects on the unique and diverse ecosystems contained in that region
B. overfishing of certain species leading to the depletion of various types of fish species
C. rampant poaching in Africa leading to the destruction and near-extinction of a number of rhino species
D. sharp increases in carbon-based emissions and greenhouse gases further widening holes in the ozone layer

STOP

If you finish before time is called, you may check your work on this section only. Do not turn to any other section.

ACKNOWLEDGEMENT FOR THIS SECTION

Passages in this section were adapted from the following sources:

Ray Bradbury, "Fahrenheit 451", first published by Ballantine Books, 1953

Helen Caldicott, "Great Barrier Reef on brink of devastation in relentless quest for coal", © 2014 by *The Sydney Morning Herald*. Originally published 4 February 2014

Calla Cofield, "25 years of Hubble Space Telescope: A History of Redemption", for space.com, 25 April 2015

Martin Luther King, Jr., "I Have a Dream" speech, 8 August 1963.

Euan McKirdy, "Australia to dump dredged sand in Great Barrier Reef Park". For cnn.com, 31 January 2014

Writing and Language Test

35 MINUTES, 44 QUESTIONS

Turn to Section 2 of your answer sheet to answer the questions in this section.

DIRECTIONS

Each passage below is accompanied by a number of questions. For some questions, you will consider how the passage might be revised to improve the expression of ideas. For other questions, you will consider how the passage might be edited to correct errors in sentence structure, usage, or punctuation. A passage or a question may be accompanied by one or more graphics (such as a table or graph) that you will consider as you make revising and editing decisions.

Some questions will direct you to an underlined portion of a passage. Other questions will direct you to a location in a passage or ask you to think about the passage as a whole.

After reading each passage, choose the answer to each question that most effectively improves the quality of writing in the passage or that makes the passage conform to the conventions of standard written English. Many questions include a "NO CHANGE" option. Choose that option if you think the best choice is to leave the relevant portion of the passage as it is.

Questions 1 – 11 are based on the following passage.

Therapeutic Art

The swimming sky of oceanic expanse in Van Gogh's *The Starry Night*; the human figure born of marble by the careful hands of Rodin; the graceful, ethereal figure of Degas's ballerina; **1** all communicate both emotion and essence in a world where aesthetic reigns supreme. Art has forever been humankind's tool of expressing **2** the ineffable, it is a form of communication when words fail or are wholly inadequate. Art challenges the artist by constructing

1

A. NO CHANGE
B. that all communicate
C. which all communicate
D. all communicating

2

A. NO CHANGE
B. the ineffable, a form of communication
C. the ineffable a form of communication
D. the ineffable form of communication

CONTINUE →

a world, which opposing forces — impulse **3** <u>and</u> <u>control, feeling and thinking</u>, ideation and actuality — must cooperate to produce a piece of art. The artist must wrestle an almost untamable creative force for control in order to grant space to its expression. The process of facing and governing this force while conveying it to others **4** <u>make</u> artistic creation an especially valuable therapeutic tool for the emotionally disturbed.

The process of creation and the created product are equally valuable parts of therapeutic art. **5** <u>Creating art requires balancing</u> two aspects of personality that are, in the case of emotionally disturbed person, especially irreconcilable. Like all artists, the emotionally disturbed person must learn to control and harness the dangerous, unpredictable forces of creation **6** <u>while remains</u> sufficiently unrestrictive to allow its expression. Balancing these forces in a constructive way while granting full play to both is an important ability to master, **7** <u>one</u> that art therapy teaches particularly well.

The emotionally disturbed artist's goal is not the perfect expression of an aesthetic ideal. **8** <u>And</u> communicating the mind's content and having it recognized by others is intensely valuable to the disturbed artist's healing. Taking ideas out of the

3

A. NO CHANGE
B. feeling, and thought,
C. emotion and thought,
D. feeling of thought

4

A. NO CHANGE
B. making
C. made
D. makes

5

A. NO CHANGE
B. Create art requires balancing
C. Create art requires balance
D. Creating art requires balance

6

A. NO CHANGE
B. but remains
C. while remaining
D. and remains

7

A. NO CHANGE
B. which
C. that
D. one ability

8

A. NO CHANGE
B. therefore
C. So
D. Yet

isolation **9** <u>impose by</u> the mind and reproducing them in a form that can be shared and understood by others releases those ideas from the mind and removes from them some of their power. Using the brush where the pen and voice fail allows others, like the therapist, to **10** <u>recognize, understand and begin</u> to deconstruct the mind's content.

Artistic creation allows emotionally disturbed people to communicate ideas they are unable to express in words, and it provides therapists with **11** <u>an opportunity to peek into</u> the mind. Examination of their artistic pieces reveals an inner world that the self of the disturbed person cannot express another way. Art then becomes a new therapeutic medium through which to understand and address the complex issues that threaten and haunt the disturbed person, and in which to free them.

9

A. NO CHANGE
B. imposing
C. imposed by
D. imposes

10

A. NO CHANGE
B. recognize, understand, and begin
C. recognize understand and begin
D. recognize, understand, and, begin

11

Which choice establishes best cohesion in the paragraph?
A. NO CHANGE
B. a chance to see
C. an otherwise unobtainable window into
D. a hint as to what's going on in

Questions 12 – 22 are based on the following passage.

The Watch

The Apple Watch promises to make **12** user's lives better in a number of ways, from helping them stay on schedule to tracking their physical activity. But early reviews of the product suggest another possible improvement: It might get us to quit staring at our phones.

At The Times, Farhad Manjoo writes that the watch "could address some of the social angst wrought by smartphones." It communicates with wearers in part via a system of taps, **13** minimizing the amount of time they have to spend actually looking at the screen. The device, Mr. Manjoo writes, "could usher in a transformation of social norms **14** just profound as those we saw with its brother, the smartphone — except, amazingly, in reverse."

Geoffrey A. Fowler at The Wall Street Journal appreciates the tapping system. The watch, he writes, "has made me more present. I'm less likely to **15** absent-mindedly reach for my phone, or feel compelled to leave it on the table during supper."

Mr. Manjoo and Mr. Fowler both report looking at the watch screen for **16** shorter stints then they'd spend on their phones, but it's certainly possible to imagine **17** users get more glued to their watch screens with time. And heavy users of photo- and video-sharing apps will likely remain tied to their

12

A. NO CHANGE
B. users lives
C. users' life
D. users' lives

13

A. NO CHANGE
B. minimizes
C. to minimize
D. minimized

14

A. NO CHANGE
B. just as profound like those
C. just as profound as those
D. just as profound those

15

A. NO CHANGE
B. absent mindedly
C. absent-minded
D. absent mind

16

A. NO CHANGE
B. shorter stints than
C. short stints then
D. short stints than

17

A. NO CHANGE
B. users who get
C. users getting
D. users who getting

CONTINUE ➔

phones for now, since the watch has no camera. **18** The device at least suggests an alternative to the status quo.

IPhones are by now notorious as thieves of attention, but it's not at all **19** clear, that people actually want to be as attentive to them as they are. The sheer frequency of public pledges to put the phone down and spend more time talking to friends and family **20** suggests that while it's certainly easy to kill an hour scrolling through Twitter, it may not actually be all that pleasant.

21 Those who argue that smartphone use is destroying society, they are overstating the case. As Nathan Jurgenson has argued, interactions that take place via digital devices aren't necessarily evil, unhealthy, or fake. But it's worth asking if we actually enjoy all the time we spend with our phones, or if we might prefer to spend less. **22** I guess that a less absorbing device might actually make us happier.

With the advent of the Apple Watch, some consumers — those able to drop at least $350, the price of the cheapest model — may have the opportunity to find out.

18
A. NO CHANGE
B. And, the device
C. Still, the device
D. Therefore, the device,

19
A. NO CHANGE
B. that clear people
C. that clear, people
D. clear that people

20
A. NO CHANGE
B. suggest
C. suggesting
D. suggested

21
A. NO CHANGE
B. Those who argue that smartphone use is destroying society are
C. Some people argue that smartphone use is destroying society, they are
D. Arguing that smartphone use is destroying society are

22
Which choice is most consistent with the tone of the passage?
A. NO CHANGE
B. It seems
C. It's arguable
D. It's distinctly possible

CONTINUE

Questions 23 – 33 are based on the following passage.

Round World? Flat World!

In 1492 Christopher Columbus set sail for India, going west. He never did find India, but he called the people he met "Indians" and came home and reported to his king and queen: "The world is round." I set **23** off for India 512 years later. I knew just which direction I was going. I went east. I came home and reported only to my wife and only in a whisper: "The world is flat."

I wish I **24** can say I saw it all coming. Alas, I encountered the flattening of the world quite by accident. It was in late February of last year, and I was visiting the Indian high-tech capital, Bangalore, **25** work on a documentary for Discovery Times Channel about outsourcing. The longer I was there, **26** the more upset I became — upset at the realization that while I had been off covering the 9/11 wars, globalization had entered a whole new phase, and I had missed it.

I guess the eureka moment came on a visit to the campus of Infosys Technologies, one of the crown jewels of the Indian outsourcing and software industry. Nandan Nilekani, the Infosys C.E.O., was showing me his global video-conference room, pointing with pride to a **27** wall size flat screen TV, **28** that he said was the biggest in Asia. Infosys, he explained, could hold a virtual meeting of the key players from its entire global supply chain for any project at any time on that supersize screen. So its American designers could be on the screen speaking with their Indian software writers and their Asian

23
A. NO CHANGE
B. of for
C. for
D. to

24
A. NO CHANGE
B. can say I see
C. could say I see
D. could say I saw

25
A. NO CHANGE
B. working on
C. works on
D. worked on

26
A. NO CHANGE
B. more upset I became
C. I became the more upset
D. I became more upset

27
A. NO CHANGE
B. wall- size flat screen TV
C. wall-size flat-screen TV
D. wall size flat-screen TV

28
A. NO CHANGE
B. which he said
C. he said that
D. he said which

CONTINUE

manufacturers all at once. That's **29** all what globalization is about today, Nilekani said.

"Outsourcing is just one dimension of a much
more fundamental thing happening today in the
world," Nilekani explained. "What **30** happened over
the last years is that there was a massive investment
in technology, especially in the bubble era, when
hundreds of millions of dollars were invested in
putting broadband connectivity around the world,
undersea cables, all those things." **31** At the same time
he added, computers became cheaper and dispersed
all over the world, and there was an explosion of e-mail
software, search engines like Google and proprietary
software that can chop up any piece of work and send
one part to Boston, one part to Bangalore and one part
to Beijing, **32** make it easy for anyone to do remote
development.

At one point, summing up the implications of all
this, Nilekani uttered a phrase that rang in my ear. He
said to me, "Tom, the playing field is being leveled."
He meant that countries like India were now able to
compete equally for global knowledge work as never
before — and that America had better to get ready
for this. As I left the Infosys campus that evening and
bounced along the potholed road back to Bangalore,
I kept chewing on that phrase: "The playing field is
being leveled."

"What Nandan is saying," I thought, "is that the
playing field is being flattened. Flattened? Flattened?
My God, he's telling me **33** the world is flattened!"

29

A. NO CHANGE
B. all globalization is about
C. what is globalization all about
D. what globalization is all about

30

A. NO CHANGE
B. happened over the last years that there
C. happened over the last years is there
D. is happened over the last years there

31

A. NO CHANGE
B. At the same time, he added computers
C. At the same time, he added, computers
D. At the same time he added computers

32

A. NO CHANGE
B. making it easy
C. to make it easy
D. makes it easy

33

Which choice is the best way to end the passage?
A. NO CHANGE
B. the world is not round!
C. the world is flat!
D. the world is leveled!

CONTINUE ➤

Questions 34 – 44 are based on the following passage.

My message to the head of the Louvre would be to come and see how we are living here," said Tariq, a carpenter's helper [34] working on construction of the Louvre Abu Dhabi, a $653 million Middle Eastern outpost of the iconic Parisian museum. [35] It was set to be completed in 2015. Its collection will include a Torah from 19th-century Yemen, Picassos, and Magrittes.

"See our living conditions and think about the promises they made," Tariq told me through a translator.

Last year, in his mid 30s, Tariq [36] leave his job at a Pakistani textile mill with dreams of [37] be a crane operator in the Gulf. He showed me his certificate of crane proficiency, pulling the worn piece of paper out of the pocket of his beige *salwar kameez*. Recruiters promised him a salary of $326 a month—for a $1,776 recruitment fee to be paid in advance. With a cousin guiding him through the process, Tariq flew to Abu Dhabi to work for the Regal Construction company, one of roughly 900 construction outfits that employ foreign workers in the emirate. [38]

34
A. NO CHANGE
B. work
C. works
D. to work

35
Which choice most effectively combines the two sentences at the underlined portion?
A. It was set to be completed in 2015, its collection
B. It was set to be completed in 2015, and its collection
C. It was set to be completed in 2015, when its collection
D. Set to be completed in 2015, its collection

36
A. NO CHANGE
B. leaves
C. left
D. has left

37
A. NO CHANGE
B. to be
C. is
D. being

38
At this point, the writer is considering adding the following sentence to end this paragraph.
"Located in the San Fernando Valley, Regal Construction Company is a family owned and operated company since 1969."
Should the writer make this addition here?
A. Yes, because it offers introductory context for the Regal Construction Company.
B. Yes, because it explains why Regal Construction Company hires so many foreign workers.
C. No, because it interrupts the paragraph's description of the Regal Construction Company.
D. No, because it introduces material unnecessary in the paragraph.

CONTINUE ➤

But when Tariq arrived, Regal didn't need him. For 24 days, he waited without pay, living in a squalid workers' camp. When work finally **39** materialized, he learned he would make only $176 a month. His boss confiscated his passport **40** and he couldn't change jobs or leave the country. He sends half his salary back to his family. After 11 months in the Gulf, he still **41** is not paid back the loan he took out to get there.

"How can I stay happy with a salary of $176?" Tariq asked, with an uncomfortable smile.

Tariq is one of dozens of construction workers laboring on Saadiyat Island **42** where I interviewed this May. He took out his flip phone and snapped a picture of the drawing I'd sketched of him. He had a gentle face that **43** lit up when he talked about cricket. He told me he'd use my drawing as a profile pic on Facebook.

Though it is now only a sunbaked construction site, Saadiyat, a ten-square-mile atoll 500 yards off the coast of Abu Dhabi, will be home to branches of the Louvre, the Guggenheim, and New York University, alongside hotels, shopping, and luxurious homes. It will be a cultural paradise, conjured by the country's vast oil wealth but built on the backs of men who are **44** living under difficult conditions.

39
A. NO CHANGE
B. offered
C. obtainable
D. available

40
A. NO CHANGE
B. for fear that
C. so that
D. lest

41
A. NO CHANGE
B. has not paid back
C. have not paid back
D. did not pay back

42
A. NO CHANGE
B. that
C. which
D. whom

43
A. NO CHANGE
B. lights up
C. lighting up
D. lit it up

44
Which choice is most consistent with the tone of the passage?
A. NO CHANGE
B. working extremely hard.
C. little more than indentured servants.
D. the real heroes.

STOP

If you finish before time is called, you may check your work on this section only. Do not turn to any other section.

Math Test – No Calculator

25 MINUTES, 20 QUESTIONS

Turn to Section 3 of your answer sheet to answer the questions in this section.

DIRECTIONS

For questions **1 – 15,** solve each problem, choose the best answer from the choices provided and fill in the circle on your answer sheet. For **questions 16 – 20,** solve the problem and enter your answer in the grid on your answer sheet. Please refer to the directions before question 16 on how to enter your answers in the grid. Your may use any available space in your test booklet for scratch work.

NOTES

1. The use of a calculator **is not permitted**.

2. All variables and expressions used represent real numbers unless otherwise indicated.

3. Figures provided in this test are drawn to scale unless otherwise indicated.

4. All figures lie in a plane unless otherwise indicated.

5. Unless otherwise indicated, the domain of a given function f is the set of all real numbers x for which $f(x)$ is a real number.

REFERENCE

$A = \pi r^2$ $A = \ell w$ $A = \frac{1}{2}bh$ $c^2 = a^2 + b^2$ Special Right Triangles

$C = 2\pi r$

$V = \ell wh$ $V = \pi r^2 h$ $V = \frac{4}{3}\pi r^3$ $V = \frac{1}{3}\pi r^2 h$ $V = \frac{1}{3}\ell wh$

The number of degrees of arc in a circle is 360.

The number of radians of arc in a circle is 2π.

The sum of the measures in degrees of the angles of a triangle is 180.

CONTINUE →

1

If $3^{n-3} - 3^2 = 18$, what is the value of n?

(A) 2

(B) 4

(C) 6

(D) 8

2

Three consecutive integers are such that five times the least integer is three times the greatest. What is the greatest of these three integers?

(A) 4

(B) 5

(C) 6

(D) 7

3

If m is an integer and $|2m - 4| < 1$, what is the value of m?

(A) −2

(B) −1

(C) 0

(D) 2

4

A bag contains apples that are either green or red. The ratio of green apples to red apples in the bag is 4 to 3. When five green apples and five red apples are removed, the ratio becomes 3 to 2. How many red apples were originally in the bag?

(A) 12

(B) 15

(C) 18

(D) 30

5

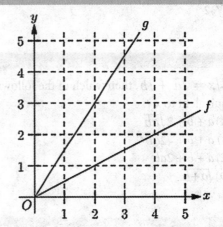

The graphs of the functions f and g are lines, as shown above. If $a = f(4)$, what is the value of $g(a)$?

(A) 1

(B) 2

(C) 3

(D) 4

65

6

Line *t* goes through points *R* and *S*, whose coordinates are (0, 1) and (*a*, 0), respectively. For which of the following values of *a* is the slope of line *t* greater than $-\frac{1}{2}$?

(A) $\frac{1}{2}$

(B) 1

(C) $\frac{3}{2}$

(D) $\frac{5}{2}$

7

If $\sqrt{x} = \sqrt{a} + \sqrt{b}$, then which of the following is equivalent to *x* ?
(A) $a + b + 2\sqrt{ab}$
(B) $a + b + \sqrt{2ab}$
(C) $a + b + 2ab$
(D) $\sqrt{a+b}$

8

Let *f* and *g* be numbers such that $30 < f < 40$ and $50 < g < 70$. Which of the following represents all possible values of $f - g$?
(A) $-40 < f - g < -20$
(B) $-40 < f - g < -10$
(C) $-30 < f - g < -20$
(D) $20 < f - g < 30$

9

Let $f(x) = (x+2)(x-2)$ for any value of *x*. What is the least possible value of $f(x)$?
(A) −4
(B) −2
(C) 0
(D) 2

10

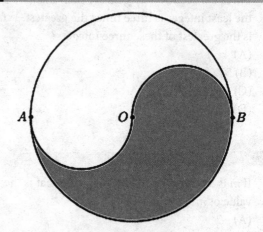

Semicircular arcs *AO* and *OB* divide the circle above with center *O* into two regions. If the length of diameter *AB* is 12, what is the area of the unshaded region?
(A) 6π
(B) 9π
(C) 18π
(D) 36π

CONTINUE

11

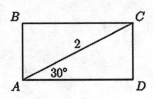

In the figure above, *ABCD* is a rectangle. What is the area of *ABCD*?

(A) $\sqrt{2}$

(B) $\sqrt{3}$

(C) $2\sqrt{4}$

(D) $2\sqrt{3}$

12

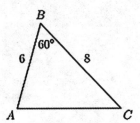

In the figure above, *AB* = 6 and *BC* = 8. What is the area of triangle *ABC*?

(A) $12\sqrt{2}$

(B) $12\sqrt{3}$

(C) $48\sqrt{2}$

(D) $48\sqrt{3}$

13

x	y
–3	15
0	3
2	–5
5	–17
7	–25

Which of the following equations is satisfied by the five pairs of numbers shown in the table above?

(A) $y = -2x + 3$

(B) $y = 2x + 6$

(C) $y = -4x + 3$

(D) $y = \dfrac{x}{3} - 12$

14

The sum of the squares of two positive consecutive integers equals 61. What is the lesser of the integers?

(A) 3

(B) 4

(C) 5

(D) 6

CONTINUE

15

If m is a positive constant and $n = 0$, which of the following could be the graph of $y = mx^2 + px + n$?

A.

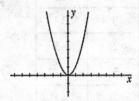

B.

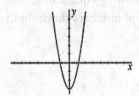

C.

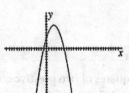

D.

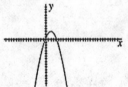

DIRECTIONS

For questions 16–20, solve the problem and enter your answer in the grid, as described below, on the answer sheet.

1. Although not required, it is suggested that you write your answer in the boxes at the top of the columns to help you fill in the circles accurately. You will receive credit only if the circles are filled in correctly.

2. Mark no more than one circle in any column.

3. No question has a negative answer.

4. Some problems may have more than one correct answer. In such cases, grid only one answer.

5. **Mixed numbers** such as $3\frac{1}{2}$ must be gridded as 3.5 or 7/2. (If $3\,1\,/\,2$ is entered into the grid, it will be interpreted as $\frac{31}{2}$, not $3\frac{1}{2}$.)

6. **Decimal answers:** If you obtain a decimal answer with more digits than the grid can accommodate, it may be either rounded or truncated, but it must fill the entire grid.

Answer: $\frac{7}{12}$ Answer: 2.5

Write answer in boxes.   ← Fraction line   ← Decimal point

Grid in result.

Acceptable ways to grid $\frac{2}{3}$ are:

Answer: 201 – either position is correct

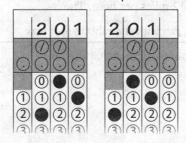

NOTE: You may start your answers in any column, space permitting. Columns you don't need to use should be left blank.

16

$$f(x) = 3x + 1$$
$$g(x) = 4x - 2$$

The two equations above define the functions f and g. If $f(c) = g(c)$ for some number c, what is the value of c?

17

Kim has a collection of nickels and dimes worth a total of $3. If she has 50 coins in all, how many nickels does Kim have?

18

During a race, Allison ran $\frac{3}{4}$ of the time with a lucky rabbit's foot, and $\frac{1}{4}$ of the time without it. With the rabbit's foot, her running speed was 6 miles per hour, and her running speed without the rabbit's foot was 12 miles per hour. The distance that Allison ran with the rabbit's foot was what fraction of the total distance that she ran?

19

If $x > 0$, and $x^2 - 5x - 6 = 0$, what is the value of x?

20

When the positive integer k is divided by 7, the remainder is 4. When $k + 26$ is divided by 7, what is the remainder?

STOP

If you finish before time is called, you may check your work on this section only. Do not turn to any other section.

No Test Material On This Page

Math Test – Calculator

55 MINUTES, 38 QUESTIONS

Turn to Section 4 of your answer sheet to answer the questions in this section.

DIRECTIONS

For questions 1 – 30, solve each problem, choose the best answer from the choices provided and fill in the circle on your answer sheet. **For questions 31 – 38,** solve the problem and enter your answer in the grid on your answer sheet. Please refer to the directions before question 31 on how to enter your answers in the grid. Your may use any available space in your test booklet for scratch work.

NOTES

1. The use of a calculator **is permitted**.

2. All variables and expressions used represent real numbers unless otherwise indicated.

3. Figures provided in this test are drawn to scale unless otherwise indicated.

4. All figures lie in a plane unless otherwise indicated.

5. Unless otherwise indicated, the domain of a given function f is the set of all real numbers x for which $f(x)$ is a real number.

REFERENCE

$A = \pi r^2$
$C = 2\pi r$

$A = \ell w$

$A = \frac{1}{2}bh$

$c^2 = a^2 + b^2$

Special Right Triangles

$V = \ell wh$

$V = \pi r^2 h$

$V = \frac{4}{3}\pi r^3$

$V = \frac{1}{3}\pi r^2 h$

$V = \frac{1}{3}\ell wh$

The number of degrees of arc in a circle is 360.

The number of radians of arc in a circle is 2π.

The sum of the measures in degrees of the angles of a triangle is 180.

CONTINUE ➡

1

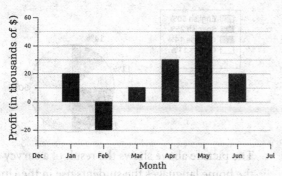

The above graph shows the profit of Sports Shack for the first half of 2015. According to the graph, the greatest loss in the profit of the Sports Shack occurred between which two consecutive months?

A. January and February
B. February and March
C. March and April
D. May and June

2

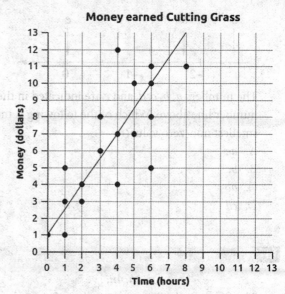

The picture above shows the money earned by cutting grass and hours worked in different places in the county; also the line of best fit is indicated in the graph. According to the graph, which of the following equations most closely models the average amount of money made cutting grass per hour?

A. $y = x + 1$

B. $y = \frac{2}{3}x + 1$

C. $y = \frac{3}{2}x + 1$

D. $y = 2x + 1$

CONTINUE ➡

3

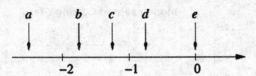

The numbers a, b, c, d, and e are indicated in the number line above. Which of the following is the smallest non-zero value?

A. ae

B. bc

C. ab

D. cd

4

$$n, 2n, 4n, \ldots$$

The first term in the sequence above is n, and each term thereafter is equal to twice the previous term. If n is an integer, which of the following could NOT be the sum of the first three terms of this sequence?

A. 14

B. 16

C. 21

D. 42

5

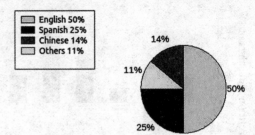

The picture above shows the result of a survey on the home languages the students use in the Upper District in the city. According to the chart, how many students are there in total if there are 5000 students has Chinese as their home language?

A. 5,814

B. 14,000

C. 35,714

D. 70,000

CONTINUE

6

If $2\sqrt{x-3} = 6$, what is the value of x ?

A. 6
B. 9
C. 12
D. 15

7

The median of a particular set of 10 integers is itself NOT an integer. Which of the following could NOT be true?
I. The integers of the set are all identical.
II. The integers of the set are consecutive.
III. The 5th largest and 6th largest integers of the set are even.

A. I only
B. II only
C. I and III only
D. II and III only

8

You own $500 worth of stock in a new company. The first five weeks you lose 50% of your money. Then there is no gain for the next 3 weeks until you decide to sell your stock. Which of the following graphs could correctly represent your stock activity over an eight-week period?

A.

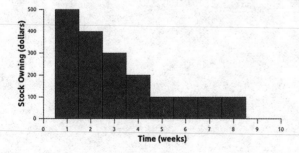

B.

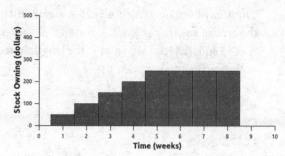

C.

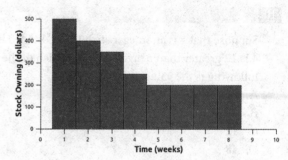

D.

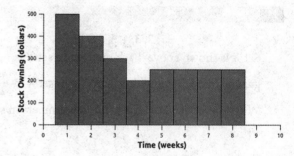

CONTINUE ➡

9

The area of square garden A is 25% greater than the area of square garden B. If the area of garden A is 45 square feet, then what is the length in feet of the perimeter of garden B?

A. 6
B. 24
C. 36
D. 72

10

Suppose that z is an integer such that z divided by 4 is 12 greater than z divided by 2. Which of the following is the value of z?

A. −12
B. −48
C. 12
D. 48

11

$$\{1, 2, 3, 4, 5, 6, 7\}$$

Set X is shown above. Each number in set Y is generated by dividing each number in set X by $\frac{1}{2}$. What is the arithmetic mean of the numbers in set Y?

A. 2
B. $\frac{7}{4}$
C. 7
D. 8

12

$\sqrt{5}$ percent of $3\sqrt{5}$ is equal to which of the following?

A. 5
B. $3\sqrt{10}$
C. $\frac{3}{20}$
D. $\frac{3\sqrt{5}}{20}$

13

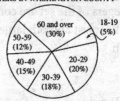

AGE DISTRIBUTION OF REGISTERED VOTERS IN WASHINGTON COUNTY

According to the graph above, if there are 12,500 registered voters aged 50 and over in Washington County, how many registered voters are under the age of 40?

A. 5,375
B. 12,798
C. 17,262
D. 29,762

14

If $6 - 4x > 18$ or $-1 > 5 - 2x$, which of the following is a possible value of x?

A. 1
B. 2
C. 3
D. 4

15

FURNITURE SETS

Set	A	B	C
Tables	1	2	3
Chairs	7	5	2

PRICES

Year	2002	2007	2012
Table	$60	$80	$100
Chair	$30	$35	$40

A furniture company sells three sets of furniture: set A, set B, and set C. Each set consists of a different number of tables and chairs as shown in the first table above. The second table shows the prices of each table and chair in three different years. Based on the prices shown, what is the lowest possible price of a furniture set bought in 2002?

A. $230
B. $240
C. $270
D. $310

16

If $2x = \dfrac{y}{3}$, which of the following is equivalent to $\dfrac{y}{6}$?

A. $\dfrac{x}{6}$

B. $\dfrac{x}{3}$

C. x

D. $\dfrac{2x}{3}$

17

A high school senior class spent 20% of its prom budget on a big box of balloons. It then spent one fourth of the remaining funds on a disc jockey. Finally, it spent $\dfrac{1}{3}$ of the remaining funds on a venue for the prom. What percentage of the original budget was spent?

A. 25%
B. 30%
C. 40%
D. 60%

18

If a line is parallel to the line $y = 3x - 4$ and passes through the point $(0, -7)$, what is the equation of the parallel line?

A. $y = 3x + 7$

B. $y = 3x - 7$

C. $y = \dfrac{-1}{3x+7}$

D. $y = \dfrac{-1}{3x-7}$

19

Which of these pairs of quadratic equations have the same solutions?

A. $-x^2 + x = -8$ and $x^2 - 2x = 4$
B. $x^2 - 3x + 6 = 0$ and $-x^2 - 3x - 6 = 0$
C. $x^2 = 2x$ and $x^2 + 2x = 0$
D. $x^2 + 2x - 3 = 0$ and $-2x^2 - 4x + 6 = 0$

CONTINUE

20

$$\frac{z}{4} = \frac{x}{y}$$

In the equation above, the numbers x, y, and z are either positive or negative. Which of the following must be equal to 8?

A. $2x$

B. $\dfrac{2yz}{4x}$

C. $\dfrac{2xz}{4y}$

D. $\dfrac{2yz}{x}$

21

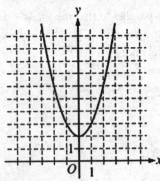

Which of the following could be the equation of the graph above?

A. $y = x^2 + 2$

B. $y = (x + 2)^2$

C. $y = -2x^2 - 4$

D. $y - 4 = 2x^2$

22

Let x be an odd integer. How many possible values of x satisfy $\sqrt{x + 7} \le 2$?

A. Two

B. Three

C. Four

D. Five

23

In the $x - y$ plane, the line $3x + 4y = 36$ intersects the x-axis at $x = m$, for some number m. What is the value of m?

A. 6

B. 7

C. 9

D. 12

24

If $(p + 1)(t + 4) = 0$ and t is positive, what is the value of p?

A. -4

B. -1

C. 0

D. 4

25

If $ab < 82$ and b is a positive multiple of 3, what is the biggest possible integer value of a?

A. 1

B. 13

C. 27

D. 81

CONTINUE

26

If x is a positive integer, which of the following are always even integers?

I. $\dfrac{x}{2}$

II. $2x$

III. $x + 2$

IV. $2x + 2$

A. I and II
B. I and III
C. III and IV
D. II and IV

27

If $f(x) = x + 10$, which of the following is a solution of $f(6a) + 2 = f(3a) + 11$? In other words, what might be the value of a?

A. There are no solutions.
B. 3
C. 9
D. 12

28

If x is 8% of y and y is 100% greater than z, when $z = 20$, what is the value of x?

A. 1.6
B. 2.3
C. 2.4
D. 3.2

29

The function g is defined by $g(x) = 28x^4 + 16x^3 - 80x^2$. In the x–y plane, the graph of $y = g(x)$ crosses the x-axis at $x = a$. Which of the following could be the value of a?

A. −1
B. −2
C. 2
D. 4

30

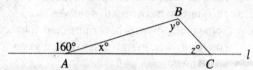

Triangle ABC and line l are shown in the figure above. What is the sum of y and z?

A. 40
B. 60
C. 160
D. 180

79

CONTINUE

DIRECTIONS

For questions 31–38, solve the problem and enter your answer in the grid, as described below, on the answer sheet.

1. Although not required, it is suggested that you write your answer in the boxes at the top of the columns to help you fill in the circles accurately. You will receive credit only if the circles are filled in correctly.

2. Mark no more than one circle in any column.

3. No question has a negative answer.

4. Some problems may have more than one correct answer. In such cases, grid only one answer.

5. **Mixed numbers** such as $3\frac{1}{2}$ must be gridded as 3.5 or 7/2. (If 3 1 / 2 is entered into the grid, it will be interpreted as $\frac{31}{2}$, not $3\frac{1}{2}$.)

6. **Decimal answers:** If you obtain a decimal answer with more digits than the grid can accommodate, it may be either rounded or truncated, but it must fill the entire grid.

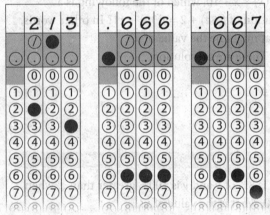

Answer: $\frac{7}{12}$ Answer: 2.5

Write answer in boxes.

← Fraction line

← Decimal point

Grid in result.

Acceptable ways to grid $\frac{2}{3}$ are:

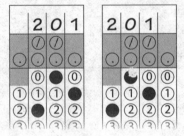

Answer: 201 – either position is correct

NOTE: You may start your answers in any column, space permitting. Columns you don't need to use should be left blank.

CONTINUE ➡

31

$$\frac{8}{4x+6} = \frac{4}{8x-2}$$

If x satisfies the equation above, then what is the value of x?

32

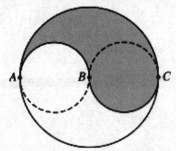

In the figure above, the smaller circles each have a radius of 4. They are tangent to the larger circle at points A and C, and are tangent to each other at point B, which is the center of the larger circle. If the perimeter of the shaded region is $a\pi$, what is the value of a?

33

A train travels at an average speed of 40 miles per hour. How many minutes will it take the train to travel 90 miles?

34

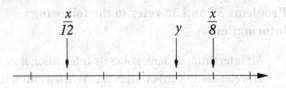

On the number line above, if each tick mark corresponds to consecutive integers, what is the value of y?

35

A family restaurant uses a secret family recipe to make their famous stewed tomatoes. The stewed tomatoes are made by combining tomatoes and sugar so that the ratio of tomatoes to sugar is 9 to 1 by weight. How many ounces of sugar is needed to make 160 ounces of stewed tomatoes?

36

If $f(x) = x^3 + 3x^2 - 6x + 14$, what is the value of $f(-1)$?

CONTINUE

Problems 37 and 38 refer to the following information.

An international bank issues its International Traveler credit cards worldwide. When a customer makes a purchase using an International Traveler card in a currency different from the customer's home currency, the bank converts the purchase price at the daily foreign exchange rate and then charges a 3% fee on the converted cost. Maria lives in the United States, but is on vacation in Brazil. She used her International Traveler card for a purchase that cost 125 reais (Brazilian currency). The bank posted a charge of $41.50 to her account that included the 3% fee.

37

What foreign exchange rate, in Brazilian reais per one U.S. dollar, did the bank use for Maria's charge? Round your answer to the nearest whole number.

38

A bank in Brazil sells a prepaid credit card worth 9,500 reais. Maria can buy the prepaid card using dollars at the daily exchange rate with no fee, but she will lose any money left on the prepaid card. What is the least number of the 9,500 reais on the prepaid card Maria must spend for the prepaid card to be cheaper than charging all her purchases on the International Traveler card? Round your answer to the nearest whole number of reais.

STOP

If you finish before time is called, you may check your work on this section only. Do not turn to any other section.

New SAT Practice Essay 1

 ESSAY BOOK

DIRECTIONS

The essay gives you an opportunity to show how effectively you can read and comprehend a passage and write an essay analyzing the passage. In your essay, you should demonstrate that you have read the passage carefully, present a clear and logical analysis, and use language precisely.

Your essay must be written on the lines provided in your answer booklet; except for the Planning Page of the answer booklet, you will receive no other paper on which to write. You will have enough space if you write on every line, avoid wide margins, and keep your handwriting to a reasonable size. Remember that people who are not familiar with your handwriting will read what you write. Try to write or print so that what you are writing is legible to those readers.

You have <u>50 minutes</u> to read the passage and write an essay in response to the prompt provided inside this booklet.

REMINDERS

— Do not write your essay in this booklet. Only what you write on the lined pages of your answer booklet will be evaluated.

— An off-topic essay will not be evaluated.

This cover is representative of what you'll see on test day.

As you read the passage below, consider how John Hawkins uses:

- evidence, such as facts or examples, to support his claims.
- reasoning to develop ideas and to connect claims and evidence.
- stylistics or persuasive elements, such as word choice or appeals to emotion, to add power to the ideas expressed.

Adapted from John Hawkins, "5 Scientific Reasons That Global Warming Isn't Happening." @townhall.com, Feb 18, 2014

1   How did global warming discussions end up hinging on what's happening with polar bears, unverifiable predictions of what will happen in a hundred years, and whether people are "climate deniers" or "global warming cultists?" If this is a scientific topic, why aren't we spending more time discussing the science involved? Many Americans have long since thought that the best scientific evidence available suggested that man wasn't causing any sort of global warming. However, now, we can go even further and suggest that the planet isn't warming at all.

2   **1) There hasn't been any global warming since 1997:** If nothing changes in the next year, we're going to have kids who graduate from high school who will have never seen any "global warming" during their lifetimes. That's right; the temperature of the planet has essentially been flat for 17 years. This isn't a controversial assertion either. Even the former Director of the Climate Research Unit (CRU) of the University of East Anglia, Phil Jones, admits that it's true. Since the planet was cooling from 1940-1975 and the upswing in temperature afterward only lasted 22 years, a 17 year pause is a big deal. It also begs an obvious question: How can we be experiencing global warming if there's no actual "global warming?"

3   **2) There is no scientific consensus that global warming is occurring and caused by man:** The primary "scientific" argument for global warming is that there is a "scientific consensus" that it's occurring. Setting aside the fact that's not a scientific argument, even if that ever was true (and it really wasn't), it's certainly not true anymore. Over 31,000 scientists have signed on to a petition saying humans aren't causing global warming. More than 1000 scientists signed on to another report saying there is no global warming at all. There are tens of thousands of well-educated, mainstream scientists who do not agree that global warming is occurring at all and people who share their opinion are taking a position grounded in science.

4   **3) Arctic ice is up 50% since 2012:** The loss of Arctic ice has been a big talking point for people who believe global warming is occurring. Some people have even predicted that all of the Arctic ice would melt by now because of global warming. Yet, Arctic ice is up 50% since 2012. How much Arctic ice really matters is an open question since the very limited evidence we have suggests that a few decades ago, there was less ice than there is today, but the same people who thought the drop in ice was noteworthy should at least agree that the increase is important as well.

5 **4) Climate models showing global warming have been wrong over and over:** These future projections of what global warming will do to the planet have been based on climate models. Essentially, scientists make assumptions about how much of an impact different factors will have; they guess how much of a change there will be and then they project changes over time. Unfortunately, almost all of these models showing huge temperature gains have turned out to be wrong.

6 Former NASA scientist Dr. Roy Spencer says that climate models used by government agencies to create policies "have failed miserably." Spencer analyzed 90 climate models against surface temperature and satellite temperature data, and found that more than 95 percent of the models "have over-forecast the warming trend since 1979, whether we use their own surface temperature dataset (HadCRUT4), or our satellite dataset of lower tropospheric temperatures (UAH)."

7 **5) Predictions about the impact of global warming have already been proven wrong:** The debate over global warming has been going on long enough that we've had time to see whether some of the predictions people made about it have panned out in the real world. For example, Al Gore predicted all the Arctic ice would be gone by 2013. In 2005, the *Independent* ran an article saying that the Arctic had entered a death spiral.

8 Meanwhile, Arctic ice is up 50% since 2012. James Hansen of NASA fame predicted that the West Side Highway in New York would be under water by now because of global warming.

9 If the climate models and the predictions about global warming aren't even close to being correct, wouldn't it be more scientific to reject hasty action based on faulty data so that we can further study the issue and find out what's really going on?

Write an essay in which you explain how John Hawkins builds an argument to persuade his audience that global warming isn't happening. In your essay, analyze how John Hawkins uses one or more of the features listed in the box above (or features of your own choice) to strengthen the logic and persuasiveness of his argument. Be sure that your analysis focuses on the most relevant features of the passage.

Your essay should not explain whether you agree with John Hawkins's claims, but rather explain how he builds an argument to persuade his audience.

YOUR NAME (PRINT) ....

LAST   FIRST   MI

TEST CENTER ....

NUMBER   NAME OF TEST CENTER   ROOM NUMBER

SAT PRACTICE ANSWER SHEET

COMPLETE MARK ● EXAMPLES OF INCOMPLETE MARKS It is recommended that you use a No. 2 pencil. It is very important that you fill in the entire circle darkly and completely. If you change your response, erase as completely as possible. Incomplete marks or erasures may affect your score.

■ TEST NUMBER   ■ SECTION 1

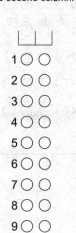

1 A B C D
2 A B C D
3 A B C D
4 A B C D
5 A B C D
6 A B C D
7 A B C D
8 A B C D
9 A B C D
10 A B C D
11 A B C D
12 A B C D
13 A B C D

14 A B C D
15 A B C D
16 A B C D
17 A B C D
18 A B C D
19 A B C D
20 A B C D
21 A B C D
22 A B C D
23 A B C D
24 A B C D
25 A B C D
26 A B C D

27 A B C D
28 A B C D
29 A B C D
30 A B C D
31 A B C D
32 A B C D
33 A B C D
34 A B C D
35 A B C D
36 A B C D
37 A B C D
38 A B C D
39 A B C D

40 A B C D
41 A B C D
42 A B C D
43 A B C D
44 A B C D
45 A B C D
46 A B C D
47 A B C D
48 A B C D
49 A B C D
50 A B C D
51 A B C D
52 A B C D

COMPLETE MARK ●   EXAMPLES OF
INCOMPLETE MARKS

It is recommended that you use a No. 2 pencil. It is very important that you fill in the entire circle darkly and completely. If you change your response, erase as completely as possible. Incomplete marks or erasures may affect your score.

SECTION 2

	A	B	C	D
1	○	○	○	○
2	○	○	○	○
3	○	○	○	○
4	○	○	○	○
5	○	○	○	○
6	○	○	○	○
7	○	○	○	○
8	○	○	○	○
9	○	○	○	○

	A	B	C	D
10	○	○	○	○
11	○	○	○	○
12	○	○	○	○
13	○	○	○	○
14	○	○	○	○
15	○	○	○	○
16	○	○	○	○
17	○	○	○	○
18	○	○	○	○

	A	B	C	D
19	○	○	○	○
20	○	○	○	○
21	○	○	○	○
22	○	○	○	○
23	○	○	○	○
24	○	○	○	○
25	○	○	○	○
26	○	○	○	○
27	○	○	○	○

	A	B	C	D
28	○	○	○	○
29	○	○	○	○
30	○	○	○	○
31	○	○	○	○
32	○	○	○	○
33	○	○	○	○
34	○	○	○	○
35	○	○	○	○
36	○	○	○	○

	A	B	C	D
37	○	○	○	○
38	○	○	○	○
39	○	○	○	○
40	○	○	○	○
41	○	○	○	○
42	○	○	○	○
43	○	○	○	○
44	○	○	○	○

■ SECTION 3

	A B C D		A B C D		A B C D		A B C D		A B C D
1	○○○○	4	○○○○	7	○○○○	10	○○○○	13	○○○○
2	○○○○	5	○○○○	8	○○○○	11	○○○○	14	○○○○
3	○○○○	6	○○○○	9	○○○○	12	○○○○	15	○○○○

Only answers that are gridded will be scored. You will not receive credit for anything written in the boxes.

16	17	18	19	20
⌐│││││	⌐│││││	⌐│││││	⌐│││││	⌐│││││
/ ○○	/ ○○	/ ○○	/ ○○	/ ○○
.○○○○	.○○○○	.○○○○	.○○○○	.○○○○
0○○○○	0○○○○	0○○○○	0○○○○	0○○○○
1○○○○	1○○○○	1○○○○	1○○○○	1○○○○
2○○○○	2○○○○	2○○○○	2○○○○	2○○○○
3○○○○	3○○○○	3○○○○	3○○○○	3○○○○
4○○○○	4○○○○	4○○○○	4○○○○	4○○○○
5○○○○	5○○○○	5○○○○	5○○○○	5○○○○
6○○○○	6○○○○	6○○○○	6○○○○	6○○○○
7○○○○	7○○○○	7○○○○	7○○○○	7○○○○
8○○○○	8○○○○	8○○○○	8○○○○	8○○○○
9○○○○	9○○○○	9○○○○	9○○○○	9○○○○

NO CALCULATOR
ALLOWED

■ SECTION 4

	A B C D		A B C D		A B C D		A B C D		A B C D
1	○○○○	7	○○○○	13	○○○○	19	○○○○	25	○○○○
2	○○○○	8	○○○○	14	○○○○	20	○○○○	26	○○○○
3	○○○○	9	○○○○	15	○○○○	21	○○○○	27	○○○○
4	○○○○	10	○○○○	16	○○○○	22	○○○○	28	○○○○
5	○○○○	11	○○○○	17	○○○○	23	○○○○	29	○○○○
6	○○○○	12	○○○○	18	○○○○	24	○○○○	30	○○○○

CALCULATOR
ALLOWED

COMPLETE MARK ● 　 EXAMPLES OF
　　　　　　　　　INCOMPLETE MARKS

It is recommended that you use a No. 2 pencil. It is very important that you fill in the entire circle darkly and completely. If you change your response, erase as completely as possible. Incomplete marks or erasures may affect your score.

■ SECTION 4 (Continued)

Only answers that are gridded will be scored. You will not receive credit for anything written in the boxes.

31	32	33	34	35

Only answers that are gridded will be scored. You will not receive credit for anything written in the boxes.

36	37	38

CALCULATOR
ALLOWED

PLANNING PAGE You may plan your essay in the unlined planning space below, but use only the lined pages following this one to write your essay. Any work on this planning page will not be scored.

Use pages 7 through 10 for your ESSAY ⟶

FOR PLANNING ONLY

Use pages 7 through 10 for your ESSAY ⟶

BEGIN YOUR ESSAY HERE.

You may continue on the next page.

STOP.

New SAT Practice Test 2

IMPORTANT REMINDERS

1

A No. 2 pencil is required for the test.
Do not use a mechanical pencil or pen.

2

Sharing any questions with anyone
is a violation of Test Security
and Fairness policies and may result
in your scores being canceled.

This cover is representative of what you'll see on test day.

Reading Test

65 MINUTES, 52 QUESTIONS

Turn to Section 1 of your answer sheet to answer the questions in this section.

DIRECTIONS

Each passage or pair of passages below is followed by a number of questions. After reading each passage or pair, choose the best answer to each question based on what is stated or implied in the passage or passages and in any accompanying graphics (such as a table or graph).

Questions 1-11 are based on the following passage.

-Adapted from Mimi Whitefield's "Havana: US Immigration Policy for Cubans Needs to Change", Miami Herald, 21 January 2015.

Cuban officials have long said they have serious concerns about the Cuban Adjustment Act and the U.S. wet foot/dry foot policy, and
Line they repeated those concerns at recent U.S.-Cuba
5 immigration talks in Havana. The adjustment act allows Cubans to be paroled into the United States and to get permanent residency and green cards after they've been here for a year and a day. Under the wet foot/dry foot policy, Cubans
10 who reach U.S. shores can stay, even if they are ferried by smugglers, and those who are picked up at sea generally are returned to Cuba. In early 2013, Cuba changed its own travel policy. Among the changes was a provision that allows
15 Cuban citizens to travel abroad for up to two years without losing their citizenship benefits. That means they could come to the United States, work legally for a period of time, and then return to the island.
20 Cuban criminal rings have used this legal loophole to come to the United States, set up criminal enterprises and then return to the island when things get hot, according to law enforcement officials. After Cuba and the United
25 States announced their policy shift recently, rafter traffic from Cuba picked up dramatically. Both

sides at the migration talks acknowledged that they had agreed to disagree on certain topics but said they planned to continue discussing the
30 complicated issues at future talks. Wet foot/dry foot is not a statute, but rather an interpretation of a court ruling, some lawyers argue. Because it involves circumventing legal proceedings, many lawmakers have expressed reluctance to have
35 a firm stance on the issue, stating that it places them in rather dubious positions with both their constituents and their respective governments.

Adding to the thicket of Cuban immigration policy is what is known as the Meissner Memo,
40 named after former U.S. Immigration and Naturalization Service Commissioner Doris Meissner. Even if Cubans sneak into the country, the memo states that as long as they immediately present themselves at an immigration office, they
45 can still be paroled into the United State and be eligible for the adjustment act. Among other topics discussed at the closed-door migration talks, which were discussed recently, were return of Cuban excludable aliens [generally
50 those with criminal records], the Cuban Family Reunification Parole Program, and the monitoring of repatriated Cubans.

There are 34,525 Cubans, most convicted of serious crimes, with final orders of deportation
55 and they fear the new relationship with Cuba could mean they will be sent back to the island. At this point, U.S. officials said there has been

CONTINUE

no change in deportation policy to Cuba. Migration talks have recently been held to revisit
60 current US-Cuban relations and migration statutes. The migration talks, which alternate between Washington and Havana, are generally low-key but recent discussions took place in an extraordinary context with the international
65 media packing the Cuban capital. Cuba and the United States generally meet twice annually to discuss the 1994 and 1995 U.S.-Cuba migration accords, which were signed to ensure safe, legal and orderly migration between the two countries.
70 The talks have been held since 1995 — except during a few periods when U.S.-Cuba relations soured.

    Meanwhile, the decision by some Cubans to take to the risky waters of the Florida Straits
75 is often influenced by frustration over their economic situation, which some said they hoped would improve with renewed ties with the United States. For 43-year-old Lazaro Lopez, who runs his own business in Havana, the only people
80 standing against better relations are those who are making money by smuggling goods in and smuggling people off the island. He said the going rate for a boat off the island is between $8,000 and $10,000 and that Cuban exiles from Miami
85 run many of the smuggling rings.

100,000
80,000
60,000   • Mariel Boatlift   32,219 arrived
                                        from **Cuba**
40,000   in 2013
20,000
0
      1960   1970   1980   1990   2000   2010

From the description of the Meissner Memo, it can be deduced that
A. it served to exacerbate strained relations by easing regulations on Cuban immigration, contrary to the wishes of the Cuban government.
B. it supported changes made to Cuban travel policy and the shifting political agenda exhibited by the Cuban government.
C. it effectively rendered the wet foot/dry foot policy obsolete by granting immediate eligibility for the adjustment act upon arriving on our shores.
D. those convicted of serious crimes are not eligible for protection under this proviso.

The primary purpose of the article is to
A. detail the ongoing "chess match" of travel policy changes being employed by both the US and Cuban governments.
B. chronicle the multiple steps both countries have attempted to implement to foster further understanding on travel restrictions and access.
C. essentially ascribe blame for current travel difficulties on the Cuban government.
D. establish a framework for future beneficial changes to travel policy which are amenable to both countries.

CONTINUE ▶

3

The term "repatriated" in line 52 most closely means:
A. exiled
B. nationalistic
C. excommunicated
D. returned

4

The graphic included with the passage most closely suggests that
A. Cuban refugee excursions peaked close to the time of the Mariel boatlift.
B. Cuban refugees have shown a steady decline since 2000.
C. since renewed talks in 1995 began, there has been a marked increase in Cuban refugees.
D. the amount of Cuban refugees during the 2000s can best be described as variable.

5

Recent policy shifts in Cuba appear to be
A. designed to foster a sense of nationalistic pride amongst Cuban people in an effort to retain more citizens.
B. unpopular with many Cubans who chose to remain in the country.
C. reflective of warmer relations with the United States and an easing of travel restrictions between the two countries.
D. overwhelmingly popular among the ruling elite who favor exile of undesired citizens from the island.

6

The best evidence for the answer to question 5 lies in
A. lines 38-42, "Adding to the thicket…"
B. lines 26-30, "Both sides at the migration talks…"
C. lines 78-82, "For 43-year old Lazaro Lopez…"
D. lines 65-69, "Cuba and the United States

7

The term "dubious" in line 36 most closely means:
A. suspect and untrustworthy
B. unclear and hazy
C. negative and complicated
D. unsure

8

From the passage, it can be inferred that
A. Cuban travel policy can best be described as pioneering.
B. popular opinion weighed greatly in recent changes to Cuban travel policy.
C. the Cuban stance on the Cuban Adjustment Act was causation of the change in their own travel policy.
D. Cuban travel restrictions have remained relatively unfettered since the mid-1960s.

CONTINUE

9

Though not a primary objective, the Cuban Adjustment Act causes the government to

A. provide a period of stagnation for Cuban refugees.

B. empower the Cuban government to implement system wide changes in their own travel policy.

C. reinforce United States suspicion of Cuba due to their reactionary policy shifts.

D. increase Cuban immigration through the easing of travel restrictions on the part of both countries.

10

The answer to question 9 is best evidenced by:

A. lines 1-5, "Cuban officials have long said…"

B. lines 24-26, "After Cuba and the United States…"

C. lines 46-52, "Among other topics…"

D. lines 57-58, "At this point, US officials…"

11

Based upon information obtained in the article, the author would most likely agree with which of the following sentiments?

A. Non-traditional residency has been the topic most influenced by recent changes.

B. Immigration has been relatively unfettered by recent policy shifts in both Cuba and the United States.

C. Individuals convicted of crimes are being unfairly victimized by both the United States and Cuba regarding recent changes in travel restrictions.

D. Cuba's stance on immigration can best be described as passively agreeable.

CONTINUE

Questions 12-21 deal with the passage below.

-Adapted from "The Giant, Underestimated Earthquake Threat to North America" by Jerry Thompson, The Extreme Earth, 13 March 2012

On a foggy spring morning just before sunrise, 27 miles northwest of Cape Mendocino, California, a pimple of rock roughly a dozen
Line miles below the ocean floor finally reaches its
5 breaking point. Two slabs of the Earth's crust begin to slip and shudder and snap apart.

The first jolt of stress coming out of the rocks sends a shock wave hurtling into Northern California and southern Oregon like
10 a thunderbolt. For a few stunned drivers on the back roads in the predawn gloom, the pulse of energy that tears through the ground looks dimly like a 20-mile wrinkle moving through a carpet of pastures and into thick stands of redwoods.

15 Cornices fall, brick walls crack, plate glass shatters. Pavement buckles, cars and trucks veer into ditches and into each other. A bridge across the Eel River is jerked off its foundations, taking a busload of farm workers with it. With computers
20 crashing and cell towers dropping offline, all of Humboldt and Del Norte Counties in California are instantly cut off from the outside world, so nobody beyond the immediate area knows how bad it is here or how widespread the damage.

25 At the US Geological Survey (USGS) lab in Menlo Park, seismometers peg the quake at magnitude 8.1, and the tsunami detection centers in Alaska and Hawaii begin waking up the alarm system with standby alerts all around the Pacific
30 Rim. Early morning commuters emerging from a BART station in San Francisco feel the ground sway beneath their feet and immediately hit the sidewalk in a variety of awkward crouches, a familiar fear chilling their guts.

35 The fault continues to rip all the way to Newport, Oregon, halfway up the state. The magnitude suddenly jumps to 8.6. A power surge blows a breaker somewhere east of town and feeds back through the system, throwing other
40 breakers in a cascade that quickly crashes the entire grid in Oregon, Washington, and parts

of California, Idaho, and Nevada. A brownout begins in six more western states. The wire line phone systems crash in lockstep.

45 Then another fragment of rock deep underneath Newport shears away. The fault unzips the rest of the way to Vancouver Island. The quake now pins seismic needles at magnitude 9.2. High-rise towers in Portland, Seattle, Vancouver,
50 and Victoria begin to undulate. The shock wave hammers through sandy soil, soft rock, and landfill like the deepest notes on a big string bass. The mushy ground sings harmony and tall buildings hum like so many tuning forks.

55 Shock waves have been pummeling the Pacific Northwest for four minutes and thirty-five seconds now, and it still isn't over. After 64 cycles, enough welds have cracked, enough concrete has spalled, enough shear walls have come unstuck
60 that some towers begin to pancake. The same death spiral everyone saw in New York on 9/11 happens all over again. Smaller buildings, but more of them. Dozens of towers go down in the four northernmost of the affected cities.

65 In the five major urban areas along the fault, tens of thousands of people have been seriously injured. Hundreds, perhaps thousands, are dead. More than a third of the oncoming shift of police, firefighters, paramedics, nurses, and doctors do
70 not show up for work. They are either stranded by collapsed buildings, bridges, and roadways, injured or dead themselves, or have decided to stick close to home to make sure their own families are OK before going to work. People who
75 survive the collapses must do their own search and rescue for family members, friends, and neighbors still trapped in the rubble. Help will come eventually, but who knows when?

People in the United States and Canada, if
80 they think at all about earthquake disasters, probably conjure up the San Andreas Fault in the worst-case scenario. In California, as they wait for "the Big One," people wonder which city the San Andreas will wreck next—San Francisco or
85 Los Angeles? But if by the Big One they mean the earthquake that will wreak havoc over the widest

CONTINUE

geographic area, that could destroy the most critical infrastructure, that could send a train of tsunamis across the Pacific causing economic
90 mayhem that would probably last a decade or more—then the seismic demon to blame could not possibly be the San Andreas. It would have to be Cascadia's fault.

12

The overall theme of the passage generally reflects:
A. a cataclysmic warning
B. geological understanding
C. infrastructure renewal
D. predictive certainty

13

The term "spalled" used in line 59 most closely means:
A. fallen
B. dislodged
C. cracked
D. removed

14

It can be assumed from the author's description of the potential final damage from this event that
A. current infrastructure may be moderately affected but generally salvageable.
B. lawlessness and rampant social problems are certain to follow this potential event.
C. strong, central leadership will provide for the citizens of the country.
D. survivors will need to be self-reliant for potentially extended periods of time.

15

Evidence for question 14 is best found in
A. lines 68-74, "More than a third…"
B. lines 74-77, "People who survive…"
C. lines 19-24, "With computers crashing and cell towers…"
D. lines 58-60, "After 64 cycles…"

16

From the tone and detail of the passage, it can be inferred that the author
A. views society as potentially avoiding a catastrophe through careful planning.
B. sees this event as generally inevitable.
C. believes current geological theory focuses on the wrong areas for protection and prevention.
D. views infrastructure as being stable enough to sustain such an event.

17

The term "undulate" used in line 50 primarily means:
A. come apart
B. shear
C. become rigid
D. sway back and forth

CONTINUE

18

The imagery conveyed by a "20 mile wrinkle" in lines 10-14 serves to illustrate

A. the steady line of falling buildings following the initial quake.

B. movement of bridges along the rivers of the areas affect by the fault line.

C. the trail of the Cascadia fault line in the Pacific Northwest.

D. the electrical surges and brownouts visible on grids throughout the region.

19

Should the events of this article occur, the author believes

A. A chain reaction of further and potentially destructive natural disasters may be set in motion.

B. Survivors will incorrectly blame the San Andreas fault line for the events which preceded.

C. There will be little damage outside of immediate surrounding area of initial epicenter.

D. Reactions to the aftermath of these events will be largely self-serving and egocentric.

20

Evidence for the answer to question 19 is primarily found in

A. lines 79-82, "People in the United States…"

B. lines 85-92, "But if by the big one they mean…"

C. lines 19-24, "With computers crashing and cell towers…"

D. lines 70-74, "They are either stranded…"

21

The author references the aftermath of 9/11 in New York primarily in order to

A. contrast the scope of human casualty between the two tragedies.

B. instill fear and wariness in the hopes of achieving preparedness.

C. demonstrate the scope of infrastructure destruction inherent with such an event.

D. plead for additional assistance to help with cleanup and rebuilding efforts after the quake.

CONTINUE ➤

Questions 22-31 deal with the passage below.

-Excerpted from "The Catcher in the Rye" by JD Salinger

"I flunked you in history because you knew absolutely nothing."

"I know that, sir. Boy, I know it. You couldn't help it."

"Absolutely nothing," he said over again. That's something that drives me crazy.

When people say something twice that way, after you admit it the first time. Then he said it three times. "But absolutely nothing. I doubt very much if you opened your textbook even once the whole term. Did you? Tell the truth, boy."

"Well, I sort of glanced through it a couple of times," I told him. I didn't want to hurt his feelings. He was mad about history.

"You glanced through it, eh?" he said--very sarcastic. "Your, ah, exam paper is over there on top of my chiffonier. On top of the pile. Bring it here, please."

It was a very dirty trick, but I went over and brought it over to him—I didn't have any alternative or anything. Then I sat down on his cement bed again. Boy, you can't imagine how sorry I was getting that I'd stopped by to say good-by to him.

He started handling my exam paper like it was a turd or something. "We studied the Egyptians from November 4th to December 2nd," he said. "You chose to write about them for the optional essay question. Would you care to hear what you had to say?"

"No, sir, not very much," I said.

He read it anyway, though. You can't stop a teacher when they want to do something. They just do it.

"The Egyptians were an ancient race of Caucasians residing in one of the northern sections of Africa. The latter as we all know is the largest continent in the Eastern Hemisphere."

I had to sit there and listen to that crap. It certainly was a dirty trick.

"The Egyptians are extremely interesting to us today for various reasons. Modern science would still like to know what the secret ingredients were that the Egyptians used when they wrapped up dead people so that their faces would not rot for innumerable centuries. This interesting riddle is still quite a challenge to modern science in the twentieth century."

He stopped reading and put my paper down. I was beginning to sort of hate him.

"Your essay, shall we say, ends there," he said in this very sarcastic voice. You wouldn't think such an old guy would be so sarcastic and all. "However, you dropped me a little note, at the bottom of the page," he said.

"I know I did," I said. I said it very fast because I wanted to stop him before he started reading that out loud. But you couldn't stop him. He was hot as a firecracker.

DEAR MR. SPENCER [he read out loud]. That is all I know about the Egyptians. I can't seem to get very interested in them although your lectures are very interesting. It is all right with me if you flunk me though as I am flunking everything else except English anyway.

Respectfully yours, HOLDEN CAULFIELD.

He put my goddam paper down then and looked at me like he'd just beaten hell out of me in ping-pong or something. I don't think I'll ever forgive him for reading me that crap out loud. I wouldn't've read it out loud to him if he'd written it—I really wouldn't. In the first place, I'd only written that damn note so that he wouldn't feel too bad about flunking me.

"Do you blame me for flunking you, boy?" he said.

"No, sir! I certainly don't," I said. I wished to hell he'd stop calling me "boy" all the time.

He tried chucking my exam paper on the bed when he was through with it. Only, he missed again, naturally. I had to get up again and pick it up and put it on top of the Atlantic Monthly. It's boring to do that every two minutes.

CONTINUE ➤

22

From this excerpt, Dr. Spencer's feelings towards Holden can best be characterized as:

A. angry for having wasted his time reviewing work that was not up to Holden's true potential

B. firm yet sympathetic towards Holden's current emotional state

C. unrepentant and derogatory, frequently demeaning Holden due to his lack of effort and understanding of the material presented in his class

D. nostalgic and warm

23

The word "chiffonier" used in line 17 is a synonym for:

A. couch

B. bed

C. chair

D. dresser

24

Holden's feelings towards his final meeting with Dr. Spencer can be best characterized as

A. originally respectful and thoughtful but deteriorating into anger and regretful.

B. indifferent towards the conversation engaged in with Dr. Spencer.

C. an attempt by Holden to correct some of his misdeeds during his tenure at Pency School.

D. appreciative and honored to have the opportunity to pay his respects.

25

The answer to question 24 is best evidenced by

A. lines 5-11, "That's something that drives me crazy..."

B. lines 69-74, "I don't think I'll ever forgive him..."

C. lines 22-24, "Boy, you can't imagine..."

D. line 49, "He stopped reading and put my paper down..."

26

It can be inferred from the passage that Holden

A. had a long history with Dr. Spencer.

B. is being asked to leave his school.

C. feels unrepentant about his behavior and performance in Dr. Spencer's class.

D. reached graduation requirements.

27

The term "innumerable" used in line 46 most closely remains

A. continual.

B. measurable.

C. recent.

D. countless.

CONTINUE ➡

28

Given the information in the passage, Dr. Spencer would most likely view Holden's future as being

A. potentially unfavorable due to his unwillingness to work and penchant to approach many situations with nonchalance.

B. immutably negative and desperate due to Holden's hostile attitude and demeanor.

C. approaching a point of critical mass wherein Holden must begin being appreciative of the benefits surrounding him.

D. somewhat favorable as Dr. Spencer appears cautiously optimistic of Holden's potential.

29

Dr. Spencer's feelings towards Holden failing his class can best be characterized as

A. regretful and solemn

B. angry and reproachful

C. justified and accusatory

D. questioning of his own ability

30

Evidence for the previous question is best found in

A. lines 51-55, "Your essay, shall we say, ends there…"

B. lines 5-8, "Absolutely nothing…"

C. lines 26-29, "We studied the Egyptians…"

D. lines 67-69, "He put my goddam paper down then…"

31

Holden's behavior during his visit with Dr. Spencer best reflects which of the following situations?

A. The defense mechanism of projection, where Holden is placing his feelings of anger and resentment over failing school on his teacher.

B. The defense mechanism of denial, where Holden is leading himself to believe that he doesn't care for much about his school, effectively overlooking his academic failures.

C. A display of passive aggressive behavior, wherein Holden is generally acting overly happy and helpful, but with vindictive undertones.

D. A display of solemn resignation to the fact that he has academically failed out of school.

CONTINUE

Questions 32-42 deal with the passage below

-Adapted from the acceptance speech of President Barack Obama, 11/6/2008

Let's resist the temptation to fall back on the same partisanship and pettiness and immaturity that has poisoned our politics for so long. Let's
Line remember that it was a man from this state who
5 first carried the banner of the Republican Party to the White House — a party founded on the values of self-reliance and individual liberty and national unity. Those are values we all share. And while the Democratic Party has won a great
10 victory tonight, we do so with a measure of humility and determination to heal the divides that have held back our progress.

As Lincoln said to a nation far more divided than ours, "We are not enemies, but friends —
15 though passion may have strained it must not break our bonds of affection." And to those Americans whose support I have yet to earn, I may not have won your vote tonight, but I hear your voices, I need your help, and I will be your
20 president too.

And to all those watching tonight from beyond our shores, from parliaments and palaces to those who are huddled around radios in the forgotten corners of the world, our stories are
25 singular, but our destiny is shared, and a new dawn of American leadership is at hand. To those — to those who would tear the world down: we will defeat you. To those who seek peace and security: we support you. And to all those who
30 have wondered if America's beacon still burns as bright: tonight we proved once more that the true strength of our nation comes not from the might of our arms or the scale of our wealth, but from the enduring power of our ideals — democracy,
35 liberty, opportunity and unyielding hope. That's the true genius of America, that America can change. Our union can be perfected. And what we have already achieved gives us hope for what we can and must achieve tomorrow.
40 This election had many firsts and many stories that will be told for generations. But one that's on my mind tonight's about a woman who

cast her ballot in Atlanta. She is a lot like the millions of others who stood in line to make their
45 voice heard in this election, except for one thing: Ann Nixon Cooper is 106 years old.

She was born just a generation past slavery; a time when there were no cars on the road or planes in the sky; when someone like her couldn't
50 vote for two reasons, because she was a woman and because of the color of her skin. And tonight, I think about all that she's seen throughout her century in America: the heartache and the hope, the struggle and the progress, the times we were
55 told that we can't, and the people who pressed on with that American creed, yes we can.

At a time when women's voices were silenced and their hopes dismissed, she lived to see them stand up and speak out and reach for the ballot.
60 Yes we can. When there was despair in the Dust Bowl and depression across the land, she saw a nation conquer fear itself with a New Deal, new jobs, a new sense of common purpose. Yes we can. When the bombs fell on our harbor and
65 tyranny threatened the world, she was there to witness a generation rise to greatness and a democracy was saved. Yes we can. She was there for the buses in Montgomery, the hoses in Birmingham, a bridge in Selma, and a preacher
70 from Atlanta who told a people that "We shall overcome." Yes we can.

CONTINUE →

32

The author discusses a victory by the Republican Party primarily

A. to sway those who may be mild dissenters or undecided persons who find themselves between parties.

B. as a means of showing his ability to foster compassion, understanding, and a spirit of good faith and camaraderie between both major political parties.

C. to show a measure of good sportsmanship in his victory over the Republican party candidate.

D. out of the obligation of political correctness.

33

Evidence for question 32 is found primarily in which of the following:

A. lines 9-12, "While the Democratic Party has won a great victory…"

B. lines 1-3, "Let us resist the temptation to fall back on…"

C. lines 14-20, "We are not enemies, but friends…"

D. lines 29-35, "And to all those who wondered if America's beacon…"

34

The style of writing in this particular passage can best be described as:

A. neutrally informative

B. centrally factual

C. vague but generally positive

D. optimistic propaganda

35

The term *partisanship* used in line 2 primarily refers to:

A. favoritism or bias

B. a conciliatory gesture

C. unity among groups

D. indifference

36

President Obama discusses the story of Ann Nixon Cooper mainly to illustrate

A. the plight of woman's suffrage during the formation of our nation.

B. the many technological advances made by the United States within the lifetime of one person.

C. the many benefits of the New Deal.

D. how the power of the will of the people to inspire change can achieve meaningful results.

37

Evidence for question 36 is best found in

A. lines 47-51, "She was born just a generation past slavery…"

B. lines 51-56, "Tonight I think about all she has seen…"

C. lines 57-59, "At a time when women's voices were silenced…"

D. lines 60-63, "When there was despair in the Dust Bowl…"

CONTINUE ➡

38

The term *creed* used in line 56 most closely means:

A. silent prayer

B. repetitive phrase

C. a core set of beliefs or ideals

D. a set of rules governing behavior

39

The author uses "Lincoln's America" most likely to illustrate

A. how American society can overcome extreme divisiveness.

B. the steadfast resolve of the American people and their willingness to fight all enemies.

C. the extent to which civil rights have progressed since President Lincoln's tenure.

D. the ability of the President to lead during times of dissention within the American people.

40

A central theme present throughout the reading selection is

A. the author's focus on civil rights as the crowning achievement of the American people.

B. a historical analysis of governmental programs and their effectiveness on stigmatized groups of individuals.

C. warnings given to foreign invaders who seek to threaten the peace and security of the American people.

D. the author's steadfast belief in the power of the will of the American people to exact meaningful change.

41

The best evidence for the answer to question 40 is found in

A. lines 27-30, "To those who would tear the world down…"

B. lines 35-39, "For that is the true genius of America…"

C. lines 16-20, "And to those Americans whose support…"

D. lines 43-46, "She's a lot like the…"

42

The author uses the imagery of the phrase, "a new dawn of American leadership is at hand," primarily

A. to symbolize and foster a sense of societal and social rebirth as evidenced by the amount of "firsts" in the election.

B. to provide evidence that multiple election outcomes have resulted in a large number of incumbents losing their positions.

C. in an effort to connect with constituents as acknowledging his relative lack of experience prior to taking office.

D. to symbolize the youthfulness of many members of his incoming Cabinet.

CONTINUE

Questions 43-52 deal with the passages below

Passage 1

-adapted from "Mars Rover Finds Stronger Potential for Life", Marc Kaufman, NY Times, 8 December 2014

For lifeless chemical compounds to organize themselves into something alive, scientists generally agree, three sets of things must be
Line present: standing water and an energy source,
5 five basic elements (carbon, oxygen, hydrogen, phosphorus and nitrogen), and time, lots of time.

In its search for environments where life might have started on Mars, the Curiosity rover has found the standing water, the energy and the
10 key elements with the right atomic charges. As a result, scientists have concluded that at least some of the planet must have been habitable long ago.

But the period when all conditions were right was counted in hundreds to thousands of years,
15 a very small opening by origin-of-life standards. That has now changed. John P. Grotzinger of Caltech, the project scientist for the mission, reported at a news conference on Monday that the rover's yearlong trek to Mount Sharp provided
20 strong new evidence that Gale Crater had large lakes, rivers and deltas, on and off, for millions to tens of millions of years. The geology shows that even when the surface water dried up, plenty of water would have remained underground, he
25 said.

Moreover, the team concluded, numerous deltalike and lakelike formations detected by orbiting satellites are almost certainly the dried remains of substantial ancient lakes and deltas.
30 None of this proves that life existed on the planet, but the case for an early Mars that was ripe and ready for life has grown stronger. And John M. Grunsfeld, a former astronaut who is NASA's associate administrator for science, said that after
35 almost 28 months on Mars, Curiosity has given scientists insight into how and where to look for clues of ancient life.

Another missing piece of the story has been the inability to detect organic compounds — the
40 carbon-based building blocks of life. That too may soon change. Last spring, several Curiosity

team members reported the detection of some simple organics that appeared to be Martian. The findings were not definitive, but NASA
45 has scheduled a news conference Dec. 14 at the annual meeting of the American Geophysical Union with "new information" about the search for organics.

Passage 2

-excerpted from "Mars Life Search: Iron Rich Rocks Could be Key", Jeremy Hsu, Astrobiology Magazine, 24 April 2015

A robotic mission's search for life on Mars
50 may seem worlds away from human scientists wandering around hot springs in Yellowstone National Park. But a study of Yellowstone's hot springs has revealed new clues about how organic materials might get preserved in similar environ-
55 ments on the Red Planet, bettering our chances of finding possible signs of life.

While previous research has focused on silica-rich rocks as proof, some researchers have begun looking at how iron-rich rocks can also
60 contain possible signs of life. Their Yellowstone hot springs study found that iron could either preserve or react with organic material in a way that helps form a fossil record. Such findings counter previous assumptions that iron-rich
65 rocks would destroy organic material through the chemical reaction known as oxidation.

The researchers collected samples from both the active Chocolate Pots hot springs in Yellowstone National Park and an "extinct" iron-
70 silica hot spring nearby that had long since dried up. They had to tread lightly on the steep slope surrounding the hot springs to avoid disturbing any loose iron sediment that might slide into the water and kill photosynthetic communities of
75 microbes by blocking their access to sunlight.

The careful sampling paid off. In a sediment core from the active hot spring, researchers found preserved lipid molecules that are part of a group of bacteria capable of converting sunlight into
80 energy. They even found preserved fragile lipids, such as fatty acids from the cyanobacteria that typically serve as food for other microbes, or are

CONTINUE

otherwise rapidly destroyed after the cells die.

85 The iron-rich hot springs may have helped preserve organic molecules such as lipids in several ways. First, iron reacts chemically with oxygen and lowers oxygen levels in the water, which prevents oxygen-dependent bacteria from consuming all the organic material such as lipids.

90 Second, iron may block certain enzymes that help break down organic material after the death of microorganisms. Third, iron can even chemically bind with organic molecules to help preserve them.

95 Robotic missions to Mars have not found signs of active hot springs. But NASA's Spirit rover discovered evidence of hydrothermal deposits in the Home Plate region that indicated an active hydrothermal system when the

100 currently dry and dusty Red Planet was younger and held more water.

43

The authors of passages 1 and 2 would most likely agree with which of the following statements?

A. The study of silica-rich rocks in the pursuit of evidence that life has existed on Mars is obsolete and inconclusive.

B. Evidence of preserved lipid molecules, particularly from cyanobacteria, present in the Yellowstone hot springs are most likely the result of an increased level of enzymes in iron-rich areas.

C. Continued research expeditions on Mars, particularly if hot springs are discovered, will likely yield greater evidence of Mars having sustained life.

D. Should life have existed on Mars, it would more likely be phosphorous or nitrogen based, rather than carbon-based life forms as we know them.

The term *assumptions* in line 64 most closely means:

A. research findings
B. contentions
C. published works
D. conjecture or speculation

The Yellowstone Research Team's findings in the Chocolate Pots' hot springs was critical to Mars research in that

A. it provided new information regarding how iron-rich rocks may help fossilization and preservation of lipid molecules.

B. researchers peripherally found ways in which cyanobacteria were relevant and critical members of intricate micro-ecosystems.

C. results obtained from research expeditions yielded new information regarding how iron molecules are unable to form covalent bonds with multiple organic molecules, detrimental to preservation.

D. it confirmed earlier hypotheses that only silica-based rocks are capable in aiding fossilization records.

46

Evidence for the answer to question 45 is best found in

A. lines 80-83, "They even found preserved fragile lipids…"

B. lines 60-63, "Their Yellowstone hot springs study…"

C. lines 63-66, "Such findings counter previous assumptions…"

D. lines 52-56, "But a study of Yellowstone's hot springs…"

CONTINUE ➡

47

Passages 1 and 2 both support the idea that
A. little critical information has been obtained to support or justify theories that life potentially existed on Mars.
B. the detection of fossilized organic compounds is critical to establishing whether or not life has existed on Mars.
C. the detection of hot springs and vast areas of former underground lakes and deltas provide the best evidence that organic, lipid-based microbes will be found on Mars.
D. the window of opportunity for Mars to have experienced the necessary conditions to support life was perhaps hundreds of thousands of years.

48

The term *habitable* used in line 12 most likely means:
A. done by routine
B. incorrigible
C. desolate
D. able to sustain life

49

From the information presented in passage 2, it can be inferred that
A. scientists will most likely recommend exploring the hydrothermal deposits of the Home Plate region.
B. further evidence of cyanobacteria in other areas of Yellowstone's hot springs are critical to providing insight into the potential of Mars sustaining life.
C. silica-rich rocks have also been found in the Home Plate region of Mars.
D. photosynthetic communities of microbes freely occurring in Yellowstone most likely have counterparts existing in underground deltas found on Mars.

CONTINUE ➔

50

The evidence provided in passage 1 indicates that

A. critical areas on Mars have shown evidence of having sustained water consistently for millions of years.

B. curiosity team members are relatively certain that the organics discovered on Mars recently are definitive evidence of microorganisms having existed in a planetary ecosystem.

C. sustained, standing water on the surface of Mars, though in existence for some time, did not occur with relative consistency.

D. though the Curiosity rover has found standing water, the correct atomic charges necessary for carbon-based life forms are relatively non-existent.

51

Evidence for question 50 is best found in

A. lines 38-40, "Another missing piece of the story…"

B. lines 18-22, "reported at a news conference…"

C. lines 1-6, "For lifeless, chemical compounds…"

D. lines 7-10, "In its search for environments…"

52

Contrary to passage 2, passage 1 focuses primarily on

A. hydrogen and carbon-based evidence laying the framework for Martian life having potentially existed.

B. evidence from iron-rich rocks providing support for the existence of microorganisms that may have indicated past life existing.

C. correlational evidence rather than evidence specific to the research at hand.

D. the impact of various chemical compounds on potential fossilization of microorganisms on Mars.

STOP

If you finish before time is called, you may check your work on this section only. Do not turn to any other section.

ACKNOWLEDGEMENT FOR THIS SECTION

Passages in this section were adapted from the following sources:

Marc Kaufman, "Mars Rover Finds Stronger Potential for Life", © 2014 by *New York Times,* originally published 8 December 2014.

Barack Obama, acceptance speech, 6 November 2008.

J. D. Salinger, "The Catcher in the Rye", © 1951 by Little, Brown and company.

Jerry Thompson, "The Great, Underestimated Earthquake Threat to North America", © 2012 by *The Extreme Earth.* First published 13 March 2012.

Mimi Whitefield, "Havana: US Immigration Policy for Cubans Needs to Change", © 2015 by *Miami Herald, originally published 21 January 2015.*

Writing and Language Test

35 MINUTES, 44 QUESTIONS

Turn to Section 2 of your answer sheet to answer the questions in this section.

Questions 1 – 11 are based on the following passage.

Shopkeepers of the World Unite

A profitable art magazine *DIS* might not do much to hasten **1** the demise of capitalism; but it could have a salutary effect on the art world. If we take the magazine at its word, part of the purpose of creating consumer-facing "diffusion lines" is to liberate emerging artists from hyper-rich collectors. **2** While many take for granted the entanglement of the art world with the ultra-elite, there was a time not all that

1
A. NO CHANGE
B. the demise of capitalism, but it could
C. the demise of capitalism but, it could
D. the demise of capitalism but it could

2
A. NO CHANGE
B. When
C. As
D. In spite of

CONTINUE

long ago **3** which close association with the very wealthy was a source of embarrassment for respected artists. The promise of the diffusion line is that it could allow artists to trade an alliance with the .01 percent for an art practice supported by the middle class. The idea is that artists could become a little more like Red Bull, **4** they make its money from the masses.

5 Throughout the run of "DISown," I heard numerous artists repeat the line, without irony, that Red Bull is "actually a media company"—the energy drinks were just a side thing. Time and again, **6** I had to explain it wasn't true: Red Bull was in fact a beverage company. **7** It's support for "DISown" and other art initiatives was a branding project to help sell energy drinks—energy drinks were not a fake-out to

3

A. NO CHANGE
B. that
C. when
D. where

4

A. NO CHANGE
B. they are making its money
C. which make its money
D. which makes its money

5

Which choice, inserted here, will most effectively establish transition from the first paragraph?

A. Red Bull has evidently done a good job of persuading people that it's really a long-lost cousin of *DIS*.
B. Many advertisements are intentionally misleading people.
C. Even today, many artists still believe in "art for art's sake."
D. Yet many artists do not really care about the diffusion lines created by *DIS*.

6

A. NO CHANGE
B. I had to explain this wasn't true:
C. I had to explain that wasn't true:
D. I had to explain that this wasn't true:

7

A. NO CHANGE
B. its support
C. his support
D. their support

help fund projects like "DISown." **8** Perhaps in the distant future, viewers of the Red Bull Network will no longer remember that the company began as a distributor of caffeine and taurine, but as of now, Red Bull's identity as a media company is largely science fiction.

Cheerleading for the middle class is **9** one thing; making money from it is something else. Many of the artists **10** they featured in "DISown" are already showing at elite galleries. *DIS* **11** it had a four-week solo show last year at Suzanne Geiss as well as prominent placement in a widely discussed exhibition, "ProBio," at MoMA PS1. They have gallery representation in Paris. The risk for "DISown," for which the Red Bull exhibition was only the launching pad, is that instead of creating an alternative funding stream for artists, it might simply allow the artists involved to peddle their wares to major collectors with greater buzz and authority.

8
A. NO CHANGE
B. Perhaps, in the distant future viewers
C. Perhaps, in the distant future, viewers
D. Perhaps in the distant future viewers

9
A. NO CHANGE
B. one thing, making money
C. one thing. Making money
D. one thing. But making money

10
A. NO CHANGE
B. who
C. which
D. DELETE the underlined portion.

11
A. NO CHANGE
B. them
C. itself
D. , it

Questions 12 – 22 are based on the following passage.

Saving Coral Reefs

Fish are the key ingredients in a new recipe **12** diagnose and restore degraded coral reef ecosystems, according to scientists from the Australian Institute of Marine Science, WCS, James Cook University, and other organizations in a new study in the journal Nature.

For overfished coral reef systems, **13** restoring fish populations will in turn restore ecological functions critical to recovery. Fish populations perform key roles. **14** For moderately or lightly fished reefs, the recipe requires knowing which fish to catch, how many, and which to leave behind.

15 The authors assessed fish biomass and functional groups from more than 800 coral reefs worldwide. The authors used them to estimate recovery periods for both lightly fished and overfished

12

A. NO CHANGE
B. to diagnose and restore
C. to diagnose and to restore
D. diagnosing and restoring

13

Which choice most effectively combines the two underlined parts?
A. Restoring fish populations, that perform key roles will in turn restore ecological functions critical to recovery.
B. restoring fish populations that perform key roles will in turn restore ecological functions critical to recovery.
C. restoring fish populations that perform key roles, will in turn restore ecological functions critical to recovery.
D. restoring fish populations will in turn restore ecological functions critical to recovery and fish populations perform key roles.

14

A. NO CHANGE
B. For moderately, or lightly fished reefs, the recipe
C. For moderately or, lightly fished reefs, the recipe
D. For moderately, or, lightly fished reefs, the recipe

15

A. NO CHANGE
B. The authors assessed … and the authors used
C. The authors assessed … and they used
D. The authors assessed … and used

CONTINUE

reefs. The scientists speculate that **16** maintaining and restoring fish populations and the functions they provide can increase the resilience of reefs to large-scale threats such as climate change.

The coral reefs of the world are in crisis, endangered by a number of coastal threats such as overfishing, pollution, and coastal development as well as **17** global threats as climate change. According to the World Resources Institute, some 75 percent of the world's coral reefs are now threatened and more than 20 percent have disappeared since climate and fishing disturbances have accelerated in the past 30 years. **18** Also, only 27 percent of the world's coral reefs are contained within marine protected areas.

19 "Studying remote and marine protected areas, we were able to estimate how much fish there would be on coral reefs without fishing, as well as how long it should take newly protected areas to recover," said M. Aaron MacNeil, Senior Research Scientist for the Australian Institute of Marine Science and lead author on the study. "This is important because we can now gauge the impact reef fisheries have had historically and make informed management decisions **20** that include time frames for recovery."

Coral reef experts agree that fishing is a primary driver in the degradation of reef function, **21** that in turn has generated growing interest in finding fisheries management solutions to support reef resilience. Removing too many herbivorous and predatory fish species deprives coral reefs of critical ecosystem functions and the capacity to respond effectively to other disturbances. Knowing the right amount to leave behind can help local fisheries set clear limits to

16
A. NO CHANGE
B. to maintain and restore
C. to maintain and to restore
D. maintain and restore

17
A. NO CHANGE
B. global threats like
C. global threats such as
D. global threats, for example,

18
A. NO CHANGE
B. Then,
C. At the same time,
D. Additionally,

19
A. NO CHANGE
B. "By studying
C. "With studying
D. "If we study

20
A. NO CHANGE
B. that includes
C. include
D. includes

21
A. NO CHANGE
B. it
C. and the degradation of reef function
D. which

CONTINUE ➡

how many fish can be taken without 22 changing the ecosystem they rely on.

Which choice is most consistent with the tone of the passage?
A. NO CHANGE
B. affecting
C. threatening
D. unbalancing

Questions 23 – 33 are based on the following passage.

The gases used to knock out surgery patients are accumulating in Earth's [23] atmosphere. In the atmosphere they make a small contribution to climate change, report scientists who have detected the compounds as far afield as Antarctica. Over the past decade, concentrations of the anesthetics desflurane, isoflurane and sevoflurane [24] have been rising globally, the new study finds.

Like the well-known climate warmer carbon dioxide, anesthesia gases allow the atmosphere to store more energy from the Sun. [25] _____, the medical gases are extra potent in their greenhouse-gas effects.

One kilogram (2.2 pounds) of desflurane, for instance, is equivalent to 2,500 kilograms (5,512 pounds) of carbon dioxide in terms of the amount of greenhouse warming potential, explained Martin [26] Vollmer an atmospheric chemist at the Swiss Federal Laboratories for Materials Science and Technology in Dubendorf, Switzerland, who led the new study. [27] "On a kilogram per kilogram basis, it's so much more potent than carbon dioxide," he said.

In a new scientific paper, Vollmer and his

Which choice most effectively combines the two sentences at the underlined portion?

A. ... atmosphere, in the atmosphere
B. ... atmosphere, and in the atmosphere
C. ... atmosphere where
D. ... atmosphere which

A. NO CHANGE
B. has been rising
C. are rising
D. were rising

Which choice, inserted here, establishes most effective transition?

A. But differently,
B. But unlike carbon dioxide,
C. Meanwhile,
D. In addition,

A. NO CHANGE
B. Vollmer an atmospheric chemist, at the Swiss Federal Laboratory
C. Vollmer, an atmospheric chemist at the Swiss Federal Laboratory
D. Vollmer, he is an atmospheric chemist at the Swiss Federal Laboratory

A. NO CHANGE
B. "On a kilogram-per kilogram basis,
C. "On a kilogram-per-kilogram-basis,
D. "On a kilogram-per-kilogram basis,

colleagues report [28] the 2014 atmospheric concentration of desflurane as 0.30 parts per trillion (ppt). Isoflurane, sevoflurane and halothane came in at 0.097 ppt, 0.13 ppt and 0.092 ppt, respectively. Carbon dioxide — which hit 400 parts per million in 2014 — is a billion times more abundant than the most prevalent of these anesthetics.

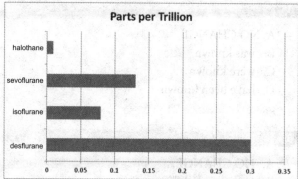

The researchers obtained their numbers by collecting samples of air from remote sites in the Northern Hemisphere since 2000, as well as aboard the icebreaker research vessel Araon during an expedition in the North Pacific in 2012 and at the South Korea Antarctic station King Sejong in the South Shetland Islands. [29] They have also been tracking the anesthetics since 2013 in two-hourly measurements at a high-altitude observatory at Jungfraujoch, Switzerland, and from ongoing air sampling from a rooftop in a suburb of Zurich, Switzerland.

[30] To turn these air samples into their global emissions estimates, the data were combined with [31] two-dimensional computer model of atmospheric transport and chemistry. The results are the first [32] so called top down estimates—based on actual atmospheric measurements—of how many metric tons of each anesthetic were released into the atmosphere in 2014. That can now be compared to "bottom-up" estimates by other researchers, which estimate atmospheric concentrations based on factors such as how much of each gas is sold annually, how much typically [33] escape through operating room vents and how much is not metabolized by patients.

28

About which anesthetic is the data wrong in the sentence, based on the graphic?
A. Desflurane
B. Isoflurane
C. Sevoflurane
D. Halothane

29

A. NO CHANGE
B. They also tracked
C. They are also tracking
D. They were also tracking

30

A. NO CHANGE
B. Turning
C. By turning
D. Turn

31

A. NO CHANGE
B. a two-dimensional
C. two dimensional
D. a two dimensional

32

A. NO CHANGE
B. so-called top down
C. so called top-down
D. so-called top-down

33

A. NO CHANGE
B. escapes
C. escaped
D. is escaped

CONTINUE

Questions 34 – 44 are based on the following passage.

It is well known that bumblebees and other pollinators can tell the difference between plants that will provide them with nectar and pollen and **34** that won't. However, until now **35** little has been known about how the arrangement of flowers affects their decision making.

Researchers from the School of Biological and Chemical Sciences at Queen Mary University of London taught bumblebees **36** to distinguish among two visually clearly different feeder types, one type containing food while the other did not. They found that bees were able to quickly learn the feeder types containing food when the feeders were arranged horizontally. **37** the bees failed to distinguish these feeder types when these were distributed vertically on a wall and significantly more often chose the wrong feeder type.

The researchers **38** are sure the bees were equally able to discriminate between the two presented feeders in both arrangements but simply chose not to waste the brain power doing so on vertically arranged feeders. They believe that this is because in a meadow typically rewarding and unrewarding flowers of different species grow side-by-side and bees benefit from visiting only flowers **39** similar to the ones that

34

A. NO CHANGE
B. those plants that won't
C. those that won't
D. the plants that won't

35

A. NO CHANGE
B. was known
C. were known
D. have been known

36

A. NO CHANGE
B. to distinguish between
C. to distinguish off
D. to distinguish from

37

Which choice most effectively connects the sentence to the paragraph?
A. And, the bees
B. Then, the bees
C. However, the bees
D. But, the bees

38

A. NO CHANGE
B. are sure of the bees
C. are sure about the bees
D. are sure that the bees

39

A. NO CHANGE
B. similar to the flowers
C. similar as the flowers
D. similar as the ones

CONTINUE ▶

have previously rewarded them. **40** On contrast, vertically clustered flowers, such as on flowering bushes or trees, the flowers in the arrangement are typically the same and paying close attention **41** on the flower features may not be needed.

Dr Stephan **42** Wolf co-author of the research said: "This is a rare example of a pollinator being able to tell the difference between different flowers but simply **43** choose not to do so."

"Further illustrating the impressive learning abilities of **44** mini brain bees, this study also shows that these capabilities may be applied in very surprising ways in different natural foraging situations," added Dr. Wolf.

40

A. NO CHANGE
B. In contrast,
C. To contrast,
D. By contrasting,

41

A. NO CHANGE
B. at
C. of
D. to

42

A. NO CHANGE
B. Wolf, co-author of the research said:
C. Wolf co-author of the research, said:
D. Wolf, co-author of the research, said:

43

A. NO CHANGE
B. choosing
C. chose
D. to choose

44

A. NO CHANGE
B. mini brained bees
C. mini-brained bees
D. mini-brained-bees

STOP

If you finish before time is called, you may check your work on this section only. Do not turn to any other section.

Math Test – No Calculator

25 MINUTES, 20 QUESTIONS

Turn to Section 3 of your answer sheet to answer the questions in this section.

$A = \pi r^2$

$C = 2\pi r$

$A = \ell w$

$A = \dfrac{1}{2}bh$

$c^2 = a^2 + b^2$

Special Right Triangles

$V = \ell wh$

$V = \pi r^2 h$

$V = \dfrac{4}{3}\pi r^3$

$V = \dfrac{1}{3}\pi r^2 h$

$V = \dfrac{1}{3}\ell wh$

The number of degrees of arc in a circle is 360.

The number of radians of arc in a circle is 2π.

The sum of the measures in degrees of the angles of a triangle is 180.

CONTINUE ▶

1

For $i = -1$, what is the quotient $\frac{3+i}{3-i}$?

A. $1 + \frac{3i}{5}$

B. $1 + \frac{3i}{4}$

C. $\frac{4}{5} + \frac{3i}{5}$

D. $\frac{5}{4} + \frac{3i}{4}$

2

If x is an integer and $|3x - 4| < 2$, what is the value of x?

A. -1

B. 0

C. 1

D. 3

3

If $x^2 = p$, where x and p are integers, which of the following could be the value of p?

A. 16

B. 17

C. 18

D. 19

4

Three consecutive integers are such that four times the least is one more than three times the greatest. Which of the following is the middle integer?

A. 7

B. 8

C. 9

D. 10

5

If k is a positive integer greater than 2, which of following could be a graph of $y = \frac{kx}{2}$?

A.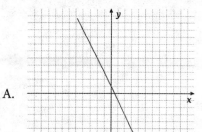

B.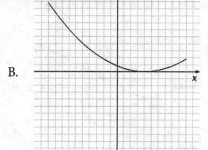

C.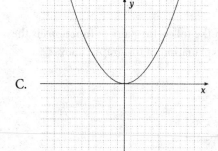

D.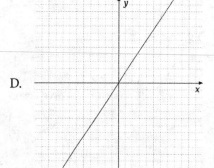

CONTINUE

6

In an isosceles triangle, one angle measures 120°. If one of the other two angles is $x°$, what is $\cos x°$?

A. $\dfrac{1}{2}$

B. $\dfrac{\sqrt{3}}{2}$

C. $\dfrac{\sqrt{3}}{3}$

D. $\dfrac{\sqrt{2}}{2}$

7

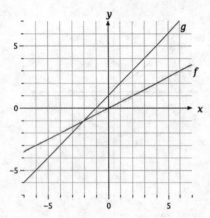

Which of the following pairs of functions is the correct explanation of the graphs above?

A. $f(x) = x - 1$

$g(x) = \dfrac{1}{2}x$

B. $f(x) = x + 1$

$g(x) = x - 1$

C. $f(x) = \dfrac{1}{2}x$

$g(x) = x + 1$

D. $f(x) = \dfrac{1}{2}x$

$g(x) = x - 1$

8

If $a^2 - 2ab + b^2 = 9$, and $a + b = 7$, which of the following is true?

A. $a = 4$, $b = 3$

B. $a = 2$, $b = 5$

C. $a = 1$, $b = 6$

D. $a = 8$, $b = -1$

9

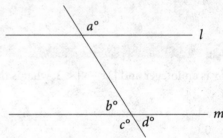

Note: Figure not drawn to scale.

In the figure above, lines l and m are parallel and $\angle a = 120°$. Which of the following is equal to the sum of $\angle b$, $\angle c$ and $\angle d$?

A. 120°

B. 240°

C. 160°

D. 250°

10

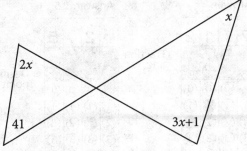

Note: Figure not drawn to scale.

In the figure above, what is the value of x?

A. 42
B. 30
C. 8
D. 20

11

GPA OF GRADUATING STUDENTS

GPA	NUMBER OF STUDENTS
3.5 − 4.0	28
3.0 − 3.4	37
2.5 − 2.9	24
2.0 − 2.4	11

The chart above is a random sample of GPAs from Mainland High School's graduating students. The entire graduating class contains 520 students. Based on the data above, which is the best estimate for the number of students in the graduating class who had a GPA of 3.0 or higher?

A. 65
B. 130
C. 260
D. 338

12

The difference of the squares of two positive consecutive integers is 15. What is the greater of the two integers?

A. 6
B. 7
C. 8
D. 9

13

If $x - y = 4$ and $2x + 3y = 20$, what is the value of $3x + 2y$?

A. 24
B. 22
C. 18
D. 35

14

If $x > 4 (x - 5) - 1$, then x must be:

A. $x > 4$
B. $x < -4$
C. $x > 7$
D. $x < 7$

15

If $3 = \dfrac{6}{\sqrt{r + 3}}$, what is the value of r?

A. 2
B. 1
C. −7
D. −1

CONTINUE

For questions 16–20, solve the problem and enter your answer in the grid, as described below, on the answer sheet.

1. Although not required, it is suggested that you write your answer in the boxes at the top of the columns to help you fill in the circles accurately. You will receive credit only if the circles are filled in correctly.

2. Mark no more than one circle in any column.

3. No question has a negative answer.

4. Some problems may have more than one correct answer. In such cases, grid only one answer.

5. **Mixed numbers** such as $3\frac{1}{2}$ must be gridded as 3.5 or 7/2. (If [3 1 / 2] is entered into the grid, it will be interpreted as $\frac{31}{2}$, not $3\frac{1}{2}$.)

6. **Decimal answers:** If you obtain a decimal answer with more digits than the grid can accommodate, it may be either rounded or truncated, but it must fill the entire grid.

Answer: $\frac{7}{12}$ Answer: 2.5

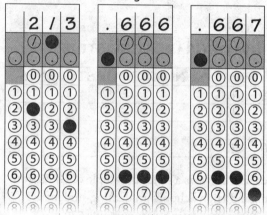

Write answer in boxes.   ← Fraction line

Grid in result.   ← Decimal point

Acceptable ways to grid $\frac{2}{3}$ are:

Answer: 201 – either position is correct

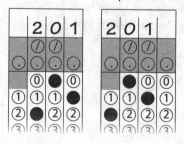

NOTE: You may start your answers in any column, space permitting. Columns you don't need to use should be left blank.

CONTINUE ➤

16

If $\frac{2x+15}{3} = x$, what is the value of x?

17

Points A, B, and C are on the same straight road. David rides his bicycle from Point B to Point C at 15 miles per hour. At the same time, Andrew drives his car from Point A to Point C at 45 miles per hour. If they both arrive at Point C after 20 minutes, what is the distance, in miles, between Point A and Point B?

18

In the figure below, ABC is an isosceles triangle. The height of the triangle, AD, is 12 inches, and $AB = AC = 15$ inches. What is the value of $\tan C$?

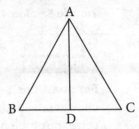

19

If $x^2 + y^2 = 34$ and $x - y = 2$, then $xy =$

20

If $\frac{x^3 - x^2}{x - 1} = \frac{4x^2 + 17x - 21}{x - 1}$ and $x > 0$, what is the value of x?

STOP

**If you finish before time is called, you may check your work on this section only.
Do not turn to any other section.**

Math Test – Calculator

55 MINUTES, 38 QUESTIONS

Turn to Section 4 of your answer sheet to answer the questions in this section.

DIRECTIONS

For questions 1 – 30, solve each problem, choose the best answer from the choices provided and fill in the circle on your answer sheet. **For questions 31 – 38,** solve the problem and enter your answer in the grid on your answer sheet. Please refer to the directions before question 31 on how to enter your answers in the grid. Your may use any available space in your test booklet for scratch work.

NOTES

1. The use of a calculator **is permitted**.

2. All variables and expressions used represent real numbers unless otherwise indicated.

3. Figures provided in this test are drawn to scale unless otherwise indicated.

4. All figures lie in a plane unless otherwise indicated.

5. Unless otherwise indicated, the domain of a given function f is the set of all real numbers x for which $f(x)$ is a real number.

REFERENCE

$A = \pi r^2$
$C = 2\pi r$

$A = \ell w$

$A = \frac{1}{2}bh$

$c^2 = a^2 + b^2$

Special Right Triangles

$V = \ell wh$

$V = \pi r^2 h$

$V = \frac{4}{3}\pi r^3$

$V = \frac{1}{3}\pi r^2 h$

$V = \frac{1}{3}\ell wh$

The number of degrees of arc in a circle is 360.

The number of radians of arc in a circle is 2π.

The sum of the measures in degrees of the angles of a triangle is 180.

CONTINUE ➤

1

If $3x + 5 = 5x - 3$, what is the value of x?

A. 3
B. −3
C. 4
D. −4

2

$2^{\frac{3}{2}} + 4^{\frac{3}{2}} + 8^{\frac{3}{2}} =$

A. $14^{\frac{3}{2}}$

B. 33

C. $8 + 18\sqrt{2}$

D. $\sqrt{3} \cdot 4^{\frac{3}{2}}$

3

If $2<a<5$ and $0<b<7$, then what is the range of $a + b$?

A. $2<a+b<12$
B. $0<a+b<7$
C. $-2<a+b<2$
D. $-2<a+b<12$

4

A circle has equation $x^2+y^2+4x-6y=0$. What is its radius?

A. $\sqrt{10}$
B. 10
C. $\sqrt{13}$
D. 13

5

What is the value of $z - 1$ if $5z - 5 = 12$?

A. 0

B. $\dfrac{12}{5}$

C. $\dfrac{17}{4}$

D. 2

6

Which of the following is a solution to the equation $\sqrt{x^2 - 3x + 9} = 4x - 9$?

A. −4
B. 4
C. −3
D. 3

Questions 7 – 10 refer to the following table of NASA data about the first six planets in the solar system.

Table 1 Fact sheet for the first six planets

Planet	Mass $(10^{24}kg)$	Density(kg/m^3)
Mercury	0.330	5427
Venus	4.87	5243
Earth	5.97	5514
Mars	0.642	3933
Jupiter	1898	1326
Saturn	568	687

7

According to the table above, what is the approximate volume of the planet Venus?

A. $1.63\times10^{20}m^3$
B. $9.28\times10^{20}m^3$
C. $1.08\times10^{20}m^3$
D. $2.55\times10^{20}m^3$

8

According to the information in the table above, approximately what fraction of the total mass of the first six planets is contributed by the mass of Jupiter?

A. $\dfrac{1}{5}$

B. $\dfrac{3}{4}$

C. $\dfrac{19}{25}$

D. $\dfrac{24}{45}$

CONTINUE

9

According to the information in the table, the volume of Earth is how much bigger than the volume of Venus, in term of percentage?

A. 1
B. 10
C. 12
D. 16

10

Suppose Mercury is an ideally perfect sphere. Use the fact that the volume of a sphere is $V=\frac{4}{3}\pi r^3$, where r is the radius of the sphere. Which of the following is the closest to the diameter of the planet Mercury, in terms of kilometers? (Note: Take $\pi = 3.14$.)

A. 3475
B. 6792
C. 4880
D. 6420

11

If $6x-2y=13$ and $-4x+2y=2$, what is the value of x?

A. 7
B. 7.5
C. 8
D. 8.5

12

How many positive integers x satisfy $-5 \le 5x \le 27$?

A. 4
B. 5
C. 6
D. 7

13

Which of the following is true about the equation $x^2+y^2-2x+6y+11=0$?

A. It represents a parabola with vertex $(1, -3)$.
B. It represents a circle centered at the point $(1, -3)$.
C. It represents a circle with radius 5.
D. It does not represent a parabola nor a circle.

14

If z is a positive number where the square of $\frac{z}{3}$ is no more than 9 and no less than 4, which of the following must be true?

A. $2 \le z \le 3$
B. $2 \le z \le 9$
C. $4 \le z \le 9$
D. $6 \le z \le 9$

15

Let $f(x)=3x^3-7x^2+x-2$. What is the value of $f(2)$?

A. -4
B. -2
C. 0
D. 2

16

If $\frac{5x+7}{x}=9$, what is the value of $\frac{21}{x}$?

A. 10
B. 11
C. 12
D. 13

CONTINUE

17

A paper company manufactures high quality printing paper. One of their most popular products, U200 series, is packaged as a ream of 500 letter size sheets (8.5in by 11in). In accordance with the regulations of a foreign market, they recently changed the measurements of the paper sheets and developed a new series, U200s. A package of the new product consists of 400 A4 size sheets (8.3in by 11.7in). Which of the following is closest to the ratio of the uncut paper needed to produce a package of U200s to that of U200?

A. 0.75
B. 0.8
C. 0.83
D. 1.25

18

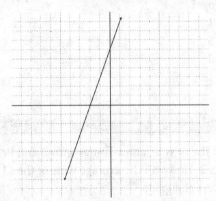

Which of the following equation expresses a line that is perpendicular to the one in the figure above?

A. $6x + 2y = 5$
B. $y - 3x + 1 = 0$
C. $y = -3x + 2$
D. $4x + 12y = 7$

19

Which of the following picture depicts the graph of the function $y = \frac{1}{2}(x - 1)(x + 2)(x - 3)$?

A.

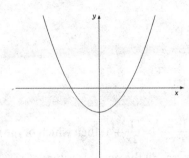

B.

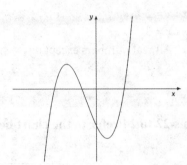

C.

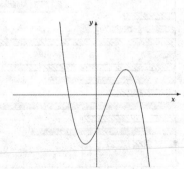

D.

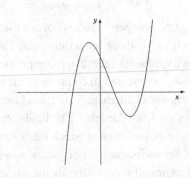

CONTINUE

20

If $a = 2b+1$ and $\dfrac{3a+b+6}{2b} = 5$, what is the value of a?

A. 7

B. 8

C. 11

D. 15

21

If $\dfrac{3(1+2x)}{6x} = \dfrac{1}{2x} + 1$, then which of the following expresses all the possible values of x?

A. $x : x = 1$

B. $x : x = 2$

C. $x : x = 3$

D. x : All real numbers except 0

Problems 22 to 24 refer to the chart below.

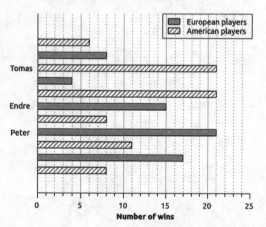

The game company Piudoo holds a tournament of their newly designed online game Piudaa. After three months of preliminary competitions, the 11 finalists are selected to compete in the world final. Among the 11 finalists, 5 are from Europe and the others are from America. The final consists of a series of games, each of which has a winner. The chart shows the number of games won when the final went half way (with only the names of three players shown).

22

According to the information above, which of the following is true?

A. If Peter wins the next match, the average wins of the European players does not change.

B. If Endre wins the next two matches, the mode of the wins of all the finalists becomes 17.

C. If Tomas wins the next 4 matches, the median of wins of American players is still less than that of the European players.

D. Currently the mode of the number of wins of European players is 8 and 21.

23

Suppose at this point Endre stops participate in the final due to personal reasons, but we keep his wins in our statistics. At least how many more games need to be played until the median of the number of wins of the European players can change?

A. 1

B. 5

C. 8

D. 12

24

If in the next 5 games Tomas wins 3 and Peter wins 2. How will the average wins of the 11 players changed?

A. It will not change at all.

B. It increases by 5.

C. It increases by $\dfrac{7}{8}$.

D. It increases by $\dfrac{5}{11}$.

CONTINUE

25

Which of the following equals $\sqrt{10}$?

A. $\sqrt[3]{100}$

B. $\sqrt[3]{20}\sqrt{20}$

C. $\sqrt[4]{2}\sqrt[4]{5}$

D. $\sqrt[4]{4}\sqrt{5}$

26

If $z \cdot (1-i)=(8+2i)$, what is the value of z?

A. $3 + 4i$

B. $1 + 3i$

C. $3 + 5i$

D. $2 - 2i$

Problems 27 to 29 are based on the information below.

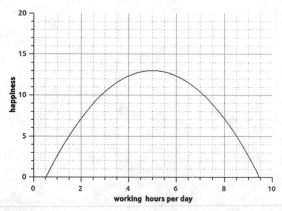

The producer of a popular television show started a project to investigate what the optimal number of working hours per day is. They carefully studied a group of hundreds of people and evaluated how happy they are as an integer score. Some of the scores are negative; these data points are used to find the curve of best fit but afterwards are treated as 0 — it would be too sad to give someone a negative happiness score. The curve of best fit thus found is depicted in the picture.

27

According to the information above, what will be the ideal number of hours to work for each day?

A. 4

B. 5

C. 6

D. 7

28

The happy interval is defined to be the interval on the x-axis (working hours axis) in the graph where the happiness is positive. What is the approximate length of the happy interval?

A. 6

B. 7

C. 8

D. 9

29

If they change the evaluation system so that each person's score decreases by 5, how would the length of the happy interval change approximately?

A. It will not change.

B. It will decrease by 2.

C. It will increase by 3.

D. It will decrease by 5.

CONTINUE

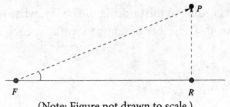

(Note: Figure not drawn to scale.)

A fox at point F observes a rabbit at point R who is moving along the line that is perpendicular to FR at the constant speed of 15m/s. The fox decides to run immediately on a straight line at the constant speed of 45m/s in order to catch the rabbit at some point P if neither of them changes directions. Which of the following is true about the angle she will choose?

A. $\sin(\angle PFR) = \dfrac{1}{2}$

B. $\cos(\angle PFR) = \dfrac{1}{3}$

C. $\sin(\angle PFR) = \dfrac{1}{2\sqrt{2}}$

D. $\cos(\angle PFR) = \dfrac{2\sqrt{2}}{3}$

CONTINUE

DIRECTIONS

For questions 31–38, solve the problem and enter your answer in the grid, as described below, on the answer sheet.

1. Although not required, it is suggested that you write your answer in the boxes at the top of the columns to help you fill in the circles accurately. You will receive credit only if the circles are filled in correctly.

2. Mark no more than one circle in any column.

3. No question has a negative answer.

4. Some problems may have more than one correct answer. In such cases, grid only one answer.

5. **Mixed numbers** such as $3\frac{1}{2}$ must be gridded as 3.5 or 7/2. (If $3\,1\,/\,2$ is entered into the grid, it will be interpreted as $\frac{31}{2}$, not $3\frac{1}{2}$.)

6. **Decimal answers:** If you obtain a decimal answer with more digits than the grid can accommodate, it may be either rounded or truncated, but it must fill the entire grid.

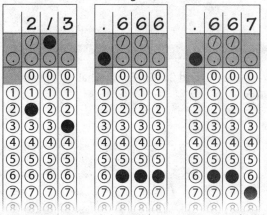

Acceptable ways to grid $\frac{2}{3}$ are:

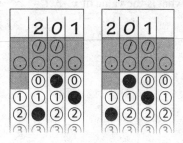

Answer: 201 – either position is correct

NOTE: You may start your answers in any column, space permitting. Columns you don't need to use should be left blank.

31

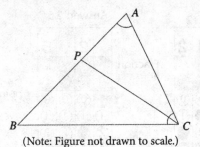

(Note: Figure not drawn to scale.)

In the figure above, CP bisects $\angle ACB$. If $\angle ACP=30°$ and $\angle A=70°$, what is the degree of $\angle B$?

32

If $a-2b+3c=13$ and $2a+5b-3c=7$, what is the value of $a+b$?

33

If $\frac{x^2-6}{x-3}=1+\frac{3}{x-3}$, what is the value of x^2-3x?

34

A restaurant offers buffet for lunch and dinner. It charges \$20 for each customer during the lunch time, and \$30 per customer for the dinner. On a particular day, the number of customers who came for lunch is 2 more than three times the number of customers who came for dinner, and the restaurant charged them \$7,240 in total. How many customers came for dinner?

35

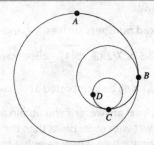

The radii of the three circles in the picture above are in the proportion of 4:2:1. The arcs AB, BC, and CD all run a quarter along their respective circle. If the length of the minor arc BC is 7π, and the length of the spiral that consists of the three minor arcs AB, BC, and CD is $a\pi$, what is the value of a?

36

The equation $2x^2-8x-k=0$ has two roots a and b. If $a-b=8$, what is the value of k?

CONTINUE

Problems 37 and 38 refer to the following information.

In the biomatics lab Iris is doing a study on the space-population relation of a certain bacterial cell. She populates the space with a fixed schedule as follows: In the beginning the space is empty. On the first day she populates x new cells. Starting from day 2, each day the number of new cells she will add to the space doubles the number of new cells she adds in the previous day. So, on the second day she introduces $2x$ additional cells, and on the third day she adds $4x$ more new cells, and so on. It is also known that in the entire process the cells do not die nor do they reproduce.

37

If $x=3$, how many cells will be there in total at the end of the fourth day?

38

Actually she populated much more than 3 cells on the first day. As a result, at the end of the seventh day, she discovered that the space was too crowded and there were already more than 20,000 cells in the space. What is the least number of cells that she added in the space on the first day?

STOP

If you finish before time is called, you may check your work on this section only. Do not turn to any other section.

New SAT Practice Essay 2

 ESSAY BOOK

DIRECTIONS

The essay gives you an opportunity to show how effectively you can read and comprehend a passage and write an essay analyzing the passage. In your essay, you should demonstrate that you have read the passage carefully, present a clear and logical analysis, and use language precisely.

Your essay must be written on the lines provided in your answer booklet; except for the Planning Page of the answer booklet, you will receive no other paper on which to write. You will have enough space if you write on every line, avoid wide margins, and keep your handwriting to a reasonable size. Remember that people who are not familiar with your handwriting will read what you write. Try to write or print so that what you are writing is legible to those readers.

You have <u>50 minutes</u> to read the passage and write an essay in response to the prompt provided inside this booklet.

REMINDERS

— Do not write your essay in this booklet. Only what you write on the lined pages of your answer booklet will be evaluated.

— An off-topic essay will not be evaluated.

This cover is representative of what you'll see on test day.

As you read the passage below, consider how Bill Clinton uses:

- evidence, such as facts or examples, to support claims.
- reasoning to develop ideas and to connect claims and evidence.
- stylistic or persuasive elements, such as word choice or appeals to emotion, to add power to the ideas expressed.

Adapted from President Bill Clinton's 1993 speech to the Congress, endorsing health care reform.

1 My fellow Americans, tonight we come together to write a new chapter in the American story. Our forebears enshrined the American dream: life, liberty, the pursuit of happiness. Every generation of Americans has worked to strengthen that legacy, to make our country a place of freedom and opportunity, a place where people who work hard can rise to their full potential, a place where their children can have a better future. Now we are in a time of profound change and opportunity. The end of the cold war, the information age, and the global economy have brought us both opportunity and hope and strife and uncertainty. Our purpose in this dynamic age must be to make change our friend and not our enemy.

2 To achieve that goal, we must face all our challenges with confidence, with faith, and with discipline. All these challenges require us to change. If Americans are to have the courage to change in a difficult time, we must first be secure in our most basic needs. Tonight I want to talk to you about the most critical thing we can do to build that security. This health care system of ours is badly broken, and it is time to fix it. Despite the dedication of literally millions of talented health care professionals, our health care is too uncertain and too expensive, too bureaucratic and too wasteful. It has too much fraud and too much greed. At long last, after decades of false starts, we must make this our most urgent priority, giving every American health security, health care that can never be taken away, heath care that is always there. That is what we must do tonight.On this journey, there will be rough spots in the road and honest disagreements about how we should proceed. But every successful journey is guided by fixed stars. And if we can agree on some basic values and principles, we will reach tills destination, and we will reach it together. So tonight I want to talk to you about the principles that I believe must embody our efforts to reform America's health care system: security, simplicity, savings, choice, quality, and responsibility.

3 Now, we all know what's right. We're blessed with the best health care professionals on Earth, the finest health care institutions, the best medical research, the most sophisticated technology. But we also know that we can no longer afford to continue to ignore what is wrong.

4 Millions of Americans are just a pink slip away from losing their health insurance and one serious illness away from losing all their savings. Millions more are locked into the jobs they have now just because they or someone in their family has once

been sick and they have what is called the preexisting condition. And on any given day, over 37 million Americans, most of them working people and their little children, have no health insurance at all. And in spite of all this, our medical bills are growing at over twice the rate of inflation, and the United States spends over a third more of its income on health care than any other nation on Earth. There is no excuse for this kind of system. My fellow Americans, we must fix this system, and it has to begin with congressional action.

5 The proposal that I describe tonight borrows many of the principles and ideas that have been embraced in plans introduced by both Republicans and Democrats in this Congress. For the first time in this century, leaders of both political parties have joined together around the principle of providing universal, comprehensive health care. It is a magic moment, and we must seize it. Both sides are willing to say, "We have listened to the people. We know the cost of going forward with this system is far greater than the cost of change." And so tonight, let me ask all of you, every Member of the House, every Member of the Senate, each Republican and each Democrat, let us keep this spirit and let us keep this commitment until this job is done. We owe it to the American people. [Applause] Thank you. Thank you very much.

6 Over the coming months, you'll be bombarded with information from all kinds of sources. There will be some who will stoutly disagree with what I have proposed and with all other plans in the Congress, for that matter. And some of the arguments will be genuinely sincere and enlightening. Others may simply be scare tactics by those who are motivated by the self-interest they have in the waste the system now generates, because that waste is providing jobs, incomes, and money for some people. I ask you only to think of this: when you hear all of these arguments, ask yourself whether the cost of staying on this same course isn't greater than the cost of change, and ask yourself whether the arguments are in your interest or someone else's. This is something we have got to try to do together.

7 I want also to say to the Representatives in Congress, you have a special duty to look beyond these arguments. I ask you instead to look into the eyes of the sick child who needs care, to think of the face of the woman who's been told not only that her condition is malignant but not covered by her insurance, to look at the bottom lines of the businesses driven to bankruptcy by health care costs, to look at the "for sale" signs in front of the homes of families who have lost everything because of their health care costs.

8 I ask you to remember the kind of people I met over the last year and a half: the elderly couple in New Hampshire that broke down and cried because of their shame at having an empty refrigerator to pay for their drags; a woman who lost a $50,000 job that she used to support her six children because her youngest child was so ill that she couldn't keep health insurance, and the only way to get care for the child was to get public assistance; a young couple that had a sick child and could only get insurance from one of the parents' employers that was a nonprofit corporation with 20 employees, and so they had to face the question of whether to let this poor person with a sick child go or raise the premiums of every employee in the firm by $200; and on and on and on.

9 I know we have differences of opinion, but we are here tonight in a spirit that is animated by the problems of those people and by the sheer knowledge that if we can look into our heart, we will not be able to say that the greatest nation in the history of the world is powerless to confront this crisis.

10 Our history and our heritage tell us that we can meet this challenge. Everything about America's past tells us we will do it. So I say to you, let us write that new chapter in the American story. Let us guarantee every American comprehensive health benefits that can never be taken away.

11 This is our chance. This is our journey. And when our work is done, we will know that we have answered the call of history and met the challenge of our time.

Write an essay in which you explain how President Bill Clinton builds an argument to persuade his audience that the current insurance system must be fixed. In your essay, analyze how President Bill Clinton uses one or more of the features listed in the box above, (or features of your own choice), to strengthen the logic and persuasiveness of his argument. Be sure that your analysis focuses on the most relevant features of the passage.

Your essay should not explain whether you agree with President Bill Clinton's claims, but rather explain how he builds an argument to persuade his audience.

■ TEST NUMBER

ENTER TEST NUMBER

For instance, for Practice Test # 1, fill in the circle for 0 in the first column and for 1 in the second column.

1 ○ ○
2 ○ ○
3 ○ ○
4 ○ ○
5 ○ ○
6 ○ ○
7 ○ ○
8 ○ ○
9 ○ ○

■ SECTION 1

	A B C D		A B C D		A B C D		A B C D
1	○○○○	14	○○○○	27	○○○○	40	○○○○
2	○○○○	15	○○○○	28	○○○○	41	○○○○
3	○○○○	16	○○○○	29	○○○○	42	○○○○
4	○○○○	17	○○○○	30	○○○○	43	○○○○
5	○○○○	18	○○○○	31	○○○○	44	○○○○
6	○○○○	19	○○○○	32	○○○○	45	○○○○
7	○○○○	20	○○○○	33	○○○○	46	○○○○
8	○○○○	21	○○○○	34	○○○○	47	○○○○
9	○○○○	22	○○○○	35	○○○○	48	○○○○
10	○○○○	23	○○○○	36	○○○○	49	○○○○
11	○○○○	24	○○○○	37	○○○○	50	○○○○
12	○○○○	25	○○○○	38	○○○○	51	○○○○
13	○○○○	26	○○○○	39	○○○○	52	○○○○

■ SECTION 2

	A B C D		A B C D		A B C D		A B C D		A B C D
1	○○○○	10	○○○○	19	○○○○	28	○○○○	37	○○○○
2	○○○○	11	○○○○	20	○○○○	29	○○○○	38	○○○○
3	○○○○	12	○○○○	21	○○○○	30	○○○○	39	○○○○
4	○○○○	13	○○○○	22	○○○○	31	○○○○	40	○○○○
5	○○○○	14	○○○○	23	○○○○	32	○○○○	41	○○○○
6	○○○○	15	○○○○	24	○○○○	33	○○○○	42	○○○○
7	○○○○	16	○○○○	25	○○○○	34	○○○○	43	○○○○
8	○○○○	17	○○○○	26	○○○○	35	○○○○	44	○○○○
9	○○○○	18	○○○○	27	○○○○	36	○○○○		

■ SECTION 3

1 A B C D
2 A B C D
3 A B C D

4 A B C D
5 A B C D
6 A B C D

7 A B C D
8 A B C D
9 A B C D

10 A B C D
11 A B C D
12 A B C D

13 A B C D
14 A B C D
15 A B C D

Only answers that are gridded will be scored. You will not receive credit for anything written in the boxes.

16

17

18

19

20

NO CALCULATOR
ALLOWED

■ SECTION 4

1 Ⓐ Ⓑ Ⓒ Ⓓ   7 Ⓐ Ⓑ Ⓒ Ⓓ   13 Ⓐ Ⓑ Ⓒ Ⓓ   19 Ⓐ Ⓑ Ⓒ Ⓓ   25 Ⓐ Ⓑ Ⓒ Ⓓ

2 Ⓐ Ⓑ Ⓒ Ⓓ   8 Ⓐ Ⓑ Ⓒ Ⓓ   14 Ⓐ Ⓑ Ⓒ Ⓓ   20 Ⓐ Ⓑ Ⓒ Ⓓ   26 Ⓐ Ⓑ Ⓒ Ⓓ

3 Ⓐ Ⓑ Ⓒ Ⓓ   9 Ⓐ Ⓑ Ⓒ Ⓓ   15 Ⓐ Ⓑ Ⓒ Ⓓ   21 Ⓐ Ⓑ Ⓒ Ⓓ   27 Ⓐ Ⓑ Ⓒ Ⓓ

4 Ⓐ Ⓑ Ⓒ Ⓓ   10 Ⓐ Ⓑ Ⓒ Ⓓ   16 Ⓐ Ⓑ Ⓒ Ⓓ   22 Ⓐ Ⓑ Ⓒ Ⓓ   28 Ⓐ Ⓑ Ⓒ Ⓓ

5 Ⓐ Ⓑ Ⓒ Ⓓ   11 Ⓐ Ⓑ Ⓒ Ⓓ   17 Ⓐ Ⓑ Ⓒ Ⓓ   23 Ⓐ Ⓑ Ⓒ Ⓓ   29 Ⓐ Ⓑ Ⓒ Ⓓ

6 Ⓐ Ⓑ Ⓒ Ⓓ   12 Ⓐ Ⓑ Ⓒ Ⓓ   18 Ⓐ Ⓑ Ⓒ Ⓓ   24 Ⓐ Ⓑ Ⓒ Ⓓ   30 Ⓐ Ⓑ Ⓒ Ⓓ

CALCULATOR
ALLOWED

COMPLETE MARK ●   EXAMPLES OF INCOMPLETE MARKS Ⓐ Ⓧ ⊖ ⊘ ◐ ⦸ ⦸ Ⓝ

It is recommended that you use a No. 2 pencil. It is very important that you fill in the entire circle darkly and completely. If you change your response, erase as completely as possible. Incomplete marks or erasures may affect your score.

■ SECTION 4 (Continued)

Only answers that are gridded will be scored. You will not receive credit for anything written in the boxes.

31

32

33

34

35

Only answers that are gridded will be scored. You will not receive credit for anything written in the boxes.

36

37

38

CALCULATOR ALLOWED

SECTION 5

○ I understand that my essay (without my name) may be reproduced in other College Board materials. If I mark this circle, I withhold my permission to reproduce my essay for any purposes beyond score reporting and the assessment of my writing skills. Marking this circle will have no effect on my score, nor will it prevent my essay from being made available to any college to which I send my SAT scores.

IMPORTANT: USE A NO. 2 PENCIL. DO NOT WRITE OUTSIDE THE BORDER!
Words written outside the essay box or written in ink **WILL NOT APPEAR** in the copy sent to be scored, and your score will be affected.

PLANNING PAGE You may plan your essay in the unlined planning space below, but use only the lined pages following this one to write your essay. Any work on this planning page will not be scored.

Use pages 7 through 10 for your ESSAY ⟶

FOR PLANNING ONLY

Use pages 7 through 10 for your ESSAY ⟶

Page 6

BEGIN YOUR ESSAY HERE.

You may continue on the next page.

SERIAL #

You may continue on the next page.

You may continue on the next page.

SERIAL #

STOP.

New SAT Practice Test 3

Reading Test

65 MINUTES, 52 QUESTIONS

Turn to Section 1 of your answer sheet to answer the questions in this section.

DIRECTIONS

Each passage or pair of passages below is followed by a number of questions. After reading each passage or pair, choose the best answer to each question based on what is stated or implied in the passage or passages and in any accompanying graphics (such as a table or graph).

Questions 1 – 11 are based on the following passage.

-Adapted from "Backwards Smiling: The Physiology of Being Happy" by Tommy Galan, Pick the Brain, 20 May 2009

Everyone smiles. From industrialized nations to remote tribes, studies have shown that smiling is universal. Even more stunning is that people
Line from all over the world smile the same way. Even
5 blind children begin to smile without seeing others smile. It's ingrained in the very code that makes us human.

Although smiling comes in many forms, most are actually fake. In fact, there is only one smile
10 that is genuine. When the corners of the mouth go up, the eyes narrow slightly creating crow's feet, and the upper half of the cheeks rise, you are experiencing the Duchenne Smile, named by Paul Ekman, an emeritus professor of psychology
15 at the University of California at San Francisco after Guillaume-Benjamin Duchenne, the French physiologist who first studied the muscle that surrounds the eye in 1862.

The Duchenne smile is the one true smile that
20 is a direct result of feeling happy. But, how do we FEEL happy? When we receive or give a gift, or see our children smile and laugh, physiological changes take place. Our hearts beat faster and the flow of blood increases. Skin temperature rises,
25 which makes the skin slightly damper and our

fingers tremble. The experience of a compliment or gift is a trigger. The trigger sets off changes in the body, which signal the brain to feel happy.

Although this may sound odd at first, try
30 forcing yourself to feeling happy when your muscles are tense, your face is frowned and your brow furrowed. The involuntary emotions cause our body reaction to signal our brain, which means that happiness arises as much from our
35 body as it does from our thoughts.

The emotions associated with feeling happy are involuntarily controlled by our automatic nervous system. This is why we cannot simply decide to be happy by influencing involuntary
40 body function. It is impossible for us to command our blood to flow faster. We do, however, have the ability to bypass the automatic nervous system. We have the ability to smile, even without a trigger.

45 Ekman's work corroborated that if feelings can come from the body, then happiness can come from a genuine Duchenne smile. Ekman trained his subjects to control the movement of the muscles that surround the eye to achieve
50 the Duchenne smile. The result was a signal of happiness without a trigger sent to the brain thereby proving that happiness doesn't flow in just one direction, and smiling alone can make us happy.
55 I suggest that we take the work of Ekman to the next level. If the bodily movement of

CONTINUE ➔

smiling can make our brains experience feelings of happiness, then why not use the smile as a trigger for others. What you put out into the
60 world comes back to you. The next time you are introduced to someone, just give your first name and watch what happens. More likely than not, they will return the introduction with their first name. Offer your first and last name, and you
65 will receive the same. Try it with a smile. I'm sure you will find a smile in return. This effect can influence your happiness and the feelings of everyone you come into contact with throughout your day. By smiling more and passing it along,
70 you truly put the Duchenne smile effect into action. Smile more…it can only make things better.

a

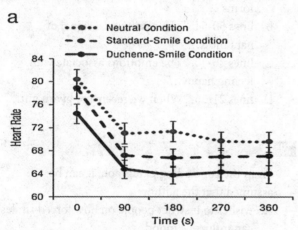

-graphic adapted from www.scicurious. scientopia.org

1

As discussed by the author, the idea of "forced happiness"

A. is firmly grounded in Ekman's work regarding the Duchenne Smile.
B. is impossible to achieve through conscious control over the autonomic nervous system.
C. occurs systematically through involuntary physical reactions in our body.
D. supports the notion that the emotion of happiness can only occur in one direction.

2

Though research and current scientific literature indicate that the action of smiling is a universal response

A. each culture possesses its own unique smiling practices governed by social situations.
B. many cultures have a smile that possesses with it the physiological reaction of a furrowed brow.
C. many smiles can be thought of as manufac-tured responses to situations.
D. the physiological reactions to smiling vary widely according to geographic region.

3

The best evidence supporting the answer to the previous question lies in

A. lines 1-6, "Everyone smiles…"
B. lines 19-23, "The Duchenne smile…"
C. lines 36-40, "The emotions associated with feeling happy…"
D. lines 8-10, "Although smiling comes in many forms…"

4

The term *ingrained* used in line 6 most closely means:

A. entrenched
B. superficial
C. heritable
D. obsolete

5

The primary purpose of the passage is to

A. discuss physiological responses to the emotion of happiness.
B. detail the work of Paul Ekman regarding his discovery of the Duchenne smile.
C. foster a sense of compassionate giving as a means of increasing happiness.
D. provide evidence of how we can influence our own emotions, particularly happiness.

CONTINUE

6

From the article, it can be inferred that
A. most people who are generally sad are choosing to possess that emotion.
B. smiling is best thought of as a physiological reflex of the mind feeling the emotion of happiness.
C. the act of purposeful smiling can increase heart rate and raise body temperature.
D. cultural norms dictate the situations in which a person is able to smile.

7

From the graphic depicted above, which of the following is true?
A. The greatest amount of heart rate change occurs between 90 seconds and 180 seconds.
B. The subjects experienced a higher level of overall heart rate in the standard condition than the neutral condition.
C. The heart rate experienced in the Duchenne condition is somewhat contradictory to the physiological evidence provided in the article.
D. There is no clear difference between any of the conditions cited.

8

The term *corroborated* used in line 45 is most synonymous with:
A. contradicted
B. remained ambivalent
C. rendered unscientific
D. authenticated

9

While physiology is most likely the strongest cause of a smile,
A. the process can be mutually reciprocal.
B. the relationship is almost certainly one directional.
C. the physiological underpinnings of smiling can be reversed.
D. willful smiling can slow heart rates considerably.

10

The best evidence for the previous answer is found in
A. lines 8-18, "Although smiling comes in many forms…"
B. lines 50-54, "The result was a signal of happiness…"
C. lines 36-40, "The emotions associate with feeling happy…"
D. lines 21-26, "When we receive or give a gift…"

11

From the concluding paragraph, it can be assumed that the author
A. wishes to instruct people on how forced smiles can influence mood.
B. considers willful governance over emotions a waste of time and energy.
C. seeks to foster more positive human contact and interaction.
D. believes that there is no such thing as a "genuine smile."

CONTINUE

Questions 12-22 deal with the passage below

-adapted from The Grapes of Wrath by John Steinbeck

Then, with time, the squatters were no
longer squatters, but owners; and their children
grew up and had children on the land. And the
Line hunger was gone from them, the feral hunger,
5 the gnawing, tearing hunger for land, for water
and earth and the good sky over it, for the green
thrusting grass, for the swelling roots. They had
these things so completely that they did not
know about them anymore. They had no more
10 the stomach-tearing lust for a rich acre and a
shining blade to plow it, for seed and a windmill
beating its wings in the air. They arose in the dark
no more to hear the sleepy birds' first chittering,
and the morning wind around the house while
15 they waited for the first light to go out to the
dear acres. These things were lost, and crops
were reckoned in dollars, and land was valued
by principal plus interest, and crops were bought
and sold before they were planted. Then crop
20 failure, drought, and flood were no longer little
deaths within life, but simple losses of money.
And all their love was thinned with money, and
all their fierceness dribbled away in interest
until they were no longer farmers at all, but
25 little shopkeepers of crops, little manufacturers
who must sell before they can make. Then those
farmers who were not good shopkeepers lost
their land to good shopkeepers. No matter how
clever, how loving a man might be with earth and
30 growing things, he could not survive if he were
not also a good shopkeeper. And as time went on,
the business men had the farms, and the farms
grew larger, but there were fewer of them.
Now farming became industry, and the
35 owners followed Rome, although they did not
know it. They imported slaves, although they did
not call them slaves: Chinese, Japanese, Mexicans,
Filipinos. They ice on rice and beans, the business
men said. They don't need much. They couldn't
40 know what to do with good wages. Why, look
how they live. Why, look what they eat. And if
they get funny—deport them.

And all the time the farms grew larger and
the owners fewer. And there were pitifully few
45 farmers on the land any more. And the imported
serfs were beaten and frightened and starved
until some went home again, and some grew
fierce and were killed or driven from the country.
And farms grew larger and the owners fewer.
50 And the crops changed. Fruit trees took the place
of grain fields, and vegetables to feed the world
spread out on the bottoms: lettuce, cauliflower,
artichokes, potatoes—stoop crops. A man may
stand to use a scythe, a plow, a pitchfork; but he
55 must crawl like a bug between the rows of lettuce,
he must bend his back and pull his long bag
between the cotton rows, he must go on his knees
like a penitent across a cauliflower patch.
And it came about that owners no longer
60 worked on their farms. They farmed on paper;
and they forgot the land, the smell, the feel of
it, and remembered only that they owned it,
remembered only what they gained and lost by
it. And some of the farms grew so large that one
65 man could not even conceive of them any more,
so large that it took batteries of bookkeepers to
keep track of interest and gain and loss; chemists
to test the soil, to replenish; straw bosses to see
that the stooping men were moving along the
70 rows as swiftly as the material of their bodies
could stand. Then such a farmer really became a
storekeeper, and kept a store. He paid the men,
and sold them food, and took the money back.
And after a while he did not pay the men at all,
75 and saved bookkeeping. These farms gave food
on credit. A man might work and feed himself;
and when the work was done, he might find that
he owed money to the company. And the owners
not only did not work the farms any more, many
80 of them had never seen the farms they owned.

12

The overall tone of the narrator during this passage suggests that the narrator

A. is communicating from a business perspective and is appreciative of the new advances farming has made during the Dust Bowl.

B. has a distaste for the manner in which farming is changing and farmers are becoming less and less involved with their own land.

C. appears to feverishly anti-immigrant and believes that the influx of individuals from varying cultures are directly responsible for the changes in farming.

D. espouses the benefits of changing banking laws and their impacts on developing young, small businesses.

13

The author's use of the word "penitent" to describe harvesting vegetables is used primarily to symbolize

A. the fact that farmers were deeply religious people who were appreciative of the crops they were able to harvest.

B. the practice of keeping Sabbath on Sundays and only farming 6 days a week.

C. the subservient relationship the farmers had with their land wherein farmers were at the mercy of their crops and farms.

D. farming practices of using a scythe and plow to farrow lines of crops.

14

Based upon the passage, the author's feelings towards the business of farming can best be described as:

A. resentful and contemptuous

B. happily nostalgic

C. respectful and proud

D. confused and questioning

15

Evidence for the previous question can best be found in

A. lines 34-38, "Now farming became an industry…"

B. lines 22-26, "And all their love was thinned with money…"

C. lines 59-64, "And it came about that owners…"

D. lines 49-53, "And farms grew larger and owners fewer…"

16

The term *feral* used in line 4 most closely means:

A. intense

B. waning

C. tame

D. wild, savage

17

The purpose of the lines, "They farmed on paper; and they forgot the land, the smell, the feel of it, and remembered only that they owned it, remembered only what they gained and lost by it" serves to indicate

A. the progressive detachment farmers had for their land.

B. the belief that farmers were better suited as managers rather than directly working their land.

C. the movement that many farmers became partial owners of their land and sold to larger corporations.

D. the effects of the Dust Bowl and Great Depression on farming profits.

CONTINUE ➡

18

The best support for the answer to the previous question can be found in

A. lines 45-49, "And the imported serfs…"
B. lines 71-75, "Then such a farmer really became a storekeeper…"
C. lines 78-80, "And the owners not only…"
D. lines 28-33, "No matter how clever…"

19

The author's characterization of the workers of many farms as "imported slaves" and "imported serfs" can best be characterized as

A. contemptuous towards immigrant workers taking jobs from current citizens.
B. reflective of commiserating with the farmers when the workers harbored a poor work ethic.
C. morally superior to farmers, believing that style of life was degrading.
D. sarcastically contemptuous, appearing to side with the owners while in effect decrying their practices.

20

The phrase, "and the owners followed Rome, although they did not know it…" is used to convey

A. the ways in which owners justified their treatment of their workers and their changing business practices.
B. the economic system that was mirrored from Ancient Roman times.
C. the rebirth of a new age of farming in America.
D. a conversion from traditional grain farming to farming more fruit trees.

21

A *scythe* in line 54 can best be described as:

A. a shovel
B. a long handled reaping tool
C. an axe
D. a device for shucking corn

22

The author uses the term, "the hunger was gone from them, the feral hunger…" primarily to illustrate

A. the abundance of crops and food available when farming profits boomed.
B. the emotional ramifications of the Great Depression on farming.
C. the growing manner in which farmers became less interested in the process of farming and more interested in the business of farming.
D. the manner in which farmers were becoming more cultured.

CONTINUE ➤

Questions 23-32 deal with the passage below:

-adapted from "100 Years Ago: Marie Curie wins 2nd Nobel Prize" in Scientific American, 28 October 2011 (originally printed in same, 25 November 1911, Vol. 105)

Feminism very nearly won a great victory in the French Academy of Sciences on January 23rd, 1911, when, in the election of a successor to the deceased academician Gernez, Marie Sklodowska
5 Curie was defeated by two votes. At a joint meeting of the five academies which compose the Institut de France, a majority had opposed the admission of women, as contrary to tradition, but each academy was left to decide the question for
10 itself.

The Academy of Fine Arts had a few women members long ago but the Academy of Sciences has never admitted a woman. It was, perhaps, the opposition of the anti-feminists that induced
15 Mme. Curie to apply as a candidate for the chair in the section of physics left vacant by Gernez, and formerly occupied by her husband and collaborator, Pierre Curie. In the preliminary grading of candidates Mme. Curie was placed
20 alone, in the first grade, while her competitors, five eminent men of science, were assigned to the second grade. Mme. Curie, however, received only 28 of the 65 votes (the Academy consists of 66 members), while 30 votes were cast for
25 Edouard Branly. There were good reasons for this choice, entirely apart from considerations of sex. Branly is a physicist of world-wide celebrity who, unlike Mme. Curie, has received few honors and emoluments. He invented the coherer for the
30 detection of electric waves and to him Marconi's first wireless message was addressed. Many of the academicians naturally desired to recognize the very important part played by their compatriot in the development of wireless telegraphy. Moreover,
35 Branly is sixty-four years old and this was his third candidacy, while Mme. Curie is only forty-three and had never before applied for admission. It is not customary to admit a candidate on the first application, and Mme. Curie's chance of
40 living until the next vacancy shall occur is greater than Branly's.

Who is this remarkable woman who so nearly surmounted these formidable obstacles? The dry and formal account of herself and her
45 work which she submitted with her application, according to custom, is perhaps more eloquent than an exhaustive biography. Marie Sklodowska was born in Warsaw November 7th, 1867. She became a student in the University of Paris where
50 she attained the degrees of licentiate in physics in 1893 and licentiate in mathematics in 1894. In 1896 she received a certificate of fitness for the secondary instruction of girls, and in 1900 became lecturer in physics in the Ecole normale
55 superieure for girls in Sevres. In 1903 she received the degree of doctor of physical science, in 1906 she became lecturer in general physics in the University of Paris, and in 1909 she was promoted to the professorship of general physics,
60 as successor to her lately deceased husband, Prof. Pierre Curie, to whom she was married in 1895.

In 1898 Mme. Curie, then thirty-one years of age, received the Gegner prize from the French Academy of Sciences, nominally for her
65 extensive researches relating to the magnetic properties of iron and steel, although the report of the awarding committee also alludes, in terms of the highest commendation, to the researches in radio-activity which she had already begun,
70 in co-operation with her husband, and to their recent discovery of the radio-active element which Mme. Curie named Polonium, in honor of her native country.

In 1903 the Nobel prize for physical science
75 was awarded, half to Mons. and Mme. Curie and half to Henri Becquerel, whose discovery of the spontaneous radio-activity of uranium ore formed the basis of all subsequent researches in radio-activity. Only a few days ago we heard the
80 news that Mme. Curie has been honored with the Nobel prize a second time, on this occasion in the division of chemistry.

Radium and polonium are not the only fruits of this ideal marriage, which was blessed by the
85 birth of two children who already give evidence of inheriting the genius of their parents. After

CONTINUE →

the shocking and untimely death of Pierre Curie, who was killed by a truck on a Paris bridge, in 1906, at the age of fifty-seven, a large majority of
90 his colleagues recommended to the ministry of public instruction the appointment of his widow and coadjutor as his successor. The result is that this gifted woman, the only one of her sex who has ever received this high honor, is now a full
95 professor in the venerable Sorbonne.

23

It can be assumed from the author's description of Mdme. Curie's first defeat to become a member of the French Academy of Sciences that

A. the author generally agrees with the decision to choose Branly over Curie.
B. due to misogynistic views, Mdme. Curie was stigmatized and, thus, lost the election due to her gender.
C. the author feels that Mdme. Curie should not have applied in the first place.
D. Mdme. Curie would have been better served applying for a position within the Academy of Fine Arts.

24

The author would most likely agree with which of the following statements?

A. Mdme. Curie simply utilized much of the research pioneered by her husband to pave the way for future scientific inquiry.
B. The French Academy of Sciences should have admitted Mdme. Curie upon her first application due to her scientific contributions.
C. Curie's attempt at gaining access to a male-dominated institution served to set feminism back, rather than moving it forward.
D. Curie's dedication and convictions eventually won over those who may have originally opposed her appointment.

25

Evidence for the previous question can best be found in

A. lines 38-41, "It was not customary…"
B. lines 11-18, "The Academy of Fine Arts had a few women…"
C. lines 89-95, "A large majority…"
D. lines 42-47, "Who is this remarkable woman…"

26

The term *emoluments* used in line 29 most closely means:

A. grants
B. earnings
C. notoriety
D. scandals

27

From the characterization of Curie given in the article, she would most likely

A. be an ardent supporter of civil rights and, in particular, the rights of women.
B. be generally extravagant and attention seeking.
C. be described by her peers as unoriginal and pedestrian.
D. avoid standing on principles in difficult situations.

28

The best evidence for the previous answer can be found in

A. lines 42-47, "Who is this amazing woman…"
B. lines 62-73, "In 1898, Mme. Curie…"
C. lines 74-79, "In 1903 the Nobel Prize…"
D. lines 13-18, "It was, perhaps, the opposition…"

CONTINUE →

29

The term *alludes*, used in line 67, most closely means:

A. to escape from
B. contradicts
C. suggests
D. describes

30

Given information contained in the article, it is clear that

A. previous research on radioactivity was nearly complete before the Curies were able to complete many of the theories.
B. scientific research on wireless telegraphy was a critical issue near the time of Curie's first attempt to enter Sorbonne.
C. studies into the radioactive properties of uranium ore were well established and documented prior to the 20th century.
D. despite considerable odds, Mme. Curie's appointment fell short by only one vote.

31

Given the background information provided for both Mme. Curie and Mons. Branly, the results of the first ballot election indicate that

A. the French Academy was somewhat justified in its choice of Mons. Branly over Mme. Curie.
B. the French Academy clearly overlooked a great many of Mme. Curie's accomplishments in an effort to elect a male over a female.
C. many voting members felt remorse for their earlier decisions and, because of this, attempted to atone for their initial mistakes by voting Mme. Curie in on her second ballot.
D. the discovery of Polonium relegated Mme. Curie to celebrity status in the scientific world.

32

In receiving the Gegner Prize, Mme. Curie was essentially being recognized for her

A. contributions to the scientific world regarding uranium ore.
B. research regarding the magnetic properties of iron and steel.
C. discovery of the element Polonium.
D. overall contributions to research in the area of radioactivity.

CONTINUE →

Questions 33-42 deal with the passage below:

-Excerpted from the Declaration of Independence, 1776

When in the course of human events, it becomes necessary for one people to dissolve the political bands which have connected them with
Line another, and to assume among the powers of the
5 earth, the separate and equal station to which the laws of nature and of nature's God entitle them, a decent respect to the opinions of mankind requires that they should declare the causes which impel them to the separation.

10 We hold these truths to be self-evident, that all men are created equal, that they are endowed by their Creator with certain unalienable rights, that among these are life, liberty and the pursuit of happiness; that to secure these
15 rights, governments are instituted among Men, deriving their just powers from the consent of the governed; that whenever any form of government becomes destructive of these ends, it is the right of the people to alter or to abolish
20 it, and to institute new government, laying its foundation on such principles and organizing its powers in such form, as to them shall seem most likely to effect their safety and happiness. Prudence, indeed, will dictate that governments
25 long established should not be changed for light and transient causes; and accordingly all experience hath shewn, that mankind are more disposed to suffer, while evils are sufferable, than to right themselves by abolishing the forms to
30 which they are accustomed. But when a long train of abuses and usurpations, pursuing invariably the same object evinces a design to reduce them under absolute despotism, it is their right, it is their duty, to throw off such Government, and
35 to provide new guards for their future security. Such has been the patient sufferance of these colonies; and such is now the necessity which constrains them to alter their former Systems of Government. The history of the present King
40 of Great Britain is a history of repeated injuries and usurpations, all having in direct object the establishment of an absolute tyranny over these

states. To prove this, let facts be submitted to a candid world.

45 In every stage of these oppressions we have petitioned for redress in the most humble terms: Our repeated petitions have been answered only by repeated injury. A prince whose character is thus marked by every act which may define a
50 tyrant, is unfit to be the ruler of a free people.

Nor have we been wanting in attentions to our Brittish brethren. We have warned them from time to time of attempts by their legislature to extend an unwarrantable jurisdiction over us.
55 We have reminded them of the circumstances of our emigration and settlement here. We have appealed to their native justice and magnanimity, and we have conjured them by the ties of our common kindred to disavow these usurpations,
60 which, would inevitably interrupt our connections and correspondence. They too have been deaf to the voice of justice and of consanguinity. We must, therefore, acquiesce in the necessity, which denounces our separation, and hold them,
65 as we hold the rest of mankind, enemies in war, in peace friends.

We, therefore, the representatives of the United States of America, in General Congress assembled, appealing to the Supreme Judge of
70 the world for the rectitude of our intentions, do, in the name and by the authority of the good people of these colonies solemnly publish and declare, That these United Colonies are, and of right ought to be, FREE AND INDEPENDENT
75 STATES; that they are absolved from all allegiance to the British crown and that all political connection between them and the state of Great Britain is, and ought to be, totally dissolved; and that, as free and independent states, they have full power
80 to levy war, conclude peace, contract alliances, establish commerce, and do all other acts and things which independent states may of right do. And for the support of this declaration, with a firm reliance on the protection of Divine
85 Providence, we mutually pledge to each other our lives, our fortunes, and our sacred honor.

CONTINUE ➡

33

The founding fathers felt justified in dissolving their allegiance to England for primarily which of the following reasons?

A. The refusal of the English monarchy to support the slave trade in a developing agrarian economy of the New World.

B. Colonial desires to grant equal rights to all inhabitants of the land.

C. England's decision to refuse to grant rights and titles to feudal lords from England who had travelled to the New World.

D. Repeated attempts by the colonies to reconcile differences with the English monarchy had been continually rebuffed.

34

Based upon the factor listed above, it can be assumed from the passage that the colonists feel

A. cultural values present in the colonies were increasingly disparate from those of England.

B. they have acted in good faith in their allegiance to the crown to this point.

C. discriminatory practices on the part of the English monarchy could no longer be tolerated or supported.

D. the feudal economy system would be best implemented in the New World due to the agrarian lifestyle adopted by the colonists.

35

It can be inferred from the tone and conjecture on the part of the colonists that

A. by granting limited colonial representation in the English Parliament, many of the landowning colonists would be satiated and order would be restored.

B. absolute and unquestioned recognition of the colonies as independent entities, along with monetary reparations for damages in transit, was the only acceptable outcome.

C. the colonists sought recognition as an independent entity, but continued to hope for mutual peace and respect with Britain.

D. establishment of a feudal monarchy in the new lands, with oversight from the English government, would help establish a sustainable economy in the New World.

36

Evidence for the answer to the previous question is best found in

A. lines 45-46, "In every stage of these oppressions…"

B. lines 56-61, "We have appealed to their native justice…"

C. lines 67-74, "We, therefore, the Representatives…"

D. lines 63-66, "We must, therefore, acquiesce…"

CONTINUE ➡

37

The word *impel* used in line 9 most closely means:
A. oblige, prompt
B. stigmatize
C. lessen
D. trivialize

38

The passage suggests that England, according to the colonists,
A. should have been willing to hear the concerns of the colonists but has found it difficult to modify their behavior towards the inhabitants of the New World.
B. had engaged in reckless quasi-imperialism, without adequate input or representation from the colonies.
C. sought to bring the outspoken leaders of the colonies back to England for legal proceedings.
D. felt it cannot be held accountable for any actions or events which had taken place away from their shores.

39

The colonists see their treatment by the English government as
A. generally warranted and deserved as they continue to be subjects of the English throne.
B. a cunning attempt by the monarchy to triangulate those who sought independence from those who were loyal to the King.
C. defensive in nature due to the English fears that the colonists will revolt.
D. an affront to unalienable rights guaranteed to them by their Creator and unable to be infringed upon by any governmental entity.

40

The term *transient* used in line 26 is synonymous with:
A. valid, worthy
B. sustained, omnipresent
C. ephemeral, fleeting
D. moving, migratory

41

The writers of the Declaration of Independence see drafting this document as
A. an obligation to themselves and their posterity.
B. an arduous and generally unworthy task.
C. useful in gaining representation in English parliament.
D. contradictory to the tenets and ideals harbored by the colonists.

42

Evidence for the answer to the previous question is best found in
A. lines 83-86, "And for the support of this Declaration…"
B. lines 30-35, "But when a long train of abuses…"
C. lines 45-48, "In every stage of these oppressions…"
D. lines 51-54, "Nor have we been wanting in attentions…"

CONTINUE ➤

Questions 43-52 deal with the passages and graphic below:

-adapted from "Large Study Finds MMR Vaccine Doesn't Cause Autism, May Lower Autism Risk" by Steven Salzberg in Forbes, 7 May 2015

We're still spending vast amounts of time and money trying to counter the ill effects of a discredited, retracted paper from 1998 that
Line claimed to find a link between the MMR (measles,
5 mumps and rubella) vaccine and autism. Even after the The Lancet retracted the study, and even after the British Medical Council revoked the medical license of its lead author, Andrew Wakefield, many people continue to withhold
10 vaccines from their children because of a fear that somehow, despite all the evidence to the contrary, vaccines might cause autism. Vaccines, I hasten to add, have saved millions of lives and are probably the greatest medical advance of the past
15 two centuries.

Now another study has appeared to add more weight to the evidence about the safety of the MMR vaccine. The New Study by Anjali Jain and colleagues, just published in the *Journal of the*
20 *American Medical Association*, looked at a huge number of children–95,727–for evidence of any link between autism and the MMR vaccine.

The results were not surprising, to those who have been following the science. Receipt of the
25 MMR vaccine was not associated with increased risk of ASD [autism spectrum disorder], regardless of whether older siblings had ASD. These findings indicate no harmful association between MMR vaccine receipt and ASD even
30 among children already at higher risk for ASD.

Here are the numbers from the new study. The authors compared vaccinated children to unvaccinated children, using a huge database of medical claims that included at least 5 years
35 of followup. (This was an "observational" study, by necessity–it would be unethical to withhold vaccines from children on purpose.) The relative risk for autism in children who had 2 doses of the MMR vaccine (the recommended amount)
40 compared to unvaccinated children was 0.74.

In other words, a child was somewhat *less* likely to be diagnosed with autism if he or she were vaccinated.

Even more surprising was the relative risk
45 among children who had an older sibling with autism: in this smaller group, children with 2 doses of MMR were just 44% as likely to be diagnosed with autism as unvaccinated children. This statistically significant finding
50 indicates, unexpectedly, that vaccines might actually *protect* children from autism.

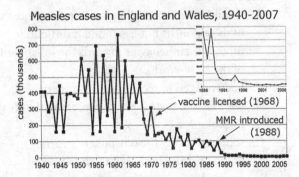

Measles cases in England and Wales, 1940-2007

-adapted from "CDC Whistleblower: CDC Covered Up MMR Vaccine Link to Autism in African American Boys", by Focus Autism in Health Impact News 11 May 2015

A top research scientist working for the Centers for Disease Control and Prevention (CDC) played a key role in helping Dr. Brian
55 Hooker of the Focus Autism Foundation uncover data manipulation by the CDC that obscured a higher incidence of autism in African-American boys. The whistleblower came to the attention of Hooker, a PhD in biochemical engineering,
60 after he had made a Freedom of Information Act (FOIA) request for original data on the DeStefano et al MMR (measles, mumps, rubella) and autism study.

Dr. Hooker's study, published August 8 in the
65 peer-reviewed scientific journal *Translational Neurodegeneration*, shows that African-American boys receiving their first MMR vaccine before 36 months of age are 3.4 times more likely to develop autism vs. after 36 months.
70 According to Dr. Hooker, the CDC whistle-blower informant — who wishes to remain anonymous — guided him to evidence that a

statistically significant relationship between the age the MMR vaccine was first given and autism
75 incidence in African-American boys was hidden by CDC researchers.

Dr. Hooker has worked closely with the CDC whistleblower, and he viewed highly sensitive documents related to the study via
80 Congressional request from U.S. Representative Darrell Issa, Chairman of the House Oversight and Government Reform Committee. The CDC documents from Congress and discussions that Hooker had with the whistleblower reveal
85 widespread manipulation of scientific data and top-down pressure on CDC scientists to support fraudulent application of government policies on vaccine safety. Based on raw data used in the 2004 DeStefano et al study obtained under FOIA,
90 Dr. Hooker found that the link between MMR vaccination and autism in African-American boys was obscured by the introduction of irrelevant and unnecessary birth certificate criteria — ostensibly to reduce the size of the study.

95 The results of the original study first appeared in the journal *Pediatrics* which receives financial support from vaccine makers via advertising and direct donations, according to a CBS News report. The DeStefano et al study is widely used
100 by the CDC and other public health organizations to dismiss any link between vaccines and autism — a neurological disorder on the rise. Dr. Hooker stated "The CDC knew about the relationship between the age of first MMR vaccine and autism
105 incidence in African-American boys as early as 2003, but chose to cover it up." The whistleblower alleges criminal wrongdoing of his supervisors, and he expressed deep regret about his role in helping the CDC hide data.

43

In comparison to passage 1, the data and information in passage 2 is

A. unclear as to the sibling effects of vaccines and Autistic Spectrum Disorders.

B. reliant heavily on a large sample of data, while the data in passage 1 is based upon a relatively small sample size.

C. statistically significant in that it found only a little correlation between vaccinated children and unvaccinated children and ASD diagnoses.

D. representative of a broad spectrum of cultures and age groups, rather than specifically focused in one particular area.

44

The authors of both of the articles would most likely agree with which of the following statements?

A. Vaccines prior to 36 months of age should be strongly discouraged, if not specifically forbidden, due to the inherent dangers at that particular age.

B. Though there is a slight risk evident for certain cultural populations, on the whole there is no link between vaccinations and ASD.

C. Siblings of individuals with ASD are at approximately a 6.8 times higher risk for developing ASD than their peers.

D. Vaccinating children after 36 months of age carries a much lower risk for developing ASD and, as such, is probably safe and beneficial.

45

A critical difference between the studies mentioned in passages 1 and 2 is:

A. Neither study makes mention of the type of data/research conducted or obtained and, as such, is subject to confounds.

B. Study 1 was conducted strictly in a laboratory setting with specific, empirically derived results.

C. Study 2 offers no specific mention of how data was obtained or why their study was designed in the manner it was.

D. Study 1 is critical and suspicious of how results were reported in previous studies, while study 2 supports previous research findings.

46

The term *contrary* used in line 12 is most synonymous with:

A. supportive, empirical
B. contradictory, antithetical
C. medically valid
D. common belief

47

The author of passage 1 would most likely disagree with which of the following research study methods?

A. A double-blind trial with placebo conditions measuring human reactions to anxious stimuli and the effects of Xanax on their reactions, with consent

B. A study of the effects of insulin on diabetic patients measuring those who chose to take medication vs. those who were opposed against medical advice

C. A study of heart rates of patients of varying body types and self-reported exercise levels

D. Testing placebo effects of depression medication on overall moods of patients who were unaware of a medication switch

48

The best evidence for the answer to the previous question can be found in lines

A. lines 35-37, "this was an observational study…"

B. lines 5-12, "Even after the Lancet…"

C. the graphic depicted at the conclusion of the passage

D. lines 16-22, "Now another study…"

49

The term *ostensibly* used in line 94 most closely means:

A. logically
B. seemingly
C. arrogantly
D. convincingly

50

The author of passage 2 believes that

A. scientific research should likely rely heavily on private donations in an effort to secure the best experimental conditions and most empirically valid results.

B. the Freedom of Information Act has effectively pioneered scientific research in many areas and is responsible for many recent scientific gains.

C. appropriations and donations tend to drive scientific research and can have effects on how outcomes are reported.

D. classically derived scientific results are now obsolete in the face of changing technology and availability of prior research.

CONTINUE →

51

The best evidence for the answer to the previous question can be found in

A. lines 95-99, "The results of the original study..."

B. lines 58-63, "The whistleblower came to the attention..."

C. lines 82-88, "The CDC documents from Congress..."

D. lines 52-58, "A top research scientist..."

52

From the graphic depicted, which of the following statements is most accurate?

A. The largest decline (%) of reported measles cases occurred after the MMR vaccine was introduced in 1988.

B. The largest spike in reported measles cases occurred in 1955.

C. There was relatively little decline in reported measles cases between when the MMR vaccine was developed and when it was introduced.

D. Though vaccines have consistently and effectively reduced measles cases, the biggest drops from year to year may be attributable to other factors.

STOP

If you finish before time is called, you may check your work on this section only. Do not turn to any other section.

ACKNOWLEDGEMENT FOR THIS SECTION

Passages in this section were adapted from the following sources:

Tommy Galan, "Backwards Smiling: The Physiology of Being Happy" © 2009 by *Pick the Brain*, published 20 May 2009

Steven Salzberg, "Large Study Finds MMR Vaccine Doesn't Cause Autism, May Lower Autism Risk" © 2015 by *Forbs*, published 7 May 015.

John Steinbeck, "The Grapes of Wrath", © 1939 by James Lloyd.

Writing and Language Test

35 MINUTES, 44 QUESTIONS

Turn to Section 2 of your answer sheet to answer the questions in this section.

DIRECTIONS

Each passage below is accompanied by a number of questions. For some questions, you will consider how the passage might be revised to improve the expression of ideas. For other questions, you will consider how the passage might be edited to correct errors in sentence structure, usage, or punctuation. A passage or a question may be accompanied by one or more graphics (such as a table or graph) that you will consider as you make revising and editing decisions.

Some questions will direct you to an underlined portion of a passage. Other questions will direct you to a location in a passage or ask you to think about the passage as a whole.

After reading each passage, choose the answer to each question that most effectively improves the quality of writing in the passage or that makes the passage conform to the conventions of standard written English. Many questions include a "NO CHANGE" option. Choose that option if you think the best choice is to leave the relevant portion of the passage as it is.

Questions 1 – 11 are based on the following passage.

A Charmed Time

[1] It was, however, until the morning that we entered the harbor of Havre that I was able to shake off my gloom. Then the strange sights, the chatter in an unfamiliar tongue and the excitement of landing and passing the customs officials caused me to forget completely the events of a few days before. Indeed, I grew **[2]** so lighthearted when I caught my first

[1]

A. NO CHANGE
B. It was not, however, until
C. It was not however, until
D. It was not however until

[2]

A. NO CHANGE
B. so very lighthearted
C. very lighthearted that
D. so lighthearted that

sight of **3** the train which was to take us to Paris, I enjoyed a hearty laugh. **4** The_____, all struck me as being extremely funny. But before we reached Paris my respect for our train rose considerably. I found that the "tiny" engine made remarkably fast time, and that the old-fashioned wheels ran very smoothly. I even began to **5** stop complaining about the "stuffy" cars for their privacy. As I watched the passing scenery from the car window, it seemed too beautiful to be real. The brightcolored houses against the green background impressed me as the work of some idealistic painter. Before we arrived in Paris there was, awakened in my heart, a love for France which continued to grow stronger, **6** a love which today makes that country for me the one above all others to be desired.

We rolled into the station Saint Lazare about four o'clock in the afternoon, and drove immediately to the Hotel Continental. My benefactor, **7** humored my curiosity and enthusiasm, which seemed to please him very much, suggested that we **8** took a short walk before dinner. We stepped out of the hotel and turned to the right into the Rue de Rivoli. When the vista of the Place de la Concorde and the Champs Elysées

3

A. NO CHANGE
B. the train it was to take us
C. the train was to take us
D. the train would take us

4

Which choice should not be included in the details here?
A. stuffy compartment cars
B. toy-like engine
C. comfortably-cushioned seats
D. old-fashioned wheels

5

Which choice is most consistent with the tone of the passage?
A. NO CHANGE
B. appreciate
C. tolerate
D. ignore

6

A. NO CHANGE
B. a love today makes
C. a love today it makes
D. a love today can make

7

A. NO CHANGE
B. humor
C. humoring
D. humors

8

A. NO CHANGE
B. taking
C. can take
D. take

CONTINUE

suddenly **9** appeared before me I could hardly credit my own eyes. I shall attempt no such supererogatory task as a description of Paris. I wish only to give briefly the impressions which that wonderful city made upon me. It impressed me as the perfect and perfectly beautiful city, and even after I had been there for some time, and seen **10** its avenues and palaces, its most squalid alleys and hovels, this impression was not weakened. Paris became for me a **11** charmed spot, and whenever I have returned there I have fallen under the spell, a spell which compels admiration for all of its manners and customs and justification of even its follies and sins.

Based on The Autobiography of an Ex-Colored Man by James Weldon Johnson, 1912.

9

Which choice is most consistent with the tone of the context?
A. NO CHANGE
B. came upon
C. burst on
D. stood in front of

10

Which choice most effectively joins the two underlined parts together?
A. NO CHANGE
B. not only its avenues and palaces, but also its most squalid alleys and hovels,
C. its avenues and palaces, and its most squalid alleys and hovels,
D. its avenues and palaces, also its most squalid alleys and hovels,

11

Which choice is the most consistent with the context?
A. NO CHANGE
B. charming
C. strange
D. adventurous

Questions 12 – 22 are based on the following passage.

The Opening of the Pandora's Box

① First, an Allied demand for an immediate unconditional surrender was made to the leadership in Japan. ② Although the demand stated that refusal would result in total destruction, no mention of any new weapons of mass destruction was made. ③ The Japanese military command rejected the request for unconditional surrender, but there were indications that a conditional surrender was possible. **12**

13 Well, on August 6, 1945, a plane called the Enola Gay dropped an atomic bomb on the city of Hiroshima. Instantly, 70,000 Japanese citizens were vaporized. In the months and years **14** to follow, an additional 100,000 perished from burns and radiation sickness. Two days later, the Soviet Union declared war on Japan. On August 9, a second atomic bomb was dropped on Nagasaki, **15** when 80,000 Japanese people perished. On August 14, 1945, the Japanese surrendered. Critics have charged that Truman's decision was a barbaric act that brought negative long-term consequences to the United States. A new age of nuclear terror led to a dangerous arms race. **16**

Some military analysts insist that Japan was on its

12

"For Truman, the choice whether or not to use the atomic bomb was the most difficult decision of his life." Where should this sentence be placed, for the sake of cohesion?
A. Before Sentence 1
B. Before Sentence 2
C. Before Sentence 3
D. After Sentence 3

13

A. NO CHANGE
B. Therefore,
C. Then,
D. Regardless,

14

A. NO CHANGE
B. following
C. that followed
D. later

15

A. NO CHANGE
B. where
C. that
D. and

16

The writer is considering deleting the previous sentence. Should the writer keep the sentence as it is or make this change?
A. Make the change, because the ending sentence is not consistent with the subject that is introduced previously.
B. Make the change, because the information presented is just repeating the preceding information.
C. Keep the sentence as is, because it provides a specific consequence in support of argument made previously in the passage.
D. Keep the sentence as is, because it provides a logical ending to the paragraph.

CONTINUE ➡

knees and the bombings **17** might not be necessary. The American government was accused of racism on the grounds that such a device **18** would never have been used against white civilians. Other critics argued that American diplomats had *ulterior motives. The Soviet Union had entered the war against Japan, and the atomic bomb could be read as a strong message for the Soviets to tread lightly. In this respect, Hiroshima and Nagasaki may have been the first shots of the Cold War **19** rather than the final shots of World War II.

Truman stated that his decision **20** for dropping the bomb was purely military. A Normandy-type amphibious landing **21** would cost an estimated million casualties. Prolonging the war was not an option for the President. Over 3,500 Japanese **kamikaze raids had already wrought great destruction and loss of American lives. Even the scientific community failed to foresee the awful effects of radiation sickness. Truman saw little difference between atomic bombing Hiroshima and firebombing Dresden or Tokyo.

The ethical debate over the decision to drop the atomic bomb will never be resolved. The bombs did, **22** well, bring an end to the most destructive war in history. Pandora's box was now open. The question that came flying out was, "How will the world use its nuclear capability?" It is a question still being addressed on a daily basis.

* ulterior—hidden

** kamikaze raids—air attacks in which planes loaded with explosives crash into targets

17
Which choice is most consistent with the tone of the paragraph?
A. NO CHANGE
B. were not really necessary
C. were simply unnecessary
D. could be avoided

18
A. NO CHANGE
B. would never been used
C. had never be used
D. were never used

19
A. NO CHANGE
B. as well as
C. but not
D. or

20
A. NO CHANGE
B. at dropping
C. about dropping the bomb
D. to drop the bomb

21
A. NO CHANGE
B. might cost
C. would have cost
D. will cost

22
A. NO CHANGE
B. however
C. then
D. therefore

CONTINUE

Questions 23 – 33 are based on the following passage.

There were a variety of Native American tribes living on the Great Plains, 23 and they were competing for scarce resources. Inevitably, the various tribes came into conflict with each other.

The Lakota (or Sioux) is actually a broad group of people 24 that includes the seven bands of the Western (or Teton) Lakota, the Dakota (Yankton and Yanktoni) and the Nakota (Santee). This group of tribes lived in the Plains for only a part of their known history. In their original northern woodland homeland, the Lakota were hard-pressed by the Anishinaabe (called Chippawa by the Lakota). The Anishinaabe were armed with guns 25 traded with trappers.

The Lakota gradually migrated south and westward and pushed aside the Omaha tribe in this early 26 migrate. At first, they were not mounted, but horses were spreading throughout the Plains from Spanish settlements in the Southwest, and by 1742 the Tetons had acquired ponies and their cultural pattern became more and more that of horse-riding nomads. In the Central Plains the Lakota came into conflict with the Pawnee, 27 it was a village tribe, that held the rich hunting lands of the Republican River Valley until the Lakota entered the region. The Pawnee war parties usually made their trips on foot, unlike other tribes. Because the Lakota 28 were a much bigger group, they had an advantage.

23

A. NO CHANGE
B. and were
C. but were
D. DELETE the underlined portion

24

A. NO CHANGE
B. that include
C. they include
D. who include

25

A. NO CHANGE
B. traded by trappers
C. trading with trappers
D. trading by trappers

26

A. NO CHANGE
B. migrated
C. migrating
D. migration

27

A. NO CHANGE
B. that was a village tribe
C. which was a village tribe
D. a village tribe

28

For the sake of cohesion, which choice most effectively completes the clause?
A. NO CHANGE
B. were more skilled warriors
C. were mounted on horses
D. were more aggressive

CONTINUE

The Omaha war parties **29** were different in size. Some had as less as seven warriors. Some had as many as a hundred warriors. All members of the party were volunteers. The leader was usually a well-known warrior **30** who had demonstrated his skill in battle. The warriors are reported to have worn a white covering of soft, dressed skin for their heads. No shirt was worn, **31** a robe was belted about the waist and tied over the breast. No feathers or ornaments could be worn at this time. In actual battle, the warriors wore only moccasins and breechcloth.

Occasionally the wives of a few of the men accompanied a large war party to assist in the care of their garments, and to do the cooking. **32** A sacred War Pack was kept in the Tent of War. It was important in any war activities. The contents of the pack were believed to protect the tribe from harm. A returning war party with the scalp of an enemy held a special

29

Which choice most effectively combines the underlined parts?
A. were different in size, some had seven warriors, some had a hundred.
B. varied from seven to a hundred warriors.
C. might have seven warriors or a hundred warriors.
D. were all different in size.

30

A. NO CHANGE
B. he had demonstrated his skill in battle.
C. had demonstrated his skill in battle.
D. demonstrated his skill in battle.

31

A. NO CHANGE
B. and a robe
C. but a robe
D. with a robe

32

Which choice most effectively combines the sentences in the underlined part?
A. A sacred War Pack was kept in the Tent of War and was
B. A sacred War Pack, kept in the Tent of War, was
C. A sacred War Pack kept in the Tent of War was
D. A sacred War Pack was kept in the Tent of War, which was

CONTINUE

scalp or victory dance. **33** Some men won special honors on the war path. They were permitted to wear an eagle feather in their scalp locks. A deer-tail headdress might also be worn by certain warriors. The large feathered headdress seen in the movies today was worn only on social occasions by noted men. Only the men wore feathers in their hair, but the women might wear them on their clothing.

33

Which choice most effectively combines the two sentences?

A. Some men won special honors on the war path, they were permitted

B. Some men won special honors on the war path were permitted

C. Men who won special honors on the war path they were permitted

D. Men who won special honors on the war path were permitted

CONTINUE

Questions 34 – 44 are based on the following passage.

Zimmermann is a cryptologist. His company, Silent Circle, encrypts voice calls, text messages, and any file attachments. If you use Silent Circle, **34** you will enjoy its privacy protection service. The service won't stop the delivery of ominous messages in range of certain base stations. But it can block eavesdropping and prevent the snooper **35** to know the number of the person you are calling or texting. Soon, access codes for Silent Circle were making their way to protest organizers in the heart of Kiev. "Those are the kinds of environments **36** where you need widespread deployment of crypto technology," Zimmermann says, with evident satisfaction.

In the past year, it's become clearer that places like Kiev are not the only environments where people might want the privacy Zimmermann can provide. Documents **37** are brought to light by former U.S. National Security Agency contractor Edward Snowden **38** suggest that the NSA gathers huge amounts of information from cloud computing platforms and wireless carriers, including the numbers ordinary

34

Which choice most effectively improves the cohesion of the paragraph?
A. NO CHANGE
B. you are guaranteed that your privacy is protected.
C. you don't worry about your personal data being leaked any more.
D. your calls to other users are sent through the company's servers and decrypted on the other phone.

35

A. NO CHANGE
B. knowing
C. from knowing
D. of knowing

36

A. NO CHANGE
B. what
C. which
D. that

37

A. NO CHANGE
B. brought to light
C. is brought to light
D. which brought to light

38

A. NO CHANGE
B. suggests
C. suggesting
D. suggested

CONTINUE

people called and the times they called them. **39** Not only the government can be watching you: so could websites, advertisers, and even retailers trying to track your movements within stores. Modern smartphones and the apps running on them are engineered to collect and disseminate enormous amounts of user data, **40** so as location, Web browsing histories, search terms, and contact lists.

By summer Zimmermann will be delivering a new way to fight back: a highly secure smartphone, called Blackphone. **41** It is now being manufactured by a joint venture that includes Silent Circle, it uses Zimmermann's encryption tools and adds other protections. It runs a special version of the Android operating system—PrivatOS— **42** block many of the ways phones leak data about your activities. **43** While custom security phones have long been in the hands of military and government leaders, this effort may signal a shift toward mass-market phones that are far more private and secure.

39

A. no change
B. Not only can the government
C. Not only could the government
D. Not only the government could

40

A. NO CHANGE
B. such as
C. such like
D. so that

41

A. NO CHANGE
B. Blackphone is
C. Which is
D. DELETE the underlined portion

42

A. NO CHANGE
B. blocks
C. that blocks
D. that block

43

A. NO CHANGE
B. When
C. That
D. Because

CONTINUE

44 Blackphone sells for $629 with subscriptions to privacy-protecting services. It is one of many measures that technologists are taking in response to the Snowden revelations. One such effort involves wider encryption of ordinary Web traffic. Stephen Farrell, a computer scientist at Trinity College Dublin who is leading that project through the Internet Engineering Task Force, says a phone that encrypts communications and seals off data leaks is a crucial part of the strategy. "Personally, I really would like to have a phone with a much more hardened and privacy-friendly configuration," he says.

44

Which choice most effectively combines the two sentences at the underlined portion?

A. Blackphone sells for $629 with subscriptions to privacy-protecting services, it is

B. Blackphone, which sells for $629 with subscriptions to privacy-protecting services, is

C. Blackphone sells for $629 with subscriptions to privacy-protecting services and is

D. Blackphone sells for $629 with subscription to privacy-protecting services, which is

STOP

If you finish before time is called, you may check your work on this section only. Do not turn to any other section.

Math Test – No Calculator

25 MINUTES, 20 QUESTIONS

Turn to Section 3 of your answer sheet to answer the questions in this section.

$A = \pi r^2$ $A = \ell w$ $A = \frac{1}{2}bh$ $c^2 = a^2 + b^2$ Special Right Triangles
$C = 2\pi r$

$V = \ell w h$ $V = \pi r^2 h$ $V = \frac{4}{3}\pi r^3$ $V = \frac{1}{3}\pi r^2 h$ $V = \frac{1}{3}\ell w h$

The number of degrees of arc in a circle is 360.

The number of radians of arc in a circle is 2π.

The sum of the measures in degrees of the angles of a triangle is 180.

CONTINUE ▶

1

$$x(3-9) + 1 = 8 + 7(3-9) - 1$$

In the equation above, what is the value of x?

A. 2

B. −6

C. −2

D. 6

2

If $2 < m < 7$ and $4 < n < 13$, then what is the range of $m - n$?

A. $-11 < m - n < 3$

B. $6 < m - n < 20$

C. $-2 < m - n < -6$

D. $3 < m - n < 11$

3

If $(x - 12)^2 = (3x + 18)^2$, what is a possible value of x?

A. 12

B. −12

C. 15

D. −15

4

If $\dfrac{2x^3 + 4x^2 - 6x}{2x} = x - 1$, what is a value of x?

A. −1

B. −2

C. −3

D. 3

5

If $x^2 - 4x - 12 = 0$, what is the value of $2x^2 - 8x$?

A. 12

B. 16

C. 24

D. 32

6

If a is a negative integer less than −2, which of the following could be a graph of $y = \dfrac{ax}{3}$?

A.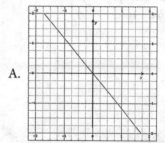

B.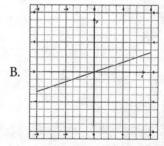

C.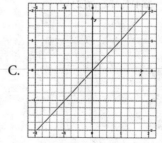

D.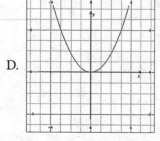

CONTINUE

7

If $-\dfrac{3}{4} < 3x - 1 < \dfrac{4}{3}$, what can be one of the values of $-6x + 2$?

A. 3
B. –3
C. 2
D. –2

8

What is the vertex of the parabola defined by the equation $y = x^2 - 6x - 16$?

A. (3, –25)
B. (–3, –25)
C. (3, 25)
D. (–3, 25)

9

If $x^2 - y^2 = 21$ and $x + y = 7$, then $x =$

A. 2
B. 10
C. 5
D. 3

10

If $f(x) = 2x^3 + 3x^2 - x + 1$, then $f(2) =$

A. 25
B. 26
C. 27
D. 28

11

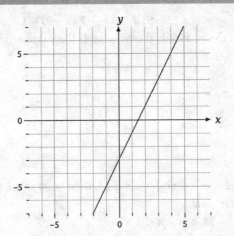

The graph of $f(x)$ is shown above. If the function is defined by $d(x) = f(x - 2)$, what is the value of $d(6)$?

A. 4
B. 5
C. 6
D. 7

12

If $5x^2 + 25x - 30 = 5x - 5$, and $x \neq 1$, which of the following can be the value of x?

A. 5
B. –5
C. –3
D. –1

CONTINUE

13

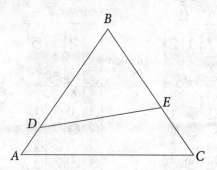

In the figure above, DE intersects triangle ABC at D and E. If $\angle ABC$ is 50°, what is the sum of $\angle ADE$ and $\angle DEC$?

A. 130°

B. 180°

C. 230°

D. 260°

14

If $\sqrt[3]{x-5} = 3$, then $x =$

A. 8

B. 27

C. –17

D. 32

15

Which of the following most completely expresses the solution set of the equation $\dfrac{2x+15}{x-3} = \dfrac{x^2}{x-3}$?

A. $x = -3, -5$

B. $x = -3, 5$

C. $x = 3, -5$

D. $x = 3, 5$

CONTINUE

DIRECTIONS

For questions 16–20, solve the problem and enter your answer in the grid, as described below, on the answer sheet.

1. Although not required, it is suggested that you write your answer in the boxes at the top of the columns to help you fill in the circles accurately. You will receive credit only if the circles are filled in correctly.

2. Mark no more than one circle in any column.

3. No question has a negative answer.

4. Some problems may have more than one correct answer. In such cases, grid only one answer.

5. **Mixed numbers** such as $3\frac{1}{2}$ must be gridded as 3.5 or 7/2. (If $\boxed{3\ 1\ /\ 2}$ is entered into the grid, it will be interpreted as $\frac{31}{2}$, not $3\frac{1}{2}$.)

6. **Decimal answers:** If you obtain a decimal answer with more digits than the grid can accommodate, it may be either rounded or truncated, but it must fill the entire grid.

Answer: $\frac{7}{12}$ · Answer: 2.5

Write answer in boxes. ← Fraction line · ← Decimal point · Grid in result.

Acceptable ways to grid $\frac{2}{3}$ are:

Answer: 201 – either position is correct

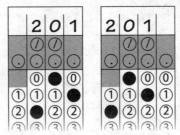

NOTE: You may start your answers in any column, space permitting. Columns you don't need to use should be left blank.

16

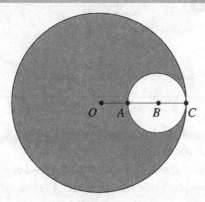

Circle O in the diagram above has a radius of 12, which is divided into three equal segments: $\overline{OA}$, $\overline{AB}$ and $\overline{BC}$. Circle B's diameter is $\overline{AC}$. The area of the shaded region is $a\pi$, what is the value of a?

17

Elias has $5.00 in quarters and nickels. The number of nickels is 10 more than the number of quarters. How many quarters does he have?

18

When the positive integer a is divided by 8, the remainder is 7. What is the remainder when $a + 12$ is divided by 8?

19

If $f(x) = \dfrac{2x}{3} + 3$, and $g(x) = \dfrac{4x}{5} + 10$, what is the value of $g(f(3))$?

20

In rectangle $PQRS$, shown below, the diagonal PR is 15 inches. If the cos of $\angle SPR$ is $\dfrac{8}{10}$, what is the value of RS?

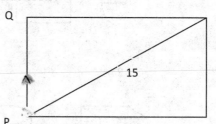

STOP

If you finish before time is called, you may check your work on this section only. Do not turn to any other section.

Math Test – Calculator

55 MINUTES, 38 QUESTIONS

Turn to Section 4 of your answer sheet to answer the questions in this section.

DIRECTIONS

For questions 1 – 30, solve each problem, choose the best answer from the choices provided and fill in the circle on your answer sheet. **For questions 31 – 38,** solve the problem and enter your answer in the grid on your answer sheet. Please refer to the directions before question 31 on how to enter your answers in the grid. Your may use any available space in your test booklet for scratch work.

NOTES

1. The use of a calculator **is permitted**.

2. All variables and expressions used represent real numbers unless otherwise indicated.

3. Figures provided in this test are drawn to scale unless otherwise indicated.

4. All figures lie in a plane unless otherwise indicated.

5. Unless otherwise indicated, the domain of a given function f is the set of all real numbers x for which $f(x)$ is a real number.

REFERENCE

$A = \pi r^2$ $A = \ell w$ $A = \frac{1}{2}bh$ $c^2 = a^2 + b^2$ Special Right Triangles
$C = 2\pi r$

$V = \ell wh$ $V = \pi r^2 h$ $V = \frac{4}{3}\pi r^3$ $V = \frac{1}{3}\pi r^2 h$ $V = \frac{1}{3}\ell wh$

The number of degrees of arc in a circle is 360.

The number of radians of arc in a circle is 2π.

The sum of the measures in degrees of the angles of a triangle is 180.

CONTINUE ➡

1

If $4 = \frac{x+6}{2}$, then $x =$

A. 1
B. 2
C. 3
D. 4

2

$(z^4+5z^2-3)-z(z^2+5z+1)=$

A. z^4-5z^3-3
B. z^4-z^3-5z-2
C. z^4-z^3-z-3
D. z^4-z^3-5z-3

3

If $-2<a<5$ and $-3<b<7$, then what is the range of $a-b$?

A. $-5<a-b<12$
B. $-2<a-b<7$
C. $-9<a-b<8$
D. $-5<a-b<9$

4

If f $0\leq\alpha\leq\frac{\pi}{2}$ (where $\frac{\pi}{2}=90°$) and $\sin\alpha = 0.618$, which of the following is correct about the range of α?

A. $0<\alpha<\frac{\pi}{8}$

B. $\frac{\pi}{8}<\alpha<\frac{\pi}{4}$

C. $\frac{\pi}{4}<\alpha<\frac{3\pi}{8}$

D. $\frac{3\pi}{8}<\alpha<\frac{\pi}{2}$

5

What is the value of x if $x+4=\frac{3x+10}{2}$?

A. -2
B. -1
C. 1
D. 2

6

Which of the following is true about the solution set of $\frac{x}{x-1} = \frac{x^2+3x-3}{x-1}$?

A. There is exactly one solution: $x=1$.
B. There is exactly one solution: $x=-3$.
C. There are no solutions.
D. There are two solutions: $x=3$ and $x=-3$.

CONTINUE

Problems 7 to 10 refer to the following information.

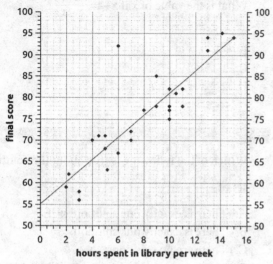

Jerry is a middle school librarian. Recently he conducted a study of the effect of using the school library on students' performance in the exams. He randomly chose a class of 26 students. On his first attempt he collected the scores of the final history exam last week. He also gathered the average number of hours each student spent in the library per week. There are no repeated points in the graph, i.e., any two students with the same final score spent different amount of time in the library. After analyzing the data, Jerry modeled the relation between the scores and the time spent in library as a linear function, shown as the graph in the picture.

7

If Jerry's model is accurate, what is the expected score for a student who does not spend any time in the library?

A. 0
B. 50
C. 55
D. 56

8

If Jerry's model is accurate, what is the expected score for a student who spends 11.5 hours per week in the library?

A. 80
B. 82
C. 84
D. 85

9

Still using Jerry's model, if a student got 75 points in the final, what is his expected number of hours per week spent in the library?

A. 7.6
B. 8
C. 9.5
D. 10

10

What is the sum of x and y, if x is the mode of the final scores and y is the mode of the hours spent in library per week?

A. 80
B. 85
C. 88
D. undefined

CONTINUE

11

Which of the following values of x satisfies $2x+7 \geq 27$?

A. 7.5

B. 8.5

C. 9.5

D. 10.5

12

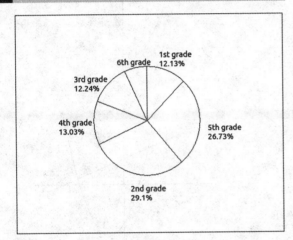

The pie graph above shows the percentage of students from each grade in a soccer camp. If 474 students are from the 5th grade, which of the following is closest to the number of students from the first through third grades?

A. 800

B. 852

C. 948

D. 1024

13

F.C. Carasus played 38 matches in a league. A team gains 3 points for each match they win, and 1 point for each match they draw. Suppose x is the number of matches where F.C. Carasus had a draw in the league, and y is the number of matches they lost. Which of the following functions, p, models the total points they get in the league?

A. $p(x,y)=114-2x-3y$

B. $p(x,y)=114-x-y$

C. $p(x,y)=x+3y$

D. $p(x,y)=38+x-3y$

14

What are the solutions to the equation $2x^2=4-5x$?

A. $\dfrac{-5 \pm \sqrt{57}}{4}$

B. $\dfrac{-5 \pm \sqrt{7}}{4}$

C. $\dfrac{-4 \pm \sqrt{56}}{2}$

D. ± 1

15

$$2x - 3y = 12$$
$$-\frac{2}{3}x + y = 7$$

Based on the above system of equations, which of the following must be true?

A. (2, 3) is the unique solution to the system.

B. (9, 2) is the unique solution to the system.

C. There are at two solutions to this system.

D. There is no solution to this system.

CONTINUE ➜

16

Joe drives a car on the highway with the speed that exactly matches the speed limit, which is 70 miles per hour. Given that there are 5280 feet in a mile, and 3 feet in a yard, which of the following is closest to the number of yards the car travels in a second?

A. 34
B. 40
C. 45
D. 52

17

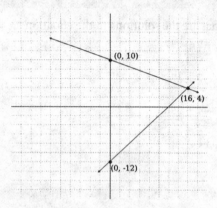

(0, 10)

(16, 4)

(0, -12)

Which of the following system of equations expresses the two lines in the picture above?

A. $x-y=-12$ and $x+2y=20$
B. $y=x-12$ and $3x+8y=80$
C. $y=2x-12$ and $x+y=20$
D. $y=x+10$ and $y-2x=8$

18

Which of the following picture depicts the equations $y=x^2-2x-3$ and $x+2y=4$?

A.

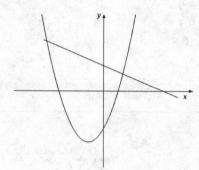

B.

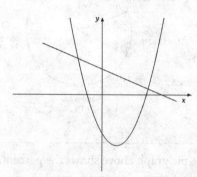

C.

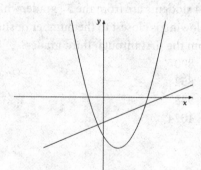

D.

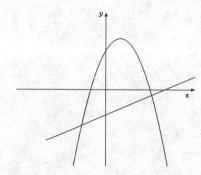

CONTINUE

19

Let $f(x)=|2x-9|$. If the function g is defined as $g(x) = f(x^2-x-1)$, then $g(-2)+g(2)=$

A. 8
B. 10
C. 15
D. 16

20

If a and b are two integers satisfying $-2<a<3$ and $-1<b<3$, and b is not 0, which of the following is true for all possible values of $\frac{a-1}{b}$?

A. $-2.5\leq\frac{a-1}{b}\leq0$

B. $-2\leq\frac{a-1}{b}\leq1$

C. $-\frac{1}{3}\leq\frac{a-1}{b}\leq2$

D. $0\leq\frac{a-1}{b}\leq3$

21

A rental company got a new car with a manufacturer's discount of 20% off the market price. They expect to rent off the car 200 days in a year at the rate of $19 per day, and then sell it after one year at the price of $33,000. The expected sell price is calculated based on the market price and the depreciation rate of 12% for the first year of this line of vehicle. What is the profit the company will gain on this car, ignoring any factors not presented above?

A. $3000
B. $4520
C. $6440
D. $6800

22

A zoologist observes the population growth of a group of rabbits. In the beginning there were 20 rabbits in the group. For the first months the population growth was slow but steady. On the 150th day it was clear that the population was already 4 to 5 times the initial value. The zoologist also observed that the rate of the population increase is somehow proportional to the population itself. According to these facts, which of the following is the most accurate graph that depicts the population of the rabbits as a function of days in the year?

A.

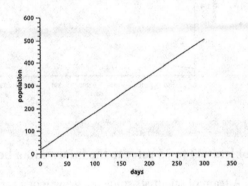

B.

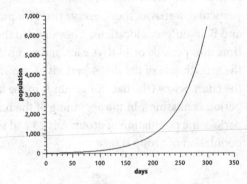

CONTINUE ➡

C.

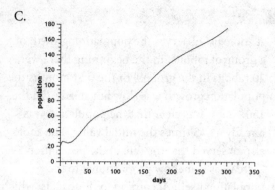

D.

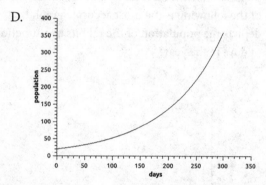

Problems 23 to 25 refer to the information below.

A team of scientists study the growth of a certain species in different environments. For this particular scenario, they observe two groups, A and B, in different locations. They divided the time into periods of 14 days each and recorded the growth rate of the first 4 periods as shown in the chart below (the data for group A in the last period is missing). In the beginning of the first period, the population of group A is 23 and the population of group B is 38.

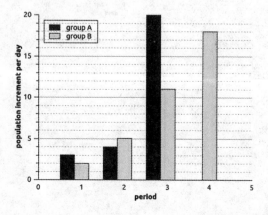

23

What is the population of group B at the end of the 2nd period?
A. 121
B. 130
C. 136
D. 150

24

Suppose that they model the growth of both groups as piecewise linear functions of the days. In other words, in each period they describe the population in each group as a linear function of the days. How many days after the experiment starts does the population of group A exceed that of group B?
A. 14
B. 30
C. 32
D. 33

25

Suppose that at the end of the 4th period both groups have the same population, which of the following is closest to the average population increase of group A in the 4th period?
A. 26
B. 9
C. 11.3
D. 10.07

CONTINUE

26

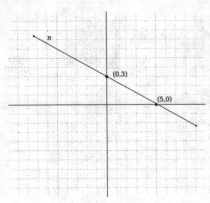

A line m has the equation $y=\frac{x}{5}-\frac{1}{5}$. What is the intersection point of the line m and line n in the figure above?

A. $(6, 1)$

B. $(5, \frac{4}{5})$

C. $(4, \frac{3}{5})$

D. $(\frac{5}{3}, 2)$

27

Suppose $x - 2x + 3x - 4x + 5x - 6x = 9$. What is the value of x?

A. 1

B. 2

C. –2

D. –3

Questions 28 to 30 refer to the following information.

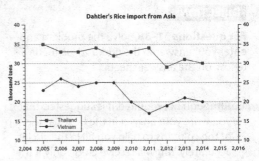

The food company Dahtier imports rice from two countries in Asia, Thailand and Vietnam. The chart above shows the amount of annual rice import from those two countries in the past 10 years.

28

According to the chart above, what percentage of Dahtier's rice import from Asia in 2014 was from Thailand?

A. 50%

B. 60%

C. 66.67%

D. 33.33%

29

According to the information above, in which year the difference of the rice import from both countries are the greatest?

A. 2005

B. 2006

C. 2008

D. 2011

30

According to the information in the chart, what is the maximum amount of yearly rice import, in thousand tons, Dahtier had from Asia?

A. 57

B. 58

C. 59

D. 60

CONTINUE

DIRECTIONS

For questions 31–38, solve the problem and enter your answer in the grid, as described below, on the answer sheet.

1. Although not required, it is suggested that you write your answer in the boxes at the top of the columns to help you fill in the circles accurately. You will receive credit only if the circles are filled in correctly.
2. Mark no more than one circle in any column.
3. No question has a negative answer.
4. Some problems may have more than one correct answer. In such cases, grid only one answer.
5. **Mixed numbers** such as $3\frac{1}{2}$ must be gridded as 3.5 or 7/2. (If $3|1|/|2$ is entered into the grid, it will be interpreted as $\frac{31}{2}$, not $3\frac{1}{2}$.)
6. **Decimal answers:** If you obtain a decimal answer with more digits than the grid can accommodate, it may be either rounded or truncated, but it must fill the entire grid.

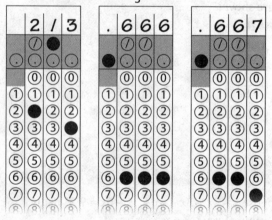

Answer: $\frac{7}{12}$ Answer: 2.5

Write answer in boxes.   ← Fraction line

Grid in result.   ← Decimal point

Acceptable ways to grid $\frac{2}{3}$ are:

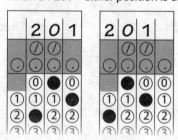

Answer: 201 – either position is correct

NOTE: You may start your answers in any column, space permitting. Columns you don't need to use should be left blank.

31

$$8a - 2b = 13$$
$$4a + 14b = 11$$

Based on the system of equations above, what is the value of $3a+3b$?

32

If $\frac{s}{2} = \frac{s+8}{3}$, what is the value of s?

Questions 33 and 34 refer to the following information.

Andy is the new manager of a software company. He observed the following table of monthly salaries for all the engineers in an engineering team.

Engineer	Experience (months)	Salary ($ per month)
Bill	0	4500
Dylon	20	5900
Randy		8084
Paul	40	10100
Leslie	72	

After careful inspection of the data, he discovered that the relation in the table between salaries and the experiences can be fit into a quadratic curve. Precisely, let y be the salary in dollars per month, and x be the working experience in the number of months, the relation between x and y can then be modeled as a parabola. Moreover, the parabola has its vertex at 0 working experience.

33

If the model is accurate, how many months of working experience does Randy have?

34

If the model is accurate, what is the percentage, rounded to the nearest integer, of Leslie's monthly salary in the total monthly salary of the team?

35

When trying to decide the infinite sum $S=1+\dfrac{1}{q}$ $+\dfrac{1}{q^2}+\cdots$, Maxwell discovered the relation:

$qS=q+S$.

Based on this, what is the value of S if $q=5$?

CONTINUE

36

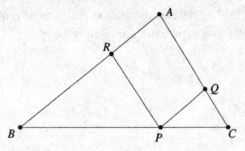

(Note: Figure not drawn to scale.)
In the figure above, $BC=15$, $AC=9$, and $AB=12$. If P is a point on BC such that $PC=5$, and Q and R are points on AC and AB, respectively, such that PQ is parallel to AB and PR is parallel to AB. What is the SQUARE of the distance between R and Q?

37

According to information in the table above, what is the ratio of densities of the heaviest planet to that of the lightest planet, among the first six planets? Your answer must be accurate to the two digits after the decimal point.

38

According to Newton's law of universal gravitation, the gravitational force between two planets is $F = G\dfrac{m_1 m_2}{r^2}$, where m_1 and m_2 are the masses of the two planets, r is the distance between them, and $G \approx 6.673 \times 10^{-11}$ N $\cdot (\dfrac{m}{kg})^2$ is the gravitational constant. If, at a certain point, the gravitational force between Earth and Venus was 48PN (1PN = 10^{15}N), and the distance between Earth and Venus was twice the distance between Earth and Mars, how many PNs is the gravitational force between Earth and Mars? Make your answer accurate to 1 digit after the decimal point.

Problems 37 and 38 refer to the following table.

Table: Fact sheet for the first six planets

Planet	Mass (10^{24}kg)	Density (kg/m^3)
Mercury	0.330	5427
Venus	4.87	5243
Earth	5.97	5514
Mars	0.642	3933
Jupiter	1898	1326
Saturn	568	687

STOP

If you finish before time is called, you may check your work on this section only. Do not turn to any other section.

New SAT Practice Essay 3

 ESSAY BOOK

DIRECTIONS

The essay gives you an opportunity to show how effectively you can read and comprehend a passage and write an essay analyzing the passage. In your essay, you should demonstrate that you have read the passage carefully, present a clear and logical analysis, and use language precisely.

Your essay must be written on the lines provided in your answer booklet; except for the Planning Page of the answer booklet, you will receive no other paper on which to write. You will have enough space if you write on every line, avoid wide margins, and keep your handwriting to a reasonable size. Remember that people who are not familiar with your handwriting will read what you write. Try to write or print so that what you are writing is legible to those readers.

You have 50 minutes to read the passage and write an essay in response to the prompt provided inside this booklet.

REMINDERS

— Do not write your essay in this booklet. Only what you write on the lined pages of your answer booklet will be evaluated.

— An off-topic essay will not be evaluated.

This cover is representative of what you'll see on test day.

As you read the passage below, consider how Martin Luther King uses:

- evidence, such as facts or examples, to support claims.

- reasoning to develop ideas and to connect claims and evidence.

- stylistic or persuasive elements, such as word choice or appeals to emotion, to add power to the ideas expressed.

Adapted from Martin Luther King, Jr.'s famous speech, "I have a dream"

1   I am happy to join with you today in what will go down in history as the greatest demonstration for freedom in the history of our nation.

2   Five score years ago, a great American, in whose symbolic shadow we stand today, signed the Emancipation Proclamation. This momentous decree came as a great beacon light of hope to millions of Negro slaves who had been seared in the flames of withering injustice. It came as a joyous daybreak to end the long night of their captivity.

3   But one hundred years later, the Negro still is not free. One hundred years later, the life of the Negro is still sadly crippled by the manacles of segregation and the chains of discrimination. One hundred years later, the Negro lives on a lonely island of poverty in the midst of a vast ocean of material prosperity. One hundred years later, the Negro is still languished in the corners of American society and finds himself an exile in his own land. And so we've come here today to dramatize a shameful condition.

4   In a sense we've come to our nation's capital to cash a check. When the architects of our republic wrote the magnificent words of the Constitution and the Declaration of Independence, they were signing a promissory note to which every American was to fall heir. This note was a promise that all men, yes, black men as well as white men, would be guaranteed the "unalienable Rights" of "Life, Liberty and the pursuit of Happiness." It is obvious today that America has defaulted on this promissory note, insofar as her citizens of color are concerned. Instead of honoring this sacred obligation, America has given the Negro people a bad check, a check which has come back marked "insufficient funds."

5   But we refuse to believe that the bank of justice is bankrupt. We refuse to believe that there are insufficient funds in the great vaults of opportunity of this nation. And so, we've come to cash this check, a check that will give us upon demand the riches of freedom and the security of justice.

6   We have also come to this hallowed spot to remind America of the fierce urgency of Now. This is no time to engage in the luxury of cooling off or to take the tranquilizing drug of gradualism. Now is the time to make real the promises of democracy. Now is the time to rise from the dark and desolate valley of segregation to the sunlit path of racial justice. Now is the time to lift our nation from the quicksands of racial injustice to the solid rock of brotherhood. Now is the time to

make justice a reality for all of God's children.

7 It would be fatal for the nation to overlook the urgency of the moment. This sweltering summer of the Negro's legitimate discontent will not pass until there is an invigorating autumn of freedom and equality. Nineteen sixty-three is not an end, but a beginning.

8 The marvelous new militancy which has engulfed the Negro community must not lead us to a distrust of all white people, for many of our white brothers, as evidenced by their presence here today, have come to realize that their destiny is tied up with our destiny. And they have come to realize that their freedom is inextricably bound to our freedom.

9 We cannot walk alone.

10 And as we walk, we must make the pledge that we shall always march ahead.

11 Let us not wallow in the valley of despair, I say to you today, my friends.

12 And so even though we face the difficulties of today and tomorrow, I still have a dream. It is a dream deeply rooted in the American dream.

13 I have a dream that one day this nation will rise up and live out the true meaning of its creed: "We hold these truths to be self-evident, that all men are created equal."

14 I have a dream that one day on the red hills of Georgia, the sons of former slaves and the sons of former slave owners will be able to sit down together at the table of brotherhood.

15 I have a dream that one day even the state of Mississippi, a state sweltering with the heat of injustice, sweltering with the heat of oppression, will be transformed into an oasis of freedom and justice.

16 I have a dream that my four little children will one day live in a nation where they will not be judged by the color of their skin but by the content of their character.

17 I have a dream today!

18 I have a dream that one day, down in Alabama, with its vicious racists, with its governor having his lips dripping with the words of "interposition" and "nullification" — one day right there in Alabama little black boys and black girls will be able to join hands with little white boys and white girls as sisters and brothers.

19 I have a dream today!

20 I have a dream that one day every valley shall be exalted, and every hill and mountain shall be made low, the rough places will be made plain, and the crooked places will be made straight; "and the glory of the Lord shall be revealed and all flesh shall see it together."

21 This is our hope, and this is the faith that I go back to the South with.

Write an essay in which you explain how Martin Luther King, Jr. builds an argument to persuade his audience that racial discrimination must end now. In your essay, analyze how Martin Luther King, Jr. uses one or more of the features listed in the box above, (or features of your own choice), to strengthen the logic and persuasiveness of his argument. Be sure that your analysis focuses on the most relevant features of the passage.

Your essay should not explain whether you agree with Martin Luther King, Jr.'s claims, but rather explain how he builds an argument to persuade his audience.

■ TEST NUMBER   ■ SECTION 1

ENTER TEST NUMBER

For instance, for Practice Test # 1, fill in the circle for 0 in the first column and for 1 in the second column.

1 ◯ ◯
2 ◯ ◯
3 ◯ ◯
4 ◯ ◯
5 ◯ ◯
6 ◯ ◯
7 ◯ ◯
8 ◯ ◯
9 ◯ ◯

1 A ◯ B ◯ C ◯ D ◯
2 A ◯ B ◯ C ◯ D ◯
3 A ◯ B ◯ C ◯ D ◯
4 A ◯ B ◯ C ◯ D ◯
5 A ◯ B ◯ C ◯ D ◯
6 A ◯ B ◯ C ◯ D ◯
7 A ◯ B ◯ C ◯ D ◯
8 A ◯ B ◯ C ◯ D ◯
9 A ◯ B ◯ C ◯ D ◯
10 A ◯ B ◯ C ◯ D ◯
11 A ◯ B ◯ C ◯ D ◯
12 A ◯ B ◯ C ◯ D ◯
13 A ◯ B ◯ C ◯ D ◯

14 A ◯ B ◯ C ◯ D ◯
15 A ◯ B ◯ C ◯ D ◯
16 A ◯ B ◯ C ◯ D ◯
17 A ◯ B ◯ C ◯ D ◯
18 A ◯ B ◯ C ◯ D ◯
19 A ◯ B ◯ C ◯ D ◯
20 A ◯ B ◯ C ◯ D ◯
21 A ◯ B ◯ C ◯ D ◯
22 A ◯ B ◯ C ◯ D ◯
23 A ◯ B ◯ C ◯ D ◯
24 A ◯ B ◯ C ◯ D ◯
25 A ◯ B ◯ C ◯ D ◯
26 A ◯ B ◯ C ◯ D ◯

27 A ◯ B ◯ C ◯ D ◯
28 A ◯ B ◯ C ◯ D ◯
29 A ◯ B ◯ C ◯ D ◯
30 A ◯ B ◯ C ◯ D ◯
31 A ◯ B ◯ C ◯ D ◯
32 A ◯ B ◯ C ◯ D ◯
33 A ◯ B ◯ C ◯ D ◯
34 A ◯ B ◯ C ◯ D ◯
35 A ◯ B ◯ C ◯ D ◯
36 A ◯ B ◯ C ◯ D ◯
37 A ◯ B ◯ C ◯ D ◯
38 A ◯ B ◯ C ◯ D ◯
39 A ◯ B ◯ C ◯ D ◯

40 A ◯ B ◯ C ◯ D ◯
41 A ◯ B ◯ C ◯ D ◯
42 A ◯ B ◯ C ◯ D ◯
43 A ◯ B ◯ C ◯ D ◯
44 A ◯ B ◯ C ◯ D ◯
45 A ◯ B ◯ C ◯ D ◯
46 A ◯ B ◯ C ◯ D ◯
47 A ◯ B ◯ C ◯ D ◯
48 A ◯ B ◯ C ◯ D ◯
49 A ◯ B ◯ C ◯ D ◯
50 A ◯ B ◯ C ◯ D ◯
51 A ◯ B ◯ C ◯ D ◯
52 A ◯ B ◯ C ◯ D ◯

■ SECTION 2

	A	B	C	D		A	B	C	D		A	B	C	D		A	B	C	D		A	B	C	D
1	○	○	○	○	10	○	○	○	○	19	○	○	○	○	28	○	○	○	○	37	○	○	○	○
2	○	○	○	○	11	○	○	○	○	20	○	○	○	○	29	○	○	○	○	38	○	○	○	○
3	○	○	○	○	12	○	○	○	○	21	○	○	○	○	30	○	○	○	○	39	○	○	○	○
4	○	○	○	○	13	○	○	○	○	22	○	○	○	○	31	○	○	○	○	40	○	○	○	○
5	○	○	○	○	14	○	○	○	○	23	○	○	○	○	32	○	○	○	○	41	○	○	○	○
6	○	○	○	○	15	○	○	○	○	24	○	○	○	○	33	○	○	○	○	42	○	○	○	○
7	○	○	○	○	16	○	○	○	○	25	○	○	○	○	34	○	○	○	○	43	○	○	○	○
8	○	○	○	○	17	○	○	○	○	26	○	○	○	○	35	○	○	○	○	44	○	○	○	○
9	○	○	○	○	18	○	○	○	○	27	○	○	○	○	36	○	○	○	○					

COMPLETE MARK ● EXAMPLES OF INCOMPLETE MARKS It is recommended that you use a No. 2 pencil. It is very important that you fill in the entire circle darkly and completely. If you change your response, erase as completely as possible. Incomplete marks or erasures may affect your score.

■ SECTION 3

	A B C D		A B C D		A B C D		A B C D		A B C D
1	○○○○	4	○○○○	7	○○○○	10	○○○○	13	○○○○
2	○○○○	5	○○○○	8	○○○○	11	○○○○	14	○○○○
3	○○○○	6	○○○○	9	○○○○	12	○○○○	15	○○○○

Only answers that are gridded will be scored. You will not receive credit for anything written in the boxes.

16 **17** **18** **19** **20**

(grid-in answer fields for questions 16–20, with digits 0–9 and fraction/decimal bubbles)

NO CALCULATOR
ALLOWED

■ SECTION 4

	A B C D		A B C D		A B C D		A B C D		A B C D
1	○○○○	7	○○○○	13	○○○○	19	○○○○	25	○○○○
2	○○○○	8	○○○○	14	○○○○	20	○○○○	26	○○○○
3	○○○○	9	○○○○	15	○○○○	21	○○○○	27	○○○○
4	○○○○	10	○○○○	16	○○○○	22	○○○○	28	○○○○
5	○○○○	11	○○○○	17	○○○○	23	○○○○	29	○○○○
6	○○○○	12	○○○○	18	○○○○	24	○○○○	30	○○○○

CALCULATOR
ALLOWED

COMPLETE MARK ●   EXAMPLES OF   Ⓐ ⊗ ⊖ Ⓟ
                   INCOMPLETE MARKS ● ⊘ ⊘ ⊛

It is recommended that you use a No. 2 pencil. It is very important that you fill in the entire circle darkly and completely. If you change your response, erase as completely as possible. Incomplete marks or erasures may affect your score.

■ SECTION 4 (Continued)

Only answers that are gridded will be scored. You will not receive credit for anything written in the boxes.

31
32
33
34
35

Only answers that are gridded will be scored. You will not receive credit for anything written in the boxes.

36
37
38

CALCULATOR
ALLOWED

PLANNING PAGE You may plan your essay in the unlined planning space below, but use only the lined pages following this one to write your essay. Any work on this planning page will not be scored.

Use pages 7 through 10 for your ESSAY ⟶

FOR PLANNING ONLY

Use pages 7 through 10 for your ESSAY ⟶

BEGIN YOUR ESSAY HERE.

SERIAL #

You may continue on the next page.

STOP.

New SAT Practice Test 4

Reading Test

65 MINUTES, 52 QUESTIONS

Turn to Section 1 of your answer sheet to answer the questions in this section.

DIRECTIONS

Each passage or pair of passages below is followed by a number of questions. After reading each passage or pair, choose the best answer to each question based on what is stated or implied in the passage or passages and in any accompanying graphics (such as a table or graph).

Questions 1-11 are based upon the passage and graphic below

-Adapted from "Forces of Divergence: Is surging inequality endemic to Capitalism?" by John Cassidy, The New Yorker, 31 March 2014. Graphic adapted from www.inequality.org

In the stately world of academic presses, it isn't often that advance orders and publicity for a book prompt a publisher to push forward
Line its publication date. But that's what Belknap,
5 an imprint of Harvard University Press, did for "Capital in the Twenty-first Century," a sweeping account of rising inequality by the French economist Thomas Piketty. Reviewing the French edition of Piketty's book, which came
10 out last year, Branko Milanovic, a former senior economist at the World Bank, called it "one of the watershed books in economic thinking." *The Economist* said that it could change the way we think about the past two centuries of economic
15 history. Certainly, no economics book in recent years has received this sort of attention. Months before its American publication date, which was switched from April to March, it was already the subject of lively online discussion among
20 economists and other commentators.

With the help of other researchers, including Saez and the British economist Anthony Atkinson, Piketty expanded his work on inequality to other countries, including Britain,
25 China, India, and Japan. The researchers

established the World Top Incomes Database, which now covers some thirty countries, among them Malaysia, South Africa, and Uruguay. Piketty and Saez also updated their U.S. figures,
30 showing how the income share of the richest households continued to climb during and after the Great Recession, and how, in 2012, the top one per cent of households took 22.5 per cent of total income, the highest figure since 1928. The
35 empirical work done by Piketty and his colleagues has influenced debates everywhere from Zuccotti Park, the short-lived home of Occupy Wall Street, to the International Monetary Fund and the White House; President Obama has said that
40 tackling inequality and wage stagnation is our foremost challenge.

The question is what's driving the upward trend. Piketty didn't think that economists' standard explanations were convincing, largely
45 because they didn't pay enough attention to capital accumulation—the process of saving, investing, and building wealth which classical economists, such as David Ricardo, Karl Marx, and John Stuart Mill, had emphasized. Piketty
50 defines capital as any asset that generates a monetary return. It encompasses physical capital, such as real estate and factories; intangible capital, such as brands and patents; and financial assets, such as stocks and bonds. In modern
55 economics, the term "capital" has been purged of its ideological fire and is treated as just another

CONTINUE ▶

"factor of production," which, like labor and land, earns a competitive rate of return based upon its productivity. A popular model of economic growth developed by Robert Solow, one of
60 Piketty's former colleagues at M.I.T., purports to show how the economy progresses along a "balanced growth path," with the shares of national income received by the owners of capital and labor remaining constant over time. This
65 doesn't jibe with modern reality. In the United States, for example, the share of income going to wages and other forms of labor compensation dropped from sixty-eight per cent in 1970 to sixty-two per cent in 2010—a decline of close to a
70 trillion dollars.

Piketty believes that the rise in inequality can't be understood independently of politics. For his new book, he chose a title evoking Marx, but he doesn't think that capitalism is doomed, or that
75 ever-rising inequality is inevitable. There are circumstances, he concedes, in which incomes can converge and the living standards of the masses can increase steadily—as happened in the so-called Golden Age, from 1945 to 1973.
80 But Piketty argues that this state of affairs, which many of us regard as normal, may well have been a historical exception. The "forces of divergence can at any point regain the upper hand, as seems to be happening now, at the beginning of the
85 twenty-first century," he writes. And, if current trends continue, "the consequences for the long-term dynamics of the wealth distribution are potentially terrifying."

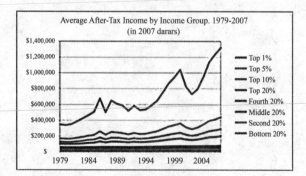

1

The author's primary purpose of this passage is to
A. discuss the global impacts of information contained in the book and the appreciation it has garnered from several countries.
B. discuss the various economic systems present throughout the world and their rates of success in attaining equality.
C. warn the reader about enmeshing politics and economics, as both are distinct entities independent of one another.
D. discuss the impacts of Marxian philosophy on the economic terminology most utilized by researchers today.

2

By referencing the economical results present in the "Golden Age," Mr. Pinketty is attempting to illustrate
A. the dangers of economic investment after periods of relative economic boom.
B. economical tendencies of steady rise or decline during various epochs in our history.
C. that although it is certainly a daunting task, the forces of economics are malleable and divergence is, at times, preventable.
D. the class system proposed by Karl Marx is most reflective of economic times in the modern world.

3

Based upon information contained in the graphic, the average after-tax income
A. has exhibited modest increases for all income groups reported.
B. has shown a slight decline for many of the income groups reported.
C. appears to have been relatively unaffected by the terrorist attacks of 2001.
D. has at least doubled for the top 5% since 1979.

CONTINUE

4

The term *empirical* used in line 35 most closely means:

A. borrowed
B. experiential
C. unsupported
D. contradictory

5

Modern theories of economics most likely favor

A. tendencies towards policies designed to achieve economic equality.
B. vocal members of various economic classes.
C. greater wealth accumulation by the top 1% of earners.
D. independent research studies offering constructive criticism and suggestion to assist in achieving results similar to the Golden Age.

6

The answer to the previous question is best found in

A. lines 58-64, "A popular model of economic growth…"
B. lines 72-75, "For his new book…"
C. lines 42-49, "The question is what's driving…"
D. lines 82-88, "The forces of divergence…"

7

Based upon the introductory paragraph, it can be inferred that

A. the author of the article agrees with many of the economical points and tenets contained in Mr. Pinketty's book.
B. there has been worldwide rebuke of the information obtained by Mr. Pinketty as "unfounded" and irrelevant.
C. popular demand for the book was not as favorable as publishers would have hoped.
D. the information contained in the book provides little new information regarding economic trends of the past 200 years.

8

Based upon the article's characterization of the research methods and writing style of Mr. Pinketty, it can be inferred that Mr. Pinketty

A. possessed a deep rooted dislike for Marxist thinking.
B. proposes a communist lifestyle as the only means of equalizing economic disparity.
C. philosophically agreed with Marxist thinking, but believes a capitalistic system can be beneficial for all, if implemented correctly.
D. is most likely within the top 5% of earners.

CONTINUE ➤

9

The term *inevitable* used in line 75 is most synonymous with
A. changing, malleable
B. unavoidable, inexorable
C. unjust, discriminatory
D. appealing, without flaw

10

From information obtained in the article, which of the following is most likely true?
A. The top 1% of earners generally have income sways reflective of economic trends.
B. Contributions by the bottom 75% of earners have a great deal of impact on overall economic policy changes due to the amount of citizens contained in that group.
C. The gap of disparity between the top 1% of earners and bottom 99% has begun to shrink gradually.
D. The top 1% of earners are relatively unaffected by national economic trends.

11

The best evidence for the answer to the previous question can be found in
A. lines 29-34, "Pinketty and Saez also updated…"
B. lines 51-54, "It encompasses physical capital…"
C. lines 75-79, "There are circumstances, he concedes…"
D. lines 21-25, "With the help of other researchers…"

CONTINUE

Questions 12-22 are based upon the passage and graphic below

-excerpted from "To Kill a Mockingbird" by Harper Lee

Being Southerners, it was a source of shame to some members of the family that we had no recorded ancestors on either side of the Battle
Line of Hastings. All we had was Simon Finch, a
5 fur-trapping apothecary from Cornwall whose piety was exceeded only by his stinginess. In England, Simon was irritated by the persecution of those who called themselves Methodists at the hands of their more liberal brethren, and as
10 Simon called himself a Methodist, he worked his way across the Atlantic to Philadelphia, thence to Jamaica, thence to Mobile, and up the Saint Stephens. Mindful of John Wesley's strictures on the use of many words in buying and selling,
15 Simon made a pile practicing medicine, but in this pursuit he was unhappy lest he be tempted into doing what he knew was not for the glory of God, as the putting on of gold and costly apparel. So Simon, having forgotten his teacher's dictum
20 on the possession of human chattels, bought three slaves and with their aid established a homestead on the banks of the Alabama River some forty miles above Saint Stephens. He returned to Saint Stephens only once, to find a wife, and with her
25 established a line that ran high to daughters. Simon lived to an impressive age and died rich.

It was customary for the men in the family to remain on Simon's homestead, Finch's Landing, and make their living from cotton. The place
30 was self-sufficient: modest in comparison with the empires around it, the Landing nevertheless produced everything required to sustain life except ice, wheat flour, and articles of clothing, supplied by river-boats from Mobile.
35 Simon would have regarded with impotent fury the disturbance between the North and the South, as it left his descendants stripped of every-thing but their land, yet the tradition of living on the land remained unbroken until well into the
40 twentieth century, when my father, Atticus Finch, went to Montgomery to read law, and his younger brother went to Boston to study medicine. Their

sister Alexandra was the Finch who remained at the Landing: she married a taciturn man who
45 spent most of his time lying in a hammock by the river wondering if his trot-lines were full.

When my father was admitted to the bar, he returned to Maycomb and began his practice. Maycomb, some twenty miles east of Finch's
50 Landing, was the county seat of Maycomb County. Atticus's office in the courthouse contained little more than a hat rack, a spittoon, a checkerboard and an unsullied Code of Alabama. His first two clients were the last two persons
55 hanged in the Maycomb County jail. Atticus had urged them to accept the state's generosity in allowing them to plead Guilty to second-degree murder and escape with their lives, but they were Haverfords, in Maycomb County, a
60 name synonymous with jackass. The Haverfords had dispatched Maycomb's leading blacksmith in a misunderstanding arising from the alleged wrongful detention of a mare, were imprudent enough to do it in the presence of three witnesses,
65 and insisted that the-son-of-a-bitch-had-it-coming-to-him was a good enough defense for anybody. They persisted in pleading Not Guilty to first-degree murder, so there was nothing much Atticus could do for his clients except be present
70 at their departure, an occasion that was probably the beginning of my father's profound distaste for the practice of criminal law.

12

The Finch family can best be characterized as being
A. completely enmeshed in Southern culture and practices.
B. non-traditional Southerners.
C. largely unsuccessful businesspeople by standards of the time.
D. an integral stop of the Underground Railroad and pioneers of emancipating slaves.

CONTINUE ▶

13

From the passage, the reader is able to ascertain that Simon Finch could be thought of as
A. an emotionally vulnerable individual.
B. compassionate and empathetic towards all people.
C. ardently supportive of Northern ideals.
D. somewhat of a hypocrite based upon his beliefs and practices.

14

Support for this can best be found by which of the following?
A. Simon's possession of slaves, contrary to what he was taught, and his feelings regarding the Civil War.
B. his support of his descendants pursuing higher educational ideals.
C. his desire to provide for his posterity by working his land independent of any assistance.
D. his decision to flee England to pursue a better life in America.

15

From the excerpt provided, we can properly ascertain that Simon Finch
A. possessed a leaning towards Atheism, causing him to leave his country in pursuit of religious freedom.
B. was in a position of high esteem in England prior to leaving for the New World.
C. most likely arrived in America somewhere between the Battle of Hastings and the Civil War.
D. enjoyed a fruitful and decorated military career.

16

The term *dictum* used in line 19 most closely means:
A. warning, caution
B. essay, position
C. lesson, moral
D. edict, decree

17

Atticus Finch's demeanor and style as a litigator can best be described as:
A. ardently anti-conciliatory
B. realistic humanism
C. confused and easily swayed
D. vicious and cutthroat

18

The best evidence for the previous answer can be found in
A. lines 55-60, "Atticus had urged them…"
B. lines 51-55, "Atticus' office in the courthouse…"
C. lines 67-72, "They persisted in pleading Not Guilty…"
D. lines 40-46, "When my father, Atticus Finch…"

19

It can be assumed from the passage that Simon Finch
A. was a spendthrift who put his amassed land and possessions at considerable risk.
B. did little to provide for his children and family.
C. prioritized being self-sufficient and providing for his family and descendants.
D. could best be thought of as indifferent and isolative.

CONTINUE ➜

20

The term *taciturn* used in line 44 is most synonymous with:

A. garrulous, chatty

B. obnoxious, wild

C. confusing, hypocritical

D. silent, reticent

21

Atticus's feelings towards his profession can best be characterized as:

A. regretful and pessimistic

B. indifferent and obligatory

C. conceited and arrogant

D. demanding and obscure

22

Evidence for the previous answer is best found in

A. lines 47-51, "When my father was admitted…"

B. lines 67-72, "They persisted in pleading…"

C. lines 40-42, "Atticus Finch went to Montgomery…"

D. lines 54-60, "His first two clients…"

CONTINUE ➡

Questions 23-32 deal with the passage below.

-adapted from Malala Yousafzai's speech to the United Nations, 12 July 2013

Dear Friends, on the 9th of October 2012, the Taliban shot me on the left side of my forehead. They shot my friends too. They thought that the bullets would silence us. But they failed.
5 And then, out of that silence came, thousands of voices. The terrorists thought that they would change our aims and stop our ambitions but nothing changed in my life except this: Weakness, fear and hopelessness died. Strength, power and
10 courage was born. I am the same Malala. My ambitions are the same. My hopes are the same. My dreams are the same.

Dear sisters and brothers, I am not against anyone. Neither am I here to speak in terms
15 of personal revenge against the Taliban or any other terrorists group. I am here to speak up for the right of education of every child. I want education for the sons and the daughters of all the extremists especially the Taliban.
20 I do not even hate the Talib who shot me. Even if there is a gun in my hand and he stands in front of me. I would not shoot him. This is the compassion that I have learnt from Muhammad-the prophet of mercy, Jesus christ
25 and Lord Buddha. This is the legacy of change that I have inherited from Martin Luther King, Nelson Mandela and Muhammad Ali Jinnah. This is the philosophy of non-violence that I have learnt from Gandhi Jee, Bacha Khan and
30 Mother Teresa. And this is the forgiveness that I have learnt from my mother and father. This is what my soul is telling me, be peaceful and love everyone.

Dear sisters and brothers, we realise the
35 importance of light when we see darkness. We realise the importance of our voice when we are silenced. In the same way, when we were in Swat, the north of Pakistan, we realised the importance of pens and books when we saw the guns.
40 The wise saying, "The pen is mightier than sword" was true. The extremists are afraid of books and pens. The power of education

frightens them. They are afraid of women. The power of the voice of women frightens them.
45 And that is why they killed 14 innocent medical students in the recent attack in Quetta. And that is why they killed many female teachers and polio workers in Khyber Pukhtoon Khwa and FATA. That is why they are blasting schools every day.
50 Because they were and they are afraid of change, afraid of the equality that we will bring into our society.

I remember that there was a boy in our school who was asked by a journalist, "Why are
55 the Taliban against education?" He answered very simply. By pointing to his book he said, "A Talib doesn't know what is written inside this book." They think that God is a tiny, little conservative being who would send girls to the
60 hell just because of going to school. The terrorists are misusing the name of Islam and Pashtun society for their own personal benefits. Pakistan is peace-loving democratic country. Pashtuns want education for their daughters and sons.
65 And Islam is a religion of peace, humanity and brotherhood. Islam says that it is not only each child's right to get education, rather it is their duty and responsibility.

Honourable Secretary General, peace is
70 necessary for education. In many parts of the world especially Pakistan and Afghanistan; terrorism, wars and conflicts stop children to go to their schools. We are really tired of these wars. Women and children are suffering in many parts
75 of the world in many ways. In India, innocent and poor children are victims of child labour. Many schools have been destroyed in Nigeria. People in Afghanistan have been affected by the hurdles of extremism for decades. Young girls have to
80 do domestic child labour and are forced to get married at early age. Poverty, ignorance, injustice, racism and the deprivation of basic rights are the main problems faced by both men and women.

Dear fellows, today I am focusing on women's
85 rights and girls' education because they are suffering the most. There was a time when women social activists asked men to stand up

CONTINUE ▶

for their rights. But, this time, we will do it by
ourselves. I am not telling men to step away
90 from speaking for women's rights rather I am
focusing on women to be independent to fight
for themselves. Dear sisters and brothers, now it's
time to speak up.

23

The author uses the adage, "the pen is mightier
than the sword," to convey
A. the notion that many Talib are illiterate and
   now have a general distaste for the disadvan-
   tages from which they were raised.
B. the perspective of fear from which the Talib
   operate, that greater knowledge translates into
   greater abilities to understand situations and
   challenge oppression.
C. her support of propaganda as an adequate and
   effective means to sway uneducated persons.
D. the belief of the Talib that books constitute
   a threat to their system of rule due to their
   support of Western ideas.

24

The best evidence for the answer to the previous
question can be found in
A. lines 60-62, "The terrorists are misusing the
   name…"
B. lines 74-75, "Women and children are
   suffering…"
C. lines 16-19, "I am here to speak up…"
D. lines 46-48, "And that is why they killed…"

25

The statement, "we realize the importance of
light when we see darkness," is used primarily to
describe
A. the belief that suffering is an inevitable
   consequence of fighting for what you believe
   in.
B. the appreciation of positive aspects of life
   when oppression reigns.
C. that perseverance and struggle can play a
   powerful role in the fight for equality.
D. the jealous manner in which the Talib view
   the rest of the world.

26

The term *ambitions* used in line 7 is most
synonymous with:
A. aspirations or intentions
B. education
C. freedoms from oppression
D. leisure

27

Based upon her depiction of her religion, we can
assume that Malala
A. was not raised in a pious or devout household.
B. is ashamed of her heritage due to the violence
   that is consistently attributed to her culture.
C. wishes to convert to a more peaceful religious
   philosophy.
D. is proud of her heritage and ashamed of those
   who misguided in her faith.

CONTINUE →

28

The best evidence for the answer to the previous question can be found in
A. lines 23-25, "This is the compassion I have learnt…"
B. lines 60-68, "The terrorists are misusing…"
C. lines 6-10, "The terrorists thought that they…"
D. lines 58-60, "They think that God is a tiny…"

29

It can be reasonably assumed from the passage that
A. Malala's family is unsupportive of her aspirations and willingness to stand up for her beliefs.
B. prior to Talib arrival to power, education was an equal right for all citizens in Pakistan.
C. though education was obtained by some girls in Pakistan, Malala was wounded while attempting to go to school.
D. education of women was strictly forbidden in all Islamic countries.

30

It can be inferred from the passage that the author believes which of the following poses the largest threat to the equal rights movement in Islamic countries:
A. fear and ignorance of change and progress
B. devout interpretations of religion
C. the influence of Western ideals and progressive thinking on current governmental structures
D. the relative sense of isolation felt by Middle Eastern countries at the hands of governments opposed to Islam

31

The term *deprivation* used in line 82 most closely means:
A. confiscation
B. poverty
C. embellishment
D. withholding

32

A common theme found throughout the passage is one of
A. absolute action with disregard for consequences.
B. impassioned advocacy garnished with understanding.
C. resolute defiance.
D. forced submissiveness.

CONTINUE

Questions 33-42 deal with the passage below.

-"The only male northern white rhino left in the world is under 24-hour protection by armed guards" by Christina Sterbenz, Business Insider Australia, 17 April 2015.

Sudan, the last male white rhino left in the entire world, is under 24-hour protection by armed guards at the Ol Pejeta Conservancy
Line in central Kenya, CNN reports. And after the
5 recent deaths of two male rhinos - named Suni and Angalifu - back in October and December, respectively, his role in his species' survival is now paramount. The entire species depends on his ability to reproduce with the two other females
10 there. However, until that happens, this big guy is being watched over 24/7 by four armed rangers to protect him from poachers.

Sudan, however, is no spring chicken. At 42, he may no longer be able to "naturally mount and
15 mate with a female," the conservancy's deputy veterinarian George Paul told CNN. He also has a low sperm count. To make matters worse, the older of the two females has weak legs and may not be able to support Sudan. The conservancy
20 has been trying to coax a conception, but so far, it's had no luck.

Unfortunately, most rhinos species can't interbreed. For example, a northern white rhino can't mate with a black rhino. There's a chance,
25 however, that a northern white rhino could mate with a southern white rhino, the only rhino species not on the endangered list.

If the entire population disappears from the globe, the result could spell catastrophe for
30 African savannas — and potentially the whole world. Poaching and habitat loss seriously threaten the rhino population. In 2013, 1,004 rhinos were poached in South Africa. That's a terrible number considering only about 20,000
35 Southern white rhinos and 5,000 black rhinos still inhabit South Africa. Rhinos, considered a "megaherbivore," are a keystone species and play a pivotal role in ecosystems.

Removal of a keystone species has huge
40 downstream effect in the ecosystem and can throw an entire community out of whack, as

Jason G. Goldman explains in Conservation Magazine. For example, when agriculture and hunting decimated the Yellowstone wolves, the
45 deer population exploded, leading to decline in plant species as well.

While we know less about how megaherbivores fit into ecosystems, a 2009 paper in the journal Science found that extinction of
50 Pleistocene megaherbivores caused similar large-scale damage in North America — one of most fundamental questions in modern ecology.

Taking that a step further, rhinos' grazing specifically helps maintain the savanna grass-
55 lands, and those grasslands sustain numerous other species, whether directly or through predation, according to a May 2014 study in the Journal of Ecology.

The study focused on Kruger National
60 Park in South Africa, where the rhinos' decline has already started to affect the structure and composition of grasslands. In areas with a high density of rhinos, the researchers found more short grasses — an important metric for biodi-
65 versity, Goldman explains. Although seemingly counterintuitive, grazers, like rhinos, increase biodiversity by selecting certain plants over others, giving other species more ability to grow.

Aside from providing food for numerous
70 species, grasslands, like the savannas, serve an important global role, as well. They act as natural "carbon sinks" — essentially storage lockers for carbon dioxide in the atmosphere, a cause of global warming. Because of industrialisation,
75 Africa's carbon emissions will likely increase substantially throughout the 21st century.

The savannas, where rhino live, are an important ecosystem, and it seems that conservation of the species is essential to preserving
80 them.

33

According to the author, industrialization in South Africa may become globally problematic largely because of
A. the increase in industrial carbon emissions on already increasing greenhouse gases, further depleting ozone layer.
B. the ecological ramifications of large-scale savannah loss by intruding corporations may increase global warming, affecting ecosystems worldwide.
C. the loss of habitat for the Northern White rhino.
D. the increase in foodstuffs consumed by mega herbivores will exceed demand levels, creating ecological imbalances worldwide.

34

The author states that rhino preservation is critical to the entire world primarily because
A. species extinction could affect tourism not only in Africa, but in zoological societies worldwide.
B. United Nations conservation efforts reflect global consciousness regarding species protection and violation of these laws negatively affects that organization.
C. the rate at which several species are reaching endangered or threatened levels are brought to consciousness by rhino population decline.
D. their place as megaherbivores in the savannah ecosystem is central to maintaining balance, and their status cannot be replaced.

35

The best evidence for the previous answer is found in
A. lines 69-74, "Aside from providing food…"
B. lines 31-33, "Poaching and habitat loss…"
C. lines 36-38, "Rhinos, considered a megaherbivore…"
D. lines 59-62, "The study focused on Kruger National Park…"

36

It can be inferred from the author's description of ecosystem disruption that
A. humans have caused the largest disruption of the ecosystems most vulnerable and affected in the article.
B. the role of over-predation by many species has caused a significant negative impact on the ecological balance in many ecosystems.
C. industrialization has less to do with savannah loss than its effects on Yellowstone National Park.
D. the fault of "carbon sinks" to moderate and store carbon dioxide are likely to blame for increased savannah loss.

37

The term *counterintuitive* used in line 66 primarily means:
A. logical
B. without care
C. harmless
D. without logical thought

38

It can be inferred from the passage that
A. rhino mating habits have previously been unstudied and, thus, difficult to replicate in captivity.
B. attempting to mate a Northern and Southern white rhino is viewed as an absolute last resort and, as such, has not been attempted yet.
C. reproductive cycles in Northern white rhinos have been most affected by poaching and industrialization.
D. it is possible, potentially, to interbreed species of rhinos with little difficulty.

CONTINUE

39

Given the information presented in the article, it is apparent that savannahs serve a crucial role due to their ability to both

A. provide naturalistic mating habitats for the remaining white rhinos and sustain ecological diversity.

B. play an important role in reducing global warming through acting as "carbon sinks" and increasing the numbers of megaherbivores in Africa.

C. sustain ecological diversity and reduce global warming by acting as "carbon sinks" in storing and managing carbon dioxide.

D. provide food for many species of animal life and increase the amount of carbon dioxide present in the atmosphere.

40

The term *paramount* used in line 8 most closely means:

A. critically important

B. final option

C. irrelevant

D. questionable

41

From the author's description of rhino decline, it can best be assumed that

A. there is a decent chance that some species of rhino can see increasing numbers in the near future.

B. their role as megaherbivores in diverse ecosystems can be assumed by other species in the food cycle.

C. the role of encroachment by industries on the savannah has only slightly affected rhino life and populations.

D. poaching continues to be a major factor in species decline of the rhino.

42

The best evidence for the answer to question 41 is found in

A. lines 74-76, "Because of industrialization…"

B. lines 32-38, "In 2013, 1,004 rhinos were…"

C. lines 53-58, "Taking that a step further…"

D. lines 28-31, "If the entire population disappears from the globe…"

CONTINUE

Questions 43-52 deal with the passages below.

-adapted from "Can This Scientist Unite Genetic Engineers and Organic Farmers?" by Jeremy Berlin in National Geographic, 4 May 2015

Eighteen scientists are sitting in a lab, talking about new ways to feed the planet. These are some of the world's foremost experts on rice.

Line Most of them are from China. Nearly all of
5 them are men. But it's an American woman—tan and fit at 54, with gray-brown hair and bright green eyes—who clearly runs the show. Her name is Pamela Roland, and this is, after all, her laboratory. Ronald is a plant pathologist
10 and geneticist—a professor at the University of California, Davis, whose lab has isolated genes from rice that can resist diseases and tolerate floods. When those genes are inserted into existing rice plants, they help farmers grow
15 high-yield harvests in places where the crop is a vulnerable staple. Last year, four million subsistence farmers in seven countries fed millions of people by planting seeds that carry a gene Ronald and her collaborators isolated.
20 But her innovations aren't limited to science. She's also trying to mend the perceived schism between genetic engineering and organic farming. To do so, she's promoting a form of sustainable agriculture that draws on both
25 practices. Only by combining elements of each, she contends, will we have a chance of feeding the world's swelling population (expected to reach 9.2 billion by 2050) while also protecting the planet's natural resources and countenancing the effects
30 of climate change.

It seems like a radical idea: There may be no more polarizing ideological debate today than the one over transgenic crops. Though there's no meaningful scientific definition of "genetic
35 modification" (GM)—virtually all the food we eat has been genetically improved in some manner—most critiques center on moving genes from one organism to another in a lab. For years many people around the world have been diametrically,
40 often bitterly, opposed to this type of genetic engineering.

But as Ronald sees it, plant geneticists and organic farmers aren't enemies. In fact, they can be bedfellows: Her husband, Raoul Adamchak,
45 is an organic farmer and co-author, with Ronald, of Tomorrow's Tale: Organic Farming, and the Future Food. Praised by Bill Gates and Michael Pollan, their book argues for an integrated theory of agriculture in which "organic farming and
50 genetic engineering each will play an increasingly important role," rather than being unnecessarily pitted against each other.

-adapted from "Will Organic Food Fail to Feed the World?" by David Biello in Scientific American, 25 April 2012

In a bid to bring clarity to what has too often been an emotional debate, environmental scien-
55 tists at McGill University in Montreal and the University of Minnesota performed an analysis of 66 studies comparing conventional and organic methods across 34 different crop species. "We found that, overall, organic yields are consid-
60 erably lower than conventional yields," explains McGill's Verena Seufert, lead author of the study to be published in *Nature* on April 26." But, this yield difference varies across different conditions. When farmers apply best management practices,
65 organic systems, for example, perform relatively better."

In particular, organic agriculture delivers just 5 percent less yield in rain-watered legume crops, such as alfalfa or beans, and in perennial
70 crops, such as fruit trees. But when it comes to major cereal crops, such as corn or wheat, and vegetables, such as broccoli, conventional methods delivered more than 25 percent more yield.
75 The key limit to further yield increases via organic methods appears to be nitrogen—large doses of synthetic fertilizer can keep up with high demand from crops during the growing season better than the slow release from compost,
80 manure or nitrogen-fixing cover crops. Of course, the cost of using 171 million metric tons of synthetic nitrogen fertilizer is paid in dead zones at the mouths of many of the world's

CONTINUE ➤

rivers. These anoxic zones result from nitrogen-
85 rich runoff promoting algal blooms that then die
and, in decomposing, suck all the oxygen out of
surrounding waters. "To address the problem of
[nitrogen] limitation and to produce high yields,
organic farmers should use best management
90 practices, supply more organic fertilizers or grow
legumes or perennial crops," Seufert says.
    In fact, more knowledge would be key to
any effort to boost organic farming or its yields.
Conventional farming requires knowledge of
how to manage what farmers know as inputs—
synthetic fertilizer, chemical pesticides and
the like—as well as fields laid out precisely via
95 global-positioning systems. Organic farmers, on
the other hand, must learn to manage an entire
ecosystem geared to producing food—controlling
pests through biological means, using the waste
from animals to fertilize fields and even growing
100 one crop amidst another.

43

The description of organic farming in passage 2
essentially indicates that:

A. this type of agriculture has the potential to be
a sustainable and ample source of food for the
world population.

B. this type of agriculture may be region specific
due to the types of crops it currently supports,
therefore underproducing for world demand.

C. it relies heavily on natural resources of
fertilization such as manure and compost.

D. this type of farming can produce up to a 25%
higher yield of legumes than conventional
farming alone.

44

A common theme shared between passage 1 and
passage 2 centers on

A. the notion that conventional farming
methods constitute a best practice model for
environmental preservation and ecological
management.

B. the belief that widespread opinion of genetic
modification of food has led to greater crop
yield and, thus, higher output from farms.

C. The process of farming is becoming
increasingly based on complex aspects of
science, rather than being strictly reliant on
agriculture.

D. An alternative to high-yield synthetic
nitrogen-based fertilizers is essential for the
survival of organic farming.

45

A critical difference between passages 1 and 2 lies
in

A. passage one offering no specific drawbacks to
organic farming while passage two outlines
critical issues which must be corrected for
organic farming to work.

B. passage two's assertion that genetic modification of plant life is universally recognized
and supported while passage one speaks of
critics to such a process.

C. passage two's omission of any potential
drawbacks to new methods of farming in
support of a more sustainable practice.

D. passage one can be considered editorial while
passage two's writing style is more exploratory
and informative.

CONTINUE ▶

46

The term *anoxic* used in line 84 is related to:

A. plant or algal growth

B. a lack of fish or marine life

C. the color green

D. a lack of oxygen

47

From passage 1 it can be inferred that

A. genetic modification of crops cannot be achieved without organic farming methods.

B. the topic of genetically altered food is a relatively new topic with little chance for public to form an opinion.

C. scientific infringement on agriculture isn't a new concept, but is seen by some as potentially dangerous.

D. current levels of rice production in Asia are relatively stable due to the fact that it is invulnerable to the elements.

48

The best evidence for the answer to the previous question can be found in

A. lines 48-52, "Their book argues…"

B. lines 33-38, "Though there's no meaningful…"

C. lines 21-25, "She's also trying to mend…"

D. lines 13-16, "When those genes…"

49

The term *diametrically* used in line 39 essentially means:

A. in direct opposition

B. fervently

C. quietly

D. unilaterally

50

From the information provided in passage 2, it can be assumed that

A. more information and research needs to be undertaken if we are to utilize organic farming methods for cereal crops.

B. synthetic, nitrogen based fertilizers have little effect on ecosystems and their impact may be somewhat overblown by environmental lobbyists.

C. global positioning systems and ecosystem management are key requirements of organic farming.

D. the fishing and tourism industry may be affected by current organic fertilizing methods designed to produce high-yield crops.

51

The best evidence for the previous answer can be found in

A. lines 80-84, "Of course, the cost of using…"

B. lines 95-100, "Organic farmers, on the other hand…"

C. lines 70-74, "But when it comes to major…"

D. lines 75-80, "The key limit to further yield…"

CONTINUE ▶

52

Support for passage 2's assertion that organic farmers must deal with the problem of high dose, nitrogen rich fertilizers and the problems of using such chemicals comes from

A. passage 1's description of the interplay present between organic farming and genetic modification, lessening the need for large amounts of fertilizers.

B. passage 1's description of Asian rice modification leading to higher yield crops in vulnerable areas.

C. passage 1's assertion that organic farming must protect natural resources and countenance climate change.

D. passage 1's description of the detractors of genetic modification as fearing transfer of genes between organisms in a lab setting.

STOP

If you finish before time is called, you may check your work on this section only. Do not turn to any other section.

ACKNOWLEDGEMENT FOR THIS SECTION

The passages in this section were adapted from the following sources:

Jeremy Birlin, "Can This Scientist Unite Genetic Engineers and Organic Farmers?" © 2015 by *National Geographic*. Originally published 4 May 2015.

David Biello, "Will Organic Food Fail to Feed the World?" © 2012 by *Scientific America*. Originally published 25 April 2012.

John Cassidy, "Forces of Divergence: Is surging inequality endemic to Capitalism?" © 2014 by *The New Yorker*. Originally published 31 March 2014.

Harper Lee, "To Kill a Mockingbird" © 1960 by *The New Yorker*.

Christina Sterbendz, "The only male northern white rhina left in the world is under 24-hour protection by armed guards." © 2015 by *Business Inside Australia*. Originally published 17 April 2015

Malala Yousafzai, Speech to the United Nations, 12 July 2013.

Writing and Language Test

35 MINUTES, 44 QUESTIONS

Turn to Section 2 of your answer sheet to answer the questions in this section.

DIRECTIONS

Each passage below is accompanied by a number of questions. For some questions, you will consider how the passage might be revised to improve the expression of ideas. For other questions, you will consider how the passage might be edited to correct errors in sentence structure, usage, or punctuation. A passage or a question may be accompanied by one or more graphics (such as a table or graph) that you will consider as you make revising and editing decisions.

Some questions will direct you to an underlined portion of a passage. Other questions will direct you to a location in a passage or ask you to think about the passage as a whole.

After reading each passage, choose the answer to each question that most effectively improves the quality of writing in the passage or that makes the passage conform to the conventions of standard written English. Many questions include a "NO CHANGE" option. Choose that option if you think the best choice is to leave the relevant portion of the passage as it is.

Questions 1 – 11 are based on the following passage.

Francis Galton

[1] Francis Galton was a relative of famed naturalist Charles Darwin, he spent much of his life dedicated to research and critical inquiries into several different subject areas, from exploration to eugenics to weather to fingerprints. He was born on February 16, 1822, and grew up in a wealthy family near Birmingham, England. At an early age [2] in his life, he began to show great intellectual promise.

At first, Galton planned to become a doctor. He studied medicine at Birmingham's General Hospital and at King's College in London in the late 1830s. But he abandoned this idea and went on to study mathematics at Cambridge University. After

1

A. NO CHANGE
B. Francis Galton, who was a relative of famed naturalist Charles Darwin, he
C. Francis Galton, a relative of famed naturalist Charles Darwin, who
D. A relative of famed naturalist Charles Darwin, Francis Galton

2

A. NO CHANGE
B. in his childhood,
C. as a young man,
D. DELETE the underlined portion

CONTINUE

his father's death in 1844, **3** Galton received a substantial inheritance. This inheritance enabled him to pursue whatever topic piqued his curiosity. And he soon decided that it was time to explore more distant shores.

Exploration and Accomplishments

In the mid-1840s, Galton made his first trip to the Middle East and Africa. He went to Egypt and traveled down the Nile River to the Sudan, among other destinations in the area. His travels inspired him **4** undertake an exploration of southern Africa. In 1850, Galton joined the Royal Geographical Society and soon set off on his journey, with the society's approval. He initially planned to travel from an area known as Damaraland **5** to Lake Ngami. He actually traveled through a Southwestern section called Ovamboland.

Galton's maps and observations and descriptions of the native peoples of these regions brought him **6** great acclaim, that includes a gold medal from the Royal Geographical Society. He published on a book on his exploration, entitled *Tropical South Africa* (1853). Two years later, Galton offered his advice for other would-be explorers in *The Art of Travel: Or, Shifts and Contrivances Available in Wild Countries* (1855).

7 Galton was married to Louisa Jane Butler in 1853, Galton ended his explorations for other scientific pursuits. He became interested in weather and created the first **8** weather map, showing different climate conditions across a geographical area. In 1863, he published a book on the subject, called *Meteorgraphica, or Methods of Mapping the WeatheHr.*

3

For the sake of cohesion, which choice most effectively combines the two sentences at the underlined part?

A. a substantial inheritance, and this inheritance enabled him

B. a substantial inheritance, it enabled him

C. a substantial inheritance, which enabled him

D. a substantial inheritance and which enabled him

4

A. NO CHANGE

B. to undertake

C. undertaking

D. undertook

5

A. NO CHANGE

B. to Lake Ngami, and he actually traveled

C. to Lake Ngami, but he went

D. to Lake Ngami, but ended up traveling

6

A. NO CHANGE

B. great acclaim, includes

C. great acclaim, including

D. great acclaim, included

7

A. NO CHANGE

B. He was married to Luisa Butler in 1853,

C. Married to Luisa Jane Butler in 1853,

D. marrying Luisa Jane Butler in 1853,

8

A. NO CHANGE

B. weather map, which showing

C. weather map, that showing

D. weather map, it showing

CONTINUE →

9 _____, Galton developed his own theories on inherited traits. He studied identical twins, and worked on the first intelligence test in his exploration of the roles of "nature and nurture"—a phrase created by Galton—in human attributes. According to some sources, Galton also coined the term "eugenics," a controversial field of study about selective breeding in humans to produce preferred traits.

Final Years

Galton spent much of his life studying heredity and eugenics, and he later thought that a person's fingerprints might be a part of human genetic puzzle. He thought that these prints might provide information on differences between people, from race to moral character to intelligence. **10** While he never made any discoveries in this area, Galton established a fingerprint classification **11** system. That is still in use today.

In 1908, Galton published his autobiography. He received a knighthood from King Edward the following year. Galton died on January 17, 1911, in Haslemere, England, at the age of 88. In his will, he donated funds for a professorship in eugenics to University College London.

9

Which choice, inserted here, best shows the possible relationship between Darwin's hypothesis and Galton's theory?
A. Following Darwin's *The Origin of Species (1859)*,
B. With clues from Darwin's *The Origin of Species (1859)*,
C. Based on Darwin's *The Origin of Species (1859)*,
D. Strongly influenced by Darwin's *The Origin of Species (1859)*,

10

Which choice is most consistent with the tone of the passage?
A. NO CHANGE
B. However, he never made any discoveries in this area. Galton established
C. Galton never made any discoveries in this area, although he established
D. Galton never made any discoveries in this area, except that he established

11

A. NO CHANGE
B. system that is still in use today.
C. system is still in use today.
D. system; it is still in use today.

Questions 12 – 22 are based on the following passage.

Imagine yourself as a farmer **12** living in Europe in the mid-19th century. **13** You own little or no land have a large debt and your taxes are due to the government. Then one day a friend comes to your door carrying a brochure printed by the "Union Pacific Railroad." The brochure says that the Union Pacific owns millions of acres in a place called Nebraska. The railroad will sell you land for a very cheap price, and **14** _____ . **15** Would you be interested in it?

The building of the railroad across the Great Plains **16** meant more settlers and more competition with the Native Americans for the land. The transcontinental railroads wanted rights-of-way through tribal lands and needed white settlers to make their operations profitable.

12
A. NO CHANGE
B. lives
C. lived
D. live

13
A. NO CHANGE
B. You own little or no land, have a large debt and your taxes are due
C. You own little or no land, have a large debt, and your taxes are due
D. You own little or no land, have a large debt and, your taxes are due

14
For the sake of cohesion, which of the following details should not be included here?
A. You can take up to ten years to pay for it.
B. Sometimes you have to fight the angry Indians.
C. The climate is mild, ideal for farming.
D. There are no heavy taxes.

15
Which choice is most consistent with the tone of the context?
A. NO CHANGE
B. Would you consider moving?
C. Would you agree to move?
D. Wouldn't you be a fool not to move?

16
A. NO CHANGE
B. mean
C. means
D. meaning

CONTINUE ➡

17 Homesteaders were getting free land from the government, large tracts of land were granted to railroads by both the states and the federal government. The goal was to encourage the railroads to construct their tracks where **18** a few people lived, and to help settle the country. The federal government was especially interested **19** to create a transportation system that would link the eastern seaboard with the western coast. **20** Not only would a transcontinental railroad help populate the Great Plains, but it would tie the country together and also provide links to the potentially rich Asian trade.

Approximately 16 percent of Nebraska's total land mass was given to various railroad companies, **21** some by the federal government, some by the state. Along the lines of the state's two major railroads, the Union Pacific and the Burlington, every other square mile of land (called a "section") went to the railroads. This checkerboard of land extended back twenty miles on both sides of the track. So, the railroads owned a total of twenty sections of land for each mile of road constructed.

Thousands of pioneers traveled to and through Nebraska in covered wagons. But after the first railroad was completed across the state in 1867, thousands more took the train to Nebraska. With the completion of the transcontinental railroad in 1869,

17
A. NO CHANGE
B. Homesteaders were getting free land from the government, but large tracts
C. Homesteaders were getting free land from the government, and large tracts
D. At the same time that homesteaders were getting free land from the government, large tracts

18
A. NO CHANGE
B. few
C. not much
D. only a little

19
A. NO CHANGE
B. creating
C. in creating
D. on creating

20
A. NO CHANGE
B. Not only a transcontinental railroad would help
C. Not only will a transcontinental railroad help
D. Not only a transcontinental railroad will help

21
A. NO CHANGE
B. either by the federal government or by the state.
C. by the federal government and by the state.
D. partly by the federal government, partly by the state.

CONTINUE

people could travel from coast to coast **22** in relatively luxury. The Oregon Trail was gradually abandoned. Railroads encouraged settlers to move to Nebraska and had a tremendous impact on settlement.

A. NO CHANGE
B. in relatively luxurious.
C. in relative luxury.
D. in relative luxurious.

Questions 23 – 33 are based on the following passage.

If you live in a northern state or Canadian province that's been buried under snow recently, you may be eagerly awaiting the first sight of an American robin digging a worm out of your front yard as 23 the sign that spring is truly here.

24 Some robins migrate and some don't, in regions with cold winters, many numbers of the familiar avian species migrate to 25 sunny Florida and Texas and many other places for a few months and then head back north when spring returns to select a breeding territory and mate. As robin expert Roland H. Wauer notes, "The spring arrival of the American robin provides many northern dwellers 26 an emotional lift."

27 However: Why do robins and other birds come back? And how do they know when to make the trip?

The timing of bird migrations is one of the most intriguing phenomena in nature, and scientists are still working 28 and trying to solve its mysteries.

23

Which choice is most consistent with the tone of the paragraph?
A. NO CHANGE
B. the sign for the returning of spring.
C. the sign that spring is back.
D. the sign of a new spring.

24

A. NO CHANGE
B. Although some robins migrate and others don't,
C. While not all robins migrate,
D. While some robins do migrate,

25

A. NO CHANGE
B. sunny Florida, Texas, or many other places
C. other place like sunny Florida and Texas
D. warmer places such as sunny Florida and Texas

26

A. NO CHANGE
B. with an emotional lift
C. for an emotional lift
D. to an emotional lift

27

Which choice is most effective transition?
A. NO CHANGE
B. Nevertheless,
C. But you may wonder:
D. People may ask:

28

A. NO CHANGE
B. and try
C. to try
D. DELETE the underlined portion

CONTINUE

According to **29** Ian Newton, he wrote the book "The Migration Ecology of Birds," many long-distance avian migrants are remarkably regular in their departure and arrival dates, and that's a crucial part of their continued survival. Regularity ensures that individuals arrive in nesting areas just as environmental conditions become suitable for breeding, and then leave before **30** it changes.

Birds such as robins aren't that much physically affected by plunging temperatures, so the key issue for migration seems to be food availability **31** as well as comfort. When the supply of insects or plant food becomes depleted in the north, they'll head southward to someplace where the food is more plentiful. As that supply becomes depleted by consumption and changing weather conditions in their winter home, that seems to trigger the urge to head back the warming north, **32** when the insects and plants are starting to become available again.

While we know what conditions attract them, scientists are still trying to figure out the mechanism **33** that actually tells birds it's time to take off. According to All About Birds, a site maintained by Cornell University's Lab of Ornithology, one hypothesis is that birds have some sort of "undis-covered interface" — basically, a sort of biological WiFi connection — that enables them to sense distant temperature and weather conditions.

29
A. NO CHANGE
B. Ian Newton, author of the book
C. Ian Newton, wrote the book
D. Ian Newton, who wrote the book

30
A. NO CHANGE
B. it changed.
C. they changed.
D. they change.

31
A. NO CHANGE
B. and
C. rather than
D. in addition to

32
A. NO CHANGE
B. where
C. while
D. as

33
A. NO CHANGE
B. that actually tell birds
C. that actually telling birds
D. that actually told birds

Questions 34 – 44 are based on the following passage.

Before people could dream of Yellowstone as a national park, three significant things had to exist. First, Yellowstone itself had to exist. **34** And, people had to experience Yellowstone. Finally, a nation had to exist. Yellowstone itself, a region of thermal activity, home to over half of the world's geysers, a region of large mountains, large high elevation lakes, abundant game and wildlife, **35** had existed beyond human history. While Yellowstone existed, people too had found Yellowstone, though not many. The area which is now Yellowstone National Park had been home to some Native Americans throughout the course of history; **36** and, the area had been largely uninhabited. The United States of America, however, did not exist until 1776 **37** nor it officially gained its independence until the Treaty of Paris of 1783. Even so, the land which is Yellowstone was not a part of the United States until the Louisiana Purchase from Napoleon in 1803. There was no person from the United States in Yellowstone until John Colter **38** walked into Yellowstone in the winter of 1807-1808.

34

A. NO CHANGE
B. Another
C. Secondly
D. Two

35

A. NO CHANGE
B. existed
C. was existing
D. has existed

36

A. NO CHANGE
B. however,
C. therefore,
D. in addition

37

A. NO CHANGE
B. nor did it officially gain
C. nor did it officially gained
D. nor didn't it officially gain

38

Which choice is most consistent with the tone in the paragraph?
A. NO CHANGE
B. went
C. wandered
D. stumbled

39 John Colter did not think of the national park idea. His fantastical stories about boiling hot streams, water shooting out of the ground, and all the characteristics of "Colter's Hell" inspired others over the decades to seek out this land, which furthermore inspired **40** others who dreamed of the national park idea in regards to Yellowstone. John Colter is not part of the specific history of the foundation of Yellowstone as a national park because he had no thought on the matter; **41** however, the possibility for its expression became real.

In 1832, the artist George Catlin may have been the first to suggest the idea of a national preserve when after ascending the Missouri River, ironically on the steamboat *Yellowstone*, he suggested that much of the West should be set aside for the Indians and buffalo **42** to live in their natural state: "A *nation's Park*, in all their wild freshness of their nature's beauty." His thoughts were also the thoughts of others. Thoreau also thought of the idea of national preserve,

39

Which choice most effectively combines the two sentences at the underlined portion?
A. John Colter did not think of the national park idea, and his
B. Although John Colter did not think of the national park idea, but his
C. John Colter did not think of the national park idea, but his
D. Even if John Colter did not think of the national park idea, but his

40

A. NO CHANGE
B. others dreamed of
C. others dream of
D. others which dreamed of

41

A. NO CHANGE
B. nevertheless,
C. on the other hand,
D. but with John Colter,

42

Which choice is most consistent with the tone of the passage?
A. NO CHANGE
B. to stay
C. to roam
D. to exist

CONTINUE

a preserve which included human exhibits. Yet, **43** like John Colter had been in Yellowstone and had not thought of the idea; they had thought of an idea without knowledge of Yellowstone. **44** Though they do not properly belong in this specific history, Catlin and Thoreau provided an intellectual precedent upon which others who came after them may have fed upon in their thoughts.

43

For the sake of cohesion, which choice best conveys the meaning?

A. NO CHANGE
B. like John Colter who had been in Yellowstone but had not thought of the idea,
C. while John Colter who had been in Yellowstone but had not thought of the idea,
D. John Colter had been in Yellowstone but had not thought of the idea,

44

A. NO CHANGE
B. Though they definitely do not belong in
C. Obviously they cannot be part of
D. As a matter of fact, they had nothing to do with

STOP

If you finish before time is called, you may check your work on this section only. Do not turn to any other section.

No Test Material On This Page

Math Test – No Calculator

25 MINUTES, 20 QUESTIONS

Turn to Section 3 of your answer sheet to answer the questions in this section.

For **questions 1 – 15,** solve each problem, choose the best answer from the choices provided and fill in the circle on your answer sheet. F**or questions 16 – 20,** solve the problem and enter your answer in the grid on your answer sheet. Please refer to the directions before question 16 on how to enter your answers in the grid. Your may use any available space in your test booklet for scratch work.

NOTES

1. The use of a calculator **is not permitted**.

2. All variables and expressions used represent real numbers unless otherwise indicated.

3. Figures provided in this test are drawn to scale unless otherwise indicated.

4. All figures lie in a plane unless otherwise indicated.

5. Unless otherwise indicated, the domain of a given function f is the set of all real numbers x for which $f(x)$ is a real number.

REFERENCE

$A = \pi r^2$
$C = 2\pi r$

$A = \ell w$

$A = \frac{1}{2} bh$

$c^2 = a^2 + b^2$

Special Right Triangles

$V = \ell wh$

$V = \pi r^2 h$

$V = \frac{4}{3}\pi r^3$

$V = \frac{1}{3}\pi r^2 h$

$V = \frac{1}{3}\ell wh$

The number of degrees of arc in a circle is 360.

The number of radians of arc in a circle is 2π.

The sum of the measures in degrees of the angles of a triangle is 180.

CONTINUE

1

The mean of the series of integers –3, 7, 12 and n is 12. What is n?

A. 48
B. 36
C. 34
D. 32

2

If $x^3 + 3 = -24$, which of the following could be the value of x?

A. –2
B. 2
C. –3
D. 3

3

If x and y are integers such that $x^2 = 16$, and $3y^3 = -192$, which of the following could be true?

I. $x = 4, y = 4$
II. $x = -4, \ y = -4$
III. $x = 4, \ y = -4$

A. I only
B. II only
C. I and II only
D. II and III only

4

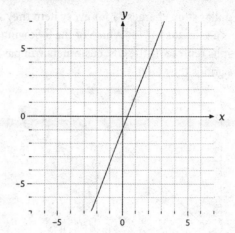

What is the equation of the line in the figure above?

A. $y = \dfrac{5}{2}x - 1$

B. $y = \dfrac{5}{2}x + 1$

C. $y = 2x - 1$

D. $y = 2x + 1$

5

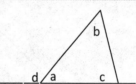

In the figure above, if $\angle d$ is 115°, what is the sum of $\angle b$ and $\angle c$?

A. 65°
B. 115°
C. 180°
D. 230°

CONTINUE

6

A dollar store charges $1 for every item they sell, plus a sales tax of 7%. Which of the following graphs represents the cost customers will pay for the goods they buy?

A.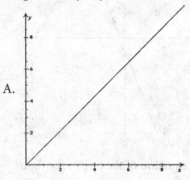

B.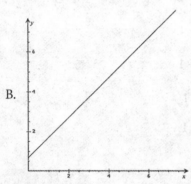

C.

D.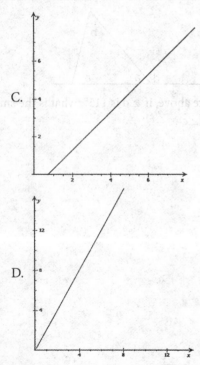

7

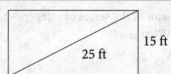

The figure above shows Mr. Thompson's rectangular garden, which is 15 feet wide and has a diagonal of 25 feet. Which of the following could be the area of his garden?

A. 200 square feet
B. 250 square feet
C. 300 square feet
D. 400 square feet

8

If $f(x) = 3\sqrt{x - 154}$, which of the following is the value of $f(218)$?

A. 192
B. 24
C. 64
D. 38

9

Which of the following expressions is equivalent to $3x\sqrt{2x}$ when $x > 0$?

A. $2x\sqrt{3x}$
B. $\sqrt{18x^3}$
C. $\sqrt{6x^2}$
D. $\sqrt{5x}$

CONTINUE

10

16 in

A locksmith needs to cut a circle out of a square metal sheet. Each side of the square is 16 inches. What is the area, in terms of π, of the biggest possible circle he can cut out?

A. 16π sq in

B. 32π sq in

C. 48π sq in

D. 64π sq in

11

x	$f(x)$
6	-3
3	-1
0	1

Which of the following equations gives a rule for the above table?

A. $f(x) = \frac{2}{3}x + 1$

B. $f(x) = \frac{2}{3}x - 3$

C. $f(x) = -\frac{2}{3}x + 1$

D. $f(x) = -\frac{1}{3}x - 1$

12

If $f(x) = \frac{3}{4}x + 1$ and $g(x) = 4x - \frac{4}{3}$, what is the value of $f(g(2))$?

A. 6

B. 4

C. 8

D. 5

13

Home Depot has a box truck rental service for the customers. The charge for this service is $19 for 20 miles or less of driving and $5 for each additional mile. If a customer's home is 25 miles away from Home Depot, what would be the cost for the rental service?

A. $44

B. $269

C. $231

D. $169

CONTINUE

14

If $\sqrt[3]{2x^2 - 7x + 30} = 3$, then $x =$

A. $3, -2$

B. $\frac{1}{2}, 3$

C. $-3, \frac{1}{3}$

D. $\frac{1}{2}, -3$

15

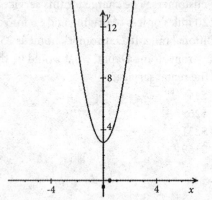

The equation $y = 2x^2 + 3$ is shown in the graph

above. Which of the following shows the graph of

$y = \frac{1}{8}x^2 + 3$?

B.

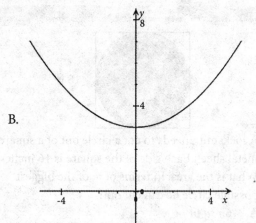

C.

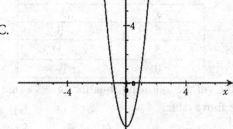

D.

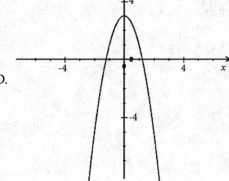

A.

CONTINUE

DIRECTIONS

For questions 16–20, solve the problem and enter your answer in the grid, as described below, on the answer sheet.

1. Although not required, it is suggested that you write your answer in the boxes at the top of the columns to help you fill in the circles accurately. You will receive credit only if the circles are filled in correctly.
2. Mark no more than one circle in any column.
3. No question has a negative answer.
4. Some problems may have more than one correct answer. In such cases, grid only one answer.
5. **Mixed numbers** such as $3\frac{1}{2}$ must be gridded as 3.5 or 7/2. (If $\boxed{3\,1\,/\,2}$ is entered into the grid, it will be interpreted as $\frac{31}{2}$, not $3\frac{1}{2}$.)
6. **Decimal answers:** If you obtain a decimal answer with more digits than the grid can accommodate, it may be either rounded or truncated, but it must fill the entire grid.

Answer: $\frac{7}{12}$

Write answer in boxes. ← Fraction line

Grid in result.

Answer: 2.5

← Decimal point

Acceptable ways to grid $\frac{2}{3}$ are:

Answer: 201 – either position is correct

NOTE: You may start your answers in any column, space permitting. Columns you don't need to use should be left blank.

CONTINUE

16

The table below shows some coordinates in the graph of a linear equation. What is the value of n?

INPUT	OUTPUT
2	6
3	8
7	a
a	n

17

Last Friday on the Shanghai Foreign Currency Exchange Market, the exchange rate of US Dollar ($) to Chinese RMB (¥) was 1: 6.16, and the exchange rate of Euro (€) to Chinese RMB (¥) was 1: 7. Based on these exchange rates, $500 was about how much Euro on that day (without checking the real USD / Euro rate)?

18

Emma walked 1.5 miles in 45 minutes. If she keeps walking at the same speed, how many miles can she walk in 2 hours?

19

Minor arc AB in circle O below is 2π, and O is the center. If $\angle ABO$ is 45°, and the area of the un-shaded region of the circle is $a\pi$ then what is the value of a?

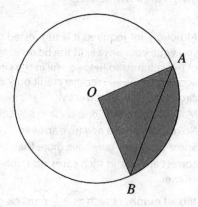

20

If $a + b + c = 6$, what is the value of $2^a \cdot 2^b \cdot 2^c$?

STOP

If you finish before time is called, you may check your work on this section only. Do not turn to any other section.

No Test Material On This Page

Math Test – Calculator

55 MINUTES, 38 QUESTIONS

Turn to Section 4 of your answer sheet to answer the questions in this section.

DIRECTIONS

For questions 1 – 30, solve each problem, choose the best answer from the choices provided and fill in the circle on your answer sheet. **For questions 31 – 38,** solve the problem and enter your answer in the grid on your answer sheet. Please refer to the directions before question 31 on how to enter your answers in the grid. Your may use any available space in your test booklet for scratch work.

NOTES

1. The use of a calculator **is permitted**.

2. All variables and expressions used represent real numbers unless otherwise indicated.

3. Figures provided in this test are drawn to scale unless otherwise indicated.

4. All figures lie in a plane unless otherwise indicated.

5. Unless otherwise indicated, the domain of a given function f is the set of all real numbers x for which $f(x)$ is a real number.

REFERENCE

$A = \pi r^2$ $A = \ell w$ $A = \dfrac{1}{2}bh$ $c^2 = a^2 + b^2$ Special Right Triangles
$C = 2\pi r$

$V = \ell wh$ $V = \pi r^2 h$ $V = \dfrac{4}{3}\pi r^3$ $V = \dfrac{1}{3}\pi r^2 h$ $V = \dfrac{1}{3}\ell wh$

The number of degrees of arc in a circle is 360.

The number of radians of arc in a circle is 2π.

The sum of the measures in degrees of the angles of a triangle is 180.

CONTINUE ➤

1

What is the biggest integer whose half does not exceed π?

A. 3

B. 4

C. 6

D. 7

2

If $3x+2<11$, which of the following describes all the possible values of x?

A. $x < 3$

B. $x > -3$

C. $x < 5$

D. $x < -5$

3

If $\frac{2-x}{2+x} = -1$, then which of the following expresses all the possible values of x?

A. $x : x = 0$

B. $x : x = 1$

C. $x : x = 4$

D. $x :$ No real numbers

4

A circle passes through the point (1, 2) and has the radius 5, which of the following is possibly the equation of such a circle?

A. $(x-3)^2 + (y-4)^2 = 25$

B. $(x-5)^2 + (y+1)^2 = 25$

C. $(x-1)^2 + (y+1)^2 = 5$

D. $(x-3)^2 + (y-6)^2 = 20$

5

$$\frac{4}{3}x - \frac{1}{2}y = 2.5$$
$$8x = 3(y + 5)$$

Which one of the following about the above system of equations is true?

A. It has no solutions.

B. It has infinitely many solutions.

C. It has exactly one solution (3, 3).

D. It has exactly one solution (6, 11).

6

A parabola P is defined by the equation $y = 2x^2 - 8x + 20$, which of the following is the equation of a parabola that shares the same vertex with P?

A. $y = (x-4)^2 + 8$

B. $y = 2x^2 - 8x - 20$

C. $y = x^2 - 4x + 20$

D. $y = (x-1)^2 - 2x + 15$

CONTINUE ➡

Questions 7 to 9 refer to the following table, where the densities of several common solids are given.

Density of some common solids

Material	Density (g/cm^3)
Aluminum	2.7
Copper	9
Gold	19.3
Iron	7.8
Lead	11.3
Platinum	?
Osmium	22.5

7

If a block of iron has the same mass as a block of 10.4m³ aluminum, which of the following is closest to the volume, in cubic meters, of the iron block?

A. 3.6
B. 4.0
C. 20.8
D. 30

8

If the density of Platinum is bigger than that of Gold, what is the median of the densities of the seven materials listed in the table, in g/cm^3?

A. 9
B. 11.3
C. 10.15
D. 15.3

9

If the density of Platinum is $8g/cm^3$ higher than the average density of the seven materials listed in the table, which of the following is closest to the density of Platinum in g/cm^3?

A. 18.0
B. 19.3
C. 20.5
D. 21.4

10

If $5b+4 \geq 2b-11$, which of the following describes all possible values of b?

A. $b \geq -5$
B. $b \leq -5$
C. $b \geq 5$
D. $b \leq 5$

11

If $x^2-4y^2=2016$ and $x+2y=4$, then $x-2y=$

A. 504
B. 1008
C. –2012
D. 8064

CONTINUE →

12

In a contest, a problem is given to all of the players, and the grand prize is awarded to the fastest problem solver. If the problem is solved within one hour, the prize is $10,000. After one hour, for each additional minute the winner spends, the prize is decreased by $300. We know Elias solved the problem in m minutes and won the competition, what was the prize (in dollars) he got? (You may assume he spent more than 1 hour and also his prize was positive.)

A. $10,000-300m$
B. $10,000-60\times300m$
C. $28,000-60m$
D. $28,000-300m$

13

Which of the following equations has exactly one value of x?

A. $(x-5)^2+3=0$
B. $(x+12)(x-21)=0$
C. $2x^2-12x=-18$
D. $x^2-4x+1=0$

14

Line a has equation $-2x+y-7=0$. Line b passes through two points $(-3, 5)$ and $(2, 15)$. Then which of the following is true?

A. a and b intersects at a point where $x>0$.
B. a and b intersects at a point where $x<0$.
C. a and b are two parallel lines.
D. a and b are the same line.

15

A popular website has 20 servers to serve the user requests. Data shows that on Monday it served 200000 user visits between 10 A.M. and 9 P.M. On average each user stayed for 5 minutes and issued 23 requests. Which of the following is closest to the average number of user requests one server handled in one second, during that particular period of time on Monday?

A. 6
B. 8
C. 10
D. 48

16

At 7:00 A.M., a tank contains 5000 gallons of water. Each minute 20 gallons of water flows into the tank, and 45 gallons of water flows out of the tank. Other than these, no water flows into or out of the tank. At what time will the tank first become empty? (Note: 1 hour = 60 minutes)

A. 10:00 A.M.
B. 10:20 A.M.
C. 10:30 A.M.
D. 11:00 A.M.

CONTINUE

17

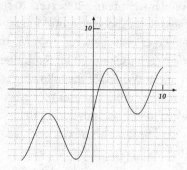

The graph of $f(x)$ is shown above. Let $g(x)=-(f(x)+4)$. Which of the following is the graph for $g(x)$?

A.

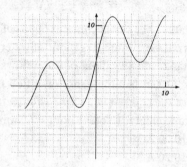

B.

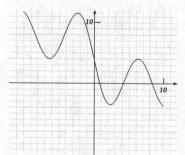

C.

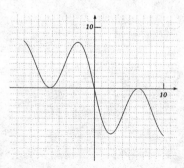

D.

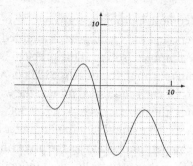

18

If $2x+y=9$ and $8(x+y)=56$, what is the value of $3x-y$?

A. 1
B. 2
C. 3
D. 4

19

Doris has an account for running her small business. She starts with 5,000 dollars on the account. She sells each item at the price of a dollars and spends 3 dollars for manufacturing and shipping every 10 items. Which of the following models the balance on her account after she sells x items, assuming x is a multiple of 10?

A. $f(a, x) = 5{,}000 + a - 3x$
B. $f(a, x) = 5{,}000 + a - 0.3x$
C. $f(a, x) = 5{,}000 + ax - 3x$
D. $f(a, x) = 5{,}000 - 3a + x$

CONTINUE

20

According to Newton's law of universal gravitation, every point mass attracts every single other point mass by a force pointing along the line passing through both points. The force is proportional to the product of the two masses and inversely proportional to the square of the distance between them, i.e., $F = G\dfrac{m_1 m_2}{r^2}$, where F is the force, m_1 and m_2 are the masses of the two points, r is the distance between them, and $G \approx 6.673 \times 10^{-11}\,\text{N} \cdot (\dfrac{m}{kg})^2$ is the gravitational constant. If the force between two points of masses is 3000N when they are 10000 m apart, what will be the force if they keep their masses and become $10000\sqrt{5}$ m apart?

A. $500\sqrt{5}$ N

B. 600N

C. $3000\sqrt{5}$ N

D. 15000N

21

Jill paid $4.15 for lunch with dimes and quarters. If he paid 25 coins in total, how many of these are dimes?

A. 12

B. 14

C. 15

D. 18

Problems 22 and 23 refer to the following information.

Forest loss has many negative impacts on the environment, including decreased forest habitat and carbon storage, but increased soil erosion, desertification and flooding. The table below shows the world forest cover, in Mha (million hectares), by regions.

	1990	2000	2010
Africa	749	709	674
Asia	576	570	593
Europe	989	998	1005
North and Central America	708	705	705
Oceania	199	198	191
South America	946	904	864

22

According to the table above, in year 2010, approximately what percentage of forests covers of the Americas are from South America?

A. 21%

B. 40%

C. 55%

D. 80%

23

According to the table, there are three regions having a drop in forest cover from 2000 to 2010. Among these three, what is approximately the biggest drop ratio among the drop ratios in these three regions?

A. 4.4%

B. 4.9%

C. 5.2%

D. 5.4%

CONTINUE

24

The traffic of a website steadily increased in the beginning of this year. Sometime later a series of hacker attack appeared. To make it worse, a competitor launched a similar website. As a result, the traffic of the website suffered a near-linear decrease. The company fought these problems by redesign the website as well as the security module of the system. After this the traffic blossomed again and quickly reached the peak of the year. For the last three months the traffic had a steadily slow decrease due to the usual winter season recession for online shopping in their category. According to the information thus mentioned, which of the following picture most accurately graphs the function of the traffic in terms of the time during the year?

A.

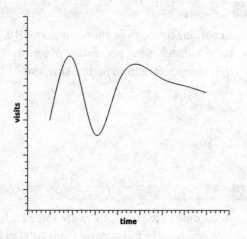

B.

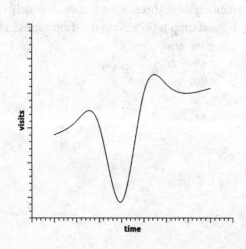

C.

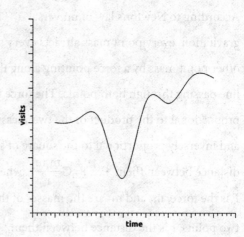

D.

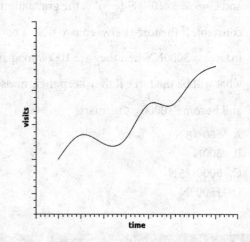

25

Which of the following accurately rewrites the expression $\frac{12^{2-t}}{3 \cdot 5^{1-2t}}$ in the form $A \cdot B^t$?

A. $\frac{48}{5}(\frac{25}{12})^t$

B. $\frac{16}{5}(\frac{12}{25})^t$

C. $\frac{48}{5}(\frac{12}{25})^t$

D. $\frac{16}{5}(\frac{12}{5})^t$

CONTINUE

Problems 26 to 28 are based on the following information.

Irene and Phoebe started working at the same time with the same starting salary of $80000 per year. As their contracts indicate, every year Irene's annual salary will increase by $9500, while Phoebe's annual salary will increase by 10%.

26

According to the information above, how much higher will be Irene's salary than Phoebe's salary after one year?

A. $0
B. $1000
C. $1500
D. $2000

27

Which of the following functions accurately models the relation between Phoebe's annual salary (y) in dollars and the number of years (x) after she starts working?

A. $y=80000+5000x$
B. $y=80000+8000x$
C. $y=80000(1.1)^x$
D. $y=80000+8000^x$

28

According to the information above and no other changes will be made to their salary, what will happen after 10 years if they still stay in the same company?

A. Irene's annual salary will be at least $10000 higher than Phoebe's.
B. Irene's annual salary will be higher than Phoebe's, but the difference will be less than $10000.
C. Phoebe's annual salary will be higher than Irene's; the difference will be less than $10000.
D. Phoebe's annual salary will be higher than Irene's by at least $10000.

29

A triangle has three sides a, b, and c. If $a=3.2$, $b=5.3$, and c is an integer, how many possible values are there for c?

A. 3
B. 4
C. 5
D. 6

30

If a is a positive integer, which of the following MUST always be an integer as well?

A. $\dfrac{(a+2)(a+3)(a+5)}{3}$

B. $\dfrac{2a+1}{2}$

C. $\dfrac{a^2+a+8}{4}$

D. $\dfrac{a(a+1)(a+2)}{6}$

CONTINUE

DIRECTIONS

For questions 31–38, solve the problem and enter your answer in the grid, as described below, on the answer sheet.

1. Although not required, it is suggested that you write your answer in the boxes at the top of the columns to help you fill in the circles accurately. You will receive credit only if the circles are filled in correctly.

2. Mark no more than one circle in any column.

3. No question has a negative answer.

4. Some problems may have more than one correct answer. In such cases, grid only one answer.

5. **Mixed numbers** such as $3\frac{1}{2}$ must be gridded as 3.5 or 7/2. (If 3 1 / 2 is entered into the grid, it will be interpreted as $\frac{31}{2}$, not $3\frac{1}{2}$.)

6. **Decimal answers:** If you obtain a decimal answer with more digits than the grid can accommodate, it may be either rounded or truncated, but it must fill the entire grid.

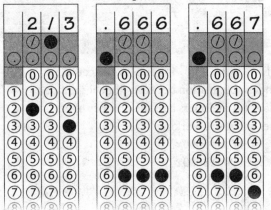

Answer: $\frac{7}{12}$ — Write answer in boxes. ← Fraction line — Grid in result.

Answer: 2.5 — ← Decimal point

Acceptable ways to grid $\frac{2}{3}$ are:

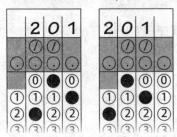

Answer: 201 – either position is correct

NOTE: You may start your answers in any column, space permitting. Columns you don't need to use should be left blank.

CONTINUE ➤

31

	Myopia	Non−myopia
Pass on first test	715	2031
Fail on first test	217	350

A local Division of Motor Vehicles (DMV) conducted a study on the effects different items may have on the new drivers' performance on their road test. The table above summarizes one of the items they observed. According to the table, what percentage, rounded to the nearest integer, of the people who have myopia failed their first road test?

32

If (a, b) is a point on the line $a-2b=1$, what is the value of $a^2+4b^2-4ab+4$?

33

If $\dfrac{3(\sqrt{2x}-3)}{4}=9$, what is the value of $\sqrt{2x}-1$?

34

Three large and one small pumps can fill a swimming pool in 3 hours; two large and two small pumps can fill the same pool in 4 hours. If we want to fill the same pool using one large and four small pumps, how many MINUTES will be needed?

35

The total cost for company M to print a collection of books is $1800 plus $9 per copy. Each copy sells for $24. The gross profit earned from printing and selling these books is the total income from sales minus the total production cost. If a collection of 3000 books is printed and sold, then what is this company's gross profit per book?

36

How many integers between 1 and 100 satisfy the equation $|x-12.56|+|x-34.56|=22$?

CONTINUE

Problems 37 and 38 refer to the following information.

Karl is learning a new language and he has a method to acquire new words. Before the first day he already knows 100 basic words in the new language. He plans to learn 5 new words on day 1, then 10 on day 2, 15 on day 3. On the x–th day he will learn $5x$ new words.

37

On the 5th day he will learn 25 new words. How many words he will know in total after 9 days?

38

The number of words he knows in this new language can be modeled as a quadratic function in the number of days. In how many days will Karl know 3000 words?

STOP

If you finish before time is called, you may check your work on this section only. Do not turn to any other section.

New SAT Practice Essay 4

 ESSAY BOOK

DIRECTIONS

The essay gives you an opportunity to show how effectively you can read and comprehend a passage and write an essay analyzing the passage. In your essay, you should demonstrate that you have read the passage carefully, present a clear and logical analysis, and use language precisely.

Your essay must be written on the lines provided in your answer booklet; except for the Planning Page of the answer booklet, you will receive no other paper on which to write. You will have enough space if you write on every line, avoid wide margins, and keep your handwriting to a reasonable size. Remember that people who are not familiar with your handwriting will read what you write. Try to write or print so that what you are writing is legible to those readers.

You have 50 minutes to read the passage and write an essay in response to the prompt provided inside this booklet.

REMINDERS

— Do not write your essay in this booklet. Only what you write on the lined pages of your answer booklet will be evaluated.

— An off-topic essay will not be evaluated.

This cover is representative of what you'll see on test day.

As you read the passage below, consider how Chris Miles uses:

- evidence, such as facts or examples, to support claims.
- reasoning to develop ideas and to connect claims and evidence.
- stylistic or persuasive elements, such as word choice or appeals to emotion, to add power to the ideas expressed.

Adapted from Chris Miles, "Benefits of Legalizing Marijuana in Colorado: Less Crime and More Profits." Sott.net March 17, 2015. Originally published July 1, 2014

1 It's now been six months since Colorado enacted its historic marijuana legalization policy, and two big things have already happened:

2 **1. Colorado's cash crop is turning out to be even more profitable than the state could have hoped.**

3 In March alone, taxed and legal recreational marijuana sales generated nearly $19 million, up from $14 million in February. The state has garnered more than $10 million in taxes from retail sales in the first four months - money that will go to public schools and infrastructure, as well as for youth educational campaigns about substance use.

4 According to his latest budget proposal, Gov. John Hickenlooper expects a healthy $1 billion in marijuana sales over the next fiscal year. That's nearly $134 million in tax revenue. Sales from recreational shops are expected to hit $600 million, which is a more than 50% increase over what was originally expected.

5 **2. Denver crime rates have suddenly fallen.**

6 Marijuana-related arrests, which make up 50% of all drug-related crimes, have plummeted in Colorado, freeing up law enforcement to focus on other criminal activity. By removing marijuana penalties, the state saved somewhere between $12 million and $40 million in 2012, according to the Colorado Center on Law and Policy.

7 According to government data, the Denver city- and county-wide murder rate has dropped 52.9% since recreational marijuana use was legalized in January. This is compared to the same period last year, a time frame encompassing Jan. 1 through April 30.

8 As the *Huffington Post* notes, this is a far cry from wild-eyed claims by legalization opponents that legal weed was the devil's work and Colorado would see a surge in crime and drug use.

9 With only a quarter of the year's data to work from, it may be too soon to definitively attribute these changes to marijuana legalization, but the possibility of a correlative pattern is certainly worth noting.

10   We are witnessing the fruits of Colorado's legal weed experiment, and those fruits are juicy indeed.

11   Of course, Gov. Hickenlooper has completely changed his tune, saying, "While the rest of the country's economy is slowly picking back up, we're thriving here in Colorado."

12   With the fall of prohibition, the marijuana industry has developed rapidly, generating thousands of new jobs. It is estimated there are currently about 10,000 people directly involved with the blossoming weed industry, with up to 2,000 people having gained employment in the past few months alone.

13   A policy gamble that anti-marijuana activists warned would turn Denver into a drug-infested hellscape has provided the city and state with numerous benefits, and set the stage for more states and cities to follow suite.

14   **Meanwhile, in Washington**

15   In yet another sign that 2014 is shaping up to be the year of marijuana reform, the Department of Drug Enforcement (DEA) is waving a white flag and surrendering on a crucial policy issue that has kept legalization from gaining traction across the nation.

16   The DEA is now asking the Food and Drug Administration to remove marijuana from its list of the most dangerous and harmful drugs. This could signal a radical shift in the way our government regulates and enforces weed.

17   Then there's the city of Washington, D.C. This November, it's all but certain that D.C. will vote on a marijuana ballot measure and even pass it, setting up a battle with Congress to legalize. This could be the most important battle yet in the marijuana prohibition fight; D.C. is considered a staging ground for many local policies that get enacted throughout the country, and a victory for pot could open the floodgates elsewhere.

18   **America agrees**

19   Public opinion has never been more in favor of decriminalizing possession of small amounts of pot. An October 2013 Gallup poll found that 58% of adults favored legalizing marijuana for adult use.

20   In 2013, 52% thought that marijuana should be legalized, with 45% opposed. According to Pew, this is a 13-point jump from 2010, when 41% thought it should be legalized and 52% opposed. The year 2010 was when Proposition 19, which would have legalized marijuana in California, was defeated with only a 53% majority. And of course, this is a dramatic swing from 1969, when nearly 8 out of 10 Americans opposed legalization.

21   Ending prohibition saves money. Since 1970, the government has spent $1.5 trillion on "drug control," though addiction rates remain constant:

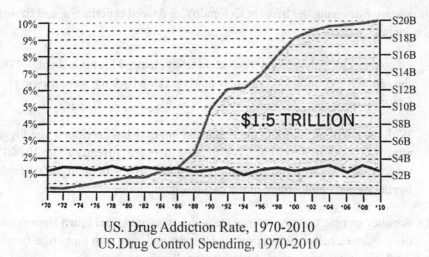

10%
9%
8%
7%
6%
5%
4%
3%
2%
1%

$1.5 TRILLION

S20B
S18B
S16B
S14B
S12B
S10B
S8B
S6B
S4B
S2B

'70 '72 '74 '76 '78 '80 '82 '84 '86 '88 '90 '92 '94 '96 '98 '00 '02 '04 '06 '08 '10

US. Drug Addiction Rate, 1970-2010
US.Drug Control Spending, 1970-2010

© Thugs Not Drugs via Mother Jones

22 If you're staring at these stark numbers and wondering why the government even bothers, you're not alone.

23 Six months after marijuana legalization, Colorado has basically proved decades of federal marijuana prohibition policy wrong. The times, they are a-changin'.

Write an essay in which you explain how Chris Miles builds an argument to persuade his audience that the federal marijuana prohibition policy is wrong. In your essay, analyze how Chris Miles uses one or more of the features listed in the box above (or features of your own choice) to strengthen the logic and persuasiveness of his argument. Be sure that your analysis focuses on the most relevant features of the passage.

Your essay should not explain whether you agree with Chris Miles, but rather explain how he builds an argument to persuade his audience.

■ TEST NUMBER   ■ SECTION 1

ENTER TEST NUMBER

For instance, for Practice Test # 1, fill in the circle for 0 in the first column and for 1 in the second column.

1 ○ ○
2 ○ ○
3 ○ ○
4 ○ ○
5 ○ ○
6 ○ ○
7 ○ ○
8 ○ ○
9 ○ ○

	A	B	C	D		A	B	C	D		A	B	C	D		A	B	C	D
1	○	○	○	○	14	○	○	○	○	27	○	○	○	○	40	○	○	○	○
2	○	○	○	○	15	○	○	○	○	28	○	○	○	○	41	○	○	○	○
3	○	○	○	○	16	○	○	○	○	29	○	○	○	○	42	○	○	○	○
4	○	○	○	○	17	○	○	○	○	30	○	○	○	○	43	○	○	○	○
5	○	○	○	○	18	○	○	○	○	31	○	○	○	○	44	○	○	○	○
6	○	○	○	○	19	○	○	○	○	32	○	○	○	○	45	○	○	○	○
7	○	○	○	○	20	○	○	○	○	33	○	○	○	○	46	○	○	○	○
8	○	○	○	○	21	○	○	○	○	34	○	○	○	○	47	○	○	○	○
9	○	○	○	○	22	○	○	○	○	35	○	○	○	○	48	○	○	○	○
10	○	○	○	○	23	○	○	○	○	36	○	○	○	○	49	○	○	○	○
11	○	○	○	○	24	○	○	○	○	37	○	○	○	○	50	○	○	○	○
12	○	○	○	○	25	○	○	○	○	38	○	○	○	○	51	○	○	○	○
13	○	○	○	○	26	○	○	○	○	39	○	○	○	○	52	○	○	○	○

COMPLETE MARK ●   EXAMPLES OF INCOMPLETE MARKS

It is recommended that you use a No. 2 pencil. It is very important that you fill in the entire circle darkly and completely. If you change your response, erase as completely as possible. Incomplete marks or erasures may affect your score.

■ SECTION 2

	A B C D		A B C D		A B C D		A B C D		A B C D
1	○○○○	10	○○○○	19	○○○○	28	○○○○	37	○○○○
2	○○○○	11	○○○○	20	○○○○	29	○○○○	38	○○○○
3	○○○○	12	○○○○	21	○○○○	30	○○○○	39	○○○○
4	○○○○	13	○○○○	22	○○○○	31	○○○○	40	○○○○
5	○○○○	14	○○○○	23	○○○○	32	○○○○	41	○○○○
6	○○○○	15	○○○○	24	○○○○	33	○○○○	42	○○○○
7	○○○○	16	○○○○	25	○○○○	34	○○○○	43	○○○○
8	○○○○	17	○○○○	26	○○○○	35	○○○○	44	○○○○
9	○○○○	18	○○○○	27	○○○○	36	○○○○		

■ SECTION 3

1 Ⓐ Ⓑ Ⓒ Ⓓ   4 Ⓐ Ⓑ Ⓒ Ⓓ   7 Ⓐ Ⓑ Ⓒ Ⓓ   10 Ⓐ Ⓑ Ⓒ Ⓓ   13 Ⓐ Ⓑ Ⓒ Ⓓ
2 Ⓐ Ⓑ Ⓒ Ⓓ   5 Ⓐ Ⓑ Ⓒ Ⓓ   8 Ⓐ Ⓑ Ⓒ Ⓓ   11 Ⓐ Ⓑ Ⓒ Ⓓ   14 Ⓐ Ⓑ Ⓒ Ⓓ
3 Ⓐ Ⓑ Ⓒ Ⓓ   6 Ⓐ Ⓑ Ⓒ Ⓓ   9 Ⓐ Ⓑ Ⓒ Ⓓ   12 Ⓐ Ⓑ Ⓒ Ⓓ   15 Ⓐ Ⓑ Ⓒ Ⓓ

Only answers that are gridded will be scored. You will not receive credit for anything written in the boxes.

16   17   18   19   20

/	○ ○	/ ○ ○	/ ○ ○	/ ○ ○	/ ○ ○
. ○ ○ ○	. ○ ○ ○	. ○ ○ ○	. ○ ○ ○	. ○ ○ ○
0 ○ ○ ○	0 ○ ○ ○	0 ○ ○ ○	0 ○ ○ ○	0 ○ ○ ○
1 ○ ○ ○	1 ○ ○ ○	1 ○ ○ ○	1 ○ ○ ○	1 ○ ○ ○
2 ○ ○ ○	2 ○ ○ ○	2 ○ ○ ○	2 ○ ○ ○	2 ○ ○ ○
3 ○ ○ ○	3 ○ ○ ○	3 ○ ○ ○	3 ○ ○ ○	3 ○ ○ ○
4 ○ ○ ○	4 ○ ○ ○	4 ○ ○ ○	4 ○ ○ ○	4 ○ ○ ○
5 ○ ○ ○	5 ○ ○ ○	5 ○ ○ ○	5 ○ ○ ○	5 ○ ○ ○
6 ○ ○ ○	6 ○ ○ ○	6 ○ ○ ○	6 ○ ○ ○	6 ○ ○ ○
7 ○ ○ ○	7 ○ ○ ○	7 ○ ○ ○	7 ○ ○ ○	7 ○ ○ ○
8 ○ ○ ○	8 ○ ○ ○	8 ○ ○ ○	8 ○ ○ ○	8 ○ ○ ○
9 ○ ○ ○	9 ○ ○ ○	9 ○ ○ ○	9 ○ ○ ○	9 ○ ○ ○

NO CALCULATOR ALLOWED

■ SECTION 4

	A B C D			A B C D			A B C D			A B C D			A B C D
1	○○○○	7	○○○○	13	○○○○	19	○○○○	25	○○○○
2	○○○○	8	○○○○	14	○○○○	20	○○○○	26	○○○○
3	○○○○	9	○○○○	15	○○○○	21	○○○○	27	○○○○
4	○○○○	10	○○○○	16	○○○○	22	○○○○	28	○○○○
5	○○○○	11	○○○○	17	○○○○	23	○○○○	29	○○○○
6	○○○○	12	○○○○	18	○○○○	24	○○○○	30	○○○○

CALCULATOR
ALLOWED

COMPLETE MARK ●   EXAMPLES OF INCOMPLETE MARKS   Ⓐ ⊗ ⊖ Ⓒ ● ⊘ ⬟ Ⓐ

It is recommended that you use a No. 2 pencil. It is very important that you fill in the entire circle darkly and completely. If you change your response, erase as completely as possible. Incomplete marks or erasures may affect your score.

■ SECTION 4 (Continued)

Only answers that are gridded will be scored. You will not receive credit for anything written in the boxes.

31 **32** **33** **34** **35**

/ ○○
.○○○○
0○○○○○
1○○○○○
2○○○○○
3○○○○○
4○○○○○
5○○○○○
6○○○○○
7○○○○○
8○○○○○
9○○○○○

Only answers that are gridded will be scored. You will not receive credit for anything written in the boxes.

36 **37** **38**

/ ○○
.○○○○
0○○○○○
1○○○○○
2○○○○○
3○○○○○
4○○○○○
5○○○○○
6○○○○○
7○○○○○
8○○○○○
9○○○○○

CALCULATOR ALLOWED

IMPORTANT: USE A NO. 2 PENCIL. DO NOT WRITE OUTSIDE THE BORDER!
Words written outside the essay box or written in ink **WILL NOT APPEAR** in the copy sent to be scored, and your score will be affected.

PLANNING PAGE You may plan your essay in the unlined planning space below, but use only the lined pages following this one to write your essay. Any work on this planning page will not be scored.

Use pages 7 through 10 for your ESSAY ⟶

FOR PLANNING ONLY

Use pages 7 through 10 for your ESSAY ⟶

BEGIN YOUR ESSAY HERE.

SERIAL #

You may continue on the next page.

You may continue on the next page.

STOP.

New SAT Practice Test 5

Reading Test

65 MINUTES, 52 QUESTIONS

Turn to Section 1 of your answer sheet to answer the questions in this section.

DIRECTIONS

Each passage or pair of passages below is followed by a number of questions. After reading each passage or pair, choose the best answer to each question based on what is stated or implied in the passage or passages and in any accompanying graphics (such as a table or graph).

Questions 1 – 11 are based on the following passage.

-Adapted from "Amazon 'deforestation' threshold causes species loss to accelerate", University of Cambridge, Science Daily, 4 March 2015.

By measuring the loss of a core tranche of dominant species of large and medium-sized mammals and birds, and using the results as a
Line bellwether, the researchers found that for every
5   10% of forest loss, one to two major species are wiped out.

This is until the threshold of 43% of forest cover is reached, beyond which the rate of biodiversity loss jumps from between two to up to
10   eight major species gone per 10% of disappeared forest.

While current Brazilian law requires individual landowners in the Amazon to retain 80% forest cover, this is rarely achieved or
15   enforced. Researchers say that the focus should be shifted to maintaining 50% cover — just half the forest — but over entire landscapes rather than individual farms, in a bid to stop whole regions losing untold biodiversity by slipping
20   below the 43% threshold at which species loss accelerates.

Unless urgent action is taken to stem deforestation in key areas that are heading towards or have just dipped below the forest cover 'threshold'
25   — which, according to the research team's models,

amounts to a third of the Amazon — these areas will suffer the loss of between 31-44% of species by just 2030.

The researchers worked across an area of
30   the North West Amazon over three million hectares in size. They then divided the region into 1,223 squares of 10,000km, and selected 31 squares representative of the spectrum of forest cover across the region (12-90% cover). 27
35   squares consisted of private land; only four were protected areas (PAs). PAs were only areas in region with almost complete forest cover.

Within the 31 squares, researchers analysed the presence of 35 key species of mammals and
40   birds for which these regions are natural habitats, such as pumas, giant anteaters and red howler monkeys. This was done through a combination of direct observation and recording evidence such as footprints and feces, as well as in-depth
45   interviews with landowners and residents, who were quizzed about species presence through photographs, animal noises and local knowledge.

They found a cut-off, conservatively given as 43% forest cover, below which the squares held
50   "markedly fewer species," with up to eight key species lost for every 10% of further deforestation beyond this threshold.

"This is not just a result of overall loss of habitat, but also reduced connectivity between
55   remaining forest fragments, causing species to

CONTINUE ➤

hunt and mate in ever-decreasing circles," one reseacher states. "This fragmentation may be the key element of the 'threshold' tipping point for biodiversity."

60   Encroaching agriculture — from beef to soya production — to feed a growing and more affluent human population means that, at the current rates, the number of 10,000km^2 landscapes in the Amazon that fall below the species loss threshold

65 of 43% forest cover will almost double by just 2030. At current rates, by 2030 only a mere 22% of landscapes in the region will be able to sustain three quarters of the key species surveyed for the study.

The expansion of agriculture in recent
70 decades means that around 41% of the original forest in the study region — some two million hectares — has been lost over just the last 40 years.

Researchers say that while PAs can counter
75 agricultural expansion — and many have increasingly called for PAs to expand across the planet amid dire evidence of rapid species decline — the limits on land that can be set aside for PAs means that biodiversity conservation success depends on
80 protecting native vegetation on private lands.

The highest priority landscapes, some 33% of land in the region, are those that either just dipped below the 43% threshold in 2010, or are expected to in the next 20 years.

85   "Avoiding deforestation and focusing reforestation in the areas that teeter on the species loss threshold will be the most direct and cost-effective way to prevent further species loss in the Amazon region," added scientists.

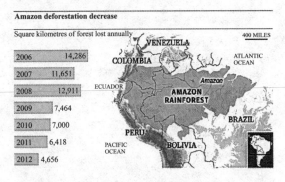

Amazon deforestation decrease

Square kilometres of forest lost annually

2006	14,286
2007	11,651
2008	12,911
2009	7,464
2010	7,000
2011	6,418
2012	4,656

-adapted from "Amazon Rainforest Deforestation Hits Record Low" in The Guardian, 28 Novem

---

1

The main purpose of the article is to
A. discuss the diverse ecosystem, flora, and fauna contained within the Amazon Rainforest.
B. sway the reader to reduce the amount of unrenewable resources consumed by the world population.
C. warn the reader of the impending effects of deforestation on biodiversity in a unique ecosystem.
D. suggest alternatives to the traditional farming methods.

2

It can be inferred from the passage that
A. the current amount of protected areas are not enough to reverse the impacts deforestation has had on reducing wildlife diversity.
B. increasing the amount of protected areas may provide little assistance in reducing the rates of deforestation.
C. species that are currently threatened or endangered are making comebacks in newly created protected areas.
D. changes to Brazilian law have provided meaningful benefits in reducing deforestation in areas of agricultural growth.

3

The term *tranche* used in line 1 most closely means:
A. population
B. representatives
C. ditch
D. portion

CONTINUE ➤

4

Based upon information contained in the article, which of the following is most likely true?

A. Animal migration due to agricultural encroachment has become a necessity for species survival.

B. Animal migration from areas that fall below the 43% forest cover threshold to more densely wooded areas is extremely difficult.

C. Agricultural encroachment has led to greater effects of poaching on biodiversity by providing accidental "access roads" to densely wooded areas of jungle.

D. There is little in the way of Brazilian law that protects species survival.

5

Evidence for the answer to the previous question can best be found in

A. lines 38-42, "Within the 31 squares, researchers analysed…"

B. lines 60-66, "Encroaching agriculture…"

C. lines 53-59, "This is not just a result…"

D. lines 69-73, "The expansion of agriculture…"

6

The term *encroaching* as used in line 60 most closely means:

A. bustling

B. expanding

C. profitable

D. intruding

7

From the research statistics cited, it can be assumed that

A. human demand for consumable products is a central factor influencing the rates of deforestation.

B. beef ranching has led to increasing demand for grains and feed products, eventually leading to higher rates of deforestation.

C. biodiversity is showing evidence of being reintroduced to protected areas.

D. economic development in rural areas is largely to blame for increased rates of deforestation in central Brazil.

8

The graphic depicted best indicates that

A. deforestation rates have been largely variable in recent years.

B. the period between 2009-2011 saw relatively stagnant deforestation rates.

C. recent law and policy changes have done little to affect rates of Amazon deforestation.

D. there were no noted increases in deforestation rates between any two years depicted in the graph.

CONTINUE

9

The author would most likely agree with the theory that

A. protected areas have provided sufficient support to curtail the effects in deforestation on biodiversity.

B. agricultural expansion must immediately be halted in all areas to best support a greater reduction in deforestation rates.

C. conservation should focus on areas that will approach the 43% forest cover threshold cited by 2030 to best preserve biodiversity.

D. current Brazilian law and policy on agricultural expansion and deforestation are enough to help reduce deforestation rates.

10

Based upon the information provided in the article, researchers likely

A. are ardently anti-agriculture and are ranching proponents intent on pursuing their environmental agenda.

B. have little faith in the ability of the Brazilian government to enforce landowner laws regarding forest cover.

C. believe protected areas are not being properly supervised and, thus, have become an ineffective means of environmental protection.

D. believe current conservation laws are focusing on incorrect areas to achieve the greatest impact of reducing deforestation.

11

Evidence for the previous question is best found in

A. lines 15-21, "Researchers say that the focus should be shifted…"

B. lines 60-66, "Encroaching agriculture…"

C. lines 74-80, "Researchers say that while…"

D. lines 7-11, "This is until the threshold…"

CONTINUE

Questions 12-21 deal with the passage below.

-Adapted from Susan B. Anthony's speech to Congress, 1873

Friends and fellow citizens: I stand before you tonight under indictment for the alleged crime of having voted at the last presidential election,
Line without having a lawful right to vote. It shall
5 be my work this evening to prove to you that in thus voting, I not only committed no crime, but, instead, simply exercised my citizen's rights, guaranteed to me and all United States citizens by the National Constitution, beyond the power of
10 any state to deny.

The preamble of the Federal Constitution says:

"We, the people of the United States, in order to form a more perfect union, establish justice,
15 insure domestic tranquillity, provide for the common defense, promote the general welfare, and secure the blessings of liberty to ourselves and our posterity, do ordain and establish this Constitution for the United States of America."
20 It was we, the people; not we, the white male citizens; nor yet we, the male citizens; but we, the whole people, who formed the Union. And we formed it, not to give the blessings of liberty, but to secure them; not to the half of ourselves and
25 the half of our posterity, but to the whole people - women as well as men. And it is a downright mockery to talk to women of their enjoyment of the blessings of liberty while they are denied the use of the only means of securing them provided
30 by this democratic-republican government — the ballot.

For any state to make sex a qualification that must ever result in the disfranchisement of one entire half of the people, is to pass a bill of
35 attainder, or, an ex post facto law, and is therefore a violation of the supreme law of the land. By it the blessings of liberty are forever withheld from women and their female posterity.

To them this government has no just powers
40 derived from the consent of the governed. To them this government is not a democracy. It

is not a republic. It is an odious aristocracy; a hateful oligarchy of sex; the most hateful aristocracy ever established on the face of the
45 globe; an oligarchy of wealth, where the rich govern the poor. An oligarchy of learning, where the educated govern the ignorant, or even an oligarchy of race, where the Saxon rules the African, might be endured; but this oligarchy of
50 sex, which makes father, brothers, husband, sons, the oligarchs over the mother and sisters, the wife and daughters, of every household - which ordains all men sovereigns, all women subjects, carries dissension, discord, and rebellion into
55 every home of the nation.

Webster, Worcester, and Bouvier all define a citizen to be a person in the United States, entitled to vote and hold office.

The only question left to be settled now is: Are
60 women persons? And I hardly believe any of our opponents will have the hardihood to say they are not. Being persons, then, women are citizens; and no state has a right to make any law, or to enforce any old law, that shall abridge their privileges or
65 immunities. Hence, every discrimination against women in the constitutions and laws of the several states is today null and void, precisely as is every one against Negroes.

12

The author seeks to point out that
A. denying women's suffrage rights is unconstitutional and misogynistic.
B. suffrage rights are state's obligation to determine on an individual basis.
C. many current politicians would agree with the idea that most women are not persons.
D. we are, in effect, living under a constitutional monarchy.

CONTINUE

13

The author's perspective that prohibiting women's suffrage is tantamount to the "disenfranchisement of one entire half of the people..." refers most to

A. the plight of African American former slaves to achieve emancipated status.
B. the prevention of some citizens by states, to be afforded rights available to others, violates Constitutional law.
C. recent voter law changes allowing women to vote in upcoming elections.
D. her desire to change wording of the Preamble to the Constitution to include the term "women."

14

The answer to the previous question is best found in

A. lines 42-46, "It is an odious aristocracy..."
B. lines 32-36, "for any state to make sex a qualification..."
C. lines 26-31, "and it is a downright mockery..."
D. lines 62-68, "being persons, then, women are..."

15

The term *odious* used in line 42 most closely means:

A. regal
B. unilateral
C. abhorrent
D. trustworthy

16

The political position of the author can generally be described as:

A. laissez-faire
B. "small government" with greater rights empowered to the state
C. a belief in a strong, centralized government where federal law supersedes state law
D. feminist-socialist

17

Evidence for the previous question can best be found in:

A. lines 6-10, "I not only committed no crime..."
B. lines 20-22, "It was we the people..."
C. lines 39-46, "To them, this government..."
D. lines 26-31, "and it is a downright mockery..."

18

It can be assumed from the author's position on women's suffrage that she believes

A. voter laws will be changed in the near future.
B. there is little legal evidence to support her claim that women are defined as "persons" by the government.
C. equal rights appear to exist in most facets of society with the exception of women's suffrage rights.
D. ramifications of this law most likely have resulted in discord and inter-family disputes due to its view of women as objects and not people.

19

The term *posterity* used in line 25 most closely means:

A. population
B. descendants
C. government
D. ancestors

CONTINUE

From the passage, it can be inferred from the author's position that she would most likely agree with which of the following statements:

A. It is hypocritical of individuals to enjoy and benefit from the rights guaranteed by the Constitution to all persons while certain populations are stigmatized.
B. Enforcement of "unalienable rights" guaranteed in the Constitution is best left to states based upon demographical information.
C. The objectification of women by our founding fathers is deeply rooted in gender roles apparent in other aristocratic nations.
D. Our current society cannot necessarily be blamed for the misogynistic perspective from which it currently operates.

It can be assumed from the tone of the selection that the author believes strongly in

A. a break from founding documents and a pursuit of more gender-equal literature to govern the land.
B. a semantic discussion regarding terminology contained in the laws or our country.
C. absolute equal rights for all "persons", or citizens, of the nation.
D. encroachment of state's rights by the federal government in an effort to create a more equal society.

Questions 22-32 deal with the passage below.

-adapted from "The Raven" by Edgar Allan Poe

Deep into that darkness peering, long I stood
there wondering, fearing,
Doubting, dreaming dreams no mortals ever
Line   dared to dream before;
5   But the silence was unbroken, and the stillness
gave no token,
And the only word there spoken was the
whispered word, 'Lenore!'
This I whispered, and an echo murmured back
10   the word, 'Lenore!'—
Merely this, and nothing more.

Back into the chamber turning, all my soul within
me burning,
Soon again I heard a tapping somewhat louder
15   than before.
'Surely,' said I, 'surely that is something at my
window lattice:
Let me see, then, what thereat is, and this mystery
explore—
20   Let my heart be still a moment and this mystery
explore;—
'Tis the wind and nothing more.'

Open here I flung the shutter, when, with many a
flirt and flutter,
25   In there stepped a stately raven of the saintly days
of yore;
Not the least obeisance made he; not a minute
stopped or stayed he;
But, with mien of lord or lady, perched above my
30   chamber door—
Perched upon a bust of Pallas just above my
chamber door—
Perched, and sat, and nothing more.

Then this ebony bird beguiling my sad fancy into
35   smiling,
By the grave and stern decorum of the countenance it wore.
'Though thy crest be shorn and shaven, thou,' I
said, 'art sure no craven,

40   Ghastly grim and ancient raven wandering from
the Nightly shore—
Tell me what thy lordly name is on the Night's
Plutonian shore!'
Quoth the Raven, 'Nevermore.'

45   Much I marvelled this ungainly fowl to hear
discourse so plainly,
Though its answer little meaning— little
relevancy bore;
For we cannot help agreeing that no living human
50   being
Ever yet was blest with seeing bird above his
chamber door—
Bird or beast upon the sculptured bust above his
chamber door,
55   With such name as 'Nevermore.'

But the raven, sitting lonely on the placid bust,
spoke only
That one word, as if his soul in that one word he
did outpour.
60   Nothing further then he uttered— not a feather
then he fluttered—
Till I scarcely more than muttered, 'other friends
have flown before—
On the morrow he will leave me, as my hopes
65   have flown before.'
Then the bird said, 'Nevermore.'

Startled at the stillness broken by reply so aptly
spoken,
'Doubtless,' said I, 'what it utters is its only stock
70   and store,
Caught from some unhappy master whom
unmerciful Disaster
Followed fast and followed faster till his songs
one burden bore—
75   Till the dirges of his Hope that melancholy
burden bore Of 'Never— nevermore.'

But the Raven still beguiling all my fancy into
smiling,
Straight I wheeled a cushioned seat in front of
80   bird, and bust and door;

CONTINUE ➤

Then upon the velvet sinking, I betook myself to linking
Fancy unto fancy, thinking what this ominous bird of yore—
85 What this grim, ungainly, ghastly, gaunt and ominous bird of yore
Meant in croaking 'Nevermore.'

This I sat engaged in guessing, but no syllable expressing
90 To the fowl whose fiery eyes now burned into my bosom's core;
This and more I sat divining, with my head at ease reclining
On the cushion's velvet lining that the lamplight
95 gloated o'er,
But whose velvet violet lining with the lamplight gloating o'er,
She shall press, ah, nevermore!

Then methought the air grew denser, perfumed
100 from an unseen censer
Swung by Seraphim whose footfalls tinkled on the tufted floor.
'Wretch,' I cried, 'thy God hath lent thee— by these angels he hath sent thee
105 Respite— respite and nepenthe, from thy memories of Lenore!
Quaff, oh quaff this kind nepenthe and forget this lost Lenore!'
Quoth the Raven, 'Nevermore.'

110 'Prophet!' said I, 'thing of evil!— prophet still, if bird or devil!—
Whether Tempter sent, or whether tempest tossed thee here ashore,
Desolate yet all undaunted, on this desert land
115 enchanted—
On this home by horror haunted— tell me truly, I implore—
Is there— is there balm in Gilead?— tell me— tell me, I implore!'
120 Quoth the Raven, 'Nevermore.'

'Prophet!' said I, 'thing of evil— prophet still, if

bird or devil!
By that Heaven that bends above us— by that God we both adore—
Tell this soul with sorrow laden if, within the
125 distant Aidenn,
It shall clasp a sainted maiden whom the angels name Lenore—
Clasp a rare and radiant maiden whom the angels name Lenore.'
130 Quoth the Raven, 'Nevermore.'

22

The initial appearance and imagery of the raven to the protagonist serves to
A. create a sense of horror and fear within the main character.
B. inspire curiosity and wonder on the part of the protagonist.
C. immediately serve as evidence of his lost love.
D. foster perplexed feelings and paranoia.

23

The literary technique of empowering the raven to speak only one word is most likely representative of which of the following:
A. supporting the main character's assertion that the bird has been trained and is lost
B. foreshadowing of the protagonist's impending descent into madness
C. illustration of the author's use of iambic pentameter to convey feelings
D. reinforcement of the protagonist's increasingly intense feelings of solitude and isolation

24

The use of the term *implore* in line 117 most closely means:
A. demand
B. wonder
C. beseech
D. hope

CONTINUE ➡

25

The main theme of the passage is most likely reflective of
A. despair and hopelessness.
B. wonder and awe.
C. hopefulness and gratitude.
D. anger and resentment.

26

Evidence for the answer to the previous question is best found in
A. lines 88-94, "This I sat engaged in guessing…"
B. lines 110-119, "'Prophet' said I, 'thing of evil'"
C. lines 62-66, "Till I scarcely more than muttered…"
D. lines 67-74, "Startled at the stillness broken…"

27

The protagonist eventually associates the raven's presence as
A. confirmation of the fact that his love is deceased.
B. an embodied spirit of Lenore.
C. representative of the afterlife.
D. an attempt by an anonymous friend to provide him with companionship.

28

Evidence for the previous question is best found in
A. lines 124-127, "Tell this soul with sorrow laden…"
B. lines 81-87, "I betook myself to linking…"
C. lines 56-61, "but the raven, sitting lonely…"
D. lines 96-102, "but whose velvet, violet lining…"

29

It can be inferred from the passage that
A. Lenore was the love of his life.
B. the protagonist feels threatened by the presence of the raven.
C. the main character harbors suspicion about his safety because of the raven's unwillingness to leave.
D. Lenore was the protagonist's mother.

30

The meaning of the word *obeisance*, used in line 27, is most closely related to:
A. spectacle, disruption
B. sound, flutter
C. objection
D. respectful gesture, deference

31

Poe consistently repeats the word "nevermore" mainly in an effort to
A. contribute to the rhyme scheme contained in the poem.
B. stress the amount of restraint exhibited by the raven.
C. convey the extent of grief felt by the protagonist.
D. objectify Lenore and demean her importance to the main character.

32

From the final stanza of the poem, what can we assume the protagonist is seeking from the raven?
A. Relief from the burden of his sorrow and melancholy.
B. Companionship to combat his increasingly intense feelings of isolation.
C. Forgiveness from any misdeeds directed towards Lenore.
D. An easing of guilt for beginning to love again.

CONTINUE

Questions 33-42 deal with the passage below.

-adapted from "Rage Against the Common Core" by David Kirp, New York Times Sunday Edition, 27 December 2014

STARTING in the mid-1990s, education advocates began making a simple argument: National education standards will level the
Line playing field, assuring that all high school
5 graduates are prepared for first-year college classes or rigorous career training.

While there are reasons to doubt that claim — it's hard to see how Utah, which spends less than one-third as much per student as New York, can
10 offer a comparable education — the movement took off in 2008, when the nation's governors and education commissioners drove a huge effort to devise "world-class standards," now known as the Common Core.

15 Although the Obama administration didn't craft the standards, it weighed in heavily, using some of the $4.35 billion from the Race to the Top program to encourage states to adopt not only the Common Core (in itself, a good thing)
20 but also frequent, high-stakes testing (which is deeply unpopular). The mishandled rollout turned a conversation about pedagogy into an ideological and partisan debate over high-stakes testing. The misconception that standards and
25 testing are identical has become widespread.

At least four states that adopted the Common Core have opted out. Republican governors who initially backed the standards condemn them as "shameless government overreach."

30 Gov. Bobby Jindal of Louisiana, a Republican and a onetime supporter of the Common Core, sued his own state and the United States Department of Education to block the standards from taking effect. When Jeb Bush, the former
35 Florida governor, recently announced his decision to "actively explore" a 2016 run for the White House, he ran into a buzzsaw of opposition because of his embrace of the Common Core.

Rebellions have also sprouted in Democratic-
40 leaning states. Last spring, between 55,000 and 65,000 New York State students opted out

of taking tests linked to the Common Core. Criticizing these tests as "unproven," the Chicago schools chief, Barbara Byrd-Bennett, declared
45 that she didn't want her students to take them.

In a Phi Delta Kappa/Gallup poll conducted last spring, 57 percent of public school parents opposed "having teachers in your community use the Common Core State Standards to guide what
50 they teach," nearly double the proportion of those who supported the goals. With the standards, the sheer volume of high-stakes standardized testing has ballooned. "The numbers and consequences of these tests have driven public opinion over the
55 edge," notes Robert A. Schaeffer of the National Center for Fair and Open Testing, known as FairTest.

Students are terrified by these tests because the results can jeopardize their prospects for
60 advancement and graduation. In New York, the number of students who scored "proficient" plummeted by about 30 percentage points in 2013, the first year of testing. Some 70 percent scored below the cutoff level in math and English;
65 the 2014 results in math were modestly better, but the English language scores didn't budge.

Many teachers like the standards, because they invite creativity in the classroom — instead of memorization, the Common Core emphasizes
70 critical thinking and problem-solving. But they complain that test prep and test-taking eat away weeks of class time that would be better focused on learning.

A Gallup poll found that while 76 percent
75 of teachers favored nationwide academic standards for reading, writing and math, only 27 percent supported using tests to gauge students' performance, and 9 percent favored making test scores a basis for evaluating teachers. Such
80 antagonism is well founded — researchers have shown that measurements of the "value" teachers add, as determined by comparing test scores at the beginning and end of the year, are unreliable and biased against those who teach both low- and
85 high-achieving students.

The Obama administration has only itself

CONTINUE →

to blame. Most Democrats expected that equity would be the top education priority, with more money going to the poorest states, better teacher
90 recruitment, more useful training and closer attention to the needs of the surging population of immigrant kids. Instead, the administration has emphasized high-stakes "accountability" and market-driven reforms. The Education
95 Department has invested more than $370 million to develop the new standards and exams in math, reading and writing.

33

The main purpose of the passage can mainly be described as:

A. attempting to influence the reader towards the potential dangers associated with high stakes standardized testing.

B. blaming Democrats for the current state of affairs in the American educational system.

C. identifying Republican responses to the Common Core and the genesis of their counterproposals.

D. pleading with current politicians to repeal the Common Core standards in an effort to increase teacher creativity.

34

While the writer discusses the dangers of high stakes standardized testing, he also

A. believes that testing in general is an accurate and beneficial indicator of teacher performance.

B. cites the relative ease with which students approach testing.

C. warns against the dangers of equating enforcing the curricular standards with implementing high stakes test measures.

D. provides indications that most teachers are in favor of such practices as a means of weeding out weaker teachers.

35

Evidence for the previous question can best be found in

A. lines 67-70, "Many teachers like the standards…"

B. lines 21-25, "The mishandled rollout…"

C. lines 39-40, "Rebellions have sprouted…"

D. lines 74-79, "A Gallup poll found that…"

36

From the tone of the article, it can be inferred that

A. the author is fiercely supportive of teachers and teacher unions.

B. the author supports the Common Core standards but opposes rigorous standardized testing.

C. the Common Core lobby group is a Republican-learning organization.

D. political supporters of the program have seen their constituency grow within their home states.

37

The term *antagonism* used in line 80 most closely means:

A. loyalty
B. support
C. pessimism
D. hostility

CONTINUE

38

It can be assumed from the article that
A. many lawmakers have shifted their stance on the Common Core due to public outcry.
B. the coalition charged with developing the Common Core received no input from teachers or political figures.
C. the main thrust of Common Core was to shift money away from poorer and lower performing districts.
D. the Common Core has creative, new, and innovative ways of teaching in classrooms across the country.

39

From all of the data presented, it is most likely the case that
A. rigorous outcome measures associated with the Common Core offer an insight into student success.
B. the majority of teachers polled do not favor common, nationwide academic standards to drive instruction.
C. rigorous outcome measures of the common core offer an unfair picture of student success and performance.
D. there is no evidence of any states opting out of implementing the Common Core.

40

The answer to the previous question is best exemplified in:
A. lines 7-14, "While there are reasons to doubt that claim…"
B. lines 58-60, "Students are terrified by these tests…"
C. lines 74-79, "A Gallup poll found that…"
D. lines 15-21, "Although the Obama administration…"

41

The term *pedagogy* used in line 22 most closely means:
A. curriculum
B. method or practice of teaching
C. implementation of a law or bill
D. educational practice

42

While lawmakers assumed that Common Core would also allow for more equitable funding,
A. roughly 10% of Race to the Top money has funded unpopular programs.
B. there has been an even distribution of funds throughout the country.
C. no appreciable increases have been realized by individual school districts.
D. increases in funding to more affluent and higher performing districts have been noticed.

CONTINUE

Questions 43-52 deal with the passages below.

-adapted from "Children with regular sleep patterns 'smarter at school" by Andrew Hough in The Telegraph, 7 June 2010.

Researchers found that children who had a regular bedtime performed better at languages, reading and math than those who went to bed at
Line different times. Scientists at SRI International, an
5 independent American research institute based in California, found the earlier a child went to bed, the better they performed at school.

The study of 8000 children who were aged four concluded those who had less than the
10 recommended 11 hours of sleep each night fell behind in their studies. "Getting parents to set bedtime routines can be an important way to make a significant impact on children's emergent literacy and language skills," said Dr Erika Gaylor,
15 an early childhood policy researcher who led the study. "Paediatricians can easily promote regular bedtimes with parents and children, behaviours, which in turn lead to healthy sleep."

It also included analysis taken from on
20 information on bedtimes that were conducted with parent during phone interviews when their child was nine months old and again when their child was four. The findings found that having a regular bedtime was the most consistent
25 predictor of positive developmental outcomes.

Scores for receptive and expressive language, phonological awareness, literacy and early math abilities were higher in children whose parents reported having rules about what time their child
30 goes to bed. Children who had an earlier bedtime also had a predictive of higher scores for most developmental measures.

Dr Gaylor said the data also disclosed that many children were not getting the recom-
35 mended amount of sleep, which may have negative consequences for their development and school achievement. She recommended parents set an appropriate time for their child to go to bed so they received sufficient levels of sleep.
40 Parents, she added, should also interact with their child at bedtime using routines such as reading

books or telling stories.

A previous study, published in Sleep Medicine in August last year, also emphasised the
45 importance of an early bedtime and consistent bedtime routine for children. It reported that children with a bedtime after 9pm took longer to fall asleep and had a shorter total sleep time. Children without a consistent bedtime routine
50 also were reported to obtain less sleep.

-adapated from" Technology in kids' bedrooms disrupts sleep patterns" by Honor Whiteman, Medical News Today, 30 July 2013

Researchers from Helsinki, Finland, conducted the first long-term study to find out whether electronic media use and electronic media presence in a child's bedroom predicted or changed sleep habits. Participants in the study
55 analyzed schoolchildren aged 10 and 11 years old from 27 schools across the Scandinavian country.

Baseline measurements for the study began in 2006, where children were asked to complete a questionnaire about their health behaviors.
60 The children were asked to do the survey again 18 months later. The children were also asked about their bedtimes and wake-up times on school days and at weekends. Television viewing and computer habits were assessed to find out
65 how many hours in the day the children watched television, videos or DVDs, and played computer games. The study also enquired whether children had a television, computer or game console in their bedroom.
70 Children who had a TV or computer in their bedroom went to bed later on school days and at the weekend, meaning they were getting less sleep. Results also revealed that when analyzing girls and boys individually, boys who had a
75 computer or TV in their bedroom went to bed later compared with the girls.

"Our main findings were that computer use and television viewing predicted shorter sleep duration and later bedtimes. The more children
80 used a computer or watched a TV, the greater was the decrease in sleep duration and the delay in

CONTINUE ➡

bedtime 18 months later.

A media presence in the bedroom was also related to irregular sleep habits: a television and
85 a computer in the bedroom among boys, and a television in the bedroom among girls."

The study authors add that since no other long-term studies exist in this research area, the results show new information that associates
90 computer and television use with sleep habits 18 months later. The authors say parents, teachers and healthcare providers should be aware that television viewing and computer use may have an adverse impact on children's sleep.
95   Teija Nuutinen of the Folkhälsan Research Center and the Department of Public Health at the University of Helsinki, says:

"Children need extra sleep as they go through puberty, but our study finds that TV
100 and computer use affect the sleep of children. This is especially true during the week and may be impacting their school work as well as their development. Media viewing habits should be considered for kids who are tired and struggling
105 to concentrate, or who have behavior problems caused by lack of sleep."

43

The authors of both passages would generally agree with which of the following statements?
A. Media influences, such as television and computers, should not be accessible to students before the completion of puberty.
B. Strict enforcement of bedtimes is the most accurate predictor of academic and develop-mental gains.
C. There is little evidence to support the claim that interrupted sleep can cause damaging effects in children's development.
D. Consistent bedtimes, predictable nighttime routines, and obtaining proper amounts of sleep have shown generally positive outcomes.

44

The author of passage 1 hypothesizes
A. that while a strict bedtime is beneficial, a consistent, relationship-focused, nighttime routine may lead to optimal child development.
B. the time at which a child falls asleep is inconsequential as long as they obtain the recommended number of hours.
C. while language and reading skills may be affected by sleep patterns, performance on measures of mathematical reasoning show little change.
D. children should also have a voice in their bedtime routines, particularly regarding what times they go to bed and the activities which occur before bedtime.

45

Evidence for the answer to question 44 is best found in
A. lines 26-30, "Scores for receptive and expressive language…"
B. lines 43-46, "A previous study…"
C. lines 37-39, "She recommended parents set…"
D. lines 8-11, "The study of 8000 children…"

46

An antonym for the term *irregular* used in line 84 may be
A. inconsistent.
B. predictable.
C. interrupted.
D. early.

CONTINUE ➡

47

Increased academic performance and educational achievement, as discussed in passage 1, is supported by which recommendation from passage 2?

A. Reducing computer use and television viewing can lead to more consistent sleep patterns and better rested children.

B. Students will recoup any skills lost once they hit puberty and media influences cease to be as negative.

C. Having a computer in a child's bedroom helps reinforce academic skills.

D. Watching television as a family unit aids in bonding and, thus, willingness from children to ask for assistance when unsure of how to complete homework.

48

The author's discussion of the importance of establishing a consistent and predictable, nighttime routine on sleep patterns for a healthy lifestyle indicates they would most likely agree with which of the following scenarios?

A. A fervent anti-smoking campaign targeted at high school students and embedded in the health curriculum serving to reduce the number of student cigarette users.

B. Lowering the drinking age to those of European countries in an effort to reduce the mystification of alcohol, leading to a decrease in the amount of alcohol abused by late teens.

C. Early swimming lessons for babies in an effort to reduce infant drowning deaths due to lack of supervision.

D. Implementing a healthy diet at home and in schools to create good-eating habits through adolescence and adulthood.

49

The author of passage 2 posits that while media influences on children's bedtimes are generally negative on average:

A. Some television and computer usage can be beneficial in assisting a child in going to sleep.

B. There is no differentiation between television viewing in the bedroom and viewing in a den or living room.

C. The roles of gender on sleep habits may also be somewhat influential.

D. Media usage before 8 p.m. is not in the least harmful.

50

Evidence for the previous question is best found in

A. lines 77-82, "Our main findings were that…"

B. lines 73-76, "Results also revealed that…"

C. lines 98-100, "Children need extra sleep as they go through puberty…"

D. lines 83-86, "A media presence in the bedroom…"

STOP

If you finish before time is called, you may work on this section only. Do not turn to any other section.

301

CONTINUE

51

The main difference between the studies cited in paragraphs one and two lies in

A. the studies in paragraph one make no determination regarding the importance or role of electronic devices on sleep patterns for children.

B. the studies in paragraph two indicate that sleep duration has no influence on academic achievement or behavior problems in children.

C. the studies in paragraph one deal with students who have passed puberty, while those in paragraph two are pre-school aged students.

D. the studies in passage one are based on self-report data of children, while the studies in passage two are not based on self-report data of children.

52

The term *phonological* used in line 27 deals primarily with

A. oral language skills.

B. the sound structure of words.

C. alphabetical awareness.

D. written language skills.

STOP

If you finish before time is called, you may check your work on this section only. Do not turn to any other section.

ACKNOWLEDGEMENT FOR THIS SECTION

Passages in this section were adapted from the following sources:

"Amazon deforestation threshold causes species loss to accelerate", University of Cambridge, Science Daily, 4 March 2015.

Susan Anthony, "Speech to Congress", 1873

Andrew Hough, "Children with regular sleep patterns smart at school", © 2010 by *The Telegraph*, published 7 June 2010

David Kirp, "Rage Against the Commom Core", © 2014 by *New York Times Sunday Edition*, published 27 December 2014.

Edgar Allan Poe, "The Raven." January 1845

Honor Whiteman, "Technology in kids' bedrooms disrupts sleep patterns", © 2013 by *Medical News today*, published 30 July 2013

Writing and Language Test

35 MINUTES, 44 QUESTIONS

Turn to Section 2 of your answer sheet to answer the questions in this section.

DIRECTIONS

Each passage below is accompanied by a number of questions. For some questions, you will consider how the passage might be revised to improve the expression of ideas. For other questions, you will consider how the passage might be edited to correct errors in sentence structure, usage, or punctuation. A passage or a question may be accompanied by one or more graphics (such as a table or graph) that you will consider as you make revising and editing decisions.

Some questions will direct you to an underlined portion of a passage. Other questions will direct you to a location in a passage or ask you to think about the passage as a whole.

After reading each passage, choose the answer to each question that most effectively improves the quality of writing in the passage or that makes the passage conform to the conventions of standard written English. Many questions include a "NO CHANGE" option. Choose that option if you think the best choice is to leave the relevant portion of the passage as it is.

Questions 1 – 11 are based on the following passage.

Striving to be a Nurse

In the summer of 2014, I partnered with an organization called Hands at Work to support vulnerable communities across Africa where **1** HIV/AIDS, poverty and the numbers of orphans and widows are a record high. I spent most of my time in Zambia, Africa in a small community called Zimba **2** when I shadowed local care workers

1

A. NO CHANGE
B. HIV/AIDS poverty and the numbers of orphans and widows
C. HIV/AIDS, poverty, and the numbers of orphans, and widows
D. HIV/AIDS, poverty, and numbers of orphans and widows

2

A. NO CHANGE
B. where
C. which
D. who

CONTINUE

3 who serve the poor and helpless in their community. Through home visits, I assessed the health and security of children, identified urgent needs, **4** and provide basic physical and emotional care. We also made it a goal to raise health awareness by securing a clean water source and by teaching the communities about HIV/AIDS transmission. The trip only strengthened my convictions to strive for equality and justice in the nursing field with the intention to serve others.

5 _____ Throughout my childhood, my parents instilled in me values **6** such as compassion and respect for others, stressing the importance of giving back to the community. Nursing would be the perfect marriage between my interest in both healthcare and people. I **7** always fascinate the intricacy and complexity of the human body. For this reason, I want to further my understanding of the body and eventually contribute my knowledge to the healthcare community. I also have a huge interest towards people and my desire to become a nurse stems from the relationships developed by helping others.

I believe this about nursing, to become a nurse to not only treat the patients' illnesses but also their quality of life. I believe nursing is a great avenue to counsel, educate, and help people live better and healthier lives. My goal as a potential health

3

A. NO CHANGE
B. they serve
C. to serve
D. which serve

4

A. NO CHANGE
B. and providing
C. and provided
D. and to provide

5

Which sentence could be added to the paragraph to most effectively establish its main idea?
A. My decision to become a nurse did not come in a moment of blinding revelation but from a result of various experiences.
B. Sometimes an early childhood dream can shape up your future career decision.
C. It's not always easy to make up your mind as to what to do in the future.
D. Some people's career decisions just came in a moment of blinding revelation.

6

A. NO CHANGE
B. about
C. of
D. for

7

A. NO CHANGE
B. always fascinated
C. am always fascinated by
D. am always fascinating

CONTINUE

professional is not only to treat **8** those are physically sick, but to care for the individual's emotional and mental level as well. I've learned that illnesses and pain are inevitable in life, but with the opportunity to become a nurse, I can comfort and aid those **9** are facing their dark and often frightening truth. As a nurse, I will be able to help people get better whether they are **10** near or far, the field of medicine should know no borders. I want to be a nurse that extends a helping hand to strangers in need since that's what the profession is all about; a desire to serve those beyond your loved ones.

In conclusion, with the Robert Wood Johnson Foundation NCIN scholarship, the mentoring program has guided my decisions in the nursing career. The program has helped me develop the skills, courage, and compassion through various experiences to excel as a well-rounded nurse. My hope is to live a life that is known for helping the poor, healing the sick, showing grace to the undeserving, and **11** love others like one would have wanted to be treated.

8

A. NO CHANGE
B. those who are
C. those they are
D. those which are

9

A. NO CHANGE
B. they are
C. that are
D. DELETE the underlined portion

10

A. NO CHANGE
B. near or far where the field of medicine
C. near or far because the field of medicine
D. near or far when the field of medicine

11

A. NO CHANGE
B. loving
C. to love
D. for loving

Questions 12 – 22 are based on the following passage.

Deforestation: Compromises of a Growing World

12 With the world growing at a pace hard to match, the increasing need for space is turning out to be an area of concern. With desperate need for land for agricultural, industrial and most importantly urban needs to contain cities and their growing population, a direct action that we have come to recognize as "Deforestation" **13** occur. Deforestation in simple term means the felling and clearing of forest cover or tree plantations in order to accommodate agricultural, industrial or urban use. It involves permanent end of forest cover to make that land available for residential, commercial or industrial purpose.

Over the last century the forest cover around the globe **14** is greatly compromised, leaving the green cover down to an all time low of about 30 per cent. According to the United Nations Food and Agriculture Organization (FAO), an estimated 18 million acres (7.3 million hectares) of forest **15** are lost each year.

Deforestation can also be seen as removal of forests **16** leads to several imbalances ecologically and environmentally. What makes deforestation alarming is the immediate and long term effects it is bound to inflict **17** if continue at the current pace. Some predictions state that the rain forests of the world will be destroyed completely if deforestation continues at

12

A. NO CHANGE
B. With the world is growing
C. With the world grows
D. With the world grow

13

A. NO CHANGE
B. occurring
C. occurred
D. occurs

14

A. NO CHANGE
B. was greatly compromised,
C. has been greatly compromised,
D. is being greatly compromised,

15

A. NO CHANGE
B. is lost
C. lost
D. loses

16

A. NO CHANGE
B. leading
C. to lead
D. lead

17

A. NO CHANGE
B. if is continuing
C. if continues
D. if continued

CONTINUE

its current pace **18** without changing.

19 _____ To get an overview, we could include the need of money, both in terms of profit-ability as well as **20** provide for one's family in most scenarios, along with lack of or no forest laws, need for land space for housing, etc., among a long list of other uses. **21** This is mainly blamed on agricultural or pastoral use, farmers fell trees for increasing space for cultivation and/or as fodder land for grazing and surviving live stock. The whole concept of 'slash and burn' agriculture is used to indicate this same process **22** when farmers employ the above chain of actions for their purposes.

18

A. NO CHANGE
B. without slowing down.
C. without stopping.
D. DELETE the underlined portion.

19

Which of the following, if inserted here, most effectively establishes the main idea of the paragraph?
A. Deforestation or clearance occurs due to several reasons.
B. Deforestation or clearance occurs when people need more land.
C. Deforestation or clearance may cause a lot of problems.
D. Deforestation or clearance affects our life in different ways.

20

A. NO CHANGE
B. providing
C. to provide
D. provided

21

A. NO CHANGE
B. What is mainly blamed on agricultural or pastoral use,
C. Which is mainly blamed on agricultural or pastoral use,
D. Mainly blamed on agricultural or pastoral use,

22

A. NO CHANGE
B. which
C. where
D. what

CONTINUE →

Questions 23 – 33 are based on the following passage.

[23] _____ Generally, I consider myself a patient person. Slow waitstaff and inefficient baristas are only a mild irritant, like seasonal allergies or when my cat knocks over a full glass of water off my bedside table. I'm effusively polite with those in the service industry, because I remember what it was like to serve demanding [24] customers which want both soy milk and half and half in their iced coffees. I tip well, I smile. But, [25] when it comes to customer service representatives, generally, I'm a giant asshole.

It's never my intention. But, if something in my apartment stops working—the internet cutting out, most likely—I'm [26] the one who call. I'm the apartment mom, the one who cagily asks everyone around the third of month to kindly Venmo me rent and who sends out cheery "reminders" when it's time to pay the utilities. I'm the one who breathes deeply around the 16th of every month, when Con-Ed automatically deducts the payment from my checking account. When the internet decides to stop working, one of my roommates generally wanders out of her room, [27] phone in hand.

"Hey, is the internet working for you?" she asks. I am usually jabbing a bobby pin into the reset button on the router and huffing. There's no need for an answer. They walk away.

Because no one else has the phone number, and because I am generally one month behind on the bill, I pick up the phone. If I've resorted [28] to call, that means that I've met my personal limit for how many times I can endure the question of whether or not the internet is working. The customer service line for things like the cable company, the electric company or your student loans are designed to build immense amounts of rage; waiting on hold while a recorded voice from Time Warner implores me to purchase a

23

Which of the following statements could be added here to most effectively establish the main idea?
A. Sometimes even a patient person may get angry, too.
B. I find few things as frustrating as dealing with service representatives.
C. It has never been easy to satisfy everybody.
D. People should not get irritated by trivial things.

24

A. NO CHANGE
B. customers want
C. customers who want
D. customers they want

25

A. NO CHANGE
B. when I talk to
C. when I talk about
D. when I deal with

26

A. NO CHANGE
B. the one to call
C. the one calling
D. the one who calls

27

A. NO CHANGE
B. a phone in hand
C. phone in her hand
D. with a phone in her hand

28

A. NO CHANGE
B. call
C. to calling
D. calling

CONTINUE ➡

phone line to save $10 on my bill **29** make me angrier than most things. By the time I actually speak to a person, I am livid.

It's not their fault, of course. They have a job, and they are gamely trying to do it. All I'm doing is making their life worse by adopting my customer service tone—sharp, imperious for no reason—and **30** speak to them as if I owned the place. (I don't, for the record.) Usually, half of my irritation is related to the fact that I'm calling because **31** a service is not working and I'll be paying for it, and the other half is because I know I still owe them money.

Being behind on your bills is embarrassing. I'm decent enough with money, **32** but there's just not much of it. With each unpaid bill that gathers dust, my credit score plummets. Sometimes, when I'm feeling flush and the automated phone calls have become too much, I call them back and pay the bill.

Recently, I discovered the actual, genuine joy of the live chat option. **33** Which would usually be a hellacious experience on the phone with a customer service representative is slightly more tolerable under the guise of a "the representative is typing…" status in a chat window. Cursing at someone who's simply trying to do their job looks a lot worse when it's written out. I can breathe easier when I'm typing in a box to someone who is trying to help me fix a problem. The angry wind is temporarily taken out of my sails.

29
A. NO CHANGE
B. makes
C. making
D. it makes

30
A. NO CHANGE
B. speaking
C. to speak
D. speaks

31
A. NO CHANGE
B. I'll be paying for it but the service is not working.
C. a service is not working, I'll be paying for it.
D. a service that I'll be paying for is not working.

32
A. NO CHANGE
B. but just not very much of it.
C. but just not that much of it to go around.
D. DELETE the underlined portion

33
A. NO CHANGE
B. That
C. It
D. What

CONTINUE →

Questions 34 – 44 are based on the following passage.

Several international groups produce routine estimates of tropical deforestation, most notably the Food and Agriculture Organization (FAO) of the United Nations, which **34** has been producing a global forest resources assessment every five to ten years since the late 1940s. The FAO report is based on **35** statistics, these statistics were provided by countries themselves, and because the ability of countries to accurately assess their forest resources varies depending on their financial, technological, and institutional resources, the estimates for some countries are likely more accurate than others. Many countries use satellite imagery as the basis for their assessments, and a few research teams have used satellite data as the basis for worldwide estimates of tropical deforestation in the 1980s and 1990s.

Some scientists and conservationists argue that the FAO provides **36** too conservative estimate of rates of deforestation because they consider any area larger than one hectare (0.01 square miles) with a minimum tree cover of 10 percent to be forested. This generous definition of "forest" means that a significant amount of degradation can occur before the FAO categorizes an area **37** to deforested. **38** _____, some satellite-based studies indicate deforestation rates are lower than even the FAO reports suggest. In the FAO's most recent forest assessment report, published in 2005, the organization itself revised downward the deforestation rates for the 1990s that it reported in 2001. Despite revisions and discrepancies, the FAO assessment is the

34
A. NO CHANGE
B. is producing
C. produces
D. have been producing

35
Which choice most effectively combines the two sentences at the underlined portion?
A. NO CHANGE
B. statistics, and these statistics were provided
C. statistics, which were provided
D. statistics provided

36
A. NO CHANGE
B. a too conservative estimate of rates of deforestation
C. an estimate of rates of deforestation too conservative
D. too conservative an estimate of rates of deforestation

37
A. NO CHANGE
B. for
C. as
D. in

38
Which choice, inserted here, establishes the best transition?
A. Also,
B. On the other hand,
C. In addition,
D. Furthermore,

CONTINUE ➡

39 most comprehensive longest-term and widely used metric of global forest resources.

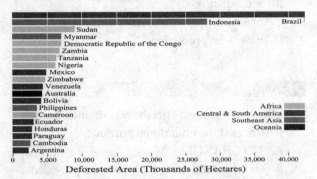

Deforested Area (Thousands of Hectares)

The FAO report does not compile statistics for tropical forest regions as a whole, but the country-by-country and regional-scale statistics provide a grim picture. The scope and impact of deforestation can be viewed in different ways. One is in absolute numbers: total area of forest cleared over a certain period. By that metric, all three major tropical forest areas, including South America, Africa, and Southeast Asia, are represented near the top of the list. Brazil led the world in terms of total deforested area between 1990 and 2005. The country lost 42,330,000 hectares (163,436 square miles) of forest, **40** roughly the size of California. Rounding out the top five tropical countries with the greatest total area of deforestation were **41** Brazil, Indonesia, Sudan, Zambia, and the Democratic Republic of Congo.

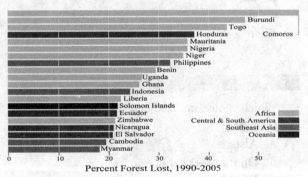

Percent Forest Lost, 1990-2005

Another way to look at deforestation is in terms of the percent of a country's forest **42** it was cleared over time. By this metric, the island nation of Comoros (north of Madagascar) fared the worst, **43** clearing nearly 60 percent of its forests between 1990 and 2005. Landlocked Burundi in central Africa was second,

39

A. NO CHANGE
B. most comprehensive, longest-term and, widely used metric
C. most comprehensive, longest-term and widely used, metric
D. most comprehensive, longest-term, and widely used metric

40

A. NO CHANGE
B. that is roughly the same size of California.
C. it is almost as big as California.
D. just like California.

41

According to the graphic, which country does not belong here?
A. Indonesia
B. Sudan
C. Zambia
D. the Democratic Republic of Congo

42

A. NO CHANGE
B. was cleared
C. that cleared
D. that was cleared

43

A. NO CHANGE
B. cleared
C. it cleared
D. that cleared

CONTINUE →

clearing 47 percent of its forests. The other top five countries that cleared large percentages of their forests were Togo, in West Africa (44 percent); Honduras (37 percent); and Mauritania (36 percent). [44] Twelve other tropical countries or island territories cleared 20 percent or more of their forests between 1990-2005.

44

A. NO CHANGE
B. Thirteen
C. Fifteen
D. Eighteen

STOP

If you finish before time is called, you may check your work on this section only. Do not turn to any other section.

Math Test – No Calculator

25 MINUTES, 20 QUESTIONS

Turn to Section 3 of your answer sheet to answer the questions in this section.

DIRECTIONS

For questions 1 – 15, solve each problem, choose the best answer from the choices provided and fill in the circle on your answer sheet. **For questions 16 – 20,** solve the problem and enter your answer in the grid on your answer sheet. Please refer to the directions before question 16 on how to enter your answers in the grid. Your may use any available space in your test booklet for scratch work.

NOTES

1. The use of a calculator **is not permitted**.

2. All variables and expressions used represent real numbers unless otherwise indicated.

3. Figures provided in this test are drawn to scale unless otherwise indicated.

4. All figures lie in a plane unless otherwise indicated.

5. Unless otherwise indicated, the domain of a given function f is the set of all real numbers x for which $f(x)$ is a real number.

REFERENCE

$A = \pi r^2$
$C = 2\pi r$

$A = \ell w$

$A = \dfrac{1}{2} bh$

$c^2 = a^2 + b^2$

Special Right Triangles

$V = \ell w h$

$V = \pi r^2 h$

$V = \dfrac{4}{3}\pi r^3$

$V = \dfrac{1}{3}\pi r^2 h$

$V = \dfrac{1}{3}\ell w h$

The number of degrees of arc in a circle is 360.

The number of radians of arc in a circle is 2π.

The sum of the measures in degrees of the angles of a triangle is 180.

CONTINUE

1

If x and y are two numbers such that $x = 2y + 1$, what is value of $10y - 5x$?

A. −5
B. −2
C. 5
D. 15

2

If $2x - 3y = -8$, which of the following expresses x in terms of y?

A. $x = 8 - 3y$

B. $x = 1.5y - 4$

C. $x = \frac{2}{3}y - 4$

D. $x = \frac{2}{3}y + 2$

3

Bob's base salary is $80,000. At the end of the year he gets an executive appreciation bonus of $20,000 plus a performance bonus that is 6% of his base salary. What is his total bonus?

A. 24,800
B. 25,000
C. 26,000
D. 30,000

4

Which of the following does NOT satisfy the inequality $x + y > 4(x - y)$?

A. $x=1$ and $y=2$
B. $x=3$ and $y=2$
C. $x=-2$ and $y=-1$
D. $x=3$ and $y=1$

5

A cylinder has a volume of 120 cubic feet. If its radius is reduced to 50% and its height is doubled, what is its volume after the change?

A. 60
B. 100
C. 120
D. 144

6

A gas station has three octane grades: regular (87 octane), mid-grade (89 octane) and premium (93 octane). A gallon of regular gas costs $2.4 and a gallon of premium gas is priced at $3.2. Amy added 16 gallons of regular grade gas to her car. With the same amount of money, how many gallons of premium grade can be added in the same gas station?

A. 10
B. 12
C. 15
D. 18

7

If the mode of the sequence of numbers (1, 4, 2, 1, 2, 2, 3, 3, 2, 4, 5, 4, x) is the single number 2, x can be any number EXCEPT for

A. 0
B. 2
C. 3
D. 4

CONTINUE

8

Which of the following is correct about all the points (x, y) such that $(x - y)^2 + (x - 1)^2 = 0$?

A. It is a circle with radius 1.

B. It is a parabola with vertex $(0, 1)$.

C. There is only one such point.

D. There are no such points.

9

All of the following expressions are equivalents EXCEPT for

A. $(x + y)^2$

B. $(x - y)^2 + 4xy$

C. $(x + 2y)^2 - 2xy$

D. $(x - y)^2 - 3y^2 + 6xy$

10

Let $f(x) = (x-1)(x-4)$. Which of the following depicts the solution set of $f(-x) \geq 0$?

A.

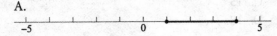

B.

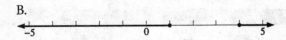

C.

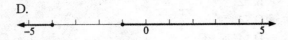

D.

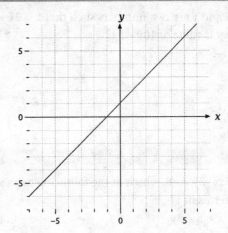

11

The picture above is the graph of a function $f(x)$, which of the following shows the graph of $|f(x - 3)|$?

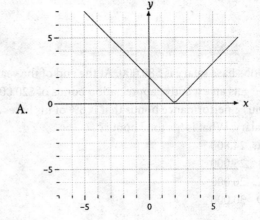

A.

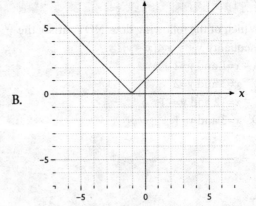

B.

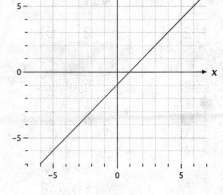

C.

D.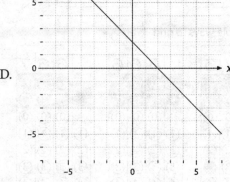

$f(x) = \dfrac{2x^2 + 3x - 1}{3x - 6}$ and $g(x) = x^2 + 3x - 2$. For which of the following situation is $f(g(x))$ NOT defined?

A. $x = 0$

B. $x = 1$

C. $x = 2$

D. $x = -2$

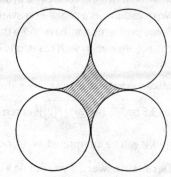

15

In the figure above, four circles with a same radius of 2 are put in a plane, where the circles in each adjacent pair touch each other. What is the area of the shaded region?

A. 4π

B. 12

C. $16 - 4\pi$

D. $12 - 2\pi$

If an angle θ is between 0 and 90 degrees, and $\sin\theta = 0.5$, what is the value of $\sin(2\theta)$?

A. 0.8

B. $\dfrac{\sqrt{2}}{2}$

C. $\dfrac{\sqrt{3}}{2}$

D. 1

Which of the following is an actual solution to the equation $\sqrt{2x + 3} - 2x = -3$?

A. 3

B. -3

C. 2

D. -2

CONTINUE

DIRECTIONS

For questions 16–20, solve the problem and enter your answer in the grid, as described below, on the answer sheet.

1. Although not required, it is suggested that you write your answer in the boxes at the top of the columns to help you fill in the circles accurately. You will receive credit only if the circles are filled in correctly.
2. Mark no more than one circle in any column.
3. No question has a negative answer.
4. Some problems may have more than one correct answer. In such cases, grid only one answer.
5. **Mixed numbers** such as $3\frac{1}{2}$ must be gridded as 3.5 or 7/2. (If [3 1 / 2] is entered into the grid, it will be interpreted as $\frac{31}{2}$, not $3\frac{1}{2}$.)
6. **Decimal answers:** If you obtain a decimal answer with more digits than the grid can accommodate, it may be either rounded or truncated, but it must fill the entire grid.

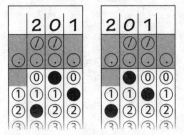

Answer: $\frac{7}{12}$ Answer: 2.5

Acceptable ways to grid $\frac{2}{3}$ are:

Answer: 201 – either position is correct

NOTE: You may start your answers in any column, space permitting. Columns you don't need to use should be left blank.

CONTINUE →

16

Cindy and Koocky the puppy are 420 feet apart, and they start to run directly towards each other with constant speeds. If Koocky's speed is five times that of Cindy's, how many feet does Koocky run before they meet?

17

A parabola has vertex (1, 3) and it goes through the points (2, 6) and (–2, t), what is the value of t?

18

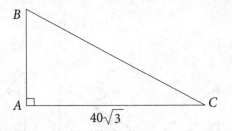

The figure above shows $\triangle ABC$. If $\angle ACB$ is 30°, what is the length of $\overline{BC}$?

19

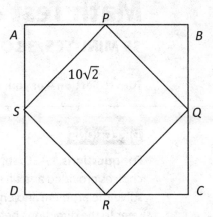

In the figure above, the P, Q, R, S are the middle points of the four sides of the square ABCD. If $\overline{PS} = 10\sqrt{2}$, what is the area of the square ABCD?

20

Carlos has 7 blocks labeled as –3, –2, –1, 0, 1, 2, 3, respectively. He picks 5 of them, and looked at the five numbers on them. He observes that the sum of these five numbers is 1, and the sum of their squares is 23. What is the sum of their cubes?

STOP

If you finish before time is called, you may check your work on this section only. Do not turn to any other section.

Math Test – Calculator

55 MINUTES, 38 QUESTIONS

Turn to Section 4 of your answer sheet to answer the questions in this section.

DIRECTIONS

For questions 1 – 30, solve each problem, choose the best answer from the choices provided and fill in the circle on your answer sheet. **For questions 31 – 38,** solve the problem and enter your answer in the grid on your answer sheet. Please refer to the directions before question 31 on how to enter your answers in the grid. Your may use any available space in your test booklet for scratch work.

NOTES

1. The use of a calculator **is permitted**.

2. All variables and expressions used represent real numbers unless otherwise indicated.

3. Figures provided in this test are drawn to scale unless otherwise indicated.

4. All figures lie in a plane unless otherwise indicated.

5. Unless otherwise indicated, the domain of a given function f is the set of all real numbers x for which $f(x)$ is a real number.

REFERENCE

$A = \pi r^2$ $A = \ell w$ $A = \frac{1}{2}bh$ $c^2 = a^2 + b^2$ Special Right Triangles

$C = 2\pi r$

$V = \ell wh$ $V = \pi r^2 h$ $V = \frac{4}{3}\pi r^3$ $V = \frac{1}{3}\pi r^2 h$ $V = \frac{1}{3}\ell wh$

The number of degrees of arc in a circle is 360.

The number of radians of arc in a circle is 2π.

The sum of the measures in degrees of the angles of a triangle is 180.

CONTINUE ➡

1

In a rating system, a player gains 30 points for each game he wins and loses 20 points for each month he does not play any game. In the past 12 months Alice has won on average 5 games per month, and there are exactly 10 months in which she played at least one game. If 12 months ago Alice's rating is 1,250, what is her rating now?

A. 2,500

B. 3,000

C. 3,010

D. 3,500

2

Look at the function $f(x)=(x-4)(ax^2+2x-c)-3$, where a and c are two constants unknown to us. Which of the following must be a point on the graph of $f(x)$?

A. $(0, -3)$

B. $(0, 3)$

C. $(-4, 3)$

D. $(4, -3)$

3

Alice spent $23.69 in total on 11 boxes of strawberries and blueberries. Among the 11 boxes, a boxes are strawberries and b boxes are blueberries. If, including tax, strawberries are $1.75 per box and blueberries are $2.49 per box, then which of the following systems of equations is true?

A. $a+b=11$
   $2.49a+1.75b=23.69$

B. $a+b=11$
   $1.75a+2.49b=23.69$

C. $a+1.75b=11$
   $2.49a+b=23.69$

D. $ab=11$
   $2.49a+1.75b=23.69$

4

A cylindrical water tank has a radius of 2m and a height of 3m. If we fill in water at the speed of 0.2m³/s, then how many seconds do we need to fill up the whole tank?

A. 30

B. 60

C. 30π

D. 60π

5

If $\dfrac{t+3}{13} = \dfrac{3t-7}{13}$, then what is the value of t?

A. 1.25

B. 5

C. 10

D. $\dfrac{21}{13}$

6

Which of the following is an equivalent to $2x^5-8x^3+6x$?

A. $2x(x+1)(x-1)(x+2)(x-2)$

B. $2x(x+1)(x-1)(x^3-3)$

C. $2x(x+1)(x-1)(x+\sqrt{3})(x-\sqrt{3})$

D. $2(x^2-1)(x^2-3)(x-1)$

CONTINUE

Questions 7 to 9 refer to the following table of letter distributions of the five English vowels in different languages. The frequencies of the accented vowels are added to their un-accented version. For example, the frequency of a in German includes that of ä.

Letter	% in English	% in German	% in Italian
A	8.167	7.094	12.380
E	12.702	16.396	12.055
I	6.966	6.550	10.173
O	7.507	3.037	9.834
U	2.758	5.161	3.177

7

If a collection of English books has 220,0000 letters in them and the distribution of the letters almost obeys the data in the table, then which of the following is closest to the number of appearances of the letter o?

A. 165000

B. 15000

C. 220000

D. 75070

8

According to the information in the table, which of the following statement is correct?

A. Among English, German, and Italian, the German language uses vowels most often.

B. Among English, German, and Italian, the Italian language uses vowels most often.

C. We cannot decide which of the three languages uses vowels most often because of the lack of data.

D. If you go to a library with a big collection of books, there will be more letter e's than letter a's.

9

The following table is the count of some letters from William Shakespeare's *King Lear*, which contains 27,605 words formed with 115,933 letters.

A	E	I	O	U
8682	14302	7172	9414	3871

Which of the following statements is accurate about Shakespeare's usage of vowels in King Lear?

A. He uses the letter *a* more frequently than the average usage in the English language.

B. He uses the first three vowels more frequently than the average usage in the English language.

C. He uses the letter *u* more frequently than the average usage in the English language.

D. None of the above is accurate due to the lack of data on the consonants.

10

If $z^2 < (\frac{2z}{3})(\frac{3z}{4}) + 1$, then which of the following describes all possible values of z?

A. $-1 < z < 2$

B. $-2 < z < 2$

C. $-\sqrt{2} < z < \sqrt{2}$

D. $-2\sqrt{2} < z < 2\sqrt{2}$

11

Circle C has the equation $x^2 + y^2 - 2x - 2 = 0$. Another circle, D, shares the same center with C, but has an area twice as much as C. What is the equation for D?

A. $2x^2 + 2y^2 - 4x - 4 = 0$

B. $x^2 + y^2 - 2x - 4 = 0$

C. $x^2 + y^2 - 2x - 5 = 0$

D. $x^2 + y^2 - 2x - 8 = 0$

CONTINUE

12

Lucas does babysitting for extra income. Each time he charges a flat rate of $30.00 per hour for the first two hours. After two hours, he charges an additional fee of d dollars for every minute. If he is asked to do a babysitting session an additional m minutes after the first two hours, which of the following functions, f, models his payment in terms of m and d?

A. $f(m, d) = 30 + m + d$
B. $f(m, d) = 30 + md$
C. $f(m, d) = 60 + 2m + 2d$
D. $f(m, d) = 60 + md$

13

The pascal (Pa) is the unit of pressure, defined as one newton per square meter. How many newtons need to be put on a surface of one square kilometer in order to keep the pressure of one pascal?

A. 1
B. 10
C. 1000
D. 1000000

14

There are 5 points in the plane, $A=(-1,5)$, $B=(1,3)$, $C=(5,5)$, $D=(-4,-1)$, and $E=(3,-2)$. Let $O=(0,0)$ be the point of origin. What is the median of the 5 slopes of the lines OA, OB, OC, OD, and OE?

A. $-\dfrac{2}{3}$

B. $\dfrac{1}{4}$

C. 1

D. $\dfrac{3}{2}$

15

Seven pieces of rope have an average length of 68 centimeters and a median length of 84 centimeters. Which of the following situations could explain the difference between the average and median lengths?

A. The lengths of these ropes are close to each other.
B. There are a few pieces that are much longer than the rest.
C. There are a few pieces that are much shorter than the rest.
D. Many of the pieces are between 68 centimeters and 84 centimeters.

16

A line passes two points (5, 7) and (8, 16). What is the equation of this line?

A. $y = x + 2$
B. $y = 2x$
C. $3x - y = 8$
D. $3x + 2y = 30$

17

If i is the complex number such that $i^2 = -1$. What is the value of $(2i-3)(1+i)$?

A. $1+i$
B. $3+2i$
C. $-3-2i$
D. $-5-i$

CONTINUE

18

If $\dfrac{9-3x}{2x} = 1 - \dfrac{1}{2x}$, then which of the following expresses all the possible values of x?

A. $x : x = 1$

B. $x : x = 1.75$

C. $x : x = 2$

D. x : All real numbers except 0

19

Alice and Bob volunteered to inflate balloons for a school event. Alice finishes 2 balloons every minute and Bob finishes 3 balloons per minute. If Alice started 5 minutes earlier than Bob, then which one of the following is true at some moment during their endeavor?

A. When Alice finishes her 20-th balloon, Bob finishes his 30-th.

B. When Alice finishes her 30-th balloon, Bob finishes his 40-th.

C. When Alice finishes her 40-th balloon, Bob finishes his 50-th.

D. When Alice finishes her 50-th balloon, Bob finishes his 60-th.

20

A cell phone dealer ordered 60 Model M products to be sold for $250 each, which represents a 20 percent markup over the dealer's initial cost for each cell phone. Of the products ordered, 6 were never sold and were returned to the provider for a refund of 50 percent of the dealer's initial cost. What was the dealer's approximate profit or loss as a percent of the dealer's initial cost for the 60 products?

A. 7% loss

B. 13% loss

C. 7% profit

D. 13% profit

21

If a and b are two integers satisfying $-20 \le a \le 30$, $-3 \le b \le 2$, and b is not 0, which of the following is true for all possible values of $\dfrac{a}{b}$?

A. $-10 \le \dfrac{a}{b} \le 10$

B. $-30 \le \dfrac{a}{b} \le 30$

C. $-\dfrac{20}{3} \le \dfrac{a}{b} \le 50$

D. $-50 \le \dfrac{a}{b} \le 15$

CONTINUE

Questions 22 to 24 refer to the following information.

Moira has some extra-large eggs at home and a container that can hold two dozens of eggs inside. Recently she got a scale as a present for her 8-year birthday. Now she likes to play with the scale with everything.

Today she did some experiments and recorded her data in the following table:

Number of eggs in the container	Weight of the container (oz)
2	9.810
4	13.520
5	16.200
7	20.360
9	24.805
14	35.813

22

What will be graph of the most accurate model for the relation between the weight of the container and the number of eggs in it?

A. A straight line passing though the origin (0, 0).

B. A straight line that does not pass though the origin (0, 0).

C. A parabola with a vertex whose x-coordinate is positive.

D. A parabola with a vertex whose x-coordinate is negative.

23

Use the correct model in the previous question, and suppose it is accurate on the last two rows in the table. Which of the following is closest to the weight of a normal extra-large egg, in oz?

A. 2.0

B. 2.2

C. 2.5

D. 2.7

24

If she puts the whole capacity of 24 eggs in the container, according to the correct model and assume again the data of the last two rows are accurate, which of the following is closest to the weight, in oz, of the container?

A. 50.2

B. 53.4

C. 55.9

D. 57.8

25

The equation of a circle with radius r that centered at (a, b) is $(x-a)^2+(y-b)^2=r^2$. Which of the following is equivalent to the equation of a circle with a radius of 5 and is centered at the point (−3, 1)?

A. $x^2+y^2+6x-2y-25=0$

B. $x^2+y^2+6x-2y-15=0$

C. $x^2+y^2-6x-2y-10=0$

D. $x^2+y^2+6x+2y-19=0$

CONTINUE

Questions 26 – 27 refer to the following information:

At the end of his first year in college, Eric calculates his grade points average (GPA). The following table gives his grades and the number of credits for each course.

Subject	Grade	Credits
Calculus I	B	4
Music	B	1
Algebra	A−	3
Intr. Physics	B+	3
English	A	2
Roman History	A	2
Basic Programming		3

Eric first calculates the grade point for each course. The grade point for a course is the number of credits, multiplied by the number corresponding to his grade: A = 4, A− = 3.7, B+ = 3.3, B=3, B−=2.7, C+=2.3, and C=2.

Then the GPA is computed by dividing the total grade points by the total number of course credits.

26

What is the median of the grade points for the 6 courses in the table corresponding to the upper 6 rows?

A. 9
B. 3
C. 8
D. 8.95

27

If Eric's GPA is 3.44, what is his grade in the Basic Programming course?

A. A
B. B
C. B+
D. B−

28

If $x \neq 3$, which of the following always equals $\dfrac{x^4 - 3x^3 - 2x^2 + 7x - 3}{x - 3}$?

A. $x^2 - x + 2$
B. $x^2 - 2x + 1$
C. $x^3 - 2x + 1$
D. $x^3 - x^2 - x + 3$

CONTINUE

29

At time 0, an object starts to move along a straight line with an acceleration of $3m/s^2$ After it reaches the speed of $60m/s$, it stops the acceleration and maintains this speed. Which of the following graphs depicts the graph of its displacement d with respect to time t? (Note: for an object moving on a straight line, starting from zero speed, with acceleration a, the displacement at time t is $d=at^2/2$.)

A.

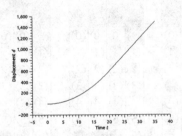

B.

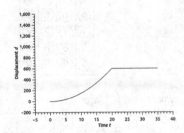

C.

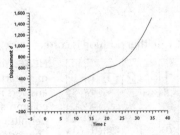

D.

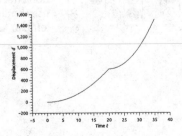

30

SALES AT AN ELECTRONIC STORE

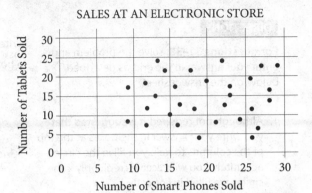

In the scatter plot above, each point represents the number of tablets and the number of smart phones sold at an electronic store on one of the days of a 30-day period. For what fraction of the days that the store sold at least 20 smart phones were over 15 tablets also sold?

A. $\dfrac{1}{2}$

B. $\dfrac{2}{3}$

C. $\dfrac{7}{30}$

D. $\dfrac{7}{15}$

CONTINUE →

DIRECTIONS

For questions 31–38, solve the problem and enter your answer in the grid, as described below, on the answer sheet.

1. Although not required, it is suggested that you write your answer in the boxes at the top of the columns to help you fill in the circles accurately. You will receive credit only if the circles are filled in correctly.

2. Mark no more than one circle in any column.

3. No question has a negative answer.

4. Some problems may have more than one correct answer. In such cases, grid only one answer.

5. **Mixed numbers** such as $3\frac{1}{2}$ must be gridded as 3.5 or 7/2. (If $3\,1\,/\,2$ is entered into the grid, it will be interpreted as $\frac{31}{2}$, not $3\frac{1}{2}$.)

6. **Decimal answers:** If you obtain a decimal answer with more digits than the grid can accommodate, it may be either rounded or truncated, but it must fill the entire grid.

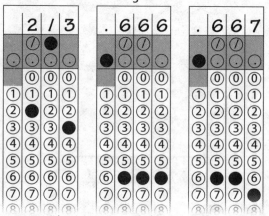

Acceptable ways to grid $\frac{2}{3}$ are:

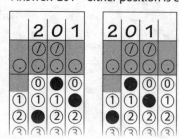

Answer: 201 – either position is correct

NOTE: You may start your answers in any column, space permitting. Columns you don't need to use should be left blank.

31

If $x^2-6x=72$ and $x>0$, what is the value of x?

32

One liter is the unit of volume that is 0.1 percent of one cubic meter. One gallon equals 3.79 liters. The density of a particular brand of milk is about 1028 kg per cubic meter, and it is priced at \$1.2 per kg. What is the price of a bottle of 1 gallon of such milk? Note: we ignore the price and weight of the bottle.

33

What is the value of x if $|x-1.1|+|x-2.2|+|x-3.3|=2.2$?

34

In the figure above, $\angle ACB=90°$. If $\cos A=\dfrac{11}{13}$ and $BC=5$, which integer is closest to the length of AC? (Note: Figure not drawn to scale.)

35

Let $P(x)=(x-5)(x-4)(x-2)(x-1)-1$. What is the value of $P(1)\cdot P(2)\cdot P(3)\cdot P(4)\cdot P(5)\cdot P(6)$?

CONTINUE

36

Consider the following lines:

l: $4x+3y=10$

m: $x=1$

n: $y=-6$

If l intersects m at point A and l intersects n at point B, what is the distance between A and B?

Problems 37 and 38 refer to the following information.

A theater sells exchange movie tickets that can be redeemed later for particular movies. There are two types of tickets with different benefits. The *golden pass* is priced at $22 each, while the *silver pass* is priced at $18 each. The tax rate is 7% for all the tickets.

37

One day Tim has $500 at his disposal, and he wants to get more varieties in his exchange tickets collection. He decides to get the same number of golden passes as silver passes. At most how many golden pass tickets he can get?

38

The following day Tim changes his mind. He wants to buy silver pass tickets only. With the same amount of $500, Tim could only buy 22 silver pass tickets because the price of the tickets goes up. (Fortunately the sales tax doesn't go up.) What is the least number of percent, in term of an integer, is the price of the silver pass increased?

STOP

If you finish before time is called, you may check your work on this section only. Do not turn to any other section.

New SAT Practice Essay 5

 ESSAY BOOK

DIRECTIONS

The essay gives you an opportunity to show how effectively you can read and comprehend a passage and write an essay analyzing the passage. In your essay, you should demonstrate that you have read the passage carefully, present a clear and logical analysis, and use language precisely.

Your essay must be written on the lines provided in your answer booklet; except for the Planning Page of the answer booklet, you will receive no other paper on which to write. You will have enough space if you write on every line, avoid wide margins, and keep your handwriting to a reasonable size. Remember that people who are not familiar with your handwriting will read what you write. Try to write or print so that what you are writing is legible to those readers.

You have 50 minutes to read the passage and write an essay in response to the prompt provided inside this booklet.

REMINDERS

— Do not write your essay in this booklet. Only what you write on the lined pages of your answer booklet will be evaluated.

— An off-topic essay will not be evaluated.

This cover is representative of what you'll see on test day.

As you read the passage below, consider how Alex Epstein uses:

- evidence, such as facts or examples, to support claims.

- reasoning to develop ideas and to connect claims and evidence.

- stylistic or persuasive elements, such as word choice or appeals to emotion, to add power to the ideas expressed.

Adapted from Alex Epstein, "Jimmy Fallon Makes the World's Best Argument Against Solar and Wind Energy." Forbes.com Nov. 12, 2014

1 Tonight Show host Jimmy Fallon, a member of "Artists Against Fracking," is, like many celebrities, in favor of banning most fossil fuel use and using wind and solar instead.

2 But a few years ago, when he was host of Weekend Update, Fallon made one of the best arguments ever why solar, wind, and other forms of renewable energy work very, very badly.

3 He was commenting on a seemingly ridiculous proposal to power cars using renewable energy from…hazelnuts.

4 Boosters of hazelnut energy made the same arguments we hear for solar and wind:

5 1. It's "renewable." It gets its energy from the sun, which will keep replenishing year after year.

6 2. It's technically possible. Engineers can extract the oil from hazelnuts and use it to power an engine.

7 But Fallon explained why these arguments are meaningless:

8 New Scientist magazine reported that in the future, cars could be powered by hazelnuts. That's encouraging, considering an eight-ounce jar of hazelnuts costs about nine dollars. Yeah, I've got an idea for a car that runs on bald eagle heads and Fabergé eggs.

9 In other words: if your form of energy is unaffordable, who cares if it's based on the sun or works in a lab?

10 Here's my question for Jimmy, given that he wants to ban fracking, a technology used in oil and gas production: Why is hazelnut energy so unaffordable? After all, hazelnuts get their energy from the sun, which is free, right?

11 I'm guessing that Jimmy would respond that while the sun is free, there were other factors in the process of producing hazelnuts that make them expensive. There are the materials needed to grow the hazelnuts. There are also all the machines needed to grow and harvest the hazelnuts and then all the work to transform them into usable energy. And there is the manpower to work the machines.

12 With hazelnuts, when you add up all the parts of the process, it's worth growing hazelnuts as a luxury food for human beings—but as fuel for the high-powered machines of modern life, it is a disaster. The same is true for solar and wind.

13 Just as it's a mistake to assume that because the sun is free, solar-powered hazelnuts will be cheap, so it is a mistake to assume that solar-powered energy can or will be cheap. Whether that's true or not depends on all the materials, manpower, and machines involved in the entire process of harnessing the sun's power.

14 The basic problem is that because sunlight and wind are dilute (low-concentration) and intermittent (unreliable) energy inputs, it takes a lot of resources to collect and concentrate them, and even more resources to make them available on-demand. These are called the diluteness problem and the intermittency problem.

15 **The diluteness problem**

16 The diluteness problem is that the sun and the wind don't deliver concentrated energy—unlike coal or oil—which means you need a lot of materials per unit of energy produced. For solar, such materials can include highly purified silicon, phosphorus, boron, and compounds like titanium dioxide, cadmium telluride, and copper indium gallium selenide. For wind, they can include high-performance compounds (like those used in the aircraft industry) for turbine blades and the rare-earth metal neodymium for lightweight, high performance magnets, as well as the steel and concrete necessary to build thousands or tens of thousands of structures as tall as skyscrapers.

17 Here's a comparison of how steel (and iron) intensive it is to generate electricity from wind as compared with coal, nuclear, or natural gas.

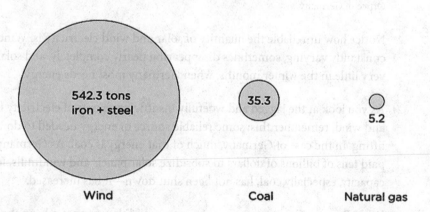

Sources: ALPINE Bau GmbH, July 2014; Peterson, Zhao, Petroski (2005); Wilburn 2011

18 This is a problem—but it's nothing compared to the intermittency problem.

19 **The intermittency problem**

20 We know from experience that the sun doesn't shine all the time, let alone with the same intensity all the time, and the wind doesn't blow all the time—and leaving aside the assurance that the sun will be "off" at night, they can be extremely unpredictable.

21 The only way for solar and wind to be truly useful, reliable sources of energy would be to combine them with some form of extremely inexpensive mass-storage system. No such mass-storage system exists. All of them require backup—except that "backup" implies that solar and wind work most of the time. It's more accurate to say that solar and wind are parasites that require a host.

22 Here's what solar and wind electricity look like in the world leader in "renewables," Germany—often cited as an example we should follow. I got this data from the European Energy Exchange, which collects data every 15 minutes.

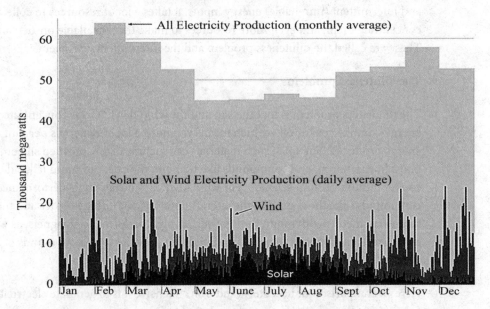

Sources: European Energy Exchange Transparency Platform Data (2013); Federal Statistical Office of Germany

23 Notice how unreliable the quantity of solar and wind electricity is. Wind is constantly varying, sometimes disappearing nearly completely, and solar produces very little in the winter months, when Germany most needs energy.

24 As you look at the jagged and woefully insufficient bursts of electricity from solar and wind, remember this: some reliable source of energy needed to do the heavy lifting. In the case of Germany, much of that energy is coal. As Germany has paid tens of billions of dollars to subsidize solar panels and windmills, fossil fuel capacity, especially coal, has not been shut down—it has increased.

25 Why? Because Germans need more energy, and they cannot rely on the renewables.

26 They might be better off relying on hazelnuts.

27 We all could stand from learning Jimmy Fallon's lesson about the hazelnut problem. Including Jimmy Fallon.

Write an essay in which you explain how Alex Epstein builds an argument to persuade his audience that we cannot rely on renewable energy. In your essay, analyze how Alex Epstein uses one or more of the features listed in the box above, (or features of your own choice), to strengthen the logic and persuasiveness of his argument. Be sure that your analysis focuses on the most relevant features of the passage.

Your essay should not explain whether you agree with Alex Epstein, but rather explain how he builds an argument to persuade his audience.

■ **TEST NUMBER** ■ **SECTION 1**

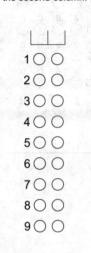

ENTER TEST NUMBER

For instance, for Practice Test # 1, fill in the circle for 0 in the first column and for 1 in the second column.

1 ○○
2 ○○
3 ○○
4 ○○
5 ○○
6 ○○
7 ○○
8 ○○
9 ○○

	A B C D		A B C D		A B C D		A B C D
1	○○○○	14	○○○○	27	○○○○	40	○○○○
2	○○○○	15	○○○○	28	○○○○	41	○○○○
3	○○○○	16	○○○○	29	○○○○	42	○○○○
4	○○○○	17	○○○○	30	○○○○	43	○○○○
5	○○○○	18	○○○○	31	○○○○	44	○○○○
6	○○○○	19	○○○○	32	○○○○	45	○○○○
7	○○○○	20	○○○○	33	○○○○	46	○○○○
8	○○○○	21	○○○○	34	○○○○	47	○○○○
9	○○○○	22	○○○○	35	○○○○	48	○○○○
10	○○○○	23	○○○○	36	○○○○	49	○○○○
11	○○○○	24	○○○○	37	○○○○	50	○○○○
12	○○○○	25	○○○○	38	○○○○	51	○○○○
13	○○○○	26	○○○○	39	○○○○	52	○○○○

SAT PRACTICE ANSWER SHEET

COMPLETE MARK ●   EXAMPLES OF INCOMPLETE MARKS

It is recommended that you use a No. 2 pencil. It is very important that you fill in the entire circle darkly and completely. If you change your response, erase as completely as possible. Incomplete marks or erasures may affect your score.

■ SECTION 2

	A B C D		A B C D		A B C D		A B C D		A B C D
1	○○○○	10	○○○○	19	○○○○	28	○○○○	37	○○○○
2	○○○○	11	○○○○	20	○○○○	29	○○○○	38	○○○○
3	○○○○	12	○○○○	21	○○○○	30	○○○○	39	○○○○
4	○○○○	13	○○○○	22	○○○○	31	○○○○	40	○○○○
5	○○○○	14	○○○○	23	○○○○	32	○○○○	41	○○○○
6	○○○○	15	○○○○	24	○○○○	33	○○○○	42	○○○○
7	○○○○	16	○○○○	25	○○○○	34	○○○○	43	○○○○
8	○○○○	17	○○○○	26	○○○○	35	○○○○	44	○○○○
9	○○○○	18	○○○○	27	○○○○	36	○○○○		

■ SECTION 3

1 Ⓐ Ⓑ Ⓒ Ⓓ   4 Ⓐ Ⓑ Ⓒ Ⓓ   7 Ⓐ Ⓑ Ⓒ Ⓓ   10 Ⓐ Ⓑ Ⓒ Ⓓ   13 Ⓐ Ⓑ Ⓒ Ⓓ

2 Ⓐ Ⓑ Ⓒ Ⓓ   5 Ⓐ Ⓑ Ⓒ Ⓓ   8 Ⓐ Ⓑ Ⓒ Ⓓ   11 Ⓐ Ⓑ Ⓒ Ⓓ   14 Ⓐ Ⓑ Ⓒ Ⓓ

3 Ⓐ Ⓑ Ⓒ Ⓓ   6 Ⓐ Ⓑ Ⓒ Ⓓ   9 Ⓐ Ⓑ Ⓒ Ⓓ   12 Ⓐ Ⓑ Ⓒ Ⓓ   15 Ⓐ Ⓑ Ⓒ Ⓓ

Only answers that are gridded will be scored. You will not receive credit for anything written in the boxes.

16	17	18	19	20

NO CALCULATOR ALLOWED

■ SECTION 4

1 A B C D
2 A B C D
3 A B C D
4 A B C D
5 A B C D
6 A B C D

7 A B C D
8 A B C D
9 A B C D
10 A B C D
11 A B C D
12 A B C D

13 A B C D
14 A B C D
15 A B C D
16 A B C D
17 A B C D
18 A B C D

19 A B C D
20 A B C D
21 A B C D
22 A B C D
23 A B C D
24 A B C D

25 A B C D
26 A B C D
27 A B C D
28 A B C D
29 A B C D
30 A B C D

CALCULATOR
ALLOWED

COMPLETE MARK ● 　 EXAMPLES OF　Ⓐ⊗⊖Ⓒ
INCOMPLETE MARKS ●◉◍◐

It is recommended that you use a No. 2 pencil. It is very important that you fill in the entire circle darkly and completely. If you change your response, erase as completely as possible. Incomplete marks or erasures may affect your score.

■ SECTION 4 (Continued)

Only answers that are gridded will be scored. You will not receive credit for anything written in the boxes.

31 　　32 　　33 　　34 　　35

36 　　37 　　38

Only answers that are gridded will be scored. You will not receive credit for anything written in the boxes.

CALCULATOR
ALLOWED

PLANNING PAGE You may plan your essay in the unlined planning space below, but use only the lined pages following this one to write your essay. Any work on this planning page will not be scored.

Use pages 7 through 10 for your ESSAY ⟶

FOR PLANNING ONLY

Use pages 7 through 10 for your ESSAY ⟶

BEGIN YOUR ESSAY HERE.

You may continue on the next page.

SERIAL #

STOP.

Answer Explanations
New SAT Practice Tests

Answer Explanations
New SAT Practice Test 1

Section 1

1. B

The best evidence for this occurs in lines 1 - 4, and 14 - 18. We see in those lines the favorable nature in which the protagonist views his job responsibilities. There is no mention of censorship, and it can only be loosely inferred from where the idea of burning books originated.

2. C

As stated previously, lines 1 - 4 introduce the reader best to the feelings of the protagonist. While lines 5 - 9 do offer insight into the way the protagonist views his job, they do not necessarily reflect the ideals of the main character.

3. A

The correct definition is a person of calm character, showing little or no emotion.

4. D

This is evidenced by Montag's desire to steal a book though he seemingly understands the consequences, the woman's assertion that they "can't ever have my books", and her stance decision to destroy her books under her own terms.

5. B

As discussed above, the woman in the story refuses to relinquish her independence and freedom, regardless of the cost.

6. C

Though he presents as a generally impersonal and indifferent individual, the passage suggests that Captain Beatty does have empathy and compassion for the victims. This is best evidenced in lines 56-61 and 77.

7. A

The correct definition of gilt is gold-leafed. Explanation provided in the next question.

8. D

Clearly, the author provides an explanation of the titles by specifically referring to their "golden eyes" glittering.

9. D

While the firefighters do need to add kerosene, a liquid, to assist with the ignition process, it is not a requirement. However, the author uses this simile to compare the inevitable fate of fishes without water to the fate the books will soon realize.

10. B

Choices (A) and (D) are incorrect because Montag shows that he is in disbelief of what he has done and tries to hide his actions quickly. Though there is evidence that some part of his action involved "conscience", the real answer to his actions lies in the word "curiosity".

11. B

The article details the events leading up to the eventual genocide, citing specific events which increased tensions between Hutus and Tutsis.

12. A

The correct definition of engender is to cause or create.

13. C

Prior to 1946, there was little intervention of any peacekeeping forces at all during the mounting tensions between Hutus and Tutsis.

14. A

The system of corvee rule served to change approaches in Rwanda due to the fact that it exacerbated an already unequal system of government. As we see in the following paragraphs, this paved the way for UN involvement.

15. C

Those lines state clearly that Belgian and UN influence were critical in causing a more equivalent distribution of power.

16. D

From the graph, there is general agreement on rough numbers with the exception of those provided by the Rwandan census of 2002 and by Gerard Prunier.

17. A

The author clearly provides evidence and support that, while tensions existed between Hutu and Tutsi factions, the tipping point came when European

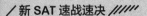

colonists began exerting their influence on one tribe over the other.

18. D

Clear definition provided in the lines which follow.

19. A

Based upon prior information, Belgians had sided primarily with Tutsis. The colonel's decision to assist Hutus was a clear break from previous Belgian decisions.

20. C

As stated previously, Belgium had primarily supported Tutsi tribes. By organizing the massacre, the colonel showed a definitive break from tradition.

21. B

The author takes care and offers insight and evidence as to why it was the Europeans who created the genocide to the level it rose. There is little evidence offered of pre-existing tensions or influences from within the country of Rwanda, only focus on European and UN intervention.

22. C

Throughout Dr. King's speech, we hear repeatedly the theme that there will be no rest until racial equality is achieved.

23. B

The imagery of being able to carve a stone from a mountain clearly illustrates the resolve of the author in achieving his goals.

24. A

Though there are multiple meanings of the word "sweltering", in context the author clearly implies that oppression and injustice are suffocating the state.

25. D

This speech clearly is made to persuade listeners to join the civil rights movement and stand up for social justice. There is little in the way of accusation with the exception of a few instances, so the main focus is garnering support.

26. B

Throughout the speech, we are greeted with passionate optimism about what can be achieved by working together towards equality. This is not said with hope, but with certainty that the goals of civil rights will be achieved.

27. C

The author is stipulating that there exists within our society the potential for us to work together peacefully to achieve beautiful results.

28. B

Referencing states who have already undergone multiple civil rights movements and, by stating that somehow this situation can and will be changed, we see that the author believes that current conditions and populations are enough to instill the tenets of the civil rights movement.

29. A

In context, the definition becomes apparent when contrasted with "every hill and mountain shall be made low".

30. D

The author references "great trials and tribulations" at the beginning of the paragraph and repeatedly attributes positive qualities to those fighting for equal rights.

31. C

By asserting that "unearned suffering is redemptive", the author is thanking those who have participated by saying greater rewards await them.

32. C

The critical portion of this statement lies in the idea that "a Negro in New York believes he has nothing for which to vote", implying that faith in political leadership to implement the ideals of African Americans is virtually nonexistent.

33. B

Given the evidence provided about the efforts undertaken prior to Hubble's launch, it is logical to assume that the initial results recorded by Hubble were far below the money and time spent in getting the project off of the ground.

34. C

In context, the term microcosm is used to illustrate the multitude of near catastrophes which seem to surround the Hubble mission.

35. A

Given the initial setbacks and various delays, the amount of information gained by Hubble, the amount of scholarly papers published because of the results obtained, and the flowery language used by the author, it is evident that Hubble has met and exceeded expectations.

36. D

The author clearly describes the incredible contribution of Hubble to the scientific world in those lines.

37. B

The best evidence for this answer lies in the comments from NASA administrator Charles Bolden who stated that Hubble has fundamentally changed our understanding of the universe.

38. A

It is evident from the comments and amount of information gained by Hubble that it will be continually utilized for quite some time. Thus, this is but the latest repair mission.

39. D

In context, the term "decades long" provides the critical explanation for the definition.

40. C

The key phrase that makes C the best answer lies in "to honor the many people who made Hubble what it is today" and subsequently describing those who gambled their careers on Hubble's success.

41. B

Zimmerman's writings clearly indicate that many researchers lost a great deal… both personally and professionally.

42. A

Direct quote that specifically states the answer to the previous question.

43. B

Passage 1 is best described as editorial based upon the style and manner of language used to convey the point. Passage 2 clearly states facts and presents information from either side of the argument.

44. D

Direct definition. In context, the author clearly uses the word to describe the manner in which policy changes go against the Authority's charter.

45. B

The author provides specific details regarding where the Australian government failed to implement or enforce regulations regarding the reef.

46. A

The author implies in those lines that the government seeks to obtain money over protecting the biodiversity contained in the reef.

47. C

The only specific event that is discussed by the Greenpeace representative in passage 2 is regarding dredge spoils and their effects on the reef.

48. D

While the reef is diverse and answer C can be somewhat correct, choice D is best as fecund essentially means fertile and productive.

49. A

From the quotation provided in the subsequent lines, it is clear that representatives of the government feel that the regulations imposed are sufficient for ecological protection.

50. B

Direct quote as mentioned above.

51. C

Both passages mention coal production and shipping as the reasons they believe these measures were passed and the dredging began. As such, letter C is the best answer.

52. A

While all choices deal with the destruction of natural resources for human gain, letter A is the only choice that deals with specific human action on ecosystems and not individual species.

SECTION 2

1. A

Choice A is the right form because "all" stands for the 3 noun phrases before it and plays the role of the subject in the sentence. Choices B and C should be eliminated because "all communicate" is not a subordinate clause; there is no need of "that" or "which." Choice D is not correct because "communicating" is not a predicate form.

2. B

"The ineffable" is a special term that needs a definition separated by a comma. Choice A is wrong because a comma cannot be a sentence connector. Choices C and D should be eliminated because there is no comma to separate "ineffable" from its definition.

3. C

Choice C is the right answer because, based in the whole sentence, obviously C sets up paralleling structure. Choices A, B, and D are incorrect because none of them creates parallelism.

4. D

Choice A is wrong because the verb doesn't agree with the subject. Choice B is a participle that cannot be a predicate by itself. Choice C mistakenly switches to past tense. Choice D is the correct form: present tense singular.

5. A

Both "creating art" and "balancing" are used as nouns. "Creating art" is the subject of the sentence, and "balancing" is the object of "requires." Choices B, C, and D should be eliminated because the verb forms "create" and "balance" cannot play the roles of subject and object.

6. C

Choices A, B, and D should be eliminated because "remains" is a finite form without a subject. Choice C is the correct answer because "while remaining" means "during the time the person is remaining."

7. A

Choice A is perfect: pronoun "one" stands for "ability" to avoid repetition. None of the other choices works.

8. D

It is like two sides of a coin: On one hand, *"The emotionally disturbed artist's goal is not the perfect expression of an aesthetic ideal;"* on the other hand, *"communicating the mind's content and having it recognized by others is intensely valuable to the disturbed artist's healing."* Only Choice D works here because "yet," meaning "but at the same time," leads to the opposite direction.

9. C

Choice C is the correct answer because the isolation was *imposed by the mind.*

10. B

To connect three listed things, the correct pattern is "<u>A</u>, <u>B</u>, and <u>C</u>." Only Choice B follows this pattern.

11. C

The previous part says that the emotionally disturbed people "*are unable to express in words*." Therefore, "*an otherwise unobtainable window*" makes the best cohesion.

12. D

The possessive forms are "user's life" (if it's singular) or "users' lives" (if it's plural.) Only Choice D shows the correct plural possessive form.

13. A

Choice A is correct: The participial *minimizing* phrase adds a supplementary action or result to the main verb *communicates*. All other choices should be eliminated: Choice B is a finite verb form without a subject; Choice C gives a purpose rather than a result; and Choice D switches to past tense for no reason.

14. C

Same degree of comparison is expressed by the structure "just as ___ as ___." Only Choice C uses this structure.

15. A

Both the adjective form "absent-minded" and the adverb form "absent-mindedly" are hyphenated. That eliminates Choices B and D. To modify a verb, "*reach*" in this case, the adverb form is needed. Choice A "absent-mindedly" is correct.

16. B

Only Choice B uses the correct comparative form "*shorter ... than.*" Choices A, C, and D are eliminated either because of "short" (without –er) or because of "then."

17. C

Choice A is wrong because it needs "that" before "users get." Choices B and D are wrong because there is no need of "who" to modify "users." Choice C is the correct answer because the verb "imagine" governs an object "users" and an object complement "getting ..."

18. C

The previous sentence indicates that some phone users *will likely remain tied to their phones for now.* This sentence states that the Apple Watch *at least suggests an alternative to the status quo*, not the logical result of the information given before it. Choice C "still" correctly shows a concession between the two sentences.

19. D

The *that*-clause is the real subject of the sentence in the structure "*It is ... that ...*" without any punctuation to break it. Only Choice D observes this rule.

20. A

The subject of the sentence is "the frequency." Therefore, the target verb should be "suggests." Choices B, C, and D should be eliminated: Choice B doesn't agree with the subject; Choice C cannot be the predicate by itself; and Choice D switches to the past without any reason.

21. B

Choice A is eliminated because of the redundancy: it's like "those they are." Choice C is wrong because it uses a comma to combine two sentences. Choice D doesn't make sense because the verb "are" doesn't have a subject. Choice B is the correct answer: The subject "those" is modified by a subordinate clause in which "who" stands for "those."

22. D

The author's tone in the whole passage is very affirmative. Choices A, B, and C all sound more or less doubtful; therefore, they should be eliminated. Choice D "distinctively possible" is the most consistent with the tone of the passage.

23. A

Only Choice A makes sense: "*Set off for*" means *started a journey to*.

24. D

The verb "wish" gives a subjunctive mood, which requires verbs in the past form. Only Choice D "*I could say I saw*" follows the rule.

25. B

Choices A and C are eliminated because "work" and "works" are finite forms without a subject. Choice D is wrong because it switches to the past. Choice B is correct: After the main sentence, an *–ing* phrase adds an accompanying action.

26. A

Only Choice A follows the correct comparative pattern: *the longer ... , the more ...*. Choice B is wrong because the second "the" is missing. Choices C and D are eliminated because of the wrong word order.

27. C

The noun "TV" is modified by two hyphenated adjectives: "wall-size" and "flat-screen." Only Choice C has both adjectives hyphenated.

28. B

Choice A is wrong because a detached subordinate clause cannot be led by "that." Choice C is eliminated because a comma cannot combine two complete sentences. Choice D is not correct either because of the wrong word order. Choice B is the only correct answer: "*which*" *stands for* the noun "wall-size flat-screen TV" and leads the modifying clause.

29. D

Choice A is eliminated because "all" can never be followed by "what." Choice B "all globalization" doesn't make sense. Choice C is wrong because it uses a question word order. Only Choice D is right: Adverb "all" emphasizes "about."

30. A

"*What happened over the last years*" is the subject of the sentence, and the clause "*that there was a massive investment in technology*" is the predicative. Choice A correctly shows this structure. None of the other choices keeps this structure.

31. C

The reporting phrase "he added," when inserted in the middle of the sentence, should be set off with two commas, as Choice C indicates.

32. B

Choices A and D should be eliminated right away because "make" and "makes" are finite verb forms without a subject. Choice C "to make it easy" indicates a purpose. Only Choice B "making it easy" shows the result.

33. C

Choice C "*The world is Flat!*" is the best answer because it echoes the beginning of the passage.

34. A

Choice A is perfect: Participial phrase "working ..." modifies the noun "helper." Choices B and C are wrong because "work" and "works" are finite verbs without a subject. Choice D is not correct either because it sounds as if they will work there in future.

35. D

Comparatively speaking, sentence "*It was set to be completed in 2015*" only gives minor information; therefore, the best way to combine the two sentences is to shorten it into a past participial phrase while keep the second sentence as the main clause, as Choice D indicates.

36. C

The time phrase "last year" calls for past tense form of the target verb; that eliminates Choices A, B, and D.

37. D

After preposition "of," a noun or its equivalent (in this case, *being*) must be used.

38. D

Choice D is the best because the whole paragraph provides a vivid description of Tariq's longing for being a crane operator, so the proposed sentence to be added is not necessary.

Choice A, B, and C are incorrect because none provides information that links the main claim made in the paragraph.

39. A

Only Choice A makes sense because "materialized" means "became real." Choices B, C, and D are eliminated because they all need to work with "was."

40. C

Only "so that" reflects the cause-effect relationship between the two parts of the sentence. Choice A is wrong because the two parts are not paralleled. Choices B and D are both wrong because they should lead to the opposite direction:
His boss confiscated his passport for fear that / lest he could change jobs or leave the country.

41. B

From the context we can infer that he started to pay back the loan 11 months ago. Therefore, present perfect tense should be used: Up till now he still "*has not paid back*" his loan yet, as Choice B indicates.

42. D

Choice D is the right answer: The author interviewed "the construction workers" in May; Only "whom" can stand for "the workers" as the object of the verb "interviewed."

43. A

"that lit up" sets up a subordinate clause and a fix collocation, and therefore Choice A is the best answer. There is no verb in the choice C and a tense error occurs in the choice B. Choice D is incorrect because it contains "it" which contradicts with "that".

44. C

Through the passage, especially the comment of "built on the backs," we can feel that the author's sympathy is on the workers' side. Each of Choices A, B, and D is partially true, but more or less neutral in tone. Only Choice C "*little more than indentured servants*" is consistent with the sympathetic tone of the passage.

SECTION 3

1. C

Substitute the answer values in for n until the equation works. Start with answer B: $n = 4$. But $3^1 - 3^2 = 3 - 9 = -6$ so answer B is incorrect. Also, we got a number that is too small, so try C or D next. When you use $n = 6$, you get $3^3 - 3^2 = 27 - 9 = 18$ so answer C is correct.

Alternatively, isolate the term with n: $3^{n-3} = 18 + 3^2 = 27$, so that $3^{n-3} = 3^3$. Since the bases are the same (both 3), the exponents must be equal: $n - 3 = 3$ which means that $n = 6$.

2. B

Use the answers, starting with C: suppose that the biggest integer is 6. Then, the three integers are 4, 5, and 6. But, $5 \times 4 = 20$ and $3 \times 6 = 18$, so answer C is incorrect. It isn't clear whether we need a bigger answer or a smaller answer, but we are close, so you should only need to try B or D. If you try answer B, the three numbers are 3, 4, and 5, and $5 \times 3 = 3 \times 5$, so B is correct.

Alternatively, let x be the greatest of the three integers. Then, the three integers from least to greatest is $x - 2$, $x - 1$, and x. Since five times the least is three times the greatest, $5(x - 2) = 3(x)$, or $5x - 10 = 3x$. Solving for x gives $x = 5$.

3. D

Working with the answers: substitute each answer into m until the inequality works. If you plug in answer D, you get $|2(2) - 4| = 0$ which is less than 1, so answer D is correct.

Alternatively, the expression $|x| < 5$, for example, means that x is less than 5 units away from 0 on the number line. In other words, x is bigger than -5 and less than 5. In math, this is: $-5 < x < 5$. So, $|2m - 4| < 1$ is the same thing as: $-1 < 2m - 4 < 1$. Adding 4 to all sides gives $3 < 2m < 5$ so that $\frac{3}{2} < m < \frac{5}{2}$, which means that m must be equal to 2.

4. B

Working with the answers may be easier. If answer A is correct, then there were 16 green apples and 12 red apples, in order to have the 4 to 3 ratio. But removing five of each gives 11 green and 7 red, which is not in the ratio of 3 to 2. If answer B is correct, then there were 20 green apples and 15 red apples, since $\frac{20}{15} = \frac{4}{3}$. Removing five of each gives 15 green and 10 red, and $\frac{15}{10} = \frac{3}{2}$, so answer B is correct.

Alternative solution: The number of green and red apples is $4n$ and $3n$, respectively, for some integer n. In this way, we can be sure that the green–to–red ratio is $\frac{4n}{3n} = \frac{4}{3}$. We need to solve the equation: $\frac{4n - 5}{3n - 5} = \frac{3}{2}$. Cross-multiplying, $8n - 10 = 9n - 15$ so that $n = 5$. There were $3n$, or 15, red apples in the bag.

5. C

Use the graph to find $f(4)$ as follows. First, go to $x = 4$ on the x-axis. Next, go vertically up until you reach the line for the function f. Then, go left horizontally to find the y-value. You should see that for function f, when $x = 4$, the $y = 2$. Since $a = f(4)$, we know that $a = 2$ and we need to find $g(2)$. Repeat the process, now using the line for the function g. You will see that $g(2) = 3$.

6. D

First, calculate the slope of line t using the given points: slope $= \frac{\text{rise}}{\text{run}} = \frac{0 - 1}{a - 0} = -\frac{1}{a}$. At this point, a good approach is to work with the answers by plugging them into the expression for slope above until you get a value greater than $-\frac{1}{2}$. For example, using answer A gives a slope of $\frac{-1}{\frac{1}{2}} = -2$, which is not greater than $-\frac{1}{2}$, so answer A is incorrect. You should find that answer D is the correct one, since $\frac{-1}{\frac{5}{2}} = -\frac{2}{5}$ is greater than $-\frac{1}{2}$.

Algebraically, calculate the slope the same as above. $-\frac{1}{a} > -\frac{1}{2} \Rightarrow \frac{1}{a} < \frac{1}{2} \Rightarrow a > 2$. (Remember to flip the inequality when multiplying by negative numbers or when taking the reciprocal of both sides.) Only answer D makes $a > 2$.

7. A

To find x, we need to square both sides of the equation: $(\sqrt{x})^2 = (\sqrt{a} + \sqrt{b})^2 = (\sqrt{a} + \sqrt{b})(\sqrt{a} + \sqrt{b})$. Now "FOIL" the right-hand side to get $x = (\sqrt{a})^2 + 2\sqrt{a}\sqrt{b} + (\sqrt{b})^2$ so that $x = a + 2\sqrt{a}\sqrt{b} + b = a + b + 2\sqrt{ab}$.

8. B

To make f–g as large as possible, we need to make f as large as possible and g as small as possible. So, f–g has to be less than 40 − 50 = −10. To make f − g as small as possible, we need to make f as small as possible and g as large as possible. So, f − g has to be greater than 30 − 70 = −40. The expression that gives all possible values of f − g is then −40 < f − g < −10.

9. A

It is helpful to recognize that $(x + 2)(x − 2) = x^2 − 4$. The equation $x^2 − y^2 = (x + y)(x − y)$ is called the difference of two squares. Since $f(x) = x^2 − 4$ and the least possible value of x^2 is zero, then the least possible value of $f(x)$ is 0 − 4 = −4, so answer A is correct.

10. C

Since O is the center of the circle, AO = 6 and OB = 6. Let's redraw the diagram, putting in the diameter of the big circle:

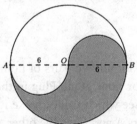

The shaded semicircle with diameter OB is equal in area to the unshaded semicircle with diameter AO. So, the area of the entire unshaded region is just half the area of the big circle. Since the radius of the big circle is 6, its area is 36π ($A = \pi r^2$). The area of the unshaded region is half the area of the whole circle, 18π, making answer C the correct one.

11. B

The diagonal of a rectangle divides it into two right triangles; in this case, 30 – 60 – 90 triangles.

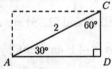

Using that information about the sides of a 30 – 60 – 90 triangle, if AC (Hypotenuse) = 2 then CD (Leg opposite the 30 degree angle = $\frac{1}{2}$ the

Hypotenuse) = 1 and AD (Leg opposite the 60 degree angle = $\frac{1}{2}$ the Hypotenuse times $\sqrt{3}$) = $\frac{1}{2} \cdot 2 \cdot \sqrt{3} = \sqrt{3}$ so the area $(l \cdot w) = AD \cdot CD = \sqrt{3} \cdot 1 = \sqrt{3}$.

12. B

In this question, you want to draw a line from A perpendicular to the opposite side of the triangle:

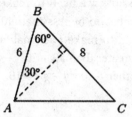

This creates a $30 - 60 - 90$ triangle with the hypotenuse, $AB = 6$. Using that information about a $30 - 60 - 90$ triangle, if AB (Hypotenuse) = 6 then the length of the side opposite the $30°$ angle (Half the hypotenuse) is 3, and the length of the side opposite the $60°$ angle (the dashed line = Half the Hypotenuse $\cdot \sqrt{3}$) is $3\sqrt{3}$. Therefore, if the base of the triangle is segment $BC = 8$, and the dashed line is the height of the triangle = $3\sqrt{3}$, then the area of the triangle ($\frac{1}{2} \cdot$ b $\cdot$h) is ($\frac{1}{2}$) $\cdot$ 8 $\cdot 3\sqrt{3} = 12\sqrt{3}$.

13. C

One of the equations works for all five pairs of numbers; the others will work for only some of the pairs, or none at all. Plug in the x and y values from the table into the equations to see which values make it true. Plug in 0 for x into the answers, $y = 3$ for answers A and C, so the other answers must be incorrect. Next plug in for x is 2. The table says for $x = 2$, $y = -5$; answer A is $y = -1$, and answer C is $y = -5$, so answer C is the correct one.

Algebraically, the equations are in slope-intercept form. $Y = mx + b$, where b is the y-intercept and m is the slope. The y-intercept is where the line crosses the y-axis or $(0,y)$. Therefore the y-intercept is listed in the table $(0,3)$. This can eliminate all equations that don't fit $y = mx + 3$, which are all answers but A and C. Then find the slope, the change in y over the change in x. Pick 2 points and find the slope using $\frac{y_1 - y_2}{x_1 - x_2}$. If $(0,3)$ and $(2,-5)$ are used the slope will be $\frac{-5 - 3}{2 - 0}$ = -4. The only equation where $m = -4$ is answer C) $y = -4x + 3$.

14. C

Use the answers, starting with B: suppose that the lesser of the integers is 4.

Then, the two integers are 4 and 5. But, $4^2 = 16$ and $5^2 = 25$, $16 + 25 = 41$, so answer B is incorrect. If you try the other answers the same way you will see that answer C is correct, $5^2 = 25$ and $6^2 = 36$, $25 + 36 = 61$.

Alternatively, let x be the lesser of the two integers. Then the next integer is $x + 1$. Since the sum of the squares of these integers is 61, $x^2 + (x + 1)^2 = 61$, or $2x^2 + 2x + 1 = 61$, move 61 to the other side of the equal sign and factor out a 2, $2(x^2 + x - 30) = 0$. Factor, $2(x - 5)(x + 6) = 0$. Solving for x gives $x = 5$ and $x = -6$. Therefore, the lesser of 2 positive integers must be 5.

15. A

Since m is positive, the U–shaped graph must open up and since n is zero, the y intercept must be zero.

16. 3

Since $f(c) = 3c + 1$ and $g(c) = 4c - 2$, $f(c) = g(c)$ is the same as $3c + 1 = 4c - 2$, which means that $c = 3$.

17. 40

Let n = number of nickels. Then, the number of dimes is $50 - n$, and we need $0.05n + 0.10(50 - n) = 3$. Solving for n gives $5 - 0.05n = 3$ so that $0.05n = 2$, or $n = 40$.

18. $\frac{3}{5}$

Let T be the total time. The distance with the rabbit's foot is then $(\frac{3}{4}) \cdot T \cdot 6 = (\frac{9}{2})T$, and the distance without rabbit's foot is $(\frac{1}{4}) \cdot T \cdot 12 = 3T$. The desired fraction is then: $\dfrac{(\frac{9}{2})T}{(\frac{9}{2})T + 3T} = \dfrac{9/2}{15/2} = \dfrac{9}{15} = \dfrac{3}{5}$

19. 6

Factor and solve the quadratic equation.

$(x + 1)(x - 6) = 0$

$x = -1$ or 6, but since we are told $x > 0$, $x = 6$

20. 2

Since the remainder is 4 when k is divided by 7, we can write $k = 7x + 4$ for some integer x. For example, if $x = 1$, then $k = 11$; if $x = 2$, then $k = 18$, and so forth. Then, substitute $7x + 4$ for k in $k + 26$ which equals $(7x + 4) + 26 = 7x + 30$. Factor (divide) out a 7 so now $7x + 7 \times 4 + 2$ so that $k + 26 = 7(x + 4) + 2$. So, the remainder is 2.

SECTION 4

1. A

Only 2 answer choices show a loss, A (January to February) or D (May to June). The loss of profit from January to February was $40,000. The loss of profit from May to June was $30,000. Answer A, with a loss in profit of $40,000, is the greatest loss the graph shows.

2. C

The equations are in slope-intercept form. $Y = mx + b$, where b is the y-intercept and m is the slope. The y-intercept is where the line crosses the y-axis or $(0,y)$. Therefore the y-intercept is $(0,1)$. Therefore the equation should read, $y = mx + 1$, which are all answers. Next compute the slope of the line of best fit, the change in y over the change in x. Pick 2 points and find the slope using $\frac{y_1 - y_2}{x_1 - x_2}$. If $(0, 1)$ and $(4, 7)$ are used the slope will be $\frac{7-1}{4-0} = \frac{6}{4} = \frac{3}{2}$. Therefore Answer C has $m = \frac{3}{2}$ and $b = 1$, so that is the correct equation $y = \frac{3}{2}x + 1$.

3. D

Since the numbers are negative except for e, multiplying two of them will result in a positive number. We can eliminate any answers with e since those answers will all be equal to 0. To get the smallest positive number, we need to multiply the two largest (least negative) numbers marked in the diagram: (D) is the correct answer.

4. B

Strategy Solution: Plug in numbers. The first three terms are n, $2n$, and $4n$. Plug in easy numbers for n to see what the sum is. For example, if $n = 1$, the sum is $1 + 2 + 4 = 7$. If $n = 2$, the sum is $2 + 4 + 8 = 14$. The sums are always multiples of 7, so answer B is correct since it is NOT a multiple of 7.

Math Teacher Solution: $n + 2n + 4n = 7n$, so that the sum of the first three terms is always a multiple of 7.

5. C

Chinese make up 14% or 5,000 of the total. To find the total number of students, let t = the total, $0.14 t = 5,000$. Solve for t, $t = 35,714$.

6. C

To solve, first divide both sides by 2, leaving $\sqrt{x - 3} = 3$. Square both sides and then you will have $x - 3 = 9$. Solve the algebraic equation. Add 3 to both sides, $x = 12$.

7. C

For choice I, suppose that the set is a group of ten 2's. The median of this set is 2, which is an integer, so choice I could NOT be true (since the median that makes it true is NOT an integer.). For choice II, note that for a set of ten numbers, there is no single "middle" number, so the median is the average of the two middle numbers (the 5th largest and 6th largest). But the average of any two consecutive integers is never an integer, so choice II is alway true. (As an example, suppose that the set is the integers from 1 to 10. The two middle numbers are 5 and 6 and the median is $\frac{5 + 6}{2}$ = 5.5.) This reasoning helps with choice III: suppose that the middle two numbers are 8 and 10. Then the median is $\frac{8 + 10}{2}$ = 9, which is an integer, so choice III could NOT be true, making answer C the only one correct.

8. D

Graph D is correct because it shows a loss of 50% of original stock ($500 × 50% = $250) over the first five weeks. At which time the graph levels off or stops showing a loss for the next three weeks. The graph then ends showing the selling of the stock.

9. B

Let x be the area of garden B. Remember that when you increase a number by a percent, you first multiply the number by the percent (divided by 100), then you add the original number. So, the equation we need is: Area of garden A = x + 0.25x = 45, so 1.25x = 45, which means that x = 36. In this case, we need the garden's perimeter, not the area. A square with an area of 36 has a side of 6, so the perimeter is 6 × 4 = 24.

10. B

First, convert the words into an equation: $\frac{z}{4} = \frac{z}{2} + 12$

From here, work with the answers by substituting them into the equation until it works. Or, use algebra to solve the equation: $\frac{z}{4} - \frac{n}{2} = \frac{z}{4} - \frac{2z}{4} = \frac{-1z}{4}$ = 12, multiply both sides by -4 so that n = -48. (You could also solve the equation by multiplying through by 4 first to get rid of the fractions.)

11. D

One way to do this is to find all the numbers in set Y, and then calculate the average or arithmetic mean of those numbers. Set Y is: 2, 4, 6, 8, 10, 12, 14, so that the average of the numbers in set Y is $\frac{56}{7} = 8$. A second way is to notice that if you divide a set of numbers by $\frac{1}{2}$, the average of the set will get divided by $\frac{1}{2}$ as well. Since the average of set X is 4, the average of set Y is 8.

12. C

$$\frac{\sqrt{5}}{100} \times 3\sqrt{5} = \frac{3\sqrt{5}\sqrt{5}}{100} = \frac{3\sqrt{25}}{100} = \frac{15}{100} = \frac{3}{20}$$

so that the correct answer is C. The radicals can also be converted to decimals and then covert the answer to a fraction.

13. B

If there are 12,500 voters age 50 and over, that is equal to 42% of the total. To find out how many voters are under the age of 40, you would have to look at the 30 –39 age group, 20–29 age group and the 18–19 age group which accounts for 43% of the total. Therefore, if you set up a proportion $\frac{42}{12,500} = \frac{43}{x}$ and cross multiply and solve for x, you will get $x = 12,798$.

14. D

Strategy Solution: Plug in the answers. Plug each one in for x until it works. For example, you can try answer B by setting $x = 2$. Then, $6 - 4x = -2$, which is less than 18 not greater than 18 and $5 - 2x = 1$, which is greater than -1 not less than, answer B is not correct. Continue doing this until you get an answer that works.

Math Teacher Solution: Solve the inequalities. You will get: $x > 3$ or $x < -3$. Only answer D is greater than 3. Since the word "or" is used, x only has to satisfy one inequality.

15. B

Consider furniture set A: it consists of 1 table and 7 chairs, which means that the price of set A in 2002 is $1 \times \$60 + 7 \times \$30 = \$270$. Similarly, the price of set B in 2002 is $2 \times \$60 + 5 \times \$30 = \$270$ and the price of set C in 2002 is $3 \times \$60 + 2 \times \$30 = \$240$. The least of these three is $240, so answer B is correct.

16. C

Strategy Solution: Plug in easy numbers for x and y, making sure that $2x = \frac{y}{3}$. An example would be $x = \frac{1}{2}$ and $y = 3$ since both sides of the equation are then equal to 1. Plug in $y = 3$ into $\frac{y}{6} = \frac{3}{6} = \frac{1}{2}$. Then plug in $\frac{1}{2}$ for x into the answers until you get $\frac{1}{2}$. Only answer C equals $\frac{1}{2}$, so it must be the correct one.

Math Teacher Solution: Since $2x = \frac{y}{3}$, solve for y, $y = 6x$. Then plug $y = 6x$ into $\frac{y}{6}$ to get $\frac{6x}{6} = x$, so answer C is correct.

17. D

Strategy: Plug in real numbers. For percent problems, the number 100 is often a good choice. With a $100 budget, the seniors spent 20% ($20) on the balloons, leaving $80. They spent one-fourth of the $80 (another $20) on the disc jockey, leaving $60. Finally, they spent 1/3 of the $60 (another $20) on the venue, leaving $40, which is 40% of the original $100. Therefore, 60% of the budget was used for the prom.

Math Teacher Solution: Let x be the original budget. After the balloons, the seniors have $x - 0.2x = 0.8x$. After the disc jockey, they have $0.8x - (\frac{1}{4})(0.8x) = 0.6x$. After the venue, they have $0.6x - (\frac{1}{3})(0.6x) = 0.4x$, so that shows that 40% of the budget remains, which means 60% of the budget was spent on the prom.

18. B

The slopes of two parallel lines are equal to each other. Since the slope of the given line is 3, the slope of a parallel line is also 3. The basic equation is then $y = 3x + b$. We need to use the point $(0, -7)$ to find b. Let's do that: $-7 = 3(0) + b$. Therefore, $b = -7$, and the complete parallel line equation is $y = 3x - 7$.

19. D

If you factor out $a - 2$ from the second equation, both equations are $x^2 + 2x - 3 = 0$, equivalent equations have the same solutions.

20. D

Strategy Solution: Plug in real numbers. Plug in easy, real numbers for x, y, and z, making sure that the numbers satisfy the given equation, $\frac{z}{4} = \frac{x}{y}$. Then, go through the answers, plugging in the values you chose until you get 8. For example, try $z = 1$, $y = 8$, and $x = 2$. Starting with A, the answers equal 4, 2, $\frac{1}{8}$, and 8, so answer D is correct.

Math Teacher Solution: Cross-multiply the given equation to get $4x = yz$. Dividing both sides by x gives $4 = \frac{yz}{x}$. Finally, to get the equation to equal 8, multiply both sides by 2, so answer D is correct.

21. A

This equation is correct because it is the only one that does have the y-intercept at positive 2.

367

22. B

Strategy Solution: Make up some odd integers, plug them in for x, and see if they work. Since you can't take the square root of a negative number, x cannot be less than -7. Also, if $x = -3$, then $\sqrt{x+7} = 2$, but any larger value of x will not work. So, looking at odd integers from -3 through -7, there are three possible values, -3, -5, and -7.

Math Teacher Solution: Solve for x. Square both sides to get $x + 7 \leq 4$. Subtract 7 from both sides, $x \leq -3$. Since you can't take the square root of a negative number and x is odd, x cannot be less than -7 but has to be no more than -3, leaving -3, -5 and -7.

23. D

Strategy Solution: Plug in the answers. The phrase "intersects the x-axis at $x = m$" is another way to say the x-intercept which means the line goes through the point $(m, 0)$. Therefore plug in each answer for x and 0 for y until they equal 36. If you try answer D, $x = 12$, the equation will read $3(12) + 4(0) = 36$. This is true so D is the correct answer.

Math Teacher Solution: If a line goes through a point, the point satisfies the equation of the line. Keeping that in mind, along with the definition of x-intercept, plug $x = m$ and $y = 0$ into the equation. $3m + 2(0) = 36$, $3m = 36$. Solve for m, $m = 12$.

24. B

One of $(p + 1)$ and $(t + 4)$ must be 0. Because t is positive, the latter will never be 0. So $p + 1$ is 0 and $p = -1$.

25. C

Suppose $b = 3n$ where n is a positive integer. From $ab \leq 81$ (because ab is an integer), we have $a \leq \dfrac{27}{n}$. It is clear when $n = 1$ we get the biggest possible $a = 27$, which is C.

26. D

Strategy Solution: Plug in a number for x, and see which of the answers are always even integers. Since all of the answers have 2 choices, two of the answers given will not always be even integers. Answer D has the 2 options that will always result in even integers.

Math Teacher Solution: I. is not even an integer, unless $x = 2$, but then $\dfrac{x}{2} = 1$ is not even. III is always increased by 2 so if x is odd, III will also be odd. II and IV are always even. Therefore answer D must be correct.

27. B

Substitute both $6a$ and $3a$ into $f(x)$ and then use the second equation to get $6a + 10 + 2 = 3a + 10 + 11$. This simplifies to $6a + 12 = 3a + 21$. Continue to solve to get $3a = 9$. Finally, divide both sides by 3 to get $a = 3$.

28. D

Strategy Solution: Plug in real numbers. Let $x = .08y$, $y = 1.00z + z$ or $y = 2z$, and $z = 20$. Plug answer D into the first equation to get $3.2 = .08y$. Solve for y by dividing each side by .08 to get $y = 40$. Since y also equals $2z$, $2z = 40$. Finally, divide each side by 2 to get $z = 20$, so answer D is correct.

Math Teacher Solution: Let $x = .08y$, $y = 1.00z + z$ or $y = 2z$, and $z = 20$. Plug $z = 20$ into $y = 2z$ to get $y = 40$. Substitute $y = 40$ into $x = .08(40)$ to get $x = 3.2$, so answer D is correct.

29. B

Strategy Solution: Plug in the answers. First, "the graph of $y = g(x)$ crosses the x-axis at $x = a$" means that a is the x-intercept, so the y-value is zero when $x = a$. Therefore, $y = g(x) = 0$ when $x = $ a. Set a (and therefore, x) equal to each answer, and check to see if $g(x)$ is zero. For example, if $x = -2$ (answer B), then $g(x) = g(-2) = 28(-2)^4 + 16(-2)^3 - 80(-2)^2 = 448 - 128 - 320 = 0$. Therefore answer B is correct.

Math Teacher Solution: Since $g(x) = 0$ when the function crosses the x-axis, set $g(x) = 0$ and solve for x by factoring. $28x^4 + 16x^3 - 80x^2 = 4x^2(7x-10)(x + 2)$. Therefore, $4x^2 = 0 \Rightarrow x = 0$, $7x - 10 = 0 \Rightarrow x = \dfrac{10}{7}$, or $x + 2 = 0 \Rightarrow x = -2$. Only $x = -2$ appears in the answers, so answer B is correct.

30. C

The $160°$ and $x \cdot$ angles lie along a line, which means that they add up to $180°$. This means that $x = 20°$. Since $x + y + z = 180°$, $20 + y + z = 180°$ so that $y + z = 160°$.

31. $x = \dfrac{5}{6}$ or .83

Cross-multiply: $8(8x-2) = 4(4x + 6)$. Apply the distributive property, leaving $64x - 16 = 16x + 24$. Solve for x, $48x = 40$. Therefore, $x = \dfrac{5}{6}$ or .83.

32. 16

The radius of each of the smaller circles is four. Therefore, Arc AB and Arc BC are both 4π, half the circumference ($2\pi r$ or $2\pi4 = 8\pi$).; The radius of the big circle is twice the radius (diameter) of the little circle or ($2 \times 4 = 8$). Therefore Arc AC is 8π, half the circumference of the bigger circle ($2\pi8 = 16\pi$). Then if you add the perimeter/circumference of the 2 halves of the smaller circles (4π + $4\pi = 8\pi$) with the perimeter/circumference of half the larger circle, $8\pi + 8\pi =$ 16π for the perimeter/circumference of the shaded region.

33. 135

Since distance equals speed multiplied by time, 90 miles = 40 mph $\cdot$ t. Solve for t, divide both sides by 40 to get $t = 2.25$ hours. Convert 2.25 hours to minutes, $2.25 \cdot 60 = 135$ minutes.

34. 11

Since the tick marks correspond to consecutive integers, it takes four "steps" (spaces) to go from $\frac{x}{12}$ to $\frac{x}{8}$. Therefore, $\frac{x}{8}$ is four greater than $\frac{x}{12}$. In equation form that is $\frac{x}{8} = \frac{x}{12} + 4$. Multiplying both sides by 24 to get rid of the fractions is $3x = 2x + 96$. Solve to get $x = 96$. Plug in x, $\frac{96}{12} = 8$. Therefore, count right 3 tick marks from 8 and $Y = 11$.

35. 16

Let t be the number of ounces of tomatoes, and s be the number of ounces of sugar. Then, $t + s = 160$ (tomatoes and sugar add up to 160 pounds), and $\frac{t}{s} =$ 9 (ratio of tomatoes to sugar is 9 : 1). Solving the second equation for t ($t = 9s$) and substituting it into the first is $9s + s = 160$ so that $10s = 160$, or $s = 16$.

36. 22
$f(-1) = (-1)^3 + 3(-1)^2 - 6(-1) + 14$
$f(-1) = -1 + 3(1) - (-6) + 14$
$f(-1) = -1 + 3 + 6 + 14$
$f(-1) = 22$

37. 3

$41.50 represents the conversion of 125 reais plus a 3% fee on the converted cost. To calculate the original cost of the item in x dollars: $1.03x = 41.50$. Solve for x to get $x = 40.29$. Since the original cost is $40.29, to calculate the exchange rate r, in Brazilian real per one U.S. dollar:

40.29 dollars $\times \dfrac{r \text{ reais}}{1 \text{ dollar}} = 125$ reais

$r = \dfrac{125}{40.29} \approx 3$ reais

38. 9233

Let d dollars be the cost of the 9,500-real prepaid card. This implies that the exchange rate on this particular day is $\frac{d}{9,500}$ dollar per real. Suppose Maria's total purchases on the prepaid card were r reais. The value of the r reais in dollars is $(\frac{d}{9,500})p$ dollars. If Maria spent the r reais on the International Traveler card instead, she would be charged $(1.03)(\frac{d}{9,500})r$ dollars. To answer the question about how many reais Maria must spend in order to make the pre-paid card a cheaper option (in dollars) for spending the r reais, set up the inequality International Traveler card $\geq$ pre-paid card, $1.03(\frac{d}{9,500})r \geq d$. Begin solving for r by dividing both sides by d, which is $1.03 (\frac{p}{9,500}) \geq 1$. Dividing on both sides by 1.03 and multiplying on both sides by 9,500 equals $r \geq 9,223$. Therefore, the least number of real Maria must spend for the prepaid card to be cheaper than the International Traveler card is 9,223 reais.

SECTION 5

Many people treat global warming as dogma. For John Hawkins, in the essay "5 Scientific Reasons That Global Warming Isn't Happening," the existence of global warming is far from proven. In fact, the evidence points against global warming. Hawkins builds his case against global warming by asking rhetorical questions, examining failed assertions, and citing encouraging recent events.

Rhetorical questions sprinkled throughout the essay encourage the readers to question their assumptions about global warming. Hawkins opens with two questions designed to establish him as a credible, even-handed voice. By juxtaposing "climate deniers" with "global warming cultists" and questioning why there is so little discussion about the science behind the supposedly scientific topic of global warming, he presents his views as a level-headed evaluation of the facts, rather than a kneejerk emotional reaction. His next question occurs at the end of the second paragraph, where his redundant wording reminds the reader of the lack of global warming since 1997. It also highlights the reductivist logic of those who propagate global warming without thoroughly examining the evidence. The essay concludes as it began, with a final question that serves as an indirect call to action. By asking the reader "wouldn't it be more scientific to reject hasty action based on faulty data...?" he allows the readers to come to his desired conclusion on their own. These carefully worded rhetorical questions set the stage for more concrete attacks on global warming.

Hawkins makes three key attacks against global warming science. First, he shows that much of the scientific consensus surrounding global warming is based on a tautology: "The primary 'scientific' argument for global warming is that there is a 'scientific consensus' that it's occurring." However, consensus is far from evident: thousands of scientists have signed petitions questioning whether humans have caused global warming or whether global warming exists at all. Second, he stresses that climate change models have consistently been incorrect. Even government-sponsored models "'have failed miserably.'" By citing respected members of the scientific community, Hawkins dismantles the notion that global warming is indisputable. Similarly, he argues that famous doomsday predictions about global warming have failed the test of time. The Artic is not in a death spiral and the West Side highway is not underwater.

The argument against global warming is rounded out with a discussion of signs that indicate a reversal in the planetary warming trend. In the second paragraph, Hawkins points out that even a respected climate change scientist acknowledges that there has been no warming over the past seventeen years. The absence of warming over the past seventeen years becomes an even stronger refutation of global warming when put in context. The alarming global warming trend was in fact only a twenty-two year period sandwiched between twenty-five years of global cooling and the steady temperatures of the past two decades. In paragraph four, he explains that Arctic ice levels, frequently lamented as proof of global warming, have actually increased significantly since 2012. Hawkins presents himself as a fair arbitrator of the evidence and calls on his ideological rivals to be open-minded by acknowledging the recent increase in ice levels and the probability that they represent good news about climate change.

John Hawkins cleverly takes on global warming from several different angles. Rhetorical questions cause the reader to begin rethinking their assumptions about global warming. Evidence that contradicts global warming demonstrates that the science is far from settled. Finally, positive trends give hope for a future that is far brighter than the one depicted by the doom and gloom prophets of global warming.

Answer Explanations
New SAT Practice Test 2

Section 1

1. C

The provisions contained in the Meissner Memo effectively expand the provisions of wet foot/dry foot by allowing quicker access to residency.

2. A

Based upon the order of policy changes and the details of both the history of political relations and discussion of ongoing diplomatic talks, it is evident that the author is seeking to outline a history of events leading to the most recent changes in travel policy.

3. D

Direct definition. Difficult to understand in context, but nationalistic and excommunicated do not fit in with the theme of the sentence.

4. C

Choices A and B are clearly not correct. Choice D is a sound option, but the overall trend since 2000 has been an increase of at least 12,000 refugees per year.

5. B

A and D are incorrect as part of the plan allows for citizens to travel abroad for greater lengths of time and include provisions to keep criminals on the island. Choice C is incorrect due to the characterization of "warmer relations".

6. C

The quote provides the best evidence of how citizens within the country feel about the policy shifts. While it is benefitting some Cubans, the majority who are reaping the rewards are those who are engaging in illegal activities.

7. A

In context, the term refers to the fact that lawmakers won't commit due to how their stance will be viewed by their constituents.

8. C

Given the timeline of events, it is evident that Cuba's stance on the Adjustment Act caused changes to their policy to address the areas where Cuba did not agree with the United States.

9. D

Statistics provided and the graphic both depict the increase in refugees entering the United States.

10. B

Direct evidence related to question 9.

11. A

As stated previously, the number of non traditional refugees entering the United States has increased steadily since policy changes eased travel restrictions to and from the island of Cuba.

12. A

The events discussed in the passage and the manner of writing all suggest the potential for cataclysmic events.

13. C

The direct definition of "spalled" is cracked. It is used appropriately in context of the sentence, particularly after "enough welds have cracked".

14. D

The author describes how isolated survivors will most likely be following these events and the potential for long-term delays is assistance.

15. B

The best evidence of the previous question comes in the last lines of the paragraph, specifically detailing the amount of time and the amount of effort survivors will need to undertake on their own.

16. B

From the tone of the article, the author speaks from a perspective of when these events may occur, not if.

17. D

In context, it is evident that the buildings are swaying with the movement of the ground due to the quake.

18. C

The image refers directly to the fault line, as described by the author's words during that particular paragraph.

19. A

The author clearly spells out the potential chain reaction of events which may occur following such a large scale quake.

20. B

In those sentences, the writer specifically defines which events are most likely to occur following a quake of that size.

21. B

By referencing such a tragedy that could be considered preventable through preparedness, the author hopes to avoid the same large scale casualties by equating an event of the magnitude of 9/11 with the potential aftermath of a large scale quake.

22. B

While Dr. Spencer does display anger, resentment, and a demeaning attitude towards Holden, his comments and questions regarding whether or not Holden blames him for failing class indicate that he harbors some warm and sympathetic feelings towards Holden.

23. D

Although all are types of furniture, a chiffonier is an antique style of dresser.

24. A

Though there is some indication that Holden is attempting to right some wrongdoings at Pency, he is clearly becoming more agitated and regretful as the conversation continues.

25. C

This particular quote directly conveys Holden's current feelings towards where the conversation and visit are going.

26. B

Although A could potentially be true, we are not given enough information to make that determination. Option C is also a potentially true answer, but it is again unclear as to how Holden feels about his performance in class. Because of this, option B is the best answer for this question.

27. D

Direct definition. The prefix in-, meaning without, and root word numer, meaning count.

28. A

While B and C could potentially be true, there is no indication that Dr. Spencer sees Holden's future as an absolute or that he should be more appreciative. Given his reading of the essay and his repeated reference to the lack of work in class exhibited by Holden, option A is the best answer.

29. C

Again, A and B are potentially correct. He is angry, reproachful, and somewhat solemn. However, Dr. Spencer's comments regarding belief that Holden didn't apply himself with any degree of consistency makes C the best choice.

30. B

Direct quote that provides specific information related to question 29.

31. A

While C is an option, Holden doesn't display quite enough overly "nice" or sympathetic behaviors during this selection to qualify as passive aggressive behavior.

32. B

The author details, in the introductory paragraph, his desires for nonpartisanship and understanding, citing specific ideals and values commonly held between both parties.

33. C

The information contained in this quote clearly reflects the author's desire to foster a sense of understanding and camaraderie between the political parties.

34. D

The speech delivered is filled with optimistic phrases and scenarios. The tone and language used in an attempt to sway the reader to the author's perspective is a clear example of propaganda.

35. A

Direct definition. Partisanship implies blindly agreeing with a particular dogma simply for acceptance.

36. D

The use of Ann Nixon Cooper and the many trials she faced en route to voting in this particular election lend credence to the notion that her example was one of overcoming discriminatory practices placed in a person's way.

37. B

The quote, particularly the last 3 words, imply that the power and willingness of the people to exact change is precisely what affects policy shifts in the United States.

38. C

Direct definition. Though it can also be used to describe a prayer, in the context of the sentence the term implies a core set of beliefs.

39. A

Given the climate of Lincoln's America, it is clear that the author is comparing the struggles and division faced by Lincoln with the divisiveness which exists between the political parties currently.

40. D

Throughout the text, we are greeted with President Obama's favorable outlook on the future of the American people. Sprinkled within this, we are provided with historical evidence of the triumphs of the American people over the difficulties they faced.

41. B

The author specifically attributes the power of change to the American people in this particular quote.

42. A

The symbolism of "dawn" implies a rebirth of sorts within the country; politically, socially, and through changes in the way society is exacting change.

43. C

The evidence provided in passage 2 suggests that the hot springs mentioned, particularly those which contain high concentrations of iron-rich rocks are critical for providing support for potential life existing on Mars.

44. D

Assumptions most directly means speculation or conjecture. The word is used correctly in context.

45. A

The Yellowstone research team found evidence that was contrary to prior research, indicating that those rocks actually assist in fossilizing carbon and lipid based materials, rather than destroying them as previously thought.

46. C

As stated previously, the current research discussed in the article countered prior research which indicated that iron-rich rocks destroyed, rather than sustained, fossilized materials.

47. B

Both articles discuss the importance of identifying and securing organic compounds as the most critical for supporting the notion that life existed on Mars.

48. D

Direct definition used correctly in context. Habitable means able to support or nurture life.

49. A

Passage 2 goes to great lengths to make correlations between the Yellowstone hot springs and areas of Mars which geographically mirror this area. It would be a logical assumption that those areas on Mars would be the next areas to be explored.

50. C

Directly taken from the article. While the authors do discuss how long a period of time Mars most likely had some type of water in existence, it is evident from the description that this was inconsistent through that time period.

51. B

The statement explicitly uses the term "off and on", indicating that this did not occur with any consistency.

52. A

Taken directly from information provided in passage 1, indicating that these life forms are critical for establishing a basis for life potentially having occurred.

SECTION 2

1. B

When "but" is used as a sentence connector, the correct way is: a comma ends the first sentence, and "but" leads the second to establish a contrast, as Choice B indicates.

2. A

The first part "Many take for granted …" and the second part "there was a time …" form a contrast, eliminating Choices B and C. Choice C shows a contrast, but "in spite of" can only used before a noun. Choice A is correct because the conjunction "while" means "in spite of the fact that."

3. C

Choice C is correct because only "when" can stand for "*a time not all that long ago.*"

4. D

The underlined part is about Red Bull, which is a company, thus eliminating Choices A and B. Choice C is wrong because "which" stands for a singular noun, and the target verb must take an –s.

5. A

The first paragraph mentions that DIS is doing something similar to Red Bull. Logically the second paragraph will discuss what Red Bull is actually doing. That's why Choices B, C, and D should be eliminated.

6. D

While a direct quotation uses quotation marks, an indirect quotation uses "that," as Choice D indicates.

7. B

The underlined part talks about "the *company's* support." Only the possessive pronoun "its" can stand for "the company's."

8. C

If the phrase "in the distant future" were taken off, the meaning and completeness of the sentence would not change. Therefore, this phrase should be set off with commas, as Choice C indicates.

9. A

This is a paired sentence. Each of the two parts has a complete sentence structure but cannot express a complete meaning without the other. That would eliminate Choices C and D. Choice B won't work because a comma is not a sentence connector. Choice A, which uses a semicolon, is the right one.

10. D

When the option to DELETE appears, give it special consideration. There must be a really good reason not to pick it. In this case, without the underlined

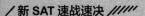

portion, the sentence works perfectly: "*Many of the artists featured in the "DISown" are already showing at elite galleries.*" Participial phrase "*featured in the DSown*" is a shortened version of "*who were featured,*" modifying "*artists.*"

11. C

Choice C is the best answer because "itself" here is used for the reflexive pronoun of "*DIS*". Choices A, B, and D are incorrect because none provides a word that is both singular and reflexive.

12. B

By definition, a *recipe* is a method or way to do something. That eliminates Choices A and D. Choice C is not the right one because of its redundancy. When two closely related infinitives appear together, only one "to" is necessary, as Choice B indicates.

13. B

Choice A should be eliminated first because a comma is not a sentence connector. When "*Fish populations perform key roles*" is changed into a *subordinate* clause appearing immediately after the modified noun, we can either use "which" to stand for "*fish populations*" and set off the clause with commas, or use "that" to stand for "fish populations" without setting off the clause with commas, as Choice B indicates.

14. A

"Lightly" is a less formal synonym of "moderately." The two adverbs joined by "or" are used as one modifying the adjective "fished." There is no need for a comma to separate any part of the phrase *For moderately or lightly fished reefs.*

15. D

The two sentences have the same subject, and they are closely related to each other. Therefore, they should be combined into a compound sentence with one subject and two predicate verbs, as Choice D indicates.

16. A

Most of the time when verbs are used as subjects, they take the *–ing* form. The original "*maintaining and restoring … can increase …*" is perfect.

17. C

All of these choices can be used to give examples of the preceding noun. In this case, only Choice C "*global threats such as*" parallels with "*coastal threats such as*" in the sentence, and is therefore the best answer.

18. C

The sentence "only 27 percent of the world's coral reefs are contained within marine protected areas" refers to the above-mentioned time frame – "in the past 30 years;" Choice C "*at the same time*" is therefore the best transition.

19. B

Choice B is the correct answer because "By studying ..." shows a way how scientists "*were able to estimate ...*"

20. A

Eliminate Choices C and D first because finite verb forms "include" or "includes" need a subject, but "decisions" cannot be the subject because it's the object of "make." Then eliminate Choice B because "that" stands for the modified plural noun "*decisions.*"

21. D

Choices A and B should be eliminated because they both use a comma to combine two sentences. Choice C is not good either because of the repetition of "the degradation of reef function."

22. C

The author's tone in the whole passage is strongly against overfishing; therefore, only "*threatening*" is consistent with it. Choices A, B, and D all sound more or less neutral.

23. C

Eliminate Choice A because a comma cannot be used to combine two sentences. Choice B is not good either because of the repetition. Choice D is wrong because "which" can only stand for "the atmosphere" but not for "in the atmosphere." Only Choice C "*where*" means "in the atmosphere" and effectively combines the two sentences into a complex structure.

24. A

The time phrase "*over the past decade*" suggests a present perfect progressive tense. That eliminates Choices C and D. Since the subject of the sentence is "concentrations," the predicate verb must be "*have been rising*" as Choice A indicates.

25. B

The previous sentence talks about how anesthesia gases are like carbon dioxide, and this sentence talks about how they are different from carbon dioxide. Therefore, Choice B "*unlike carbon dioxide*" most effectively connects them together.

26. C

After the name, some personal information can be inserted to identify the person. Since the identification is not absolutely necessary for meaning or completeness of the sentence, it should be set off with commas. In the case, Wallmer's identification is "an atmospheric chemist at the Swiss Federal Laboratories for Materials Science and Technology in Dubendorf, Switzerland;" and it should be separated with commas, as Choice C indicates.

27. D

When a group of words is used as an adjective to pre-modify a noun, it should be hyphenated, such as *a five-year-old boy, a hundred-dollar bill, etc*. In this case, Choice D is the right form: "Kilogram-per-kilogram" is used as an adjective to modify the noun "basis."

28. D

The graphic shows that halothane is less than 0.01. The accurate data is *0.0097* rather than *0.097*.

29. A

The time phrase "since 2013" requires the target verb to be in the present perfect progressive form. Choices B, C and D should be eliminated because "tracked" indicates that they did it in the past, "are tracking" indicates that they are doing right now, and "were tracking" indicates that they were doing it at a certain time in the past. Only Choice A "have been tracking" indicates that they started doing it at a past time and never stopped doing it; and they are still doing it today.

30. A

Only Choice A "*to turn*" can serve as an adverbial of purpose, which explains why the data were combined with a two-dimensional computer model.

31. B

Eliminate Choices A and C because "model" is a countable noun; therefore, it has to be "a … model." If a computer model is two dimensional, we may call it "*a two-dimensional computer model*," as Choice B indicates.

32. D

Choice D is the correct answer because both adjectives "so-called" and "top-down" should be hyphenated.

33. B

Choice C is obviously wrong because there is no reason to switch to the past. Choice D is not right either because "escape" is not a transitive verb, which cannot be used in the passive voice. The subject "how much of each gas" is singular, eliminating Choice A. Choice B "*how much escapes*" is the right one.

34. C

The sentence indicates that bumblebees can tell the difference *between plants that will* provide nectar and pollen *and plants that won't*. Eliminate Choice A because "*plants that will*" and "*that won't*" are not balanced. Choices B and D should be eliminated too because of the repetition of "plants." Choice C is the right choice: To avoid repetition, the second *plants* should be replaced by *those*.

35. A

The time phrase "*until now*" suggests that present perfect tense should be used, eliminating Choices B and C. Choice D should also be eliminated because the subject "*little*" is singular, agreeing with "has been known."

36. B

There are three correct patterns of using "*distinguish*": *to distinguish A and B; to distinguish between A and B; to distinguish A from B*. Choice B "to distinguish between" is one of them.

37. C

The previous sentence tells that bees were able to distinguish the right type of feeders arranged horizontally, and this sentence says that bees failed to distinguish the right type of feeders arranged vertically. Choices A and B should be eliminated because "and" and "then" can only connect something similar. Both "but" and "however" introduce something on the contrary; "but" appears after a comma, while "however" appears after a period. In this case, Choice C "However" is the correct transition.

38. D

The rule for using "*to be sure*" is: Before a noun or a phrase, use "to be sure of;" Before a sentence, use "to be sure that." In this case, ask yourself: What are the researchers sure of? The answer is: The bees were equally able to discriminate the two presented feeders in both arrangements. That is a complete sentence. Therefore, Choice D "*are sure that*" is the correct answer.

39. A

The correct usage of describing similarity is: "same as" but "similar to." That will eliminate Choices C and D. Choice A is better than Choice B because pronoun "ones" stands for "flowers," avoiding repetition.

40. B

Eliminate Choices A and D first, because the usages are "*on the contrary*" and "*by contrasting*." While "to contrast" shows a purpose of the action, "in contrast" introduces the other side of the fact. In this case, Choice B "in contrast" is the right transition.

41. D

You can only pay attention *to* something or somebody.

42. D

The phrase "co-author of the research" is an identification of Wolf. If it were taken out, the meaning and completeness of the sentence would not change. The phrase is therefore not essential to the meaning of the sentence and should be set off with commas, as Choice D indicates.

43. B

Only Choice B "*choosing not to*" parallels with "*being able to*."

44. C

If someone uses his left hand dominantly, he is a *left-handed* person. Similarly, bees with mini brains are called "*mini-brained* bees," as Choice C indicates.

SECTION 3

1. C

$$\frac{3+i}{3-i} = \frac{(3+i)^2}{(3-i)(3+i)} = \frac{3^2+6i+i^2}{3^2-i^2} = \frac{9+6i-1}{9+1} = \frac{8+6i}{10} = \frac{4}{5} + \frac{3i}{5}$$

2. C

Working with the answers: substitute each answer into x until the inequality works. Plug in answer C, to get $|3(1) - 4| = |-1| = 1$ which is less than 2, so answer C is correct.

Another way to solve it: The inequality, $|3x - 4| < 2$, is the same thing as: $-2 < 3x - 4 < 2$. Adding 4 to all sides gives $2 < 3x < 6$. Divide by 3 so that $\frac{2}{3} < x < 2$, which means that x could be equal to 1.

3. A

Only Choice A satisfies the condition that both x and p are integers: $\sqrt{16} = \pm 4$.

4. B

Let x be the least integer. The three consecutive integers from the least to the greatest will be x, $x + 1$, and $x + 2$. Since four times the least integer is one more than three times the greatest, $4x = 3(x + 2) + 1$. Solve it and you get $x = 7$. The middle integer $x + 1 = 8$.

5. D

Just plug in: If $x = 0$, $y = 0$. That means the line must go through the 0 point of both x-axis and y-axis, eliminating Choices A and B. Since k is greater than 2, if $x = 2$, $y > 2$; if $x = -2$, $y < -2$. That eliminates Choice C because Choice C shows that y can never be negative. Therefore, D is the correct choice.

6. B

If one angle of an isosceles triangle measures 120°, then each of the other two angles is 30°. $\cos 30° = \dfrac{\sqrt{3}}{2}$

7. C

The graph shows that f goes through the 0 point. That means $f(0) = 0$, or if $x = 0$, $y = 0$. When you plug in, you can eliminate choices A and B. The correct answer must be either choice C or D. Then, take a look at line g. It crosses the y-axis at 1. That means $g(0) = 1$, or if $x = 0$, $y = 1$. When you plug in, you'll see that (C) is the correct answer.

8. B

Start by "de-foiling" the left part: $(a - b)^2 = 9$. Therefore, $a - b = 3$, or $a - b = -3$. Add them up with $a + b = 7$ one by one, and you get $2a = 10$, $a = 5$, or $2a = 4$, $a = 2$. Then, you arrive at the answer: $a = 2$, and $b = 5$.

9. B

Because line l and line m are parallel, the unlabeled angle on line m equals to $a°$, and $a = 120$. Therefore, $a + b + c + d = 360$, $b + c + d = 360 - 120 = 240$.

10. D

In the figure, two triangles are formed by two lines that cross each other plus two additional lines. Each triangle has an unlabeled angle, both of which are formed where the two longer lines cross. That means these two angles are equal to each other. In each triangle, the two labeled angles plus the unlabeled angle equals 180. Therefore, $2x + 41 = (3x + 1) + x$.

Solving it for x, you get: $2x + 41 = 4x + 1$, $2x = 40$, $x = 20$.

11. D

First, find the percentage of the students who had a GPA of 3.0 or higher. The total number of the students being sampled is 100. Among them, 65 had a GPA of 3.0 or higher. That means 65% of the 520 graduating students had a GPA of 3.0 or higher: $520 \times \dfrac{65}{100} = 338$. Choice D is the correct answer.

12. C

Use the answers: Start from $7^2 - 6^2 = 49 - 36 = 13$. Very close. Next, you will get the right answer: $8^2 - 7^2 = 64 - 49 = 15$. The greater of the two numbers is 8. Another way to solve it: Set x as the greater number, and the lesser will be $x - 1$. So, $x^2 - (x-1)^2 = 15$. Expand it, you get: $x^2 - x^2 + 2x - 1 = 15$. Solving for x, you get $x = 8$. Therefore, the greater integer is 8.

13. A

There are different ways to solve it.
1) Simply stack and add:

$$2x + 3y = 20$$
$$+ \quad x - y = 4$$
$$\overline{3x + 2y = 24}$$

2) Plug in:

$x - y = 4$, so $x = 4 + y$
$2x + 3y = 20$
$2(4 + y) + 3y = 20$
$5y = 12$
$y = 2.4$
$x = 6.4$
$3x + 2y = 3(6.4) + 2(2.4) = 24$

14. D

To solve, distribute 4 on the right side of the inequality to get $x > 4x - 21$. Subtract $-4x$ from both sides to get $-3x > -21$. Divide both sides by -3, making sure to flip the inequality sign since you are dividing by a negative number. This results in $x < 7$.

15. B

To find the value of r, we must first find the value of $\sqrt{r+3}$. Since $3 = \dfrac{6}{\sqrt{r+3}}$ we can get $\sqrt{r+3} = 2$. Square both sides: $r + 3 = 4$, $r = 1$

16. 15

First, multiply both sides by 3 to clear fraction:
$2x + 15 = 3x$

Then subtract $2x$ from both sides: $15 = 3x - 2x$

The answer is: $x = 15$

17. 10

The distance between Point A and Point B is $AC - BC$.

AC is the distance Andrew drives for 20 minutes at 45 miles per hour, so

$$AC = 45 \times \frac{20}{60} = 15$$

BC is the distance David rides a bicycle for 20 minutes at 15 miles per hour, so

$$BC = 15 \times \frac{20}{60} = 5$$

Therefore, $AC - BC = 10$

The distance between Point A and Point B is 10 miles.

18. $\frac{4}{3}$ or 1.33

The height of the isosceles triangle forms a right triangle with the base. Because

you know BD is 12 and BC is 15, you can either use the Pythagorean Theorem

or Pythagorean triple to determine that CD is 9. tan C is opposite / adjacent,

which is $\frac{12}{9} = \frac{4}{3}$.

19. 15

Square both sides of $x - y = 2$:
$(x - y)^2 = 2^2$
So, $x^2 - 2xy + y^2 = 4$
Because $x^2 + y^2 = 34$,
$34 - 2xy = 4$
$-2xy = -30$
Therefore, the answer is: $xy = 15$

20. 7

Factor the numerators:
$\frac{x^2(x-1)}{x-1} = \frac{(x-1)(4x+21)}{x-1}$, so

$x^2 = 4x + 21$
$x^2 - 4x - 21 = 0$

Factor it:
$(x + 3)(x - 7) = 0$
$x = -3$, $x = 7$. Only 7 is bigger than 0; therefore, 7 is the right answer.

SECTION 4

1. C

Plug in. Or subtract both side by $3x$ and increase both side by 3, we get $8 = 2x$; therefore $x = 4$, which is (C).

2. C

$2^{\frac{3}{2}} = 2^{1+\frac{1}{2}} = 2\sqrt{2}$; $4^{\frac{3}{2}} = (4^{\frac{1}{2}})^3 = 8$; $8^{\frac{3}{2}} = (2^3)^{\frac{3}{2}} = 2^{\frac{9}{2}} = 2^{4+\frac{1}{2}} = 16\sqrt{2}$. Their sum is $8 + 18\sqrt{2}$, which is (C).

3. A

Stack and add:

$$2 < a < 5$$
$$+ \quad 0 < b < 7$$
$$\overline{2 < b < 12}$$

The correct answer is (A).

4. C

Write the equation in the standard form,

$x^2 + 4x + 4 + y^2 - 6y + 9 = 13$;

$(x + 2)^2 + (y-3)^2 = (\sqrt{13})^2$.

The radius is $\sqrt{13}$, which is (C).

5. B

Note that the value in question is $z - 1$, we can solve it without calculating z first. Divide both sides by 5, we get $z - 1 = \dfrac{12}{5}$, which is (B).

6. D

The answers are quite simple, plug them in. For (A) or (C), the right hand side is negative, it will never equal the left hand side. For (B), the right hand side is 7 while the left hand side is $\sqrt{13}$. For (D), both sides equals 3. So the correct answer is (D).

7. B

Although it's common sense, it can also be easily guessed even by just looking at the units, the formula for computing the volume is

$$\text{Volumn} = \frac{\text{Mass}}{\text{Density}}$$

So the approximate volume of Venus is $\dfrac{4.87 \times 10^{24}}{5243} \approx 9.28 \times 10^{20}\,(m^3)$, which is (B).

Note that (A) is the volume of Mars. (C) and (D) both used wrong formulas.

8. C

Fix the unit of 1024kg, The total mass of the first six planets is 0.33 + 4.87 + 5.97 + 0.642 + 1898 + 568 = 2477.812. Jupiter contributed the fraction $\dfrac{1898}{2477.812}$ $\approx$0.765. None of the answers is in this form, but we can calculate them (possibly first eliminate some obvious wrong answers) as (A) 0.2, (B) 0.75, (C)0.76, (D) 0.82. The correct answer is (C).

9. D

Keeping the same units in the calculation, we can express the ratio of the volume of Earth to the volume of Venus as $\dfrac{5.97/5514}{4.87/5243} \approx 1.16562$. So the volume of Earth is approximately 116.56% of the volume of Venus, it is about 16.56% bigger, which is closest to (D).

10. C

We first calculate the volume of Mercury: $0.33 \times \dfrac{10^{24}}{5427}\,(m^3)$. So the radius satisfy

$$\frac{4}{3}\, 3.14\, r^3 = 0.33 \times \frac{10^{24}}{5427}$$

In order to keep the answer accurate, we do not calculate the intermediate values, instead we rearrange

$$r^3 = \frac{0.99}{4 \times 3.14} \times \frac{10^{24}}{5427}$$

so

$$r = \sqrt[3]{\frac{0.99}{4 \times 3.14 \times 5427}} \times 10^8\,(m).$$

Use a calculator we get the diameter is 2r, which is roughly 4879686 m ≈4880 km. (C) is the correct answer.

11. B

To compute x, the most natural thing is to cancel out y, and it is easy to do in this problem. Simply add these two equations together we get $2x = 15$. So $x = 7.5$, which is (B).

12. B

All the positive integers satisfy $-5 \leq 5x$. The biggest integer satisfying $5x \leq 27$ is 5. So all the integers satisfying the inequality are {1, 2, 3, 4, 5}, there are 5 of them. (B) is the correct answer.

13. D

Be careful, $x^2 + y^2 - 2x + 6y + 11 = (x-1)^2 + (y+3)^2 + 1$, which is always positive, never equals 0. So no point in the plane satisfies the equation. The correct answer is (D).

14. D

The problem translates into $4 \leq (\frac{z}{3})^2 \leq 9$. Note that z is positive, so is $\frac{z}{3}$. Taking the square roots, $2 \leq (\frac{z}{3}) \leq 3$. Multiply by 3 we get (D).

15. A

$f(2) = x^2 (3x-7) + (x-2) = 4(-1) + 0 = -4$, which is (A).

16. C

Try to observe the answer without explicitly solving x. The left side is $\frac{5x}{x} + \frac{7}{x} = 5 + \frac{7}{x}$, so $\frac{7}{x} = 4$. Multiply both sides with 3, we get $\frac{21}{x} = 12$, which is (C).

17. C

The productions are different in sizes and otherwise of the same quality. Without other information, the material needed is proportional to the total area of paper sheets in one package in both series. So the ratio is $\frac{400 \times 8.3 \times 11.7}{500 \times 8.5 \times 11} \approx 0.8308877$. The correct answer is (C).

18. D

Observe the x-intercept and y-intercept of the line in the figure, it has slope 3. So, a line perpendicular to it has slope $-\frac{1}{3}$. Rewrite the answers in the slope form, we have:

(A) $y = -3x + \frac{5}{2}$

(B) $y = -3x - 1$

(C) $y = -3x + 2$

(D) $y = -\frac{1}{3}x + \frac{7}{12}$

Therefore, (D) is the correct answer.

19. D

The function has one negative root –2, and two positive roots 1 and 3. Thus (A) and (B) are not correct answers. Note that when $x>3$, which is the biggest root, $(x–1)(x + 2)(x–3)>0$. Thus the function has positive values to the right of the rightmost intersection with the x-axis. The correct answer is (D).

20. A

Plug in the answers. If $a = 7$, since $a = 2b + 1$, so $b = 3$. $\frac{3a+b+6}{2b} = \frac{21+3+6}{6} = \frac{30}{6}$ = 5. So (A) is the correct answer.

21. D

Plug in the answers. When $x = 1$, the left hand side is $\frac{9}{6} = 1.5$, the right hand side is $0.5 + 1 = 1.5$. Since the question asks all the possible values of x, (B) and (C) are ruled out. To decide which one of (A) and (D) is correct, plug in any other non-zero value, for example, $x = –1$; the left hand side is $\frac{-3}{-6} = 0.5$, the right hand side is $–0.5 + 1 = 0.5$, so (A) is ruled out. (D) is the correct answer.

Algebraically, multiply both sides by $6x$ we get $3(1 + 2x) = 3 + 6x$; expand the left hand side we get $3 + 6x = 3 + 6x$, which is always true as long as the original fraction is well defined, i.e., x is not 0. (D) is the correct answer.

22. C

If Peter wins the next match, the average of the wins of the European players certainly increase; (A) is eliminated. The mode currently is 8 and 21, each has 3 occurrences. Even Endre wins the next two matches and makes his total wins 17, there will be only two occurrences of 17 in the list. (B) is eliminated. (C) is correct, Tomas has more wins than the median of the American players, increasing it will never change the median. Finally (D) is not correct because there are no modes of the wins of European players; for them each number only occur once.

23. C

Currently the European players has the number of wins, sorted in ascending order, is (4, 8, 15, 17, 21). Endre's number, 15, cannot be changed. Increasing the numbers bigger than 15 will not change the median. We need to at least change 8 to 16 in order to change the median. (C) is the correct answer.

24. D

No matter who wins the next 5 games, each game will have one win and it will be averaged over 11 players. So the increase in average is always $\frac{5}{11}$, which is (D).

25. D

One way is to write everything in the form $2^a 5^b$. $\sqrt{10} = 2^{\frac{1}{2}} 5^{\frac{1}{2}}$

For (A), $\sqrt[3]{100} = \sqrt[3]{2^2 5^2} = 2^{\frac{2}{3}} 5^{\frac{2}{3}}$.

For (B), $\sqrt[3]{20}\sqrt{20} = (20)^{\frac{1}{3}+\frac{1}{2}} = (20)^{\frac{5}{6}} = (2^2 \times 5)^{\frac{5}{6}} = 2^{\frac{5}{3}} 5^{\frac{5}{6}}$.

For (C), $\sqrt[4]{2}\sqrt[4]{5} = 2^{\frac{1}{4}} 5^{\frac{1}{4}}$.

For (D), $\sqrt[4]{4}\sqrt{5} = (2^2)^{\frac{1}{4}} 5^{\frac{1}{2}} = 2^{\frac{1}{2}} 5^{\frac{1}{2}}$.

So the correct answer is (D).

26 . C

One may plug in the answers and verify that (C) is the correct answer.
Or let $x = a + bi$. $x(1-i) = (a + bi)(1-i) = a - ai + bi + b = (a + b) + (b - a)i$. So we have $a + b = 8$ and $b - a = 2$, which solves to $a = 3$ and $b = 5$.

27. B

The curve achieves its maximum y-value (happiness) around the point (5, 13). The correct answer is (B).

28. D

In the graph, when x is roughly between 0.5 and 9.5 (note that each mark is an increment of 0.5), the happiness value is positive. All other points have happiness 0. So the happy interval is approximately (0.5, 9.5); it has length 9, which is (D).

29. B

Each data point is moved 5 units downwards, so is the best fit curve. So, we just need to move the curve in the graph down by 5 units and find its intersection with the x-axis. But there is a better way to think about it, we may leave the curve and move the coordinate system. Observe the intersection of the curve with the line $y = 5$, which is viewed as the new x-axis. The happy interval has length 7, which makes (B) the correct answer.

30. D

If the fox and the rabbit arrive at P at the same time, the distances they travelled,

FP and RP, should be proportional to their speed, i.e., 1:3. So, $\sin \angle PFR = \dfrac{PR}{FP}$ $= \dfrac{1}{3}$, which eliminates (A) and (C).

Suppose $PR = x$ and $FP = 3x$. Because FRP is a right angle, we have

$x^2 + FR^2 = 9x^2$.

This implies $FR = \sqrt{8}x$ and $\cos(\angle PFR) = \dfrac{\sqrt{8}x}{3x} = \dfrac{2\sqrt{2}}{3}$. (D) is the correct answer.

Also one may use the relation $\cos^2(\angle PFR) = 1 - \sin^2(\angle PFR) = 1 - \dfrac{1}{9}$.

31. 50

CP bisects the angle ACB and $\angle ACP = 30°$, so $\angle ACB = 60°$. $\angle ACB$, $\angle A$, and $\angle B$ are three inner angles of a triangle, they sum to 180°. So the degree of $\angle B$ is $180 - 60 - 70 = 50$.

32. $\dfrac{20}{3}$ or 6.66

There are three variables in two linear equations. This kind of equation system do not have unique solutions. But the problem indicates that there is a unique value for $a + b$.

Adding the two equations together, c is cancelled. We have the same coefficient for a and b, $3a + 3b = 20$, so divide both sides by 3, we get $a + b = \dfrac{20}{3}$.

33. 10

Multiply both side by $x - 3$, we get

$$x^2 - 6 = x - 3 + 3.$$

Rearrange, we get

$$x^2 + x - 6 = 0$$

The left hand side can be easily factored into $(x-3)(x + 2)$, so it has solutions $x = 3$ and $x = -2$. However $x = 3$ makes the denominator of the original equation 0. So, $x = -2$, and $x^2 - 3x = 10$.

34. 80

Algebraically, suppose x customers came for dinner, then $(3x + 2)$ came for lunch, and

$$20(3x + 2) + 30x = 7240$$

Divide both sides by 10 and expand we get $9x + 4 = 724$. Solve this we get $x = 80$.

Another way to solve this: $7240 minus two lunches is $7200. Then it divides into groups of one dinner and three lunches, which is $90 for each group. So there are $7200/$90 = 80 such groups. So the number of dinner customers is 80.

35. 24.5 or $\dfrac{49}{2}$

The easiest way is to understand that the radii are in the proportion 4:2:1, so are the circumferences of the three circles, and so are the respective quarters of these three circles. So the arc lengths have $AB:BC:CD = 4:2:1$. Arc BC has length 7π, so the arc AB has length 14π and the arc CD has length 3.5π. Their sum is 24.5π.

36. 24

The parabola $y = 2x^2-8x-k = 2(x-2)^2-8-k$ is symmetric around its vertex, which has x-coordinate 2, so the two roots (which are 8 apart from each other) are $2-4 = -2$ and $2 + 4 = 6$. Both of them satisfy the equation. Substitute any of them, for example, $2 \times 4-8(-2)-k = 0$ gets $k = 24$.

37. 45

The number of cells she adds on the first four days are 3, 6, 12, 24. $3 + 6 + 12 + 24 = 45$.

38. 158

The number of cells she adds on the first seven days are x, $2x$, $4x$, $8x$, $16x$, $32x$, $64x$. So, at the end of the seventh day, the number of cells in the space is
$$(1 + 2 + 4 + 8 + 16 + 32 + 64)x = 127x \geq 20000.$$
This implies $x \geq \dfrac{2000}{127} \approx 157.48$. Because x is an integer, the answer is 158.

SECTION 5

Former President Bill Clinton is a famously gifted orator. In his 1993 speech to the Congress, he attempts to persuade the legislature, as well as the American public, to endorse health care reform. In the speech, the critical need for health care reform is established by repeating key words and phrases, invoking patriotism, and humanizing the issue.

Repetition is used throughout the speech to emphasize key ideas and strengthen powerful imagery. In the first paragraph, Clinton begins three clauses describing the United States with "a place." This reminds his audience of the kind of country their homeland ought to be, a place that embodies the ideals enshrined in the Declaration of Independence. In the second paragraph, the repetition of "too" and "too much" underscores the harsh realities of the American health care system. By describing the health care system as "too uncertain and too expensive, too bureaucratic and too wasteful" and full of "too much fraud and too much greed", he depicts a broken system in desperate need of reform. Repetition appears again in paragraph five as Clinton builds towards his proposed solution. The reiteration of "both" and "every" encourages members of Congress from both sides of the aisle to work together for change. The use of repetition effectively illuminates the problem and encourages a solution.

Clinton invokes the patriotism of his audience in order to promote his desired health care reforms. He opens with "My fellow Americans," indicating that his message is not only for Congress, but also for the entire nation. He urges his countrymen to collaborate to guarantee the American dream for everyone in their generation. This sets the stage for his first plea to his listeners to be open to change, a theme fleshed out more fully later on. In paragraph two, he urges his audience to bravely weather a bumpy journey toward change by listing a series of very American principles that ought to be at the heart of health care: "security, simplicity, savings, choice, quality, and responsibility." Finally, in paragraph three, he makes an appeal to his listeners' vanity as he espouses how American exceptionalism is manifest in the health care system. Reminded of what is so great about America and American health care, the audience becomes receptive to making major changes.

Clinton makes health care reform all the more urgent by putting a human face on it. Potent statistics are interspersed with real-life scenarios, helping the audience to imagine how disastrous the loss of their health insurance would be. This also allows Clinton to explain technical concepts such as preexisting conditions and rising medical costs in approachable layman's terms. Later on, even hypothetical opponents to health care reform are humanized. By offering plausible reasons why someone might favor the current system, the costs of sticking with the status quo are balanced against the imperative for reform. Clinton intensifies the stakes of his argument by describing a series of heart wrenching stories of people struggling to afford health care for themselves and their children. These true stories take the issue of health care reform out of the realm of the theoretical and push it to the forefront of the listener's mind. Humanizing health care reform makes it a "we" issue and challenges the nation to accept change for the collective good.

Clinton uses his signature rhetorical flair to convince Congress to pursue health care reform. Throughout the speech, repetition highlights both the strengths of the American nation and the disappointing weaknesses of its health care system. Willingness to embrace change is depicted as patriotic. Finally, devastating human stories make health care reform seem like the only logical course of action.

Answer Explanations
New SAT Practice Test 3

Section 1

1. B

The author details the ways the autonomic nervous system provides involuntary responses to situations. Because of this, it would be impossible to exert any type of voluntary control over physiological responses.

2. C

Because the author provides evidence that many of our smiles are fake, smiling can be considered manufactured responses to situations...made up to make ourselves and others feel better about our responses.

3. D

These particular lines explicitly delineate the notion of fake smiles and state that, in essence, there is only one true smile, or physiological reaction, to situations.

4. A

Used in context, the author seeks to convey the point that smiling is embedded in who we are. Although heritable may be viewed as somewhat correct, the correct meaning as it is intended in the sentence is embedded or entrenched.

5. D

While the article does touch on the types of physiological responses we have to our emotions, the primary purpose is to convey that we do have the ability to choose how we feel.

6. B

The details provided regarding the autonomic nervous system lend credence to the answer that smiling is generally an involuntary reflex to feeling happy. The brain feels it, the body does it.

7. C

The article makes mention about increased heartrate during smiling or happiness. However, the only genuine smile condition produced the lowest values of heart rate, in contradiction to research.

8. D

The term, used correctly in context, means supported or lent evidence to.

9. A

Based upon assertions by the author, happiness causes individuals to smile and reap the physiological benefits of smiling. Additionally, he states that the act of smiling can send a signal to the brain to feel happy. As such, it is a mutually reciprocal relationship.

10. B

The lines specifically contain the phrase, "the result was happiness without a trigger sent to the brain..." proving that smiling and happiness have a dichotomous relationship.

11. C

In the final paragraph, the author discusses the ways that smiling at someone produces a reaction of smiling back. By doing this, both people are likely to feel happiness. By pointing this out, the author is seeking to foster greater human interaction and encouragement of assisting others in feeling happy.

12. B

The narrator, throughout the text, continues to point out the way in which farmers are becoming indifferent to their profession and displaying little appreciation for their land. From the tone of the passage, it appears the narrator is in disagreement.

13. C

The author uses the word penitent and the image of farmers on their hands and knees, as if in prayer or begging for crops to grow, to indicate that they were in effect at the mercy of their crops.

14. A

As stated previously, the overall tone of the passage is somewhat sarcastically contemptuous. Positive attributes are continually used to describe the old way of farming, while the new way is generally described in sterile, manufactured, indifferent terms.

15. B

Here, the author indicates that greed is at the root of the ills of current farming practices. The manner in which new farming practices are described clearly indicates a distaste for where farming was headed.

16. D

Feral directly means wild or untamed. In context, it represents human's innate and primal nature and it's connection with the land.

17. A

Ascribing sensory descriptions to the changes in farming serves to indicate the depth in which the author feels land owners are now detached from their farms and land. It conveys a powerful, primal point.

18. C

Being storekeepers, they would be "working" inside and not directly with the Earth or soil or crops.

19. D

Though the author uses demeaning terms towards the immigrant workers, the most vitriolic comments occur from the perspective of the farmers. From the tone of the passage, the author conveys distaste contempt for the manner in which the workers are viewed.

20. A

This is reflective of the feudal system and the fact that many owners, then and in this passage, felt that they were justified in their business practices and victimized when worker output was not what it should be.

21. B

A scythe is a long handled tool, with a long blade at the end, used to thresh crops.

22. C

Here the author is conveying the point that the farmers are losing their innate love of the land, their connection with their farms and soil, and their feelings that farming is below them.

23. A

The author takes great pains in detailing the qualifications of both Branly and Curie. Though the deciding factor may not have been specifically rooted in contributions to science, the author does justify the election of Branly over Curie.

24. D

While Curie did depend on her husband's research to continue her experiments, she clearly swayed her distractors into believing that her scientific inquiry and advancements warranted admission into the elite Sorbonne.

25. C

These lines clearly indicate that Curie had definitively changed the opinions of her detractors into the favorable.

26. B

The term emoluments literally means profits made through economic gains.

27. A

Given Curie's personality history, it seems clear that she would be a supporter of equal rights for people, specifically regarding the stigmatization of women. This is rather apparent in her decision to apply to Sorbonne.

28. D

These lines provide evidence that the fact that no women were previously admitted to Sorbonne as justification and motivation to apply. Because of this, it is conceivable that Curie sought to provide a level playing field, regardless of gender.

29. C

The term alludes specifically means suggests or hints. The word is used correctly in context.

30. B

The author indicates that Bronly's advances for wireless telegraphy were critical in the decision to elect Branly over Curie.

31. A

While there was an overabundance of misogynistic thought during this time, the author points out many qualifications that justify the appointment of Branly over Curie.

32. B

All answers but choice A are generally correct. However, it was specifically the advances Curie made in the area of the magnetic properties of iron and steel that bestowed upon her the Gegner award.

33. D

Within the text of the document, the colonists state on several occasions that they had made attempts to reconcile or mend relations with England, but their requests have been met with a deaf ear or further redress.

34. B

The colonists reference their attempts at being loyal subjects within the document. From their perspective, the language and terms they use, and their position that they have not broken any English law to this point, they are asserting that they have acted in good faith in following the laws established by the monarchy.

35. C

The colonists imply throughout the document and, explicitly at certain points, that they seek only mutual respect and understanding but will no longer tolerate the treatment afforded to them by the English government. While they remain angry and vigilant, the tone is that things will be fine as long as England respects their wishes.

36. D

The words contained in these lines reflect the desires of the colonies to maintain an open and positive relationship with England and that, though there are some differences between them, they are willing to move forward as a new nation.

37. A

The term impel means to oblige or provide cause. This is synonymous with the term compel.

38. B

According to the colonists, the King of England has acted as a "despot" who recklessly and aggressively imposed his will over those of the people and has threatened or harmed those who have opposed his rule.

39. D

Within the first paragraph of text the framers of the Declaration of Independence cite specifically the rights guaranteed to them by their Creator and the fact that no government or person can infringe upon them.

40. C

This is a direct definition of the word transient. The term means fleeting or short lived.

41. A

Throughout the document, the framers repeatedly convey the perspective that they have been forced into this position by the behavior of the King and the English parliament. As such, they feel they have an obligation to right the wrongs of injustice.

42. B

These particular lines deal directly with the obligation felt by the colonists to change the manner in which they are governed or are treated by the English government.

43. A

Passage 2 offers no specific evidence of the effects on siblings regarding ASD and vaccines. Their primary focus is on African-American boys, a very narrow representative population.

44. D

Though the author of passage 2 does not specifically state this opinion, from the data provided and the tone of the passage, it can be inferred that vaccinations after 36 months of age are a safe and beneficial intervention.

45. C

Passage 2 mentions a previous study and a re-examination of the data in that particular research, but the reader really has no idea how that data was acquired and the reliability of the original data collection and interpretation.

46. B

The term contrary is used correctly in context. It means contradictory, as the author uses it to say that even though there is considerable evidence opposed to this school of thought, individuals ascribe to it regardless.

47. D

The authors of passage 1 have no difficulties with outside the box research as long as it is conducted in an ethical manner. This scenario represents the only unethical research method.

48. A

These lines provide direct evidence for the need to make ethical decisions, the only ones which support the previous answer.

49. B

Though A and D could conceivably be utilized in this sentence, the true definition is seemingly. This makes the most sense in context of the sentence and perspective the author is attempting to convey.

50. C

The author of passage 2 expresses pessimism and suspicion of how the results were obtained and reported from the original study. Given that the author is reporting contradictory findings and relying on a whistleblower for the most information, it is clear that they are generally giving pause when interpreting the original findings.

51. A

These lines provide the best evidence of support for the answer listed above. The author is attempting to directly tie appropriations and funding to the manner and type of data reporting.

52. D

The graphic depicted shows considerable variability prior to the MMR vaccine being discovered and implemented. In actuality, measles was declining considerably prior to the vaccine being given. Therefore, it is possible other factors (hygiene, communication, detection) may have played a large role as well.

SECTION 2

1. B

The sentence means "I was *not able* to shake off my gloom *until* the morning that we entered the harbor." In another way, "It was *not until* the morning that we entered the harbor that I *was able* to shake off my gloom." Eliminate Choice A because "*not*" must appear either with "until" or with "was able." "However" can be placed at the beginning of the sentence or inserted in the middle. At the beginning, set it off with a comma; in the middle, insert it between two commas, as Choice B indicates.

2. D

Both "so" and "very" can be used to modify adjective "lighthearted;" "so" goes with "that," but "very" doesn't. Choice D is the correct answer: I grew *so lighthearted that* when I caught the first sight of the train, I enjoyed a hearty laugh.

3. A

In the sentence, "*the train*" is the object of the phrase "*caught the first sight of*;" it cannot be the subject of the clause "(the train) *was to take us to Paris.*" That will eliminate Choices C and D. Choice A correctly uses "which" to stand for "the train" and be the subject of the subordinate clause modifying "the train."

4. C

The sentence states that something "*struck me as being extremely funny*." The stuffy compartment cars could be funny. The toy-like engine could be funny. The old-fashioned wheels could be funny. Only "the comfortably-cushioned seats" cannot be "funny." Therefore, Choice C is the correct answer.

5. B

The author's tone is lighthearted and joyful. He loved everything he saw. Choices A, C, and D should be eliminated because "stop complaining," "tolerate" or "ignore" the "stuffy" cars do not sound joyful at all. Only Choice B, "*appreciate" the "stuffy" cars for their privacy,* is consistent with the joyful tone.

6. A

Here it needs a which-clause to modify the noun "a love," so as to parallel with "a love for France which continued to grow stronger." Only Choice A shows this structure.

7. C

Choices A, B, and D should be eliminated because *humored, humor* and *humors* are finite verb forms, which cannot stand alone without a subject. Choice C *"humoring" my curiosity and enthusiasm* is the right choice because an inserted participial phrase can add an accompanying action to the main verb.

8. D

The formal form is: *He suggested that we should take a walk.* However, "should" is optional, as Choice D indicates.

9. C

From the context "I could hardly credit my own eyes," we know that the author was greatly shocked by what he saw. Only Choice C *"burst on"* is consistent with the tone of the paragraph.

10. B

Of the two underlined parts, one is the best part of the city – *its avenues and palaces;* the other is the worst – *its most squalid alleys and hovels.* Therefore the best way to combine them is *"not only … but also …"* as Choice B indicates.

11. A

The author says that whenever he has returned to Paris, he has *"fallen under the spell,"* blindly loving it, as if some magic power had put a curse on it. That's why Paris for him was not a charming, or strange, or adventurous place, but rather, *a charmed spot,* as Choice A indicates.

12. A

When we put this sentence together with the paragraph, we can easily see that the whole paragraph explains why "*For Truman, the choice whether or not to use the atomic bomb was the most difficult decision of his life.*" Therefore this main idea sentence should be placed at the beginning of the paragraph, as Choice A indicates.

13. D

The first paragraph indicates that there was a possibility that the Japanese might accept a conditional surrender to avoid being bombed. Choices A, B or C will lead to a logical development, which is not the case. Only Choice D "*regardless*" most effectively transitions from the information given in the previous paragraph to the opposite.

14. C

Choice A is wrong because "in the months and years to follow" indicates a future time. Choice B is not correct either because "following" should be a pre-modifier, like "in the following months and years." Choice D should be eliminated because "later" means "not immediately." Choice C "*in the months and years that followed*" is the correct expression.

15. B

Nakasake is a place. Therefore, only Choice B "*where*" can stand for "in Nakasake" and thus join the next part to the main sentence.

16. C

Choice C is the best answer. It precisely demonstrates the disastrous consequence of Truman's decision and thus supports the previous statement of "barbaric act". Choice A, B, and D are not correct because none successfully recognizes the reason why the sentence is relevant to this particular location in the passage.

17. C

The tone of the paragraph is very severe when presenting the opponents' criticism against the bombing decision made by Truman. Eliminate Choices A, B, and D because expressions such as "*might not be necessary,*" "*were not really necessary,*" or "*could be avoided*" are too weak to match the tone of the whole paragraph. Only Choice C "*were simply unnecessary*" works well.

18. A

The subjunctive structure consists of two parts: a condition and a result. The present subjunctive structure uses the simple past form in the condition and "would do" in the result. The past subjunctive structure uses the past perfect form in the condition and "would have done" in the result. Eliminate Choices C and D first because "would" must appear in the result part. Choice B should also be eliminated because "*would never be used*" is for the present. In this case, the action happened in the past: the A-bombs were used against Japanese. However, if it *had been against white civilians*, such a device *would never have been used*, as Choice A indicates.

19. B

Choices A, C and D should be eliminated because terms such as "rather than," "but not," and "or" tend to negate one of the two equally correct claims: *the first shot of the Cold War* and *the last shot of the World War II*. Only Choice B "as well as" correctly expresses the meaning of "in addition to."

20. D

You may make *a decision to* do something, *for doing* something or *against doing* something. In this case, Truman made *a decision to drop* the bomb, as Choice D indicates.

21. C

Here Truman was talking about a past scenario: If we had taken a Normandy-type amphibian landing. It is a past subjunctive structure. The correct result part is: It would have cost an estimated million casualties, as Choice C indicates.

22. B

This sentence presents a contrast to the previous one. Therefore the correct transition is "*however*," as Choice B indicates.

23. D

When the choice to DELETE appears, there must be a really good reason not to pick it. In this case, none of the other choices add anything that is necessary to the meaning or structure of the sentence. Without the underlined portion, the participial phrase "*competing for scarce resources*" perfectly adds further information to the sentence. Therefore, the best choice is to DELETE the underlined portion.

24. A

Eliminate Choice C because "*they include*" starts a new sentence without ending the previous one with a period. Then, eliminate Choice D because the modified word is "*a broad group*" instead of "*people.*" Since "that" stands for a singular noun "*group*," the target verb must be "includes," as Choice A indicates.

25. B

Choices C and D do not make sense. The trappers traded their guns for gold with Indians. Therefore, the guns were "*traded by trappers,*" as Choice B indicates.

26. D

"*This*" can only modify a noun, eliminating Choices A, B, and C because "migrate," "migrated," and "migrating" are different verb forms. The correct noun form is Choice D "*migration.*"

27. D

The underlined portion is to give *the Pawnee* a definition. The correct way is just inserting the definition itself "*a village tribe,*" as Choice D indicates.

28. C

This paragraph compares the two groups how they moved. On one side, the Lakota's *cultural pattern became more and more that of horse-riding nomads.* On the other side, *the Pawnee war parties usually made their trips on foot.* Based on this comparison, the Lakota had an advantage because they *were mounted on horses,* as Choice C indicates.

29. B

Choice A should be eliminated because sentences cannot be combined by commas. Choice C gives incorrect information, as if there were only two options: either seven warriors or a hundred. Choice D "*different in size*" is not specific. Only Choice B contains all the necessary information: The parties might have as less as seven warriors or as many as a hundred warriors.

30. A

Choices C and D are wrong because finite verb forms "had demonstrated" or "demonstrated" cannot stand alone without a subject. Choice B is not correct either because "he had demonstrated" starts a new sentence without ending the previous one with a period. Choice A is a perfect subordinate clause led by "who" modifying the noun "warrior."

31. C

Choice A should be eliminated because it combines two sentences with a comma. The first sentence "No shirt was worn" and the second "a robe was belted about the waist and tied over the breast" form a contrast, eliminating Choices B and D as they suggest a continuation. All that remains is Choice C, which fits in the usage "*no ... but*" to mean *only*.

32. B

Choice A is not good because the two sides of "*and*" are not balanced. Choice D actually means *the Tent of War,* instead of *the Sacred War Pack,* was important in any war activities. An inserted past participial phrase adding minor information to the main clause should be set off by commas, as Choice B indicates.

33. D

Eliminate Choice A because a comma cannot combine two sentences. Choice B can also be eliminated because "*were permitted*" doesn't have a subject. Choice C is not correct either because, if "*who won special honors on the war path*" were taken out, the remainder "*men they were permitted*" doesn't make sense. Only Choice D uses a subordinate clause "*who won special honors on the war path*" to modify "*men*" without changing completeness of the main clause.

34. D

After introducing Zimmamann and his company, it is the time to introduce its service: how it works. Choices A, B, and C are more like comments rather than introduction. Choice D explains how it works: *your calls to other users are sent through the company's servers and decrypted on the other phone.*

35. C

The correct pattern is "to prevent somebody from doing something." In this case, The Silent Circle's service can *prevent* the snooper *from knowing* the number of the person you are calling or texting, as Choice C indicates.

36. A

Choice A is correct because an environment is like a place. Here "*where*" means "in those environments." If we put it back, the subordinate clause means: You need widespread deployment of crypto technology *in those environments.*

37. B

Basic structure of the sentence is "Documents suggest ..." To modify "documents," we can either use a subordinate clause "which are brought to light by..."or simply shorten it to a past participial phrase "*brought to light by...*" as Choice B indicates.

38. A

Choice B "*suggests*" is wrong because it doesn't agree with the subject "documents." Choice C "suggesting" is a participial phrase which cannot be a predicate by itself. Choice D is the past tense form, not appropriate for presenting a fact.

39. C

For the sake of consistence, "could" is the right word choice, eliminating Choices A and B. After "not only," a reverse word order must be used. In this case, the word order is like this: "not only could the government be watching you, so could ...," as Choice C indicates.

40. B

To list some examples of the "user data," only "such as" is the correct way.

41. D

When choice to DELETE appears, give it special consideration. There must be a really good reason not to pick it. In this case, none of the other choices are grammatically appropriate: Choices A and B would make two sentences combined with a comma; Choice C is a subordinate clause without a modified noun. Without the underlined portion, participial phrase *"now being manufactured by a joint venture that includes Silent Circle"* works fine, adding more information to the main clause *"it uses Zimmermann's encryption tools and adds other protections."* Choice D is therefore the correct answer.

42. C

Eliminate Choices A and B because "block" and "blocks" are finite verb forms without a subject. Since relative pronoun "that" stands for a singular noun "system," the target verb must take an –s, as Choice C indicates.

43. A

The original is perfect because "while" is a conjunction that means "in spite of the fact that."

44. B

Choice A is wrong because two sentences cannot be combined by a comma. Choice C should be eliminated because it is a run-on sentence. Choice D is wrong because a "which" clause must immediately follow the noun it modifies. Choice B is the correct answer because it uses a subordinate clause "which sells for $629" to modify "Blackphone."

SECTION 3

1. D

Start by distributing: $-6x + 1 = 8 - 42 - 1$

The solve for x: $-6x = -36$

The answer is: $x = 6$

2. A

If we times $4 < n < 13$ by -1, we can get $-13 < -n < -4$. Because $2 < m < 7$, we can get $2 + (-13) < m - n < 7 + (-4)$, and this means $-11 < m - n < 3$.

3. D

Square root both sides: $x - 12 = 3x + 18$, or $x - 12 = -3x - 18$

Solve it for x: $-2x = 30$, so $x = -15$, which is (D);

Or $4x = -6$, so $x = -1.5$, which is not among the choices.

4. B

Simplify the left side by dividing:

$$\frac{2}{2}x^{3-1} + \frac{4}{2}x^{2-1} - \frac{6}{2}x^{1-1} = x^2 + 2x - 3 = (x-1)(x+3)$$

Now the equation looks like this:

$$(x-1)(x+3) = (x-1)$$

There is a possibility: $x-1 = 0$, so $x = 1$, which is not among the choices.
Divide both sides by $(x-1)$;

$$(x+3) = 1$$

Subtract 3 from both sides: $x = -2$

5. C

In this question, you don't have to solve for x. Look at the question carefully, you'll see that $2x^2 - 8x = 2(x^2 - 4)$. From $x^2 - 4x - 12 = 0$, we get $x^2 - 4 = 12$. Therefore, $2x^2 - 8x = 2(12) = 24$.

6. A

Since a is less than -2, and $y = \frac{ax}{3}$, y will be negative when x is positive; or y will be positive when x is negative. Just take a look at these graphs, you'll see that only (A) satisfies this.

7. D

The question doesn't ask for the value of x. Comparing $3x-1$ and $-6x + 2$, you'll see that $-2(3x-1) = -6x + 2$. So we can multiply the inequality by -2, remembering to flip the inequality signs:

$$-\frac{3}{4}(-2) > (3x-1)(-2) > \frac{4}{3}(-2)$$

$$\frac{6}{4} > -6x + 2 > -\frac{8}{3}$$

Only -2 satisfies this inequality.

8. A

If you remember that, given a quadratic function in the form $y = ax^2 + bx + c$, the x-value of the vertex is at $-\frac{b}{2a}$. In this case, $a = 1$ and $b = -6$, so the vertex will be at the point when $x = 3$, eliminating Choices B and D. By plugging in, you can get $y = -25$. The correct answer is (A).

Another way to solve it: Set $y = 0$, you can factor $x^2 - 6x - 16 = 0$ as $(x - 8)(x + 2) = 0$; therefore, $x = 8$ or -2. The midpoint is the average of the x-values: $\frac{8+(-2)}{2} = 3$.

9. C

Factor the left side as $(x + y)(x - y) = 21$. Substitute $x + y = 7$, you get $x - y = 3$. Stack and add: $x + y = 7$

$$+ \quad x - y = 3$$
$$2x \quad = 10$$

Therefore, $x = 5$. The correct answer is (C).

10. C

To find the value of $f(2)$ when given the equation of $f(x)$, you need to make $x = 2$ every time it appears in the function:

$f(2) = 2 \times 2^3 + 3 \times 2^2 - 2 + 1$

$f(2) = 16 + 12 - 2 + 1$

$f(2) = 27$

This is (C).

11. B

Start to solve it by plugging in: $d(6) = f(6 - 2) = f(4)$. Then use the graph to find the value of $f(4)$. The answer is 5.

12. B

Factor both sides: $5(x - 1)(x + 6) = 5(x - 1)$.
Note that $x \neq 1$, divide both sides by $5(x - 1)$, we get: $(x + 6) = 1$. Therefore, $x = -5$.

13. C

Because $\angle ABC$ is 50°, $\angle ACB + \angle BAC = 180° - 50° = 130°$.
Since $\angle ACB + \angle BAC = 130$, $\angle ADE + \angle DEC = 360 - 130 = 230$. That is Choice C.

14. D

To clear a cube root, cube both sides of the equation:

$(\sqrt[3]{x - 5})^3 = 3^3$

$x - 5 = 27$

Add 5 to both sides, you get $x = 32$.

15. B

Multiply both sides by $x-3$ to clear the fraction: $2x + 15 = x^2$

Because this equation is a quadratic, set it equal to 0: $x^2 - 2x - 15 = 0$

Factor: $(x-5)(x+3) = 0$

This means: $x = -3$ or $x = 5$.

Double check that neither of them makes the denominator in the original equal to 0.

16. 128

The un-shaded region, circle B, is inside Circle O. So the area of the shaded region equals to the area of circle O minus circle B. Circle O's radius is 12, and circle B's $12/3 = 4$. Therefore, $12^2\pi - 4^2\pi = (144 - 16)\pi = 128\pi$.

17. 15

Set x as the number of quarters, so the number of nickels is $x + 10$. Elias's money can be expressed by this equation: $25x + 5(x + 10) = 500$

Solve it for x: $25x + 5x + 50 = 500$

$$30x = 450$$

$$x = 15$$

18. 3

Distribute the quotient:

$$\frac{a+12}{8} = \frac{a}{8} + \frac{12}{8}$$

Since $\frac{a}{8}$ has a remainder of 7, and $\frac{12}{8}$ has a remainder of 4, the two remainder together will be 11. As 11 is still greater than 8, the division should go on until we get a remainder of 3. Therefore, the answer is 3.

19. 14

First, find the value of $f(3)$:

$$f(3) = \frac{2 \times 3}{3} + 3 = 5, \text{ that means } g(f(3)) = g(5).$$

Then, plug it in and get the answer:

$$g(5) = \frac{4 \times 5}{5} + 10 = 14$$

20. 9

If the cos of $\angle SPR$ is $\frac{8}{10}$, that means $\frac{PS}{PR} = \frac{8}{10}$.

Step 1. Set up a proportion:

$\frac{PS}{15} = \frac{8}{10}$

Solve this proportion, we get $PS = 12$

Step 2. Use the Pythagorean Theorem or Pythagorean triple to determine:

$RS / PS / PR = 3 / 4 / 5$

$RS / 12 / 15 = 3 / 4 / 5$

Solve this proportion, we get the answer: $RS = 9$

SECTION 4

1. B

Plug in. Or multiply both sides by 2, we get $8 = x + 6$, therefore $x = 2$, which is (B).

2. C

$(z^4 + 5z^2 - 3) - z(z^2 + 5z + 1) = (z^4 + 5z^2 - 3) - (z^3 + 5z^2 + z) = z^4 - z^3 - z - 3$, which is (C).

3. C

Find the lower limit and upper limit of $a - b$. To make $a - b$ as small as possible, we make a small (close to -2) and b big (close to 7), and $a - b$ close to -9. To make $a - b$ as big as possible, we make a big (close to 5) and b small (close to -3), and $a - b$ close to 8.

Alternatively, the second inequality can be written as $-7 < b < 3$. Adding to the first inequality we get (C).

4. B

Use a calculator, $\sin\frac{\pi}{8} \approx 0.38$, and $\sin\frac{\pi}{4} = \frac{1}{\sqrt{2}} \approx 0.707$. Because the sine function is monotone increasing in the range $[0, \frac{\pi}{2}]$, our angle must lie between $\frac{\pi}{8}$ and $\frac{\pi}{4}$. The correct answer is (B).

5. A

Plug in. Or observe that the right hand side is $1.5x + 5$, so $x + 4 = 1.5x + 5$, we get $0 = 0.5x + 1$; therefore $x = -2$, which is (A).

6. B

Plug in the answers. $x = 1$ makes the denominators of the equation 0, so (A) is eliminated. When $x \neq 1$, we only need to check if $x^2 + 3x - 3$ equals x. When $x = -3$, $x^2 + 3x - 3 = 9 - 9 - 3 = -3 = x$, so -3 is a solution to the equation. This eliminates (C) and leaves (B) and (D) possible. When $x = 3$, $x^2 + 3x - 3 = 9 + 9 - 3 \neq 3$. This eliminates (D). Thus the correct answer is (B).

7. C

If he does not spend any time in the library, his average number of hours per week in the library is 0. It is clear from the line in the graph that the expected score is 55, which is (C).

8. D

The x-coordinate 11 and 11.5 are not marked in the graph. 11.5 is the third mark after 10. Start from there and the vertical line intersects the graph of the linear function at $y = 85$, which is (D).

9. A

The score line $y = 75$ intersects the linear function at a point whose x-coordinate what is slightly bigger than 7.5. Note that the fact there is student scored 75 and spent 10 hours per week is not important here. The correct answer is (A).

10. C

The mode is the most frequent number occurs in the data. There are 4 points on the vertical line at $x = 10$, and 3 points on the horizontal line at $y = 78$. No other number of hours appears more than 3 times, and no other scores appear more than twice. So the two modes are 78 and 10, respectively. Their sum is 88, which is (C).

11. D

Solve the inequality. Subtract both sides by 7, $2x \geq 20$; then divide both sides by 2, $x \geq 10$. Alternatively, observe that the $2x + 7$ is monotone (bigger x gives bigger $2x + 7$), so if there is a correct answer, it must be (D).

12. C

The three lower grades consists of $12.13 + 29.1 + 12.24 = 53.47\%$ of the total number. It is almost twice as 26.73%. The answer is roughly $474 \times \dfrac{53.47}{26.73} \approx 948$, which is (C).

13. A

If they have x draws and y loses, the number of matches they won is $(38 - x - y)$.

So the total number of points is $x + 3(38 - x - y) = x + 114 - 3x - 3y = 114 - 2x - 3y$, which is (A).

14. A

There are no obvious solutions to this equation. So we use the quadratic formula. The equation can be written as $2x^2 + 5x - 4 = 0$. It has roots $\frac{-5 \pm \sqrt{5^2 - 4 \cdot 2(-4)}}{4} = \frac{-5 \pm \sqrt{57}}{4}$, which is (A).

15. D

Multiply the second equation with -3, we get $2x - 3y = -21$, contradicts the first equation. So (D) is the correct answer.

16. A

Since 1 mile is 5280 feet and 1 yard is 3 feet, there are $5280/3 = 1760$ yards in a mile. So the car travels at the speed 70×1760 yards per hour. There are 3600 seconds in an hour, so in each second it travels $70 \times 1760 \div 3600 \approx 34.22$ yards, which is closest to (A).

17. B

Plug in the answers. The two lines has y-intercepts 10 and -12, respectively. Substitute $x = 0$ in the equations.

The two y-intercepts in (A) are -12 and 10.
The two y-intercepts in (B) are -12 and 10.
The two y-intercepts in (C) are -12 and 20.
The two y-intercepts in (D) are 10 and 8.

So we may rule out (C) and (D). To decide which of (A) and (B) is correct, note that $(16, 4)$ is on both lines.

In (A), $16 + 2 \times 4 = 24 \neq 20$. So (A) is not correct. This leaves (B) as the correct answer. It is easy to check that $(16, 4)$ indeed satisfies both equations in (B).

18. B

$x + 2y = 4$ has x-intercepts and y-intercepts $(4, 0)$ and $(0, 2)$, respectively. So (C) and (D) are eliminated. $y = x^2 - 2x - 3 = (x - 1)^2 - 4$, which has vertex $(1, -4)$. (B) is the correct answer.

19. A

$g(-2) = f((-2)(-2) - (-2) - 1) = f(4 + 2 - 1) = f(5) = |10 - 9| = 1$.
$g(2) = f((2)(2) - 2 - 1) = f(4 - 2 - 1) = f(1) = |2 - 9| = 7$.
So $g(-2) + g(2) = 8$, which is (A).

20. B

Note that a can only take values from $\{-1, 0, 1, 2\}$, and b can only takes values from $\{1, 2\}$. Try all the combinations, the smallest $\frac{a-1}{b}$ is -2, achieved when $(a, b) = (-1, 1)$; the biggest $\frac{a-1}{b}$ is 1, achieved when $(a, b) = (2, 1)$. The correct answer is (B).

21. D

The selling price will be 88% of the market price for the new car. So the market price is $33000/0.88$, and the price at which the rental company bought the car is $\left(\frac{33000}{0.88}\right) \times 0.8 = 30000$ dollars. The profit is $33000 + 19 \times 200 - 30000 = 6800$ dollars, which is (D).

22. D

Note that the model should not be a linear function where the population changes proportional to the number of days, but the increase rate never changes. Instead, when the rate is proportional to the population, the function is exponential – the slope of the tangent line represents the increase rate, and the slope should get bigger and bigger as the days passes. This leaves (B) and (D) as possible answers. But only (D) has population between 80 and 100, which is 4 to 5 times of the initial 20. The correct answer is (D).

23. C

The population after two periods is $38 + 14 \times 2 + 14 \times 5 = 136$, which is (C).

24. B

Similar to the previous question, but this time we list the populations after each period.

	A	B
Initial	23	38
After period 1	65	66
After period 2	121	136
After period 3	401	290
After period 4		542

The piecewise functions first cross in period 3, because in the two early periods, the population of B is higher than the population of A on both ends. At the beginning of period 3, group A has 15 less than group B, but each day its increment is 9 more than that of group B. So in 2 days its population exceeds B. The answer is (B).

It is nice to keep the following picture of the piecewise functions in mind.

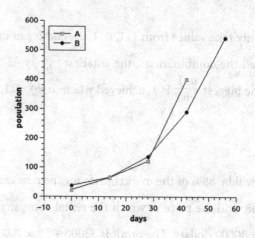

25. D

Use the table in the solution to the previous question. The missing cell should also be 542. Group A has its population increase of 141 in the 4th period of 14 days, so the average increase is $\frac{141}{14} \approx 10.07$, which is (D).

26. C

We can first work out the equation for n:
$\frac{y}{x-5} = \frac{3}{0-5} = -\frac{3}{5}$ which means
$3x + 5y = 15$.

Now we can solve the system of linear equations for m and n. Or we may plug in the answers. Among the options, only (C) satisfies both $3x + 5y = 15$ and $y = \frac{x}{5} - \frac{1}{5}$. So (C) is the correct answer.

27. D

You may plug in the values. It is better to simplify the equation first,
$x - 2x + 3x - 4x + 5x - 6x = (x - 2x) + (3x - 4x) + (5x - 6x) = (-x) + (-x) + (-x) = 9$. From here it is clear $x = -3$, which is (D).

28. B

Be careful that the chart does not begin with the 0 amount import. The import in 2014 from Thailand and Vietnam are 30 and 20, respectively. Thailand's proportion is $\frac{3}{3+2} = 60\%$, which is (B).

29. D

The difference is represented by the gap between the two curves. It is clear from the picture that in 2011 the gap is biggest. The correct answer is (D).

30. C

Now we need to look for the maximum sum of the imports from both countries. We can compute the sum for each year and find the maximum. One faster way is to first look at the two peak values in each country. That is 35 and 26, which is not achieved in the same year. So the maximum possible would be 60. To make it 60, the import from Thailand should be at least 34; there are only three such points, but none of them has corresponding Vietnam import of 26. Thus a sum of 60 is also not possible. 59 is achieved in both years of 2006 and 2008. (C) is the correct answer.

31. 6

The simpler way is to get $3a + 3b$ directly, without solving a and b. Adding the two equations together, $12a + 12b = 24$, divide both sides by 4 we get $3a + 3b = 6$.

32. 16

Multiply both sides with 6, we get $3s = 2s + 16$; thus $s = 16$.

33. 32

Let us first find the equation of the parabola. It has vertex (0, 4500), and obviously y increases with x when $x>0$. So it has the form

$$y = 4500 + ax^2$$

for some constant a. We can plug in either Dylon's data or Paul's data to find a. For example, plug in the point corresponds to Dylon, we have $5900 = 4500 + 400a$, this solves to $a = 3.5$. So, the equation Andy has as the model is

$$y = 4500 + 3.5x^2$$

For Randy, we have $8084 = 4500 + 3.5x^2$, which gives $x^2 = 1024$ and thus $x = 32$.

34. 44

Use the equation we found in the last problem, Leslie's salary can be computed as $4500 + 3.5(72)^2 = 22644$. The fraction of this salary in the total is

$$\frac{22644}{4500 + 5900 + 8084 + 10100 + 22644} \approx 0.44202 \approx 44.2\%.$$ So the answer is 44.

35. $\frac{5}{4}$ or 1.25

When $q = 5$, the relation becomes $5S = 5 + S$; subtract S from both sides, $4S = 5$. So, $S = \frac{5}{4}$.

36. 52

A nice thing to notice is that the ratio between the three sides of *ABC* is 3:4:5. So ∠*A* is a right angle and *ARPQ* is a rectangle. The triangles △*ABC*, △*RBP*, △*QPC* are all similar; they all have the sides in the ratio 3:4:5. In particular, *PC* = 5 implies *QC* = 3 and *PQ* = 4. So *RA* = *PQ* = 4 , and *AQ* = *AC-QC*. Because $RQ^2 = AR^2 + AQ^2 = 52$, so $RQ = \sqrt{52} = 2\sqrt{13}$. Its square is 52.

37. 0.24

According to the MASS column (or to the common knowledge), the heaviest planet in the whole solar system is Jupiter, and the lightest among the first six is, as the name suggests, Mercury. The ratio of the density of Jupiter to the density of Mercury is 1326 to 5427, which is approximately 0.244.

38. 25.3

We first find the ratio of the two forces (use index 1 for Mars, 2 for Venus):

$$\frac{F_1}{48} = \frac{F_1}{F_2} = \frac{m_1}{r_1 r_1} \frac{r_2 r_2}{m_2} = \frac{m_1}{m_2} \left(\frac{r_2}{r_1}\right)^2 = \frac{642}{4870} \times \frac{4}{1}.$$

This gives us 25.31PN.

SECTION 5

Martin Luther King, Jr.'s "I have a dream" speech is one of the most frequently referenced speeches in American history. In it, King argues that racial discrimination must end now. In order to persuade his audience to embrace racial equality, he uses irony, extended metaphor, and repetition.

Irony is used to highlight both the disappointments faced by African Americans and their hopes for a brighter future. As he opens his remarks, King alludes to Abraham Lincoln and his signing of the Emancipation Proclamation. The Emancipation Proclamation should have radically transformed the lives of freed slaves. Unfortunately, the reality for African Americans in King's time is nothing like the future Abraham Lincoln dreamt of. Even with slavery abolished, "one hundred years later, the Negro still is not free." Toward the end of his speech, King uses irony again to boldly put forth his vision for the future. Even in Alabama, notorious for "its vicious racists," King envisions a day when children of different races will be able to hold hands "as brothers and sisters." King powerfully employs unexpected contrasts to underscore the ongoing racism in America and advocate for a truly egalitarian alternative.

Extended metaphors are an effective vehicle for depicting the stark realities of racism and proposing restitutions. In paragraphs four and five, King compares inequality to a broken banking system. King explains that Declaration of Independence's guarantees of life, liberty, and the pursuit of happiness comprise a promissory note that ever single American is entitled to, regardless of race. Much like attempting to cash a bad check, African Americans find themselves shut out from the rights that should be theirs. King will not give up hope for his people or his country by refusing "to believe that there are insufficient funds in the great vaults of opportunity in this nation." Later, he invokes the seasons to describe African Americans' "legitimate discontent." King has faith we can move forward from the "sweltering summer" of racial injustice to "an invigorating autumn of freedom and equality." These extended metaphors enrich King's arguments and increase the potential for change by planting unshakeable images in the listener's mind.

The repetition of key words and phrases moves the audience from despair over the state of race relations to hope for the future. In the beginning of the speech, King repeats the phrase "one hundred years later" to stress how frustratingly little things have changed for African Americans between the signing of the Emancipation Proclamation and the year 1963. With his audience sufficiently outraged about inequality, King makes his call to action. The repetition of "now is the time" marks the need for immediate action. The final third of the speech pivots from anger to optimism as King recites his mantra of "I have a dream", each time adding something new to his vision for a better future. This repetition helps the listener to hone in on crucial points and walk away from the speech sharing King's vision.

The "I have a dream" speech was a watershed moment during the Civil Rights movement that helped to accelerate the end of segregation. Martin Luther King, Jr. was a compelling speaker with impressive oratorical skills. Juxtaposition, analogy, and reiteration were among the techniques he wielded to increase the potency of his message.

Answer Explanations
New SAT Practice Test 4

Section 1

1. A

The first two paragraphs deal primarily with world reception of the book and the trend towards expanding the economic theories contained in it to other parts of the world. He specifically cites several other countries where research is being conducted.

2. C

Towards the end of the article, particularly in the last paragraph, the author clearly states that Pinketty does not feel that trends are a certainty to continue. While economics favors that trajectory, there are ways in which we can slow the growing economic gap.

3. D

The graphic depicts that the income for the top 5% of earners has gone from under $200,000 in 1979 to over $400,000 in 2004, conceivably at least doubled during that time.

4. B

The term empirical is closely related to a style of scientific study that is research and experiment-based. This type of research is favorable due its reliance on evidence-based conclusions.

5. C

Based upon current economic trends and information contained in Mr. Pinketty's book, greater wealth accumulation by the top 1% is a continuing trend despite warnings and evidence that this is shrinking the amount of money available for typical wage earners.

6. D

Pinketty explicitly states that, after a period of slowed earnings for the top wage earners, the income gap has begun to steadily increase again. The consequences of this are dire.

7. A

Given the style of writing and the description of the information contained in the book, along with the references of world reception, it appears clear that the author of the article is impressed with the findings contained in Pinketty's book.

8. C

Pinketty's choice for title, borrowing from Marxist terms, shows the respect in which he views some of the ideas possessed by Marx. He cites Marx in a few places as being somewhat correct in his economical theory, but is also quick to point out how capitalism can succeed under the right conditions.

9. B

The term inevitable directly means unavoidable or unable to be changed. In context, Mr. Pinketty is relaying his belief that we are able to reverse economic trends should we choose to do so.

10. D

The author specifically points to the effects of the Great Recession and how the effects of this economic event had relatively little effect on the top wage earners.

11. A

The statistics contained in those lines point directly to the fact that top wage earners seem somewhat impervious to the negative economic trends most likely felt by typical wage earners in America.

12. B

The first few lines of the excerpt shed insight into how the Finch family differed from traditional Southerners in their absence from the Battle of Hastings. Additionally, descriptions of Simon's actions later in the passage lend evidence to this.

13. D

From the description of Simon Finch, he appears to want to reap the benefits of slavery while decrying the South's military actions against the North because it negatively influenced his family and possessions. This is generally a hypocritical action.

14. A

As explained previously, his actions do not necessarily match his ideas. Additionally, it seems that Simon felt others could sacrifice for his gains.

15. C

Given the timelines provided, it is evident that Simon arrived after the Battle of Hastings. His feelings regarding the impacts of the Civil War on his family and possessions indicate that he was already here and established by that time.

16. D

While lesson could be used correctly in context of this sentence, a dictum more closely resembles the term edict or decree. Less of a lesson, more of a demand.

17. B

We receive a glimpse into the demeanor of Atticus by his stance that, though he knows his clients are guilty, he wishes their lives spared above capital punishment. However, he is also aware of the heinousness of their crimes and thus, urges them to plead guilty.

18. A

These lines contain direct evidence of the compassionate understanding, yet effort to bring to justice, he has for his two clients. It is reflective of his demeanor as a human being as well.

19. C

Contained within the passage, we see that Simon Finch has established a small compound for himself and his family. By future generations continually returning to work the land and keep it profitable, we are able to ascertain that Simon wished to not only provide for his family, but establish a safe haven should his family members struggle.

20. D

From the use of the word in context, we see that Alexandra met and married a very unassuming man who spent a good deal of time alone and in silence.

21. A

Atticus' job, protecting many clients from capital punishment or imprisonment, appears to be somewhat different from the reasons he initially began to study law. Though this is only an assumption, we see that his office decorations and overall demeanor reflect an individual questioning his decisions.

22. B

The last lines of the excerpt deal specifically with Atticus and his distaste for his profession and what his job entails.

23. B

The author demonstrates throughout her writing that the motivation for the denial of rights by the Taliban is rooted in fear and ignorance. She implies that knowledge and understanding are power in that they allow people to question what is being told to them, rather than blindly accepting and obeying.

24. D

In these lines specifically, the author mentions fear of what is being taught. This is not necessarily because the Taliban disagrees, but understanding breeds questioning. The author implies that the Taliban fear those who may question their authority.

25. C

Though topically it can mean an appreciation of what is not possessed, the true meaning of the phrase comes in the following line. The implication is that struggle while being oppressed leads to greater appreciate of what has been sought.

26. A

The direct, correct definition for ambitions is aspirations or goals. It is used correctly and directly in context.

27. D

Though Malala is quick to point out the shortcomings of the zealots who seem to be garnering the majority of the headlines regarding Islam, she is just as quick to point out the errors in thinking that these individuals are representative of the entire religion. She speaks glowingly of her religion while decrying those who abuse its message for their own personal gain.

28. B

In these lines, the author specifically points out the discrepancy between the overall message of Islam and the ill-conceived practices that some implement. Her belief is that those who are using it to oppress are misrepresenting the religion as a whole.

29. C

From her depiction of events and the situations surrounding her attack, we can reasonably assume that Malala was injured while attempting to obtain an education.

30. A

The author references fear several times during her speech. It is the focal point of her rationale for the attacks perpetrated by the Taliban and, to her, a critical component of the reason they oppress in the manner described.

31. D

Though deprivation can also mean confiscation, in the context of this sentence, it is used to describe the withholding of basic rights by the Taliban to certain portions of the population. Therefore, withholding is the correct choice for the word in context.

32. B

The author is pleading for patience and understanding, though she is ardent in her advocacy for basic and equal rights for all. Her mention of several non-violent leaders lend credence to her position that change can come through peaceful means.

33. B

The author documents the ecological ramifications of savannah loss on overall global environmental outlooks. This is mainly through an increase in carbon emissions and a reduction of savannah grasslands.

34. D

The author draws parallels to the rhino's place in ecosystems to those of the wolves in Yellowstone National Park. He details the effects that rhino decline will have on this ecosystem and, subsequently, the world.

35. C

These lines provide support for the answer to question 34 in that they specifically assign certain roles to rhino place in the ecosystem. As such, their contribution to the ecosystem cannot be replaced and is of critical importance.

36. A

The author repeatedly points out the causes of savannah and habitat loss in South Africa. Those contributions, poaching and industrialization, are all caused by humans.

37. D

In context, the term generally means illogical and defying rational thought. Therefore, option D is the best choice.

38. B

Given the information provided in the article, rhinos cannot interbreed. However, cross breeding within species (white rhinos) is a distant possibility. Given the manner in which the author describes this potential, it has obviously not been attempted yet.

39. C

The description of savannahs supporting vast arrays of flora and fauna support the first part of the answer. The critical part comes from their role as carbon sinks in assisting in storing carbon dioxide and reducing greenhouse gases.

40. A

Though Sudan does represent the final option for white rhino survival at this point, the correct answer would be critically important. It is correctly used in context of the sentence.

41. D

Though potions of the other answers are correct, the only truly certain possibility is option D. We are certain that poaching has had a negative effect on rhino populations given the statistics provided in the article.

42. B

These are the statistics necessary to obtain the correct answer to question 41. The numbers of rhinos poached has had a dire effect on overall populations, not just due to being killed, but a reduction.

43. B

Passage 2 details the types of crops most successful with organic farming. Given the regions these crops are grown in and the types of crops which are not as responsive to organic farming, this would be a region specific intervention. Current info provided indicates that organic farming underproduces for the world demand.

44. C

Both articles deal with scientific advancements in farming and the reliance on more complex aspects of science (ecosystem management, GPS technology) to be successful. There is less emphasis on agriculture and more on engineering.

45. A

Passage 1 deals primarily with the benefits of organic farming. The only specific drawbacks are related to genetic modification. Passage 2 outlines several topics which must be rectified for organic farming to be successful.

46. D

Anoxia relates directly to a lack of oxygen.

47. C

As the author states, genetically altered food isn't something new or that we haven't already dealt with, but critics are becoming increasingly concerned over the impacts of genetic engineering on foodstuffs.

48. B

These lines directly convey the points of the critics and their positions on the type of genetic modification acceptable and those that are more concerning.

49. A

Diametrically means in opposition to. In this sentence, it is somewhat redundant, but used properly. It implies there are strong feelings on both sides with little middle ground.

50. D

Given the anoxic areas of water, the algal blooms, the starvation of oxygen, and the term "dead zones", it can be assumed that areas most affected would see a dramatic reduction in marine life. As such, fishing and tourism would be affected.

51. A

The lines contained here deal directly with the anoxic areas and the effects of high dose nitrogen fertilizer on the marine life and water quality.

52. C

Passage 2 discusses the environmental ramifications of the process necessary for organic farmers to reap high yield crops. They further assert that organic farmers need to be well versed in ecological management. Passage 1 discusses the need for organic farmers to protect natural resources in an effort to countenance global warming, supportive of passage 2.

SECTION 2

1. D

Eliminate Choice A because two sentences cannot be combined by a comma. Choices B and C can also be eliminated because when the inserted part were taken off, the remainder couldn't be a good sentence. When the underlined part is changed into a noun phrase "*a relative of famed naturalist Charles Darwin,*" it becomes an identification, which can be inserted immediately after Francis Galton and set off with commas, or immediately before Francis Galton and set off with a comma, as Choice D indicates.

2. D

When the option to DELETE appears, give it special consideration. There must be a really good reason not to pick it. In this case, there is no such a reason because none of the other choices add anything essential to the phrase "*at an early age.*" The best answer is therefore Choice D.

3. C

Choice A is good in meaning, but it's not the best in structure because it repeats *"inheritance."* Choice B can be eliminated because two independent sentences cannot be combined by a comma. Choice D can be eliminated too because *"which"* is a relative pronoun that doesn't need "and" to connect to the main clause. Choice C is the correct answer because *"which"* stands for the modified noun *"inheritance"* and leads the subordinate clause.

4. B

There are two ways to use verb to inspire correctly: *to inspire somebody to do something; to inspire somebody with something.* In this case, the correct expression is: Galton's travels *inspired him to undertake* an exploration of southern Africa, as Choice B indicates.

5. D

Choices A, B and C all tell that Galton got to a different place; but how did it happen? Did he change his mind? Only Choice D *"but ended up traveling"* shows that he unintentionally traveled to a new place, not as *he initially planned.*

6. C

Eliminate Choice A because a comma cannot combine two independent sentences. Choices B and D should also be eliminated because "included" and "includes" are finite verb forms that cannot work without a subject. Choice C is the correct expression because it uses a participial phrase *"including a gold medal from the Royal Geographical Society"* to give further information and it is set off by a comma.

7. C

The rule that two independent sentences cannot be combined by a comma eliminates Choices A and B. Choice D means "He was marrying Luisa Butler in 1853," which makes no sense. All that remains is Choice C, *"married to Luisa Butler in* 1853," a participial phrase that adds more information to the main clause, making it the correct answer.

8. A

A participial phrase does not need a subject, eliminating Choices B, C and D. It just needs a comma to set off from the main clause, as Choice A indicates.

9. D

From the description in this paragraph, we can hardly see any direct relationship between Galton's *own theory* and The Origin of Species. Therefore, words like "following," "with clues from" or "based on" are not appropriate for describing the relationship between the two. Most possibly Galton was *"strongly influenced by*" Darwin and developed his own theory, as Choice D indicates.

10. A

None of Choices B, C, or D is consistent with the tone of the passage because they all emphasize his failure rather than his accomplishments. In the original, "while" means "in spite of the fact that," setting aside his failure and emphasizing his accomplishments. That's why there should be NO CHANGE.

11. B

Eliminate Choice C because "is still in use today" doesn't have a subject. Choice D is grammatically correct, but it doesn't combine the two sentences. When relative pronoun "that" stands for the modified noun "system" and leads the subordinate clause, it cannot be set off by a comma or a period. The correct answer is therefore Choice B.

12. A

Choices B, C and D should be eliminated because "live," "lived," and "lives" are finite verb forms that cannot stand alone without a subject. No change is needed in the original: a participial phrase *living in Europe in the mid-19th century* modifies the noun "farmer."

13. C

To list three items, the correct pattern is: "A, B, and C." Only Choice C shows the correct way to punctuate three listed items.

14. B

The purpose of the brochure is to attract people to Nebraska; therefore, only positive facts should be included. Among all the choices, "*sometimes you have to fight the angry Indians*" is the only negative fact, making Choice B the correct answer.

15. D

The brochure describes a dreaming picture in front of the poor farmers in Europe: cheap land, long grace period for payment, ideal climate, and no heavy taxes. To such a great opportunity, Choices A, B and C all sound too neutral. Only Choice C, "*Wouldn't you be a fool not to move?*" is consistent with the tone of the paragraph.

16. A

The whole paragraph is written in the past tense, and the underlined word "meant" is the past tense form of *mean*. Therefore, NO CHANGE is needed here.

17. D

The rule that two independent sentences cannot be combined by a comma eliminates Choice A. Choice B can be eliminated also because the two parts do not form a contrast. Choice C combines the two sentences with "*and*", as if "*Homesteaders were getting free land from the government*" and "*large tracts of land were granted to railroads by both the states and the federal government*" were equally important. Actually the whole paragraph only deals with the land granted to the railroads, thus eliminating Choice C. By changing the first sentence to a time phrase, Choice D indicates that "*large tracts of land were granted to railroads by both the states and the federal government*" is the main idea sentence. Choice D is therefore the correct answer.

18. B

Choices C and D should be opted out because neither *much* or *a little* can modify countable nouns, such as "people." While both *a few* and *few* can be understood as "not many," *a few* has a positive meaning (some), but *few* has a negative meaning (almost none.) Therefore, Choice B is the correct answer.

19. C

The usage is *to be interested in something / doing something*. In this case, the federal government was *interested in creating* a transportation system. Choice C is therefore the correct answer.

20. A

Choices C and D should be opted out for the tense error: "*will*" cannot be used when talking about things that happened long ago. In the pattern "not only … but," the first part needs a flipped word order, eliminating Choice B and making the original correct and NO CHANGE is needed.

21. B

Since there are only two options, "*either … or*" is the best expression, as Choice B indcates.

22. C

Preposition "in" requires a noun "*luxury*," eliminating Choices B and D. A noun can only be modified by an adjective; Choice C, "*in relative luxury*," is therefore the correct answer.

23. A

When all the choices are grammatically correct and basically mean the same thing, a closer look would be necessary. By comparing all the choices, you would find that the original is the best of all because the word "*truly*" echoes "*eagerly awaiting*" in the context. Therefore, Choice A is the correct answer: NO

CHANGE is needed.

24. C

Eliminate Choice A because two sentences cannot be combined by a comma. The main clause states that *many numbers of familiar avian species migrate*. Logically the first part should point out that some robins do not migrate so as to make a contrast. Choices B and D do not work because they both emphasize that some robins do migrate. Only Choice C, *"While not all robins migrate,"* establishes a contrast to the main clause.

25. D

Why do birds migrate to the south? It's warmer there. Choice D contains the key word *"warmer"* and uses *"such as"* to list examples, making it the best choice.

26. B

You can *provide* somebody *with* something; or you can *provide* something *for* somebody. In this case, the return of the robin *provides many northern dwellers with* an emotional lift, making Choice B the correct answer.

27. C

While all of these choices can be used as a transition to a new topic, Choice C *"you may wonder"* serves the best as a transition here because the author is talking to *you* all the time.

28. D

When the option to DELETE appears, give it a special consideration. There must be a really good reason not to pick it. In this case, there is no such reason because none of the other choices add anything to the meaning and completeness of the sentence. The best answer is Choice D.

29. B

The rule that two sentences cannot be combined by a comma eliminates Choice A. Choice C is wrong because *"wrote the book"* doesn't have a subject. While Choice D is grammatically correct with a subordinate clause *"who wrote the book"* modifying Ian Newton, Choice B is more explicit with a noun phrase inserted after Ian Newton as his identification. Therefore, Choice B, *"author of the book,"* is the best answer.

30. D

Eliminate Choices B and C because there is no reason to switch to past tense. The context tells us that birds arrive *just as environmental conditions become suitable for breeding,* so the birds leave before *"the environmental conditions"* change. If the noun is plural, the pronoun must be plural as well, eliminating

Choice A and making Choice D "*they change*" the correct answer.

31. C

The first part of the sentence, "*Birds such as robins aren't that much physically affected by plunging temperatures,*" clearly denies "comfort" as a key factor affecting birds' migration, eliminating Choices A, B and D and making Choice C "*rather than*" the correct answer.

32. B

The underlined portion is a subordinate clause modifying "*the warming north,*" a place rather than a time, which eliminates Choices A, C and D, and makes B "*where*" the correct answer.

33. A

A subordinate clause must have its own subject and predicate. Eliminate Choice C because "telling" is not a predicate form. Choice D can also be eliminated because there is no reason to switch verb tense. In the subordinate clause, "that" stands for "mechanism," a singular noun, making "that actually tells" the correct answer and NO CHANGE is necessary.

34. C

To parallel with *First* and *Finally* in the context, the right word is Choice C "*Secondly.*"

35. A

The time phrase always determines the tense form of the target verb. In this case, "*beyond human history*" gives the clue as to which verb form should be used: Human history began in a past time; therefore, Yellowstone "had existed" beyond that past time, as Choice A indicates.

36. B

The previous sentence states, *The area which is now Yellowstone National Park had been home to some Native Americans throughout the course of history.* This sentence describes the area as "*largely uninhabited.*" Therefore, the transition should signify a contrast to the previous sentence. Choice B "however" does this effectively, while other choices are either irrelevant or indicating a continuation.

37. B

Choice C is wrong because "*nor didn't*" is double negative. Choice D can be eliminated also as "*did gained*" being double past. Choice A fails to follow a flip word order as required by "nor." Choice B is the correct answer.

38. D

Throughout the paragraph, the author is using a lighthearted, leisurely tone to tell the history of Yellowstone. Here Choice D *"stumbled"* sounds more humorous, therefore more consistent in the tone of the paragraph, while other choices are too neutral.

39. C

The first sentence states, *John Colter did not think of the national park idea.* The second sentence says that John Colter's fantastical stories *inspired others who dreamed of the national park idea in regards to Yellowstone.* These two facts about John Colter form a contrast, eliminating Choice A because "*and*" signifies a continuation. Choices B and D are both wrong because "*although*" or "*even if*" can never get along with "but." All that remains is Choice C, which effectively uses "but" to establish a transition of contrast.

40. A

Choices B and C should be eliminated because "dream" or "dreamed" are finite verb forms which cannot stand alone without a subject. The modified noun "others" requires "who" instead of "which" in the subordinate clause. Therefore, Choice A is the correct answer and NO CHANGE is necessary to the original.

41. D

While all of these choices signify a contrast, only the phrase "*but with John Colter*" shows the link between John Colter and the idea of the national park. Choice D is the correct answer.

42. C

Throughout the passage, the author is using a lighthearted, leisurely tone to tell the history of Yellowstone. Choices A, B, and D should be eliminated because words like "live", "stay," and "exist" all sound too neutral. Choice C, "much of the West should be set aside for the Indians and buffalo *to roam* in their natural state," is most consistent with the tone of the passage.

43. B

This paragraph tells about George Catlin and Thorau who made some contribution to the idea of a national park regarding Yellowstone. This sentence tries to describe the similarity between them and John Colter, eliminating Choice C because "while" signifies a difference. Choice D can be eliminated too because two sentences cannot be combined by a comma. Choice A is not correct because in writing, "like" is a preposition that only links a noun, not a sentence. Choice B, "*like John Colter who had been in Yellowstone but had not thought of the idea,*" is the correct answer.

44. A

The author views John Colter, Catlin and Thorau as early contributors to the idea of the Yellowstone National Park. The original, "*though they do not properly belong in this specific history*," suggests that in one way or the other, they were still related to it, fairly giving them some credits. All other choices have a strong negative connotation in them, making Choice A the best answer and NO CHANGE is needed.

SECTION 3

1. D

Set up the equation based on the information given:

$$\frac{-3+7+12+n}{4} = 12$$

Solve it for n:

$$\frac{16+n}{4} = 12$$

$$n = 48 - 16 = 32$$

2. C

Subtract 3 from both sides: $x^3 = -24 - 3 = -27$
The answer is $x = -3$.

3. D

From $x^2 = 16$, we get $x = 4$ *and* $x = -4$. The difference among the choices lies in the value of y. From $3y^3 = -192$, we get $y^3 = -64$, so $y = -4$, eliminating choice I. Therefore, the answer is only II and III are true, which is D.

4. A

The figure shows that when $x = 0$, $y = -1$, eliminating choices B and D. It also shows that when $x = 2$, y = 4. Plug it in, you'll see that only choice A is correct.

5. B

We know that $\angle b + \angle c + \angle a = 180°$, and $\angle d + \angle a = 180°$. Therefore, $\angle b + \angle c = \angle d = 115°$. This is B.

6. A

If you don't buy anything, you don't pay any money. That means when $x = 0$, $y = 0$, eliminating Choice B. You don't get anything free in a dollar store, eliminating Choice C. The sales tax is 7%, so $y = 1.07x$; the slope is close to 1.

Therefore, the correct graph is A.

7. C

We only need to figure out the length of the rectangular. The rectangle's diagonal cuts it into two equal right triangles, with the diagonal as their shared hypotenuse, which is 25 feet. According to the right triangle trigonometry, the adjacent (length of the rectangle) is 20 feet. Therefore, the area of the rectangle is: $15 \times 20 = 300$.

8. B

Solve this problem by plugging in:
$f(218) = 3\sqrt{218 - 154}$
$f(218) = 3\sqrt{64}$
$f(218) = 24$

9. B

Remember the relationship between the square root and the numbers in front of it is multiplication. So, $3x\sqrt{2x} = \sqrt{3^2x^2 2x} = \sqrt{18x^3}$. The correct answer is (B).

10. D

Since the side of the square is 16 in, the radius of the biggest possible circle will be 8 in. Therefore, its area is: $A = \pi r^2 = 8^2\pi = 64\pi$

11. C

Apply the rule to the equations one by one: First, if $x = 6$,

A. $f(6) = \frac{2}{3}(6) + 1 = 5$, wrong.

B. $f(6) = \frac{2}{3}(6) - 3 = 1$, wrong.

C. $f(6) = -\frac{2}{3}(6) + 1 = -3$, right.

D. $f(6) = -\frac{1}{3}(6) - 1 = -3$, right.

Continue with C and D only, if $x = 3$,

C. $f(3) = -\frac{2}{3}(3) + 1 = -1$, right.

D. $f(3) = -\frac{1}{3}(3) - 1 = -2$, wrong.

The correct answer is (C).

12. A

First, find out the value of $g(2)$
$g(2x) = 4(2) - \frac{4}{3} = 8 - \frac{4}{3} = \frac{20}{3}$

Then, plug in to get the value of $f(g(2))$

$$f(\frac{20}{3}) = \frac{4}{3}(\frac{20}{3}) + 1 = 6$$

13. D

Based on the information given, if the driving mileage is x when $x \geq 20$, the rental cost will be: $f(x) = 5(x-20) + 19$.

The customer's home is 25 miles away, so a round trip is 50 miles. Plug in to find the cost: $f(50) = 5(50-20) + 19 = 169$.

14. B

Cube both sides: $(\sqrt[3]{2x^2-7x+30})^3 = (3)^3$

$2x^2-7x + 30 = 27$

$2x^2-7x + 3 = 0$

Factor it: $(2x-1)(x-3) = 0$

This is the answer: $x = \frac{1}{2}$ or $x = 3$.

15. B

Both equations are in the vertex form of a quadratic. They have the same vertex, which is 3. That means when $x = 0$, eliminating choices A and C. When compared with the original graph, we see that choice D flipped the graph, which shows a negative variable. Therefore, choice B is the correct answer.

16. 34

From the first two sets, you can find that the rule is: $y = 2x + 2$. Apply the rule to figure out the value of a: $a = 2(7) + 2 = 16$. Apply the rule again: $n = 2(16) + 2 = 34$.

17. 440

Based on the information given, the rate of US Dollar to EUR is: 6.16: 7 = 0.88. Therefore, $500 \times 0.88 = €440$.

18. 4

Set x as the number of miles Emma can walk in two hours, or 120 minutes. Then set up the ratio:

$1.5: 45 = x: 120$

$$x = \frac{1.5(120)}{45} = \frac{180}{45} = 4$$

19. 12

Because OA and OB are radii, triangle AOB is isosceles. This means that if $\angle ABO$ is 45°, so is $\angle BAO$. That makes $\angle AOB$ 90°, so arc AB is $\frac{1}{4}$ the circumference of the circle. Because the minor arc AB is 2π, the circumference of the circle O ($2\pi r$) is 8π. From there, you can find the radius of the circle r, which is 4, making the area of circle O 16π. Since the shaded region is $\frac{1}{4}$ of the circle, which is 4π, the area of the unshaded region of the circle is 12π, so $a = 12$.

20. 64

$2^a \cdot 2^b \cdot 2^c = 2^{a+b+c} = 2^6 = 64$

SECTION 4

1. C

π is approximately 3.14. The half of 6 is 3; the half of 7 is 3.5, which exceeds π. (C) is the correct answer.

2. A

Subtract 2 from both sides, we get $3x<9$. Then divide both sides by 3, we get $x<3$, which is (A).

3. D

Plug in. When $x = 0$, $\frac{2-x}{2+x} = \frac{2}{2} = 1$. When $x = 1$, $\frac{2-x}{2+x} = \frac{1}{3}$. When $x = 4$, $\frac{2-x}{2+x} = \frac{-2}{6} = -\frac{1}{3}$. So (A), (B), (C) are all incorrect, and (D) is the correct answer.

Alternatively, multiply both sides by $(2 + x)$ gives $2-x = -2-x$, adding x to both sides gets $2 = -2$, which is impossible. So no real numbers satisfy this equation. (D) is the correct answer.

4. B

The equations in all the answers are in the standard center-radius form. The right hand side should be the squared radius. So (C) and (D) are eliminated. The circle passes through (1,2), so (1,2) should satisfy the equation of the circle. It is easy to check (1,2) does not satisfy (A) but satisfies (B). Therefore, (B) is the correct answer.

5. B

It is easy to plug in (C) and (D). We see that both (3,3) and (6,11) are solutions to the system of equations above. So none of (A), (C), and (D) is an accurate statement. This leaves (B) as the correct answer.

6. D

First write the equation for P in the vertex form: $y = 2(x-2)^2 + 12$. Its vertex is (2,12).

(A) is already in the vertex form; its vertex is (4, 8).

(B) is a translate of P along the y-axis (moving downwards by 40); so it cannot share the same vertex with P.

(C) has the vertex form $y = (x-2)^2 + 16$, which has vertex (2, 16).

So (D) is left as the correct answer. The form of (D) is a little tricky, but it can be rewritten as

$$y = x^2 - 2x + 1 - 2x + 15 = x^2 - 4x + 16 = (x-2)^2 + 12.$$

7. A

Mass equals the production of volume and density. When the masses are the same, the volumes are in inverse proportion to their density. Let x be the volume of the iron block in cubic meters. $x:10.4 = 2.7:7.8$, so $x = \dfrac{2.7 \times 10.4}{7.8} = 3.6$, which is (A).

8. B

If the density of Platinum is bigger than that of Gold, the median must be the density of Lead — there are three densities less than it, and three (including Platinum, because it is bigger than Gold, which is in turn bigger than Lead) bigger than it. So the median is 11.3, which is (B).

9. D

We introduce two solutions. In both solutions we first note down the sum of the densities of the other six materials, which is $2.7 + 9 + 19.3 + 7.8 + 11.3 + 22.5 = 72.6$.

Now we can plug in the answers. Note that (A) can be quickly eliminated, since the average, even count Platinum's density as 0, is already bigger than 10, and 18 will not be 8 higher than the average. For (B), the average will be $\dfrac{72.6+19.3}{7} \approx 13.1$, 19.3, which is not close to 13.1 + 8. For (C), the average will be $\dfrac{72.6+20.5}{7} \approx 13.3$, 20.5, which is not close enough to 13.3 + 8. And for (D), the average will be $\dfrac{72.6+21.4}{7} \approx 13.4$, which is 21.4−8. Therefore, (D) is the correct answer.

We can also set the equation

$$x = \frac{72.6+x}{7} + 8,$$

The solution is around 21.4333, which is closest to (D).

10. A

Subtract $2b$ from both sides, we get $3b + 4 \geq -11$. Then subtract 4 from both sides, we get $3b \geq -15$. Finally divide both sides by 3, we get $b \geq -5$, which is (A).

11. A

Note the factorization $x^2 - 4y^2 = (x + 2y)(x - 2y)$. So, $2016 = 4(x - 2y)$. Thus $x - 2y = \frac{2016}{4} = 504$, which is (A).

12. D

Elias spent $(m-60)$ additional minutes, so the prize is $10000 - 300(m-60)$. Simplify it, we get $28000 - 300m$, which is (D).

Or plug in some values. For example, take $m = 60$, the prize should be 10000. Only (D) gives the correct answer.

13. C

It is clear that (A) has no real roots because the left hand side is always greater than 0. It is also clear that (B) has two roots -12 and 21. (D) is equivalent to $(x-2)^2 = 3$, which has two roots. (C) is equivalent to $x^2 - 6x = -9$, i.e., $(x-3)^2 = 0$, has exactly one value $x = 3$. So (C) is the correct answer.

14. C

Plug in $(-3,5)$ into the equation for a and see that a does not go through $(-3,5)$; thus (D) is eliminated. The equation for a can be written as $y = 2x + 7$, so its slope is 2. The slope of b is $\frac{15-5}{2-(-3)} = 2$ as well. Therefore, these two lines are parallel and (C) is the correct answer.

15. A

There are many choices to approach this problem. We can first imagine the users are uniformly distributed to the servers, so each server gets 10000 users, hence 230000 requests. Between 10 A.M. and 9 P.M. there are 11 hours, i.e., 11 × 3600 seconds. So on average each second a server handles $\frac{230000}{11 \times 3600} = \frac{2300}{376} \approx 6.117$ user requests, which is closest to (A).

Note that the 5 minutes average stay time is of no use in this problem.

16. B

Combining the incoming water (as positive) and outgoing water (as negative), the tank loses 25 gallons per minute. It takes $\frac{5000}{25} = 200$ minutes to empty the tank. 200 minutes equals 3 hours and 20 minutes. So the time is 10:20 A.M., which is (B).

17. C

Translate the graph 4 units upwards, and then flip it about the x-axis. Or use $g(x) = -f(x) - 4$, first flip it about the x-axis then translate it 4 units downwards.

Another way is to observe the y-intercept. From the picture $f(0)$ is around -4. So $g(0)$ is around $-(-4 + 4) = 0$. Only (C) has y-intercept close to 0. The correct answer is (C).

18. A

The second equation can be simplified to $x + y = 7$ by dividing both sides by 8. Combining with the first one we get $x = 2$, then $y = 5$, and $3x - y = 1$, which is (A).

19. B

Plug in with $a = 1$ and $x = 10$, i.e., each item sells at \$1, and she sold 10 items. The selling price earned her \$10, and she spent \$3 for manufacturing and shipping them. So the account ends with \$5007.

At this stage both (B) and (D) gives the correct number. But simply plugging in again with $a = 2$ and $x = 10$ will rule out (D). So (B) is the correct answer.

20. B

Their distance is multiplied by $\sqrt{5}$, $r2$ is 5 times the original. The force, when the two masses are unchanged, is inversely proportional to the square of the distance, so it is $\frac{1}{5}$ of the original. $\frac{3000N}{5} = 600N$, which is (B).

21. B

Solution 1. Plug in. If there are 14 dimes, then there are 11 quarters. $10 \times 14 + 11 \times 25 = 415$.

Solution 2. Suppose there are x dimes and $(25-x)$ quarters, then we have $10x + 25(25-x) = 415$, which solves to $x = 14$.

Solution 3. First suppose all the coins are dimes, then the total will be 250 cents, which is 165 less than 415. Changing one dime to a quarter will add 15 cents for us, so we need to change 11 coins to quarters to make up the 165 cents. The number of dimes remained is 14, which is (B).

22. C

The total forest of the Americas is 864 + 705 = 1569, in which 864 is about 55%, which is (C).

23. B

The drop ratio in Africa is $\frac{35}{709} \approx 0.049$; the drop ratio in Oceania is $\frac{7}{198} \approx 0.035$; the drop ratio in South America is $\frac{40}{904} \approx 0.044$. Although South America has the bigger absolute drop in Mha, it is Africa that has the biggest drop ratio of about 4.9%, which is (B).

24. B

In (A) the peak of the year occurred too early. In (C) the peak occurred too late. (D) is not really close to the description. The correct answer is (B).

25. A

Plug in the answers with some special values of t. When $t = 0$, the expression evaluates to $\frac{144}{15} = \frac{48}{5}$, this rules out (B) and (D). When $t = 1$, the expression evaluates to 20, while (A) evaluates to 20 and (C) evaluates to $\frac{576}{125}$. So the correct answer is (A).

26. C

Phoebe's salary will be increased by $80000 \times 10\% = \$8000$, while Irene's is increased by \$9500. Start with the same salary, after one year Irene's will be \$1500 higher than Phoebe's. (C) is the correct answer.

27. C

Each year the salary is increased by 10%, i.e., the previous year's salary multiplied by 1 + 10% = 1.1. We can also plug in the values for 1 or 2 years and see that (C) is the correct answer.

28. D

Irene's salary after 10 years will be $80000 + \$9500 \times 10 = 175000$. At the same time, Phoebe's salary will be $80000 \times (1.1)^{10} \approx \$207500$. Phoebe's salary will be at least \$30000 higher than Irene's. The correct answer is (D).

29. D

In a triangle the sum of any two sides is larger than the third. So we need $c + 3.2 > 5.3$ and $3.2 + 5.3 > c$. These implies c is in the range $(2.1, 8.5)$. (It is also easy to convince oneself that for any value of c in this range, there is a valid triangle.) Thus all the possible integer values for c are 3, 4, 5, 6, 7, 8. The correct answer is (D).

30. D

While it can be mathematically proven that (D) is always an integer, for this problem it is easy to eliminate the wrong answers. (B) might be the easiest; plug in $a = 0$, it gives a value of 0.5. Make $a = 1$, (C) evaluates to $\frac{10}{4} = 2.5$. (A) is a little trickier. When $a = 0$ or $a = 1$, (A) evaluates to an integer. But when $a = 2$, it evaluates to $\frac{140}{3}$, which is not an integer. The correct answer is (D).

31. 23

The people have myopia in the table is $715 + 217 = 932$. Among the 932 drivers, 217 failed on their first test. The percentage is roughly $\frac{217}{932} \approx 23.28\%$.

32. 5

There are infinitely many points on this line. The form of the problem indicates that there is only one answer. So we may pick any point, say, $(1,0)$. And $a^2 + 4b^2 - 4ab + 4 = 1 + 0 + 0 + 4 = 5$.

Algebraically, square the relation $a - 2b = 1$, we get $1 = (a - 2b)^2 = a^2 + 4b^2 - 4ab$, so $a^2 + 4b^2 - 4ab + 4 = 5$.

33. 14

Our aim is $\sqrt{2x} - 1$, we can solve this without computing x explicitly. Multiply both side by 4 and then divide by 3, we get $\sqrt{2x} - 3 = 12$. Add 2 to both side we get $\sqrt{2x} - 1 = 14$.

34. 320

Suppose in one hour each large pump can fill the volume of x and each small can fill volume y. We have $3(3x + y) = 4(2x + 2y)$, because both sides represent the volume of the pool. We have only one equation but that is enough to solve the ratio between x and y. Expand and simplify, we get $x = 5y$. This means one large pump equals five small pumps. So the first conditions now says 16 small pumps will fill the pool in 3 hours; that means 1 small pump can do the job in

48 hours. One large and four small pumps are equivalent to 9 small pumps, so we need $48 \times \dfrac{60}{9} = 320$ minutes.

35. $14.4

The cost to print one book is $\dfrac{\$1800}{3000} + \$9 = \$9.6$, then the gross profit per book is $24 - $9.6 = $14.4

36. 22

A good way to understand this is from the geometric point of view. $|x-12.56| + |x-34.56|$ is the sum of distances from x to the points 12.56 and 34.56 on the real axis. If $x < 12.56$, then $|x-34.56|>22$; if $x > 34.56$, then $|x-12.56|>22$. If $12.56 \leq x \leq 34.56$, then $|x-12.56| + |x-34.56| = (34.56-x) + (x-12.56) = 22$. So x satisfies the equation if and only if $12.56 \leq x \leq 34.56$. There are 22 such integers.

37. 325

For the first 9 days, on average Karl learns 25 new words (because the 5th day is in the middle). So at the end of the 9th day, he will know $100 + 25 \times 9 = 325$ words.

38. 34

The number of words Karl knows after 1, 2, 3 days are 5, 15, and 30, respectively. We can use the points (1, 105), (2, 115), and (3, 130) to determine the quadratic function as $f(x) = 2.5 x^2 + 2.5x + 100$.

Also one can derive the sum of the arithmetic progression and reach the same $f(x) = 100 + \dfrac{(5+5x)x}{2}$.

Solve $2.5x^2 + 2.5x + 100>3000$. It is equivalent to $x(x + 1)>1160$. Because we want x to be an integer, it is good to estimate and test some x values. Because $33 \times 34 = 1122$ and $34 \times 35 = 1190$, we see that the smallest such x is 34.

SECTION 5

Throughout the course of American history, public opinion about marijuana has ebbed and flowed. Of late, the tides seem to be shifting in favor of marijuana legalization as states like Washington and Colorado repeal their prohibitions against the drug. In the essay "Benefits of Legalizing Marijuana in Colorado: Less Crime and More Profits", Chris Miles argues that the federal marijuana prohibition policy is wrong. Miles builds his case by citing meaningful statistics, cleverly using colloquial language, and exploring nationwide trends.

Bold statistics appear throughout the article that demonstrate the benefits of legal marijuana. Miles presents Colorado, which legalized marijuana in 2013, as a case study in the far-reaching advantages states can enjoy by ending their prohibitions on pot. "Taxed and legal recreational marijuana sales" have been a financial boon for the state. To counter negative perceptions about marijuana, he explains that the massive tax revenues, projected to be nearly $134 million over the next decade, will be used for critical civic projects including public schools and "youth educational campaigns about substance use." He then turns to an even more crucial benefit: crime. Murders in the Denver area have fallen a stunning 52.9% in the months following legalization and police officers, freed from the burden of enforcing draconian drug laws, are able to focus their resources on more serious crimes. These statistics urge expanded legalization of marijuana by showing some of the concrete benefits that Colorado has already enjoyed in a very short period of time.

Miles adds extra heft to his explanations about the benefits of legalization by following them with cheeky refutations of marijuana detractors. After describing Colorado's drop in crime, he writes that these positive outcomes are worlds apart from fearful claims "that legal weed was the devil's work". In the same vein, the thousands of newly created Colorado jobs in no way resemble the "drug-infested hellscape" prophesied by the drug's opponents. Contrary to the best hopes of marijuana's opponents, national efforts to curb drug addiction through drug control policies have failed miserably. The Colorado experiment is a bold alternative to ineffective federal policies, showing that "The times, they are a-changin'." This folksy expression is a gentle way of saying that the foes of legalization have all but lost the battle. The author's glib rebuttals portray marijuana opponents as reactionary at best and foolish at worst and make legalization appear to be the only logical option.

Finally, Miles argues that nationwide trends make eventual legalization seemingly inevitable. Miles cites polls to show growing momentum for ending prohibition. As of 2013, more than half of those surveyed nationwide support decriminalizing marijuana for adult use. In the nation's capital, the epicenter of harsh drug enforcement, DC residents are posed to pass a ballot initiative legalizing marijuana. Even the Drug Enforcement Agency is softening its hardline stance and "asking the Food and Drug Administration to remove marijuana from its list of the most dangerous and harmful drugs." This hints that the federal government is beginning to experience a paradigm shift regarding how marijuana ought to be regulated. For Miles, Colorado has shown that legalization can be a success and that other states would be wise to follow suit.

Miles makes a strong argument that marijuana should be legalized nationwide. The evidence in Colorado points to strong economic benefits and steep drops in crime. The worst fears propagated by marijuana opponents have not materialized. Now other states are getting ready to continue what Colorado started and repeal a prohibition that has not worked.

Answer Explanations
New SAT Practice Test 5

Section 1

1. C

The author provides in detail the rates of deforestation and the amount of biodiversity that has been impacted by deforestation and agriculture. While A and B are discussed, they are not the central theme of the article.

2. A

The author cites statistics and research that explicitly details that current efforts are not enough to reverse the effects of deforestation. The opposites of the other answers are correct.

3. D

Though this is generally an economic term meaning a portion of profits or investments, the author uses it synonymously with a portion of the wildlife.

4. B

The author cites a specific researcher who states that animal migration has been made extremely difficult by both deforestation and farming. The impact has had lasting effects on mating and hunting rituals.

5. C

The quote from the research explicitly delineates the difficulties deforestation has on biodiversity

6. D

Although encroaching can also mean expanding, in this case the term is used to mean intruding in areas it shouldn't.

7. A

The author specifically states that human demand for products has had far reaching impacts on rates of deforestation in the rain forest.

8. B

The rates of deforestation have not been variable, they have generally shown decline since 2008. Further, deforestation rates increased between 2007 and 2008. Therefore, the only possible correct choice is B.

9. C

This answer is best provided towards the end of the article, in lines 81-84.

10. B

The author's proposal that landowner laws should be modified or adapted to better fit the government's ability to regulate them speaks to their belief in the ability of the Brazilian government to enforce the current laws in effect.

11. A

These lines provided direct evidence to the opinions of the author.

12. A

The author continually points out references in the Constitution that guarantee equal rights to all citizens of the nation. Her repeated references to women as citizens and "persons" indicates that current law violates constitutional precedent.

13. B

The author references the fact that state rights do not overpower federal law. She points out that the Constitution does not differentiate between male and female citizens and, as such, states have no right to do so.

14. D

Specifically, the author states that states enacting laws to prevent certain citizens from reaping the benefits of rights guaranteed in the Constitution is illegal.

15. C

Direct definition. The term odious, used correctly in this context, denotes significant negativity and displeasure with an entity.

16. C

The author's continual reliance on the Constitution as precedent setting regarding rights afforded to citizens, her reference to it as the "supreme law of the land", and her assertion that states have no right to make laws preventing implementation of the Constitution all point towards her belief in a strong, centralized government.

17. A

The author cites her actions as a direct result of her acting upon what she felt were her intrinsic rights as a citizen.

445

18. D

The author discusses the impacts of denying rights to certain citizens as creating a climate of "dissention, discord, and rebellion in every home of the nation". Clearly, she feels that enacting laws such as these lead to significant familial strife.

19. B

Direct definition. Posterity means descendants or future generations.

20. A

Given her ardent stance on unequivocal equal rights for all, it is clear that the author would most likely support the idea that it is hypocritical to enjoy rights guaranteed to all while certain populations are stigmatized.

21. C

Again, given the tone and nature of her argument, coupled with her references to the denial of rights to the "Negroes", it is clear that her position is that of absolute equal rights.

22. B

The main character is originally mystified by the bird. He makes several positive references to his regal appearance and his general easy nature. It isn't until the bird says "nevermore" after the author references his loneliness that he begins to harbor negative feelings towards the bird.

23. D

By using a singular word to communicate with the main character, the author is attempting to illustrate that the bird, an animal, senses the loneliness and isolation felt by the main character. The singular word is representative of the singular person in the poem.

24. C

The term implore most closely means beseech, or beg. While hope is a close synonym, it doesn't convey the depth and strength of feeling possessed by the protagonist. Demand is correct in the context of the sentence, but the poem deals more with anguish and hopelessness. A main character would more likely be aggressively begging, rather than demanding, in this situation.

25. A

As stated previously, the poem runs the gamut of emotions. Laughter, hopefulness, sadness, anger, etc. However, the overpowering theme... the emotion most frequently and intensely felt by the main character...is a pervasive sense of hopelessness and lack of control over his life.

26. C

His reference to the fact that other friends, in addition to Lenore, have left him illustrates the main character's feeling of powerlessness to maintain meaningful relationships in his life.

27. B

While the raven does confirm that Lenore is most likely deceased, there is really no specific proof that she is dead. We only know she is gone and not returning to the main character's life in this world. Therefore, the raven is representative of her embodied spirit.

28. D

The description of the facets of his life that Lenore will no longer touch, and the physical representations of this, lead the reader to understand that the raven is most likely the spirit of the lost Lenore.

29. A

Given the terminology ascribed to Lenore and the manner in which the author and main character describe how much she has meant, it is evident that she was the love of his life. His despair and isolation have only grown since her passing.

30. D

While A and B could probably be used correctly in this sentence in context, the term obeisance specifically relates to gestures of respect. In actuality, it works incredibly well in this line. The raven has little regard for formalities. His mission is clear...show the main character that he will carry Lenore with him always.

31. C

By using the word "nevermore" so frequently, the writer conveys a feeling of never-ending pain and suffering. Though grief typically abates over time, the repeated use of the word "nevermore" indicates that the main character will never experience a lessening of this feeling.

32. A

Though companionship may be somewhat of a secondary goal for the protagonist, the main issue he seeks to resolve is his unrelenting sense of sorrow.

33. A

Much of the data and analysis presented has little to do with the Common Core as a whole, and focuses primarily on the effects of high stakes testing on teacher opinion and student performance.

34. C

The author clearly rallies against high stakes testing. However, in the course of making his argument heard, he specifically states that there is a clear difference between favoring educational and curricular reform and favoring high stakes testing.

35. B

These lines clearly indicate the writer's assertion that there exists a difference between testing and curriculum reform.

36. B

Through careful example and discussion, the author does make the case that the Common Core and national educational standards can lead to better teaching practices. Conversely, he eloquently points out that high stakes testing is unpopular among citizens, teachers, students, and politicians.

37. D

While antagonism can also entail a certain degree of pessimism, the context of the word usage clearly indicates extremely strong negative feelings. As such, option D is the best answer.

38. A

Citing specific politicians, it is evident that public outcry and rebellions have caused many politicians to shift their stance on the Common Core.

39. C

The author discusses the displeasure with which teachers view testing and its related effects on student performance on those measures along with describing student attitudes towards the test. Taken together, it is clear that he feels standardized testing unfairly stigmatizes students and teachers.

40. B

In these lines, we are offered specific evidence from students regarding their views on the test taking experience.

41. B

Specifically, pedagogy means the practice or art of teaching. Correctly used in context. However, it can be misinterpreted in context as curriculum.

42. A

The author cites 370 million dollars going to fund high stakes accountability and market driven reforms, both unpopular with voters. Given the 4.3 billion spent on Race to the Top, the 370 million represents about 10% of the money.

43. D

Both passages provide evidence that those 3 influences have been shown to favor positive outcomes. There is little discussion on the importance of one of the factors above any of the others.

44. A

The author does point out the importance of a strict bedtime and consistent routine, but also discusses the importance of parental interaction on child development. It is assumed this may also play a role in phonological development.

45. C

Citing a specific source, the author again discusses the importance of interaction on child development and sleep routines.

46. B

In context, the term is used to convey that there is little consistency to the bedroom routine...time going to bed, length of sleep, etc. The opposite would be a predictable time to go to bed, routine, and amount of sleep.

47. A

The author of passage 1 indicates that sound, consistent, and appropriate amounts of sleep are good predictors of favorable academic outcomes. Passage 2's support comes from the argument that electronic devices negatively influence the amount of sleep a child receives, supporting passage 1's perspective.

48. D

The key element here is an encompassing lifestyle change that leads to a healthy lifestyle, both at home and at school. While option A is a good choice, the negative behavior is already established and under the control of the student. Option D is promoting a healthy lifestyle before negative habits are formed.

49. C

The author cites, on separate occasions, the influence of gender on sleep patterns and routines. Though they are not well thought out arguments or studies, there is some credence to the notion that gender plays a role.

50. B

Direct citation of a gender-specific study.

51. A

Passage one does not offer any other negative influence on child sleep patterns other than that of bedtime and nighttime routine.

52. B

Phonology is the study of the sound structure of words.

SECTION 2

1. D

To list three items, the correct pattern is "<u>A</u>, <u>B</u>, and <u>C</u>." Only Choice D shows the correct way to punctuate them.

2. B

A relative pronoun stands for the noun immediately before it: *who* stands for a person, *when* stands for a time, and *which* stands for a non-person element. In this case, Zimba is a place; the relative pronoun that stands for it therefore is "where," as Choice B indicates.

3. A

In the original, relative pronoun "*who*" stands for "*workers*" as the subject of the subordinate clause. There is no error in it; therefore, NO CHANGE is necessary. All other choices are grammatically incorrect.

4. C

There is a parallel structure in this sentence: "I *assessed* the health and security of children, *identified* urgent needs, and ..." Choices A, B and D should be eliminated because "provide," "providing," and "to provide" do not match "assessed" and "identified." Only Choice C "*and provided*" is paralleled with the other two past tense verbs in the sentence.

5. A

The paragraph explains how the author made her career decision to be a nurse. There are three factors that helped shaping her decision: values instilled by parents, fascination about human body, and interest in people. Choice A states that the author's decision came "*as a result of various experiences,*" which covers all the three factors that influenced her decision making. Therefore, Choice A can be the main idea sentence of this paragraph. All other choices are either too general or too narrow.

6. A

It is a good way to use "such as" to list examples. In this case, *compassion and respect for others* are examples of "*values;*" Choice A is therefore the correct answer and NO CHANGE is necessary to the original.

7. C

We can either say "Something is fascinating," or "I am fascinated by something." In this case, the author must be fascinated by the intricacy and complexity of the human body. Therefore, Choice C "*I am always fascinated by*" is the correct answer.

8. B

Choice A can be eliminated because "*those*" is the object of "*treat,*" and "*are physically sick*" cannot stand alone without a subject. Choice C is wrong because "They are physically sick" is an independent sentence, and two sentences jammed together make a run-on. Choice D is not correct either because "which" cannot stand for people. Choice B is therefore the correct answer.

9. D

When option to DELETE appears, give it special consideration. There must be a really good reason not to pick it. In this case, there is no such reason. When the underlined portion is taken out, the remainder becomes a perfect sentence: *I can comfort and aid those facing their dark and often threatening truth.*

10. C

The rule that two sentences cannot be combined by a comma eliminates Choice A. When we take a close look at the two sentences, we can see that "*the field of medicine should know no borders*" is the reason why a nurse can help needy people "*whether they are near or far.*" This relationship eliminates Choices B and D, and makes Choice C the correct answer.

11. B

This sentence shows a parallel structure: "*My hope is to live a life that is known for helping …, healing …, showing …*" Choices A, C and D should be eliminated because neither "love," "to love" or "for loving" matches the three previous participial phrases. Only "*and loving*" fits in the structure, making Choice B the correct answer.

12. A

Choices B, C and D. should be eliminated because preposition "with" can only be followed by a noun, not a sentence. The original "With the world growing" is perfect, because "the world" is the object of "with," and the participial phrase "growing at a pace hard to match" modifies "the world." Choice A is the correct answer, and NO CHANGE should be made to the original.

13. D

Eliminate Choice B because "*occurring*" is a participle that cannot be a predicate by itself. Also eliminate Choice C because there is no reason to switch to the past tense. In this long sentence, the subject is "*a direct action*;" the predicate verb must therefore take an *s*, as Choice D indicates.

14. C

The time phrase "*over the last century*" indicates that deforestation started a century ago and continues up to now. To describe such an action, it needs present perfect tense, making Choice C, "the forest cover *has been greatly compromised*," the correct answer. All other choices are inappropriate either for being a past form or a present.

15. A

Choices C and D should be eliminated because forests can only *be lost* or *get lost*. In this sentence, the subject "acres" (rather than "forest") is plural; therefore, the verb should be "are." Choice A is the correct answer and NO CHANGE should be made to the original.

16. B

Choices A and D should be eliminated because "leads" and "lead" are finite verb forms that cannot stand alone without a subject. Choice C is wrong because "to lead" indicates a purpose, as if the purpose of removal of forest is to lead to several imbalances ecologically and environmentally, making no sense. All that remains is Choice B, which works well with a participle phrase "*leading to several imbalances*" modifying "*removal of forest.*"

17. D

None of Choices A, B and C works because "continue," "is continuing," and "continues" are finite verb forms that cannot stand alone without a subject. Only Choice D works because "continued" is a participle and "*if continued*" is the simplified form of "*if it is continued.*"

18. D

When the option to DELETE appears, give it special consideration. There must be a really good reason not to pick it. In this case, we don't see such reason because none of the other choices will add more meaning that *"continue"* doesn't cover. Therefore, the underlined portion is absolutely unnecessary, making Choice D the correct answer.

19. A

The whole paragraph explains why deforestation happens: for money, for land, and lack of law. Therefore, Choice A can be inserted as the topic sentence of the paragraph. All of the other choices are either too narrow or irrelevant.

20. B

The phrase "as well as" is a conjunction joining two equal elements. In this case, the underlined portion must be a noun because the other element is "profitability," a noun. That eliminates Choices A, C and D. Only Choice B works because "providing" is a gerund, a noun equivalent.

21. D

The rule that two sentences cannot be combined by a comma eliminates Choices A and B. Choice C can also be eliminated because it is a subordinate clause without a modified noun. All that remains is Choice D, *"mainly blamed on agricultural and pastoral use,"* which is appropriate because a past participle phrase can be used as an adverbial in the sentence.

22. C

The last part of the sentence means: farmers employ the above chain of actions for their purposes *in the same process.* When we change it back to a subordinate clause, only "where" can stand for "in the process," eliminating Choices A, B and D, and making Choice C the correct answer.

23. B

The passage explains why the author often gets frustrated when dealing with service representatives. Therefore, Choice B, *"I find few things as frustrating as dealing with service representatives,"* will most effectively establish the main idea. All of the other choices are either too general or irrelevant.

24. C

Choices B and D should be eliminated because they are grammatically incorrect. In the sentence, the subordinate clause modifies "Customers;" the relative pronoun should therefore be "who," eliminating Choice A and making Choice C the correct answer..

25. A

"When it comes to" is an idiomatic phrase usually used to switch the topic and get to the opposite side. In this case, the author describes herself as a patient person, tolerating most offences, polite, tipping and smiling; however, dealing with customer service representatives is the only thing that frustrates her. Therefore, "when it comes to" is a perfect transition between the two parts. Choice A is the correct answer. All other choices work no better.

26. D

The subordinate clause modifies 'the one," singular, the target verb should therefore be "calls." Also, only "the one who calls" parallels with "the one who asks" and "the one who breathes" in the context, making Choice D the correct answer.

27. A

Noun phrase "in hand" is an idiom meaning "available for using instantly." In this case, "phone in hand" is an idiomatic usage that means the same as "holding a phone in her hand." All of the other choices are not as effective as the original, making Choice A the correct answer and NO CHANGE to the original is necessary.

28. C

The usage is either *to resort to something* or *to resort to doing something*. In this case, *"If I've resorted to calling"* is the correct expression, eliminating Choices A, B and D and making Choice C the correct answer.

29. B

To decide what verb form is to use, we have to find the subject first. In the sentence, the subject is *"waiting on hold,"* the agreeable verb should therefore be *"makes me angrier,"* as Choice B indicates.

30. B

Take out the inserted part, we can easily see that preposition "by" governs two verbs: adopt and speak. As objects of "by," both verbs should take the gerund form: adopting and speaking. Only Choice B is the correct answer, while other choices are grammatically incorrect.

31. D

Choice B should be eliminated because pronoun "it" cannot appear before the noun it stands for. The rule that two sentences cannot be combined by a comma eliminates Choice C. While Choice A is grammatically correct, Choice D is better because it emphasizes "a service is not working" as the main reason for calling. Choice D is therefore the correct answer.

32. C

When the option to DELETE appears, give it special consideration. There must be a really good reason not to pick it. In this case, there is such a reason: Without the underlined portion, the sentence doesn't sound logically right, as if "*I'm decent enough with money*" were the reason for "*being behind the bills*." Choices A and B can be eliminated because they are both vague in meaning: How much is much? Even a millionaire could feel having not much. All that remains is Choice C, "just not that much to go around," perfectly explaining why the author has bills unpaid. Choice C is therefore the correct answer.

33. D

Relative pronoun "which" must immediately follow the modified noun, eliminating Choice A. Choices B and C should be eliminated too because "that" or "it" will make two sentences combined by a comma, which is a grammatical error. Choice D works in the context, with relative pronoun "what" leading the subordinate clause as the subject of the sentence.

34. A

The time phrase "since the 1940s" requires the target verb to be in the present perfect tense form, eliminating Choices B and C. In the subordinate clause "which" stands for the Food and Agriculture Organization (FAO) of the United Nations, a singular noun, making Choice A the correct answer.

35. D

The rule that two sentences cannot be combined by a comma eliminates Choice A. While all of the other choices are grammatically correct, Choice D is the most concise one, with a past participle phrase "provided by countries themselves" modifying the noun "statistics." Choice D therefore most effectively combines the two sentences.

36. D

A singular countable noun, such as "estimate," must have the indefinite article *a* (*an*) before it, eliminating Choice A. While all of the other choices are grammatically correct, Choice D is the best because "too conservative" is emphasized.

37. C

"To categorize" means to put in a category, or to classify. You may categorize a person *as* a bully, *as* a stranger, or *as* a friend. Choices A, B, and D should be eliminated because neither "to," "for" or "in" works with *categorize*. Choice C is the correct answer.

38. B

Choices A, C, or D are much similar because "also," "in addition," and "furthermore" are all transitions of continuation. Only Choice B, "on the other hand," is a transition of contrast. Choice B is therefore the correct answer.

39. D

Three adjectives modifying a noun should be separated by commas in the pattern of A, B, and C, as Choice D indicates.

40. A

The original is a noun phrase that gives additional information to the sentence. It is concise in meaning and correct in grammar. Choices B and C should be eliminated because two sentences cannot be combined by a comma. Choice D does not convey clear meaning of comparing the size. Choice A is therefore the correct answer.

41. C

The graphic shows that the top five countries were Brazil, Indonesia, Sudan, Myanmar, and Democratic Republic of Congo. Zambia is not among the top five. Choice C is therefore the correct answer.

42. D

Choices B and C do not make sense. Choice A, "it was cleared over time," makes two sentences jammed to a run-on. Only Choice D works, as a subordinate clause "that was cleared over time" modifying the noun "forest." Choice D is the correct answer.

43. A

The rule that two sentences cannot be combined by a comma eliminates Choices C and D. Choice B does not work as it needs relative pronoun "which" to form a subordinate clause. The original works, as a participle phrase adding more information to the sentence. Choice A is therefore the correct answer,

44. B

The graphic shows that 18 tropical countries or island territories had 20 percent or more of their forest cleared during the period. Take out the top five, there are thirteen left. Choice B is the correct answer.

SECTION 3

1. A

From $x = 2y + 1$, subtract x and 1 from each side we get $-1 = 2y - x$. So $10y - 5x = 5(2y - x) = 5(-1) = -5$, which is (A).

We can also plug in $y = 0$ and get $x = 1$, then see that only (A) satisfies.

2. B

When $y = 0$, we can solve that $x = -4$. So the choices (A) and (D) are eliminated. Next use $y = 2$, we can solve $x = -1$. This eliminates (D) and satisfies (B). The correct answer is (B).

Another way to solve it:

Add $3y$ to both sides, and we get $2x = 3y - 8$

Divide both sides by 2, and we get $x = \dfrac{3}{2}y - \dfrac{8}{2}$. That is Choice B: $x = 1.5\,y - 4$

3. A

His bonus is

$$20000 + 80000 \times \frac{6}{100} = 20000 + 4800 = 24800,$$

which is (A).

4. D

Before plugging in the answers, it is slightly better to simplify the inequality a little. It is equivalent to $x + y > 4x - 4y$ and in turn the same as $3x < 5y$. Now plug in the answers.
(A) $3x = 3$ and $5y = 10$, the inequality is satisfied.
(B) $3x = 9$ and $5y = 10$, the inequality is satisfied.
(C) $3x = -6$ and $5y = -5$, the inequality is satisfied.
(D) $3x = 9$ and $5y = 5$, the inequality is NOT satisfied.

5. A

Suppose the radius and height of the original cylinder is r and h, respectively, it has volume $\pi r^2 h = 120$. The volume of the new cylinder is $\pi(\dfrac{r}{2})^2 (2h) = \dfrac{1}{2}\pi r^2 h = 60$.

6. B

The answer is $16 \times \dfrac{2.4}{3.2}$. Note that it is much better to cancel out common factors before doing the multiplication:

$$16 \times \frac{2.4}{3.2} = \frac{16 \times 24}{32} = \frac{24}{2} = 12$$

That is (B).

7. D

It is better to write the numbers (other than the last x) in sorted order: $(1,1,2,2,2,2,3,3,4,4,4,5,x)$. So x can be any value without affecting the fact that 2 is the sole most frequent number in the list, except when $x = 4$, which will make both 2 and 4 the mode of the sequence.

8. C

The sum of two squares is 0, then both of them must be 0. This means any point satisfying the equation must have $x - y = 0$ and $x - 1 = 0$. This is true if and only if $x = y = 1$. So there is only one such point, namely (1,1). (C) is the correct answer.

9. C

We can expand and then simplify all the choices.

A quicker way is to plug in some special 0 values. Substitute $x = 1$ and $y = 1$, (A), (B), and (D) evaluate to 4, while (C) evaluates to 7.

10. D

When $x<1$, both $(x - 1)$ and $(x - 4)$ are negative, so $f(x)$ is positive; when $x>4$, both $(x - 1)$ and $(x - 4)$ are positive, so $f(x)$ is positive; when $1<x<4$, $(x - 1)$ is positive and $(x - 4)$ is negative, so $f(x)$ is negative; $f(1) = f(4) = 0$. From this analysis, $f(x) \geq 0$ if and only if $x \leq 1$ or $x \geq 4$. (The same conclusion can also be achieved by drawing the graph of $f(x)$.) So $f(-x) \geq 0$ if $-x$ satisfies $-x \leq 1$ or $-x \geq 4$, which is equivalent to $x \leq -4$ or $x \geq -1$. (D) is the correct answer.

11. A

$|f(x - 3)|$ is always non-negative, so (C) and (D) are first eliminated.

When $x = 3$, $|f(x - 3)| = |f(0)|$, from the graph of $f(x)$ we see its value is 1. So (3, 1) should be on the graph of $|f(x - 3)|$. It is now easy to see that (A) is the correct answer.

12. C

Use the special right triangle from the reference sheet on the test paper. We find that θ has 30 degrees. So 2θ has 60 degrees. Use the same picture of the special right triangle again, we find that $\sin(2\theta) = \dfrac{\sqrt{3}}{2}$, which is (C).

13. A

The easiest way is to plug in the answer. Since negative numbers are tricky to work with, better try a positive number first. Let's try A. Make $x = 3$ in the equation:

$\sqrt{6 + 3} - 6 = -3$

$3 - 6 = -3$

It works! So pick A for the answer.

Of course you can also solve it by using algebra. Start by adding $2x$ to both sides:

$\sqrt{2x+3} = 2x - 3$

Square both sides:

$2x + 3 = (2x - 3)^2$

$2x + 3 = 4x^2 - 12x + 9$

$4x^2 - 14x + 6 = 0$, so $2x^2 - 7x + 3 = 0$

Factor it:

$(2x - 1)(x - 3) = 0$

$x = \dfrac{1}{2}$, which is not in the options, and $x = 3$, which is (A).

14. B

$f(g(x))$ is not defined when the denominator is 0. This happens when $3g(x) - 6 = 0$, i.e., $g(x) = 2$. So we need an x such that $x^2 + 3x - 2$. We can easily solve this equation to get $x = 1$ or $x = -4$. Because the choices involve only very small numbers, it is also easy to plug in the numbers and see only (B) satisfies our requirement.

15. C

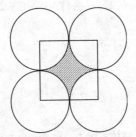

Connect the four centers of the circles as in the picture above, it is a square of side length 4. The shaded area equals the area of the square minus the four sectors. It is clear that the four sectors add up to one complete circle with radius 2. So the shaded area is $4 \cdot 4 - \pi 2 \cdot 2 = 16 - 4\pi$, which is (C).

16. 350

From they start to they meet, both spend the same amount of time. The ratio of the speed is 5:1, so is the ratio of the distance they covered. Divide the 420 feet into 6 equal parts, Cindy covers 1 and Koocky covers 5. So that is $70 \cdot 5 = 350$ feet.

17. 30

Write the parabola in the vertex form, $y = a(x - 1)^2 + 3$. Because $(2,6)$ is on the curve, so it satisfies the equation. We get $6 = a \cdot 1 + 3$, which gives us $a = 3$. Now

$(-2,t)$ satisfies the equation as well, so $t = 3(-2-1)^2 + 3 = 30$.

18. 80

The right triangle has one angle 30 degrees, it is one of the special triangles shown in the reference of the test paper. The segments incident to the 30-degree angle are $x\sqrt{3}$ and $2x$. Because $\overline{AC} = 40\sqrt{3}$, so $\overline{BC} = 40 \cdot 2 = 80$.

19. 400

The triangle ASP is a isosceles right triangle. Use the reference sheet from the test paper, we find $\overline{AP} = 10$. Therefore the side of the square, $\overline{AB} = 2\overline{AP} = 20$. And the area is $20 \times 20 = 400$.

20. 7

The key trick to avoid extensive brute-force search is to work on the two missing blocks. Suppose the two missing blocks has numbers a and b, we have

$$a + b = (-3) + (-2) + (-1) + 0 + 1 + 2 + 3 - 1 = -1$$

and

$$a^2 + b^2 = (-3)^2 + (-2)^2 + (-1)^2 + 0^2 + 1^2 + 2^2 - 23 = 5.$$

Now it is easy to plug in different choices of a, or simply solve the quadratic equation. We find the missing numbers are -2 and 1. So the sum of the cubes on the five selected blocks is $(-27) + (-1) + 0 + 8 + 27 = 7$.

SECTION 4

1. C

During the last 12 months, Alice has won 60 games, gaining 1800 points; and there are 2 months she did not play any game, losing 40 points. So her rating now is $1250 + 1800 - 40 = 3010$, which is (C).

2. D

Plug in the answers, $f(4) = (4-4)(ax^2 + 2x - c) - 3 = 0 - 3 = -3$. No matter what a and c are, the graph passes through $(4, -3)$, which is (D).

3. B

The correct answer is (B). Note that (A) has the prices interchanged for strawberries and blueberries. It is not necessary to solve, but the solution is that $a = 5$ and $b = 6$.

4. D

The volume of the tank is $\pi r^2 h = 12\pi (m^3)$. Therefore the time needed to fill the tank is simply $\dfrac{12\pi\,(m^3)}{0.2(m^3/s)} = 60\pi\,(s)$. The correct answer is (D).

5. B

The equation actually tells that $t + 3 = 3t - 7$. From there we get $10 = 2t$; thus $t = 5$, which is (B).

6. C

One can factorize the expression as $2x^5 - 8x^3 + 6x = 2x(x^4 - 4x^2 + 3) = 2x\,(x^2 - 1)$ $(x^2 - 3) = 2x\,(x + 1)(x - 1)(x + \sqrt{3})(x - \sqrt{3})$, which is (C).

Also note that it is easy to eliminate the other answers. (B) is a polynomial of degree 6, while the expression in question has degree 5. (D) does not evaluate to 0 when $x = 0$ as the expression in question does. Finally, when $x = 2$, (A) evaluates to 0, but $2x^5 - 8x^3 + 6x = 12$. So, only (C) could be the correct answer.

7. A

$2200000 \times 7.507\% = 165154$, which is closest to (A).

8. B

(D) is not correct because we do not know the distribution of the languages in the library. For example, if all the books in the collection is in Italian, then a appears more often than e. The data in the table is enough to calculate the frequency of the vowels in each language — the frequency is just the sum of the columns. We do not need to calculate the accurate results. Instead we just need to compare the columns row by row. For example, Italian beats English because it gains a big margin in 4 rows and only in the second row the percentage is slightly less. To compare Italian and German, observe that Italian has 5 + more in the first row, 5– less in the second row, so it wins in the first two rows; similarly it wins in the last two rows, as well as the middle row. So Italian uses vowels most often. (B) is the correct answer.

9. C

We compute the frequencies of the letters as the following table:

A	E	I	O	U
7.488%	12.336%	6.186%	8.120%	3.339%

He uses a, e, and i less frequently than the percentages in the original table, and both o and u more frequently. The correct answer is (C).

10. C

First simplify $(\frac{2z}{3})(\frac{3z}{4}) = (\frac{z^2}{2})$. So the inequality is equivalent to $z^2 < \frac{z^2}{2} + 1$. Multiply both sides by 2 and subtract z^2, we get $z^2 < 2$, which solves to (C).

11. C

Write the equation of C in the standard form,

$x^2 - 2x + 1 + y^2 = 3$;

$(x - 1)^2 + (y)^2 = 3$.

So, the center of C is $(1,0)$; and the square of the radius of C is 3. The area of a circle is πr^2. So the area of two circles are proportional to the square of their radii. Thus the square of radius of D is 6. Because D shares the center with C. The equation for D is

$(x - 1)^2 + (y)^2 = 6$;

$x^2 - 2x + 1 + y^2 = 6$,

which rearranges to (C).

12. D

First it should be clear the payment for the first two hours is $60. Now plug in, for example, Lucas did one extra minute with a rate of 1 dollar ($m = 1$ and $d = 1$), his payment should be $61. Only (D) gives the correct answer.

13. D

Here is partly a physics problem, partly a word puzzle, and partly a joke. There are 1000000 pieces of square meters in a square kilometer. In order to put the same pressure, we need one newton standing on each of the pieces. So 1000000 newtons are needed, which is (D).

14. B

If we sort the 5 slopes, the median is the number in the middle. It is clear that we have 2 negative slopes (those for OA and OE). So we are after the smallest non-negative slope among OB, OC, and OD. They have the slopes 3, 1, and $\frac{1}{4}$, respectively. So the median is $\frac{1}{4}$, which is (B).

15. C

Obviously the distribution of the lengths of these seven ropes is not symmetrical, otherwise the average and median would have been equal. The example in the question has an average that is smaller than the median, so an appropriate conjecture is that small outliners are present in the data; that is, there are a few pieces that are much shorter than the rest.

16. C

Plug in the answers. (8,16) eliminates (A); (5,7) eliminates (B); and both points satisfy (C), which is the correct answer.

17. D

$(2i - 3)(1 + i) = 2i + 2i \cdot i - 3 - 3i = 2i + 2(-1) - 3 - 3i = -5 - i.$

18. C

Plug in the answers. When $x = 1$, the left hand side is 3, and the right hand side is 0.5. This rules out both (A) and (D). To decide which of (B) and (C) is correct, we plug in the simpler one. When $x = 2$, both sides equals $\frac{3}{4}$. So (C) is the correct answer.

19. D

Alice started 5 minutes earlier. When Bob started, Alice has her 10-th balloon finished. We may modify the statement of the options to the form "when Alice finishes x additional balloons (other than the first 10), Bob finishes his y-th". In a correct answer x and y should be proportional to their speed. Among the answers, only (D) has 40:60 = 2:3, the others are not even close.

Algebraically, suppose the at a moment Alice finishes her x-th balloon and Bob finishes his y-th. x and y satisfy a linear equation. When Bob starts, $y = 0$, $x = 10$. One minute later $y = 3$ and $x = 12$. From here we can see the equation $y = \frac{3x}{2} - 15$ models the relation between x and y. Plus in the answers, the correct one is (D).

20. D

Since the price of each product consists of the initial cost plus 20% markup, the dealer's profit per product for these 54 products would be 20%. This gives us 54 numbers of 20%. The dealer also returned 6 products and got a refund of 50% of the initial cost for each unsold product, and this means the dealer's profit per product for these 6 products is –50%. Now we can calculate the average profit for all 60 products as following:

$$\frac{20\% \times 54 + (-50\%) \times 6}{60} = 13\%$$

21. B

When $(a,b) = (30,1)$, the ratio is 30; this rules out (A) and (D). When $(a,b) = (-30,1)$, the ratio is –30; this rules out (A) and (C). So the correct answer is (B).

22. B

One can either graph the data in the table and discover it's a line with a positive y-intercept; or model it directly: suppose normally each egg weights b oz and the container weights a oz ($a>0$), then we have the relation $y = a + bx$, which makes (B) the correct answer.

23. B

The function $y = ax + b$ passes through both points (9, 24.805) and (14, 35.813). One may solve the equation and get $b \approx 2.2$. One slightly faster way to solve this is to observe the difference between the last two rows, and see that 5 eggs weigh 11.008 oz. So each egg weighs 11.008/5 $\approx$ 2.2oz, which is (B).

24. D

The easiest way is, because the data in the last row and the answer to the previous question are accurate, add 10 eggs to the last row, which makes the weight approximately 35.8 + 22 = 57.8(oz), which is (D).

25. B

The standard form of the equation is $(x + 3)^2 + (y - 1)^2 = 25$. Expand we get

$x^2 + 6x + 9 + y^2 - 2y + 1 = 25$;

Simplify, we get

$x^2 + y^2 + 6x - 2y - 15 = 0$.

which is (B).

Note that one can also find special points on the circle and check if they are satisfied by the equations in the answers. Four obvious points are (–3,6), (–3,–4), (–8,1), and (2,1).

26. D

The grade points for the first 6 courses are $3 \times 4 = 12$, $3 \times 1 = 3$, $3.7 \times 3 = 11.1$, $3.3 \times 3 = 9.9$, $4 \times 2 = 8$, $4 \times 2 = 8$. The median is the average of 8 and 9.9, which is 8.95. The correct answer is (D).

27. C

Plug in the answers, or solve it algebraically. The total number of credit points is 18, so the total grade points should be 61.92. From the solution to the previous problem, the grade points of the first six courses add up to 52, so the grade point for the last course is 61.92 – 52 = 9.92. With three credits, this means the points corresponding to the grade is approximately 3.3. The grade is B +, which is (C).

28. C

Make $x = 0$, the expression evaluates to 1. Now we plug in the answers. Only

(B) and (C) evaluates to 1. If you know some theory of polynomials, then you see (C) has the correct degree. Otherwise, make $x = -1$ (note that $x = 1$ will not differentiate (B) and (C)), the original expression evaluates to 2. (B) evaluates to 4 and (C) evaluates to 2. The correct answer is (C).

29. B

The movement of the car can be separated into two stages at the time when it reaches speed 60m/s. In the first stage the curve is a parabola; in the second stage the car moves at a constant speed, which is the slope of the straight line. In (A) the slope is 0, i.e., the car does not move after 20 seconds (the displacement does not chance). The correct answer is (B).

30. D

The question is about fraction. In this fraction, the denominator is the number of the days that the store sold at least 20 smart phones, which is 15, while the numerator is the number of the days that the store also sold over 15 tablets, which is 7.

31. 12

First set the equation to 0. $x^2 - 6x - 72 = 0$. There are many factors of 72. It is easier to further write it in the vertex form. $(x - 3)^2 = 81$, so $x - 3$ is 9 or -9. Thus x is either -6 or 12. Because $x > 0$, so $x = 12$.

32. 4.67 or 4.68

There are 1000 liters in 1 cubic meter, so the density of the milk is 1.028 kg per liter. One gallon has 1.028×3.79 kg, the price should be $\$1.2 \times 1.028 \times 3.79 \approx \$4.675$

33. 2.2

From a geometric point of view, $|x - 1.1| + |x - 3.3|$, the sum of distances from x to 1.1 and 3.3, is always no less than $|3.3 - 1.1| = 2.2$. So, for the equation to hold, $|x - 2.2|$ must be 0, which implies $x = 2.2$

A slower solution is to discuss the relative greatness of x and the numbers 1.1, 2.2, 3.3. There are up to 7 cases and only when $x = 2.2$ is the equation possible.

34. 8

Suppose $AC = 11t$ and $AB = 13t$. Because $\triangle ACB$ is a right angle, we have

$AC^2 + BC^2 = AB^2$,

i.e. $121t^2 + 25 = 169t^2$.

This implies $48t^2 = 25$ so $t = \dfrac{5}{\sqrt{48}}$. Thus $AC = 11t = \dfrac{55}{\sqrt{48}} \approx 7.94$.

Another way to use the calculator is as follows. The angle A is $\cos^{-1}(\frac{11}{13})$, and $\frac{BC}{AC} = \tan A$, so

$$AC = \frac{BC}{\tan(\cos^{-1}(11/13))} \approx 8.$$

35. 117

Note that when $x = 1,2,4,5$ will make $(x - 5)(x - 4)(x - 2)(x - 1)$ zero, so $P(x) = -1$.

$P(1) \cdot P(2) \cdot P(3) \cdot P(4) \cdot P(5) \cdot P(6) = (-1)(-1)([-2][-1] \cdot 1 \cdot 2 - 1)(-1)(-1)(1 \cdot 2 \cdot 4 \cdot 5 - 1) = 3 \cdot 39 = 117.$

36. 10

The point on l with $x = 1$ satisfies $4 + 3y = 10$, which solves to $y = 2$. So A = (1,2).

The point on l with $y = -6$ satisfies $4x + 3(-6) = 10$, which solves to $x = 7$. So B = (7,-6).

So the distance between A and B is $\sqrt{(7 - 1)^2 + (-6 - 2)^2} = \sqrt{36 + 64} = 10$.

37. 11

The price of one golden pass and one silver pass combined, including tax, is ($22 + $18) × 1.07 = $42.8. $\frac{500}{42.8} \approx 11.68. So Tim can buy as many as 11 tickets such bundles, which has 11 golden pass tickets.

38. 13

Suppose the price of the silver pass is increased by x perent, where x is an integer. The new price will be $18 \times (1 + \frac{x}{100})$. We have $\frac{500}{18(1 + \frac{x}{100})1.07} < 23$.

Solving this we get x>12.8719. So the integer x should be at least 13.

SECTION 5

In recent years, the debate over how to best source energy has intensified as criticisms have rained down on fracking and other techniques used to extract fossil fuels from the earth. In the essay "Jimmy Fallon Makes the World's Best Argument Against Solar and Wind Energy," Alex Epstein argues that we cannot rely on renewable energy. To build his case against renewables, he analyzes an extended metaphor, breaks down complex scientific concepts, and includes relevant diagrams.

On his Weekend Update sketch on Saturday Night Live, comedian and anti-fracking advocate Jimmy Fallon once jokingly suggested that hazelnuts are the solution to the world's energy problems. While Fallon was only kidding, Epstein explains how hazelnuts are the perfect metaphor for renewable energy sources like solar and wind power. Just like hazelnuts, solar and wind power initially appear to be free because they come from nature. However, a deeper investigation into the process used to produce them reveals that the materials and manpower required to convert raw resources into usable energy are prohibitively expensive. In short, "Just as it's a mistake to assume that because the sun is free, solar-powered hazelnuts will be cheap, so it is a mistake to assume that solar-powered energy can or will be cheap." By seriously assessing Fallon's hazelnut proposition, Epstein makes solar and wind power seem just as silly as hazelnut power.

Having shown the reader that solar and wind power are far more impractical than the initially appear, Epstein provides accessible scientific explanations for why they are not the answer to the world's energy woes. Epstein first introduces the problem of diluteness—the energy that comes from the sun and wind is not concentrated energy. To underscore how challenging it is to concentrate their power, he lists a series of the many rare and expensive materials required to transform dilute sun and wind energy into electricity. Then, Epstein invites the readers to recall their own experiences with sun and wind in order to describe the intermittency problem. Everyone knows that "the sun doesn't shine all the time" and "the wind doesn't blow all the time." Suddenly, solar and wind power are transformed in the mind of the reader from environmentally responsible to intuitively unreliable. By gently walking his audience through the complicated science, the author makes a compelling case against renewable energy.

Armed with the basic scientific facts, the reader is ready to interpret charts that provide further damning evidence against solar and wind power. In the section on the diluteness problem, Epstein presents a chart showing the comparative amounts of steel required to produce different forms of energy. Before the audience even reads the numbers, they see that the circle for wind power dwarfs the circles for coal and natural gas. Later, in the section on the intermittency problem, another chart starkly depicts the unreliability of wind and solar power. The black and gray bars on the graph show solar and wind power to be wildly erratic. These carefully selected charts add an impressive visual to Epstein's other arguments.

For Alex Epstein, Jimmy Fallon's tongue-in-cheek gibe about hazelnut power perfectly parallels the unreliability of solar and wind power. Epstein convinces his audience to abandon hopes of replacing fossil fuels with renewables by explaining the scientific obstacles in layman's terms while user-friendly graphs make the impact of his arguments even more dramatic.